MERE CATHOLICISM

Faith in the Third Millennium

DANIEL AGATINO

SUNBURY
P R E S S

Mechanicsburg, PA USA

Published by Sunbury Press, Inc.
Mechanicsburg, Pennsylvania

SUNBURY
P R E S S
www.sunburypress.com

For information about special discounts for bulk purchases, please contact Sunbury Press Orders Dept. at (855) 338-8359 or orders@sunburypress.com.

To request one of our authors for speaking engagements or book signings, please contact Sunbury Press Publicity Dept. at publicity@sunburypress.com.

ISBN: 978-1-62006-685-0 (Trade Paperback)

Library of Congress Control Number: 2018963715

FIRST SUNBURY PRESS EDITION: December 2018

Product of the United States of America
0 1 1 2 3 5 8 13 21 34 55

Set in Bookman Old Style
Designed by Crystal Devine
Cover by Lawrence Knorr
Edited by Jennifer Cappello

Continue the Enlightenment!

To

Gabriel, my fiery angel

and

Leo, my gentle lion

✝

ABBREVIATIONS

ANF   *The Ante-Nicene Fathers*, ed. Alexander Roberts &
           James Donaldson, 10 vols., 1885–87

CCC   *Catechism of the Catholic Church*, 2nd ed.

CIC   *Code of Canon Law* (1983 ed.; *Codex Iuris Canonici*)

DH   Heinrich Denzinger, *Compendium of Creeds,
           Definitions, and Declarations on Matters of Faith and
           Morals*, 43rd ed., rev., enl., & ed. Peter Hünermann
           (San Francisco: Ignatius Press, 2012)

ISV   International Standard Version Bible

KJV   King James Bible

NABRE   New American Bible-Revised Edition

NIV   New International Version

NPNF[1] *The Nicene and Post-Nicene Fathers*, 1st ser., ed. Philip
           Schaff, 10 vols., 1886–1889.

NPNF[2] *The Nicene and Post-Nicene Fathers*, 2nd ser., ed.
           Philip Schaff & Henry Wace, 14 vols., 1890–1900.

PL   Patrologia Latina

ST   Thomas Aquinas, *Summa Theologiae*

Tanner   Norman P. Tanner, ed., *Decrees of the Ecumenical
           Councils*, 2 vols. (Washington, DC: Georgetown Univ.
           Press, 1990)

✝

CONTENTS

Preface   ix

Introduction: Christianity in the Third Millennium   1

Chapters

   1. Faith and Reason   11

   2. Freedom and Responsibility   34

   3. Work and Prayer   63

   4. Sin and Salvation (Hamartiology and Soteriology)   83

   5. Suffering and Love   107

   6. God (Theology)   127

   7. Jesus (Christology)   143

   8. Mary (Mariology)   188

   9. Saints and Angels (Hagiology and Angelology)   201

  10. The Church (Ecclesiology)   219

  11. The Bible (Bibliology)   249

  12. Humankind, Creation, and Last Things
      (Anthropology and Eschatology)   273

Notes   305

About the Author   347

"ERROR IS MANIFESTLY ANCIENT;
BUT TRUTH WHICH REPROVES IT
IS EVER MORE ANCIENT STILL."
—SAINT COLUMBANUS

✝
PREFACE

C. S. Lewis' *Mere Christianity* is the obvious inspiration for the title of this book. In that book, Lewis uses the example of a person standing in a hall that is lined on both sides by rooms: Each room represents a different Christian tradition. He wanted to get readers into the hallway and let them choose for themselves whether to enter Christianity by the door of Anglicanism, Catholicism, and so forth.[1]

Mere Christianity brilliantly focuses on what essentially all Christians agree upon; namely, the Creed, the canon of the New Testament, etc. However, many of the great controversies between Protestants and Catholics are purposely not discussed. There were ecumenical reasons for avoiding topics like papal primacy, purgatory, Marian devotions, and so forth. But, by avoiding these sorts of topics, *Mere Christianity* can be read as *Mere Protestantism*.

I wrote *Mere Catholicism* to address some of those missing topics. Even though I am both intellectually and emotionally convinced of the truth of Catholic Christianity, I am indebted to C. S. Lewis (an Anglican) for helping me better understand how Christianity offers the most compelling *raison d'être*. His work, and I hope my own, is an exploration of "faith seeking understanding," to quote St. Anselm of Canterbury.[2]

For me, the search was quite personal. As a newborn baby, I died; or nearly died—the accounts vary. In preparation for my impending death, I was baptized. There was little time remaining in my life; and, so, a kind Jewish woman who worked at the hospital stood in as my "godmother."[3] After my exigent baptism, there was not much else to do but pray and wait. It was then that a miraculous event occurred. My parents were visited by a nurse who asked one of them: "Do you believe in God?" After answering in the affirmative, the nurse gave them a green scapular of the Immaculate Heart of Mary. This nurse then boldly proclaimed that I would recover. To the relief and delight of my parents, and to the utter surprise of my doctor, I actually did. Family members sought out that nurse among the sea of other nurses, who in those days all wore white uniforms. However, she was nowhere to be found. According to the other employees at the hospital, no such nurse matching her description even worked at the small hospital where all this had taken place.

I grew up hearing this story over and over again. I freely admit that this experience may have been the catalyst to my lifelong yearning to know God. I still have the scapular, which sits in a gilded frame above my desk as I type this. However, I don't tell many people about this event. After all, if someone were to tell me a similar kind of story, I'd be extremely skeptical. I could find a thousand rational explanations for what happened, none of which would have involved miracles or the supernatural. I would point out that just because two events coincide—in this case, an encouraging visit from an ostensible nurse and the recovery of a baby—does not mean one caused or even influenced the other.

I have worked both as a professor and an attorney, and whether I'm in the classroom or the courtroom, one of my goals is to discover truth. I try to keep in mind Oscar Wilde's quip: "The truth is rarely pure and never simple."[4] I remember one client whose story just didn't make sense. I reviewed it with him again and again, but still something didn't seem right. Just prior to appearing before the judge, I asked him one more time to clarify his story. He pondered for a moment and finally responded, "Do you want the truth, or do you want the 'true truth'?" I had to laugh but should not have been surprised, because getting to the "true truth" is not always easy.

Truth can be defined philosophically, semantically, and in other ways. Aristotle, for example, taught that truth is that which corresponds to reality.[5] In the Bible, the word "truth" is translated from the Hebrew word "*emet*," or from the Greek word "*alētheia*." "Emet" means, "faithful," "dependable," or "true." "Alētheia" means "sincere," or "accurate."

I have to ask myself what, if anything, makes my purported miracle story dependable or accurate? How is it any different than a claim made by someone who insists that his grilled cheese sandwich bears the image of Jesus Christ? This is just a variation of the broader question: What makes belief in God the "true truth"? The Church encourages and sometimes challenges all of us to seek out what is true and good for God's greater glory and for our own unending joy. This takes hard work. According to the Roman sage Seneca: *Res severa est verum gaudium* ("True joy is a serious matter").

In a society distinguished by such abundant plurality and diverse opinions, discussions about issues of truth and goodness and faith can be complicated. As a college professor, I regularly encounter students who have grown up accepting certain "truths," only to come to college and encounter ideas and perspectives that directly challenge those beliefs. I try to convince them that Shakespeare was right: "There are more things in heaven and earth, Horatio,/Than are dreamt of in our philosophy."[6]

While being introduced to new or unfamiliar ideas can be exciting and liberating, it can also be quite frightening and confusing. We can easily feel threatened or overwhelmed by unfamiliar concepts. Sorting through all the competing philosophies our culture has to offer can cause anxiety, distress, and (in severe cases) despair. A foolish alternative to facing such encounters is choosing simply to move from one mindless distraction to another, never really engaging with the ideas our world presents. Saint Thomas More observed that you have to "Occupy your minds with good thoughts, or the enemy will fill them with bad ones. Unoccupied they cannot be."[7]

Perhaps you don't believe in God at all; or, you are someone who believes that he is disinterested in your life. Regardless of whether you are a believer or a skeptic, one thing we all share is that we have questions—deep and puzzling questions, such as: "How do I live a good life?" In response, the Church declares that we are all called to live in God's love, work in God's love, rest and play in his love, and one day, die, so as to rise to the eternal presence of the God who is love.

✝

CHRISTIANITY IN THE THIRD MILLENNIUM

We live in a fast-paced, perception-altering world. For some, encountering such rapid changes makes life a "great blooming, buzzing confusion."[1] Advances in science and technology and frequent alterations in social beliefs and practices can be frustrating for believers who struggle to reconcile Church teachings with secular culture. Believers could ignore all this, but escapism is the mortal enemy of all Christians. The Church encourages us to critically examine the ever-changing world in which we live and, equally important, examine ourselves—though gently, and not with a merciless scrutiny. The message of the Gospels is that Jesus Christ came into the world to declare in a commanding and unapologetic voice certain inviolable truths. But, in their most authentic form, these truths do not demand small-minded, fanatical conformity and submission. The Church has always recognized this, and while Catholic teaching is neither vague nor unintelligible, there is a richness and diversity to Church doctrine.[2]

Certainly, one cannot claim to be a good Catholic and, for example, deny the existence of the Trinity, but Catholicism is not always univocal. Dogma cannot change, but teachings on non-dogmatic issues can change and sometimes do. The Church of today is the one and same Church that Jesus founded and the Apostles promulgated, but it is more prolific and expansive. The faith of over a billion Catholics is multifaceted and rich in variant traditions and theologies. Part of the genius of the Church is the plurality that subsists within the One Church. "To differ, even deeply, one from another, is not to be enemies, it is simply to be. To recognize and accept one's own difference is not pride. To recognize and accept the difference of others is not weakness. If union has to be, if union offers any meaning . . . it is above all in the recognition and acceptance of difference . . ."[3]

Valuing difference does not mean adopting an "anything-goes" ideology. C. S. Lewis observed: "What would really satisfy us would be a God who said of anything we happened to like doing, 'What does it matter so long as they are contented?' We want, in fact, not so much a Father in Heaven as a grandfather in heaven—a senile benevolence who, as they say, 'liked to see young people enjoying themselves' and whose plan for the universe was simply that it might be truly said at the end of each day, 'a good time was had by all.'"[4]

We might think we'd like a God like this, but really, we don't even want a parent who is so disinterested that there are absolutely no rules, regardless of the consequences that may follow. God has rules. He does not grade on a curve comparing us to each other but to his objective norm. The Church, too, has rules. The problem, the perennial problem, which plagued both ancient Judaism and contemporary Christianity, is these rules can become ends in themselves instead of means to an end. I was in class with a student who described her experience of Christianity as "pray, pay, and obey." She is one of countless people discontented with organized religion. Most of us can certainly sympathize with her. In most of my encounters with lapsed Catholics, I learn of some personal hurt or injustice, perceived or authentic, that drove the person to leave the Church.

The parable of the Good Samaritan (Luke 10:25-37) exemplifies the hypocrisy of two outwardly religious people. The story is about an injured man left on the side of the road. Passersby who are supposed to be pious Jews, a priest and a Levite, ignore the injured man's plight; but a Samaritan, an anti-religious-establishment figure, is the hero of the story. He is the one who helps. When Jesus asks the rabbi which man treated the injured man like a neighbor, the priest, the Levite, or the Samaritan, the rabbi who responded to Jesus hated the Samaritans so much he could not even answer Jesus by uttering the word "Samaritan." Instead, the rabbi simply said, "The one who treated him with mercy." (It is possible the priest and the Levite in the story represent the old law and how ineffectual it is when not coupled with love. Like the old law, the rules of the Catholic Church are incomplete when absent of love and compassion.)

Many of us have our own Good Samaritan story to tell; a story of religious indifference. It has been my experience that many lapsed Catholics have either been personally or indirectly hurt or offended by someone in the Church. A friend of mine tells of a deeply offensive experience during a baptism he attended. The priest who celebrated the sacrament asked everyone in the church to stand. Some of the elderly people in the pews chose to remain seated; I think due to fatigue or arthritis. The priest then interrupted the baptism to announce that since Jesus hung on the cross in torment for hours, everyone in the church could bear to stand for at least a few minutes. He refused to continue until everyone was up on their feet.

What can be said other than Catholics, like all humans, are sinners? "The Church," says Cardinal Newman, "is ever ailing, and lingers on in weakness, 'always bearing about in the body the dying of the Lord Jesus, that the life also of Jesus might be made manifest in her body.'"[5] I'm not judging this priest. In fact, he simply may have been trying to bring a sense of reverence to the ceremony. Perhaps he was thinking of St. John of the Cross' advice, "Whenever anything disagreeable or displeasing happens to you, remember Christ crucified and be silent."[6] But St. John was counseling people to make this observation on their own and not have it imposed upon them from someone else. Unfortunately, my example is somewhat benign.

We all know there are much more serious instances that could be cited. In recent times, the pedophile scandal identified an unconscionable number of priests, thousands across the globe, along with numerous bishops, who have participated in gravely immoral and criminal acts. The decades-long abuse that has been revealed is profoundly disturbing and ranks among the greatest scandals in Church history. As an attorney, I have represented victims of clergy sexual abuse and have personally witnessed the devastation and lifelong trauma they suffer. The sins of those Catholics involved are reprehensible and merit punishment from both ecclesiastical and secular authorities. Not only have victims been irreparably injured, betrayed, and hurt, but the entire Church has been affected. Due specifically to the sexual abuse scandal, many have left the Church for other Christian denominations; others have abandoned belief in God altogether. The once-influential moral authority of the Church has been decimated. There are no excuses. There are no justifications. We can, however, contextualize the information by pointing out that, while this sinful behavior is gravely evil and damnable in the eyes of God, Jesus is the source of our faith—not pedophile priests or conspiring bishops. Moreover, the vast majority of priests and religious clergy reflect God's goodness. They epitomize the words of Father Joseph Girzone, who wrote, "In every age there exist quiet heroes who, in their selfless devotion, lay aside their own needs and comforts and consecrate their energies and talents to healing the wounds of a troubled humanity."[7]

We do well to remember that our faith is in God and not in any particular human or organization. Saint Paul encouragingly reminds us that, no matter how surprising or disturbing our journey may become: "neither death, nor life, nor angels, nor rulers, nor things present, nor things to come, nor powers, nor height, nor depth, nor anything else in all creation, will be able to separate us from the love of God in Christ Jesus our Lord" (Romans 8:38–39). Nonetheless, challenges still exist. To better grasp them, I sometimes use psychological language; but more often, concepts from philosophy and theology prove most helpful. Superficially, it seems like an easy task to summarize Catholic teaching and practices. Just pick up an official catechism. Even when Church teaching is unpopular or unfamiliar, the *Catechism of the Catholic Church* proves to be an authentic resource.[8] A quick scan of its index reveals teachings on every topic from "Abortion" to "YHWH" (that is, the Tetragrammaton). Yet, while the *CCC* is an invaluable resource, it is necessarily a mere summary of the faith. As such, there is much that is left out. More importantly, it can be difficult to ascertain which teachings are central to the faith and which are ancillary.[9] Equally, some topics are addressed with a finality that may sometimes belie the fact that some of their aspects may continue to be debated even among orthodox Catholics.

Sometimes, the process of understanding and of communicating Christianity is messy. Some people question how it is that the simple message to love God and one another, which was preached by a homeless, first-century itinerant rabbi, transformed into numerous capricious rules and obligations, promulgated by a bureaucratic, hierarchically-ordered, ritualistic institution known as the Catholic Church. The response to this is simple:

> The Church does not make the divine law of faith and morals, but only authoritatively attests it, its contents and its validity. The law is the requirement of God, nor is it as such an arbitrary dictate of the divine will. . . . Its positive ordinances represent the ideal of humanity as the eternal Wisdom and Love desire it to be realized, and the new man as God's design would have him. Of its essence, therefore, the law of God does not impose a burden on human nature, but is an enriching, fulfilling and perfecting of it. It is a life-giving truth and a life-giving law. And therefore the Catholic affirms it in the light of his practical reason and by a free choice of his will makes it his own, so that it becomes his own law, an act of his moral freedom, a determination of his moral conscience.[10]

Furthermore, like any institution, a complex organization such as the Catholic Church demands a complex structure.

I had a history professor who used to say that there is always a "good" and a "bad" version of any story. I was advised to write this book with a policy of "no ink to the opposition"; that is, I should present Catholic teaching without regard either to the Church's dirty laundry or to opposing viewpoints. I chose not to adopt this policy.

In order to better understand our subject, occasionally I rely on technical, philosophical, and theological concepts (e.g., words like "epistemology" and "Christology"). I have also tried to strike a balance by using scholarly jargon to clarify, and not obfuscate, certain points. After all, as the philosopher Blaise Pascal pointed out, we are seeking the "God of Abraham, God of Isaac, God of Jacob, not of the philosophers and the scholars."[11] Saint Paul warned that it is possible to get too caught up in confounding philosophies. "See to it that no one takes you captive through philosophy and empty deceit, according to human tradition, according to the elemental spirits of the universe, and not according to Christ" (Colossians 2:8).

In deference to this realization, I have not always opted to be strict with my use of precise theological or philosophical language.[12] Also, I am not always clear about which teachings are central to the faith, (e.g., a dogma like the Trinity) and which ones are peripheral, (e.g., a theologoumenon, or mere theological opinion, like "all dogs go to heaven"). The same holds true for certain practices. I sometimes fail to distinguish among pious traditions, scholarly consensus, and formal teachings. For example, there are some Catholic practices, such as reciting the Rosary, that have a long tradition—but they are purely voluntary. Other practices, such as fasting for one hour before receiving holy Communion[13], are codified in the Church's canon law. At a minimum, the Precepts of the Church outline behaviors for maintaining a Catholic identity.[14]

This book does more than examine minimal Catholic beliefs and practices; it explores the faith, albeit sometimes in a meandering fashion. According to J. R. R. Tolkien, "Not all those who wander are lost."[15] Tolkien's sentiments may seem a bit romantic, but exploring different options is useful. After all, there is no guru who can simply impart to us instantaneous wisdom. I had a professor who jokingly said that, if you want to become a guru, the first thing you would learn in "guru school" would be that, whenever someone asked you a deep and puzzling question, your answer should always be: "You are asking the wrong question." There is an anecdote in philosophical circles: A student asks, "What is the meaning of life?" To which the philosopher answers, "Who wants to know?" This sort of deflection is not what this book is about.

The famous Socratic Method is all about getting a person to ask the right questions. Socrates responded to questions with directed, critical questions of his own. In doing so, he helped his students to discover truth. This process often leads to doubt and controversy, but the fruit of such frustrations can be a deeper understanding of the subject. That said, there isn't necessarily one right way to go about this questioning. The process as it relates to faith is very personalized. Questions that plague you may be of little or no concern to me; answers that I may find satisfying may be remarkably inadequate for you.

Among the most important questions we can ask is the one Jesus famously asked his Apostles, "Who do you say that I am?" (Mark 8:29). The answer to this question is not only the basis of this book but also the very foundation of Christianity.

What we believe is important. But, *how* we believe is equally important. For example, tradition holds that after St. Peter betrayed Christ he wept so bitterly that permanent lines formed on his face from the copious tears. Did this really happen? Not likely. This is more reasonably mere legendary hagiography. While the story of St. Peter's tears having caused permanent scars on his face might not be real, his utter and complete repentance and sorrow were undoubtedly real (cf. Mark 14:72). The story of his tear-scarred face helps to communicate Peter's abject regret. So, Peter's scarred face may be just a legend, but it is one that communicates an important truth.[16]

Another example of my use of certain narratives to point out a greater truth comes from my repeated references to Adam and Eve. Is the story true? Yes, Catholics must believe it to be true. The question is: In what way is it true? The biblical authors sometimes deal with Adam and Eve as real historical persons—though, not inescapably as the universal biological progenitors of all humans. At other times, they are symbols for all humanity . . . or, symbols for Israel . . . or, even literary figures. Are we dealing with poetry, allegory, parable, or something else? Believing the story to be true is not the same as believing everything in the Bible to be literal history. Jesus' parables communicated truth, but they were not accounts of historical events.

By applying this insight to all of divine revelation, we find that Catholic theology is richly complex, nuanced, layered, and (sometimes) not easily subject to simple formulations. While the Church embraces and assents to all sincere efforts to seek out truth, be they based in science or emotion or elsewhere, there is recognition that sin can and historically has distorted this pursuit. Pope St. Gregory the Great said, "Error is manifestly ancient, but truth which reproves it is ever more ancient still."[17] The Church responds not with a single "Catholic" way to see and understand the world. Instead, she offers a rich intellectual tradition of over two millennia that approves of and encourages both unity and diversity. One of the best ways to mix flexibility with resoluteness is to remember the following axiom: "In essentials, unity; in non-essentials, liberty; in all things, charity."[18]

The challenge is to act on such principles, even when doing so is difficult. According to the biblical scholar J. B. Phillips, Jesus "would have discouraged any sentimental flying to His bosom and often told men to go out and do most difficult and arduous things. . . . He left His followers to carry out a task that might have daunted the stoutest heart. Original Christianity had certainly no taint of escapism."[19] Although Jesus loved every person he encountered, we find him telling people to do such things as to take up their crosses (Matthew 16:24); to leave their families to follow him (Luke 14:26); and to abandon their riches for his sake (Luke 18:22). Among those closest to him (the saints and martyrs), we find many who were tortured and killed in a terrifying variety of ways. Saint Teresa of Avila used to joke with God about how much suffering he allowed into her life. If this is the way God treats his friends, she'd say to him, it's no wonder he has so few of them.

These days, he may have fewer friends due to other factors. Contemporary, secular culture often invites us to adopt either one of two extreme worldviews: Sometimes, we are counseled to be totally scientific-minded rationalists, devoid of any sense of mystery or the supernatural. Other voices advise us toward the opposite extreme by promoting a non-judgmental kind of emotionalism that embraces all opinions, religious ideas included, as being equally justifiable.

If we adopt this second philosophy, then what we call "God" becomes nothing more than a projection of our own egos. John Calvin warned that human nature is like an idol factory: Our hearts conjure countless replacements for God habitually.[20]

It is only by that grace that we can come to understand even the difficult elements of the Catholic faith. No doubt every reader will not agree with all that I have written. If everyone did then I probably haven't really written anything worth reading but only pandered by offering what Dietrich Bonhoeffer criticizes as "cheap grace." According to a sermon by Bonhoeffer, "Cheap grace is the grace we bestow on ourselves. Cheap grace is the preaching of forgiveness without requiring repentance, baptism without church discipline, communion without confession. . . . Cheap grace is grace without discipleship, grace without the cross, grace without Jesus Christ, living and incarnate."[21]

Rejecting cheap grace does not equate with rejecting innovations. Although blasphemy and sacrilege are commonplace in modern life, the antidote is not to retreat into a saccharine piety or overly sentimental spirituality. Sometimes I think some Christians need to reclaim a sense of holy irreverence. Here's an example of what I mean: Outside the US Conference of Catholic Bishops building in Washington DC is a statue of Jesus. It depicts him with one hand raised as if he were blessing a crowd. Well, that is what it is supposed to look like; some think it looks more like Jesus is hailing a taxi cab. This is not the forum for a critique of aesthetics, but it is a reminder once again that we too often fall into the shallow satisfaction of substituting skepticism instead of faith, positive-thinking instead of hope, and sentiment in place of love.

So, nothing herein should be read as a wholesale critique of the modern world, as if looking back nostalgically to the *via antiqua* reveals a golden age while looking upon the *via moderna* reveals some flawed version of Christianity. The Holy Spirit, in undiminished love, is ever at work renewing, regenerating, sanctifying, and reforming his Church. So, taking a cue from the prophet Isaiah, this book is an invitation to broaden both our thinking and practices: "Enlarge the site of your tent, and let the curtains of your habitations be stretched out; do not hold back; lengthen your cords and strengthen your stakes" (Isaiah 54:2).

Isaiah's message is clear: God is a big and generous God. Jesus emphasizes and the Old Testament attests to a God who is the God of lavish, excessive, abundant, extravagant, tender, empathetic, selfless, cleansing, empowering, redeeming love. He is the God who gave not just a few types of fruits but plants of every kind from which to eat (Genesis 1:29); who sent an excess of manna from heaven to feed his people and who led them to a land flowing with milk and honey (Exodus 16); he hosts a banquet and pours our libations until the cup overflows (Psalms 23:5). Jesus reconfirms this munificence, proclaiming God to be like the forgiving father who rushes out to greet his prodigal son (Luke 15:22-23). He is like the good shepherd who leaves the 99 sheep to go after the one that is missing. He is the generous king who forgives a massive debt (Luke 17:3-4). He is the giver of the good measure, pressed down, shaken together, running over and overflowing (Luke 6:38). Jesus' own miracles attest to this character. He changed an enormous amount of water into the very finest-tasting wine (John 2). Jesus fed the hungry crowds with just a few fish and loaves, with much left over (Matthew 14:13-21, and Matthew 15:32-16). Above all, he is the only begotten son who sacrificed himself so that we may live.

†

CHAPTER ONE

FAITH AND REASON

BIG STORIES

There are two basic metanarratives, or big stories, that offer competing views about the way in which Christianity affected the world. To simplify matters, we'll call the first one the "Catholic" view and the second one the "secular" view. (Perhaps the word "humanist" would be appropriate, given the *Humanist Manifesto*[1] does a good job of summarizing this metanarrative. But, given there are great Catholic humanists, such as St. Thomas More, I chose not to use this moniker to avoid confusion.) The Catholic view conceives of the world as having fundamentally changed due to the incarnation of Jesus Christ. His life, death, and resurrection initiated an ontological shift with consequences not just for every individual but for all of creation. More than merely offering a guide for a nice way to live, Jesus' ministry re-launched the kingdom of God—the new creation. Time and again, Jesus gave hints of this restorative power during his life. He calmed the storm, healed the sick, and raised the dead. The parables he told also point us to a new reality that is breaking forth into our broken world. The beatitudes he proclaimed give us a glimpse into the kind of behavior expected of people living in his kingdom. The Church he inaugurated provides the sacraments to strengthen, to encourage, and to redeem us.

The Church claims no expertise outside of the subject matters of faith and morals. However, the Christian perspective categorically rejects elements of the competing secular metanarrative (really, we ought to say "metanarratives" in the plural, as there many varied positions), which posits that prior to Christianity the world was advancing along, and then the Church came about promoting arbitrary, inconsistent, narrow-minded, separatist, intolerant, irrational, and superstitious fear mongering. From the secular perspective, civilization was doing quite nicely without Christianity—just look to the glories of the ancient Greco-Roman world, for example. Though tainted by a variety of barbarisms, the world before Jesus was steadily progressing. This progress, under the influence of Christianity in the West, brought us into a darkness from which we would only begin to emerge when rational thinking challenged faith, during the Age of Enlightenment.

These summaries are vastly oversimplified—secularism is not merely defined by a rejection of theism, as Catholics have been champions of many humanist causes. The point is merely to distinguish the two opposing worldviews. What I have labeled as "Catholic" and "secular" worldviews are examples of the broader categories of faith and reason.

For centuries, many believed these two competing views were wholly irreconcilable; and in some ways that is true. However, insisting that the two perspectives are in an unavoidable titanic struggle likens us to children on a beach, making two crabs who would prefer to be left alone duke it out in a sand pit for our amusement. "Faith and reason are like two wings on which the human spirit rises to the contemplation of truth; and God has placed in the human heart a desire to know the truth—in a word, to know himself—so that, by knowing and loving God, men and women may also come to the fullness of truth about themselves."[2]

What we are really talking about here are very separate disciplines that explore the physical and metaphysical realms from different, but not mutually exclusive, perspectives. In the history of the Church there have certainly been clashes between Church and science (science is simply one example of a way of reasoning), Church and state, Church and culture. When the Church acts according to its best principles, these encounters inevitably prove enriching and rewarding. From her very inception, the Church was meant to continually grow and mature in new and sometimes unexpected ways.

This Catholic worldview both lauds and incorporates many of the contributions of thinkers who reject the Christian narrative. The Church believes that all who seek truth really seek God, even if unknowingly.

Actually, many secular advances roused lax Christians from their dogmatic slumber.[3] If superstition is the byproduct of an unscientific mind, then materialism is the byproduct of an overly scientific mind. Science provides us with great answers to scientific questions, but not all questions are scientific in nature.

> The history of Catholicism is the history of a bold, consistent, comprehensive affirmation of the whole full reality of revelation, of the fullness of the divinity revealed in Christ according to all the dimensions of its unfolding. It is the absolute, unconditional and comprehensive affirmation of the whole full life of man, of the totality of his life-relations and life-sources. And it is the unconditional affirmation, before all else, of the deepest ground of our being, that is to say of the living God. And Catholicism insists on the whole God, on the God of creation and judgment, and is not content with any mere Father-God of children or sinners, still less with the miracle-shy God of the Enlightenment and of Deism, a sort of parliamentary deity. And it would have the whole Christ, in whom this God was revealed to us, the Christ of the two natures, the God-man, in whom heaven and earth possess their eternal unity . . .[4]

Christianity, therefore, is best understood and best lived not as an insulated experience, divorced from everything else we do and know, but in full and confident interaction with the other. Amidst all this interaction, the Church puts forth no single Catholic philosophy[5] but recognizes a variety of legitimate ways of knowing; that is, expressions of faith and of reason. In our world of competing ideas, the Church does not offer the single truth on all topics but subjects the cacophony of rival truth claims and all the world's various philosophies and ideas to scrutiny in light of the Gospel of Jesus Christ. This scrutiny can be understood as faith and reason being in a relationship that can take various forms: symbiotic (they have a positive relationship); separate and distinct (they have no relationship); or as being contradictory (they have a negative relationship).

Catholics tend to see faith and reason as symbiotic; like two hands of an expert violinist, working together to build the melody of a magnificent symphony. For some believers, however, this symbiosis is based on perplexities they cannot resolve. I once heard a deacon preach about how much he liked to scuba dive. He explained that when a diver goes underwater, it is easy to get disoriented and not know which way is up. There is no need to panic, however, because all you have to do is follow the bubbles. The bubbles always rise to the surface. His point, as he later explained, was that we should all follow the bubbles of God in our life.

Honestly, I have absolutely no clue what the bubbles of God are, let alone how to follow them. Yet I suspect there was a bit of wisdom concealed in that sermon, if only it could have been communicated more clearly. Some people find Christianity as confusing as I found the deacon's sermon. To them, the entire *mysterium fidei* (Latin: "mystery of faith"), including the story of Jesus, sounds interesting, and there seems to be a bit of wisdom in it. But mostly Christianity really doesn't make all that much sense to them, much of it appearing naïve, old-fashioned, or simply ridiculous. There are claims of spectacular miracles and ludicrous assertions about a God who loves us, but nonetheless he allows—or worse, he inflicts—so much suffering on us. For them, faith is not all that different from watching a movie. When we see a film, we pretend for two hours or so that what we are viewing could actually happen. We engage in the willful suspension of disbelief and simply ignore the fact that much of what we see in the movie cannot possibly happen in real life. As the philosopher Nietzsche said, "'Faith' means not wanting to know what is true."[6]

Some believe that we have absolutely no access whatsoever to truth; that we are prisoners of our own minds. This sort of extreme skepticism inevitably leads to solipsism—or worse, nihilism. The Chinese philosopher Chuang Tzu posed the following scenario. As a man, one night he dreamt he was a butterfly. Now that he was awake he cannot help but wonder if he is not a butterfly dreaming he is a man. How can he know? How does one differentiate between real life and mere dreams? Well, to begin with, in the example of the butterfly dream, that very fact that we use the word "dream" means there is a recognized difference between real life and dreamed life. That is not a bad place to start.

There is a rich history in Eastern philosophy that explores how we all create illusions that we exchange for reality. The Buddha is credited with devising an entire code of living based on the belief that much of our lived experience is an illusion. The ultimate goal of a Buddhist is to attain *Nirvana* (Sanskrit: "no wind"). That place of no wind is where we see clearly.

Traditionally, Abrahamic faiths bristle at this notion that the world is illusory. YHWH is a creator God, and to deny the reality of creation is to drift into Gnosticism. There is no genuine happiness aside from an encounter with truth. Truth exists independently of our desires, opinions, or feelings. When truth uncomfortably clashes with faith, we need not retreat to an uncritical fundamentalism that seeks to ignore developments in science and culture, nor should we simply rest in ambiguity. As Cardinal Newman explained,

> . . . he who believes Revelation with that absolute faith . . . is not the nervous creature who startles at every sudden sound, and is fluttered by every strange or novel appearance which meets his eyes. He has no sort of apprehension, he laughs at the idea, that any thing [sic] can be discovered by any other scientific method, which can contradict any one of the dogmas of his religion. . . . He is sure, and nothing shall make him doubt, that, if anything seems to be proved by astronomer, or geologist, or . . . in contradiction to the dogmas of faith, that point will eventually turn out, first, not to be proved, or, secondly, not contradictory, or thirdly, not contradictory to any thing [sic] really revealed, but to something which has been confused with revelation . . .[7]

Truth, however solid and substantial, can and often is misunderstood. Saint Paul warned, "For now we see in a mirror, dimly, but then we will see face to face. Now I know only in part; then I will know fully, even as I have been fully known" (1 Corinthians 13:12). The Greek philosopher Plato explored this potential for misunderstanding in his "Allegory of the Cave." Plato speculates about how people would react to the real world if they had experienced it for the first time after a long imprisonment of being chained in a dim cave where they only saw shadows cast on a wall illuminated by a distant fire.

Notwithstanding this failing, Christianity teaches that we can access truth via many routes. Saint Augustine's writings relied heavily on Plato; St. Thomas Aquinas often argued from the perspective of Aristotle. Saint Francis of Assisi avoided philosophical arguments in favor of a more mystical approach. Which of the Catholic spiritualities is the best fit for you? Inevitably, in matters of faith, we sometimes must continue in discomfort and even puzzlement for a time, perhaps a long time, just wrestling with how to make sense of certain teachings and how to live out our faith. Discovering the truth is not an easy task. I use the word "discover," because truth is not something we create like an artist but something we find like a treasure hunter.

And we should expect, from time to time, to fall prey to doubts, just as we should be confident that atheists, too, have such instances. The difference is that growing in the life of faith tempers those doubts, giving way to a deeply personal relationship with God. Faith is, therefore, more than mere subjective belief, more than the result of a conclusion reached after a rigorous intellectual investigation or personal soul searching. Christianity is a transformative encounter with Jesus; a relationship that gives the Christian new possibilities and perspective. Jesus often preached about faith and did so in terms of what Martin Buber, centuries later, identified as the "I–Thou" relationship, as opposed to the "I–It" relationship. (I-Thou defines a relationship between a subject and a subject—there is mutual respect—whereas an I-It relationship is between subject and object—involving disregard and even control of one party by the other.) For Christ, faith was not an abstract concept but a relationship; it is a gift that eludes a precise definition.

First and foremost, faith is a gracious gift from God, which a person can accept or reject. This acceptance or rejection is shaped, in part, by an individual's emotional and intellectual commitments. Faith is bigger than the individual, however, and emanates from the Body of Believers, as witnesses to the Gospel. The gift of faith is the bestowal of a share in God's own knowledge about himself. Faith is a belief in God and the truths he has revealed. (Hope, on the other hand, is the confidence that these truths have application in life.)

"Now faith is the assurance of things hoped for, the conviction of things not seen" (Hebrews 11:1). Faith is a gift that cannot be earned, bargained for, or simply chosen. Faith is always responsive to God's invitation. Some years ago, a Christian denomination was advertising with the catchphrase "Catch the Spirit," in reference to the Holy Spirit. I'd drive by this church, thinking that the slogan was kind of catchy, though it was theologically suspect since God is always the initiator. The sign ought to have read, "Get caught by the Spirit." We do not initiate the relationship with God. He is always reaching out to each one of us in love. So, any change that comes about through his grace, whether it be conversion, forgiveness, etc. is never a change in God but always a change in the person.

The best we can do is to prepare ourselves to receive his invitation. The Christmas carol "Joy to the World" has a verse with the words, "Let every heart, prepare him room." Maybe this reckons back to the infancy narrative of the Gospel of Luke, which records that there was no room in the inn for the pregnant Mary and her husband, Joseph, and so Jesus was born outside in a manger. What can be done to make room for God in our lives? One way is by adopting an openness to God, a "Here I am" attitude. The great patriarch, Abraham, was addressed by God, and he responded with the Hebrew word "*hineni*," which means, "Here I am." When God spoke to the prophet Samuel, he too answered with "hineni."

Abraham and Samuel's openness—their willingness to encounter the mystery of God—is important, but hineni is only a start. Oxford University displays a famous painting of Christ standing outside a door, knocking to gain entrance; but the door has no handle or doorknob. The artist, Holman Hunt, explains that the door represents the human heart, and the human heart can only be opened from the inside. The decision to open the door is a choice, an act of one's will. Too many of us act only when we feel inspired to do so. The most successful among us realize that, more often, action generates inspiration, not the other way around. A good student does not wait for the inspiration to study; a good athlete does not wait for the feeling to train.

Faith in God certainly can involve one's feelings; in a positive sense, a believer can experience consolation. However, aridity or an absence of emotion, even a negative emotional experience, can accompany a strong faith. To love God does not always mean having strong emotional feelings for him.

While faith is not synonymous with or dependent upon feelings, neither is it simply a kind of intellectual assent. Some have come to faith through intellectual persuasion, like St. Augustine's experience recounted in his famous *Confessions*. For Augustine, critical thinking played an important role in preparing him to receive the transforming gift of faith. Yet, as St. Ambrose put it, "*Non in dialectica placuit Deo salvum facere populum suum*," ("God does not save his people with arguments")[8]. Others experience a more emotional conversion. John Wesley described his faith with the words: "I felt my heart strangely warmed." The Latin phrase "*cor cordi loquitur*," which translates to "heart speaks to heart," is another example along the lines of Wesley's experience.

Consider the Buddhist story of a certain master whose guest inquired about Zen. The master agreed to discuss the matter over tea. The two sat down, and the master began to pour, but when the cup was full, he continued pouring. The astonished guest protested that the cup could hold no more tea. The master replied that, like the teacup, the guest was full to the brim with his own theories. If he were to learn anything new, it would simply spill over like the tea. To be serious about learning Zen, he would first need to be emptied, to lose himself. In imitation of Jesus' kenosis, Christianity also invites each one of us to become emptied, though, perhaps, in a different way than the Zen master intended. Jesus advised, "For those who want to save their life will lose it, and those who lose their life for my sake, and for the sake of the gospel, will save it" (Mark 8:35).

God's love presupposes that he created beings with genuine freedom. Exercising this freedom is every person's right, even at times a duty, but if God instructs us to reject what we wish most to succumb to, then without anger or regret, that is what we are called to do. Failing to yield to God's wishes, however, does not negate his love. Even if we deny or ignore him, God's love for us remains. I have an atheist colleague who incessantly used to kid me whenever I went to an on-campus Mass at the Catholic college where I taught. I'd pass by his office and he'd ruefully ask me, "Going to see your imaginary friend again?" He is a gentle and jovial professor with whom I have developed a valued friendship. We'd debate sometimes but often seemed to drift into extreme examples. As a general rule of debate, it is unfair to compare your side's best examples with the other side's worst examples. I've encountered Christians who make ignorant claims such as equating all atheists with Stalin. On the other hand, I've encountered atheists who take extremist positions, suggesting, for instance, that parents who take their child to a worship service should be prosecuted for child abuse.

Nevertheless, my colleague and I kept it pleasant. Yet, even if he weren't my friend, if he were acerbic, crude, or mocking, I still would try not to react belligerently. As Brother Thomas Merton explained, "Do not be too quick to assume that your enemy is an enemy of God just because he is your enemy. Perhaps he is your enemy precisely because he can find nothing in you that gives glory to God. Perhaps he fears you, because he can find nothing in you of God's love and God's kindness and God's patience and mercy and understanding of the weaknesses of men. Do not be too quick to condemn the man who no longer believes in God, for it is, perhaps, your own coldness and avarice, your mediocrity and materialism, your sensuality and selfishness that have killed his faith."[9]

My friend in this story is only one of many atheists I know and love. As a lawyer, I recognize that knowing the ins and outs of the opposition's argument can be remarkably helpful for dialogue, and with that in mind I often expose myself to arguments against my faith. So, I've learned that it is much better to have conversations rather than arguments about faith. The difference is inestimable. An argument wants a winner and a loser. It is confrontational and can degrade into toxic personal attacks very easily. Genuine conversation, on the other hand, starts off with an equal playing field. Neither party should presuppose what the other side is going to say. And each side needs to respect the evidentiary standards of their respective disciplines. Further complicating the matter is that what leads you to faith may drive me away. "The same sun that melts wax also hardens clay," goes the saying.

So, if I were going to argue in favor of atheism I would start by pointing out the remarkable variety of religions the world has produced. Even if we focus on just the world's greatest religions, the ones that have lasted for not just centuries but millennia, I would point out that no one has yet been able to persuade members of opposing belief systems that they are incorrect. So, for example, Hindus have not yet convinced Christians, and Christians have not yet convinced Buddhists, and so on. Additionally, the reality is that disparate beliefs are not just a matter of one faith convincing another, but also finding a single faith that has kept an unbroken continuity of observances and teachings. Even within single-faith communities we will find a plethora of different beliefs that often change over time. There are many examples of religions where practices and beliefs that were once thought to be acceptable are now considered abhorrent (e.g., some "good" Christians thought it quite appropriate to own slaves).

The reasons why no one religion reigns supreme over all the others is simply because each and every one of them is nothing other than sheer and utter fantasy. It's all made up. Or, perhaps, that is too extreme a claim. We may worship the great chief in the sky because for millennia *Homo sapiens* have formed social groups that looked toward an authority figure for leadership. Primitive societies had chieftains, and as history progressed, we simply projected this experience out into the cosmos.

After making this bold claim, I would point out that all religious belief is socialized, while atheism is discerned. When life ends, existence ceases. This is not a pleasant thought, but millions of people adopt this view in preference to religious fantasies. Theists may suffer from what psychologists call optimism bias; our brains are wired to prefer believing in better rather than worse outcomes. Yet the reason why atheism continues not only to persist but to thrive is because it is the only honest conclusion at which any rational person can arrive. More than being honest and rational, atheists are truly courageous, more so than any religious zealot or martyr who acts only to gain favor with or please their God. Atheists bravely reject millennia of religious superstitions and oppressive attempts to instill societal conformity. Although, for much of history, atheists have long been pariahs in society, and they still exist despite so many efforts to eradicate them. Atheists all subscribe to the same beliefs concerning the supernatural—it is nonexistent, while theists maintain vastly different theologies. The reason atheism can't be extinguished is the same reason truth can't be extinguished; because rational minds will inevitably gravitate toward reality.

Atheism is both noble and democratic. Atheists believe in individual human value while rejecting any notion that such value is the result of a top-down hierarchy, a dignity imparted by some deity. We can all trace our ancestry to the primitive life from which we evolved. The reality is that while there are psychological, sociological, cultural, and, perhaps, even biological compulsions to believe in a god, there is really only one reason to be an atheist; because atheism is correct. Traditionally, children are taught about God at the same time they learn about other fairy tales. Belief in God, for the child, is really no different than believing in Santa Claus or the Tooth Fairy. In adulthood, all such fantasies should be disregarded. Actually, we all do disregard them and become atheists as we mature; even the most ardent believer must admit to being an atheist with respect to other religions. Ask a Catholic to craft an argument that establishes the historicity of the visitation of the Angel Gabriel to the Virgin Mary, as recounted in the Gospels, while simultaneously applying similar criteria to dismiss the alleged angelic visitations purported by other religious traditions. "Yes, of course, Gabriel visited Mary." "No, of course, the Mormons are wrong, and the angel Moroni did not visit Joseph Smith Jr.; that's ridiculous." You see the challenge this presents.

Carl Sagan said that, "extraordinary claims require extraordinary evidence"[10]; and there is simply no such evidence for the supernatural. You may want it all to be true because of fear or loneliness, but something as uncomplicated as the classic unsolvable question of theodicy—the topic of why an all-good, all-powerful god allows injustice and suffering in the world—proves atheism to be true. The notion that any deity intervenes, providentially, in the lives of believers more so than in the lives of nonbelievers, is laughable. Theists in general, and Christians in particular, make bold claims about the power of a loving God at work in our world. Really? Just look around, or better yet, look back through history to the many wars, slavery, torture, disasters, etc., all of which show that we live in a distinctly non-supernatural world governed by the laws of nature and definitively not overseen by the providence of a benevolent, omnipotent God. The Church then is comprised of masses of self-deluded people who shamefully exchange rational thought and objective truth for a false sense of security. Worse, this harmful fantasy is all the more poignant given that parents and authority figures vainly foist their superstitions onto others. Consider parents who rely on prayer instead of medicine for a sick child.

In a more general sense, it is simply an indisputable fact that believers don't seem to fare any better in life than non-believers. Can anyone truly argue that men and women of faith are richer, healthier, or rewarded in some visible way for all their prayers and devotions? As a corollary, look to the extraordinarily successful individuals who either dismissed or were highly skeptical about the existence of any god or the supernatural (e.g., scientists including Albert Einstein and Stephen Hawking; titans of business including Andrew Carnegie and Warren Buffet; authors Mark Twain and Isaac Asimov, etc.).

Consider how would-be assassins tried to kill Adolf Hitler over ten times, yet he survived. Joseph Stalin was arrested and exiled to Siberia on multiple occasions but managed to live to become the leader of the Soviet Union and murder over twenty million people. If these ordeals were paralleled in the life of some great saint, believers would ascribe God's providential intervention to their survival. For instance, in 1981, Pope St. John Paul II survived an assassin's bullet. He was nearly killed but credited his survival to the intercession of Mary. (A bullet from this incident was given by Pope St. John Paul II to the then-bishop of Fátima, Portugal, where it was added to the crown adorning a statue of Our Lady of Fátima). Did Mary save Hitler and Stalin and the pope?

Traditional Judeo-Christian so-called morality is merely a product of crude socialization to keep us organized and "in line." The sheer amount of suffering imposed by theists on the world is inestimable. Religious zealots have burned heretics, "witches," and books with glee. They have imposed a prudish sexual moral code that has oppressed countless people throughout the ages. But, by divorcing ourselves from such pointless religious ideals, we can create a world filled with goodness, compassion, and justice; minus all the religious trappings and attendant biases. Once we realize we are not the crowning creation of some celestial deity, we will free ourselves from the arrogance associated with such religious claptrap and start to create a truly moral society. Many scholars have noted that we did not move out of the Stone Age due to a lack of stones; instead, our knowledge advanced, and so we left a more primitive culture behind. The same kind of culture-changing opportunity presents itself today. There is no teleology, no ultimate goal for our existence, except that which we choose for ourselves. In that liberating truth we should find our happiness.

Well, that's my pitch for atheism. I suppose if I were really trying hard to convince you then I'd throw in a few insults that describe men and women of faith as dull-minded or naïve. Regardless, I sincerely hope you were not even slightly persuaded by what I have written. The arguments I made may have sounded convincing at a surface level, but my entire defense of atheism is filled with erroneous presumptions, fallacious reasoning, and all sorts of metaphysical nonsense. I employed a number of rhetorical tricks to make my arguments sound convincing when really they are poorly argued, misleading, and weak. Let me give you just two simple rebuttals to a couple of the points I made above. (Other counter-arguments follow throughout the book.)

First, let me counter the argument that atheists discern truth independently while theists are indoctrinated—it is a fallacious claim. We don't have to drift off into an unsophisticated pluralistic theology in order to point out certain important similarities in the concept of God developed independently of each other across the world's great religious traditions. As to those topics on which the world's great religions disagree, while there may appear to be countless different opinions and teachings, they can be categorized and grouped. "There isn't really, for an adult mind, this infinite variety of religions to consider. We may divide religions, as we do soups, into 'thick' and 'clear.' By Thick I mean those which have orgies and ecstasies and mysteries and local attachments. . . . By Clear I mean those which are philosophical, ethical and universalizing. . . . Now if there is a true religion it must be both Thick and Clear: for the true God must have made both the child and the man, both the savage and the citizen, both the head and the belly."[11]

Second, I'll rebut the absurd claim that believers correlate our experience of our own parents with our concept of God while atheists do not. One can just as easily proclaim that it is Freud, one of the proponents of this theory, who had daddy issues and was merely projecting his own self-admitted ambivalence for his own dad into the realm of the divine.

In short, even a modestly informed Catholic can easily refute each argument I made in my feigned defense of atheism. But those who struggle with belief in God in the face of such arguments do well to recall Martin Luther King Jr.'s words, "Peace is not merely a distant goal that we seek, but a means by which we arrive at that goal."[12] The same can be said about faith. Faith is not a distant goal that we seek, but a means by which we arrive at that goal. In the words of St. Augustine, "Understanding is the reward of faith. Therefore seek not to understand that you may believe, but believe that you may understand."[13]

To understand that there is a God is not enough. "You believe that God is one; you do well. Even the demons believe—and shudder" (James 2:19). Belief, then, is authentic when it inspires action. C. S. Lewis compares authentic faith with the sort of mere belief James wrote about. He uses the analogy of paint and dye. Mere belief is like surface paint, while authentic faith is more like a penetrating dye. "Painted" Christians go through all the motions of a true convert, but always with a sense of resentment.[14] Some of the resentment Lewis talks about stems from the false idea that Christ demands we love him to the exclusion of all others. Although

God is to be our primary love, "I do not mean that God would have even His closest presence make us forget or cease to desire that of our friend. God forbid! The Love of God is the perfecting of every love."[15] That perfecting love should permeate our entire lives.

There is, however, a potent difference between superficial faith and sincere skepticism. Faith often progresses in stages or degrees. *Fides quaerens intellectum* (faith seeking understanding) was a theme of St. Anselm's writing. A person's faith is expected to be troubled by duplicity, confusion, anxiety, and a host of other impediments. Believers are not without uncertainties.[16] An argument can be made that God appreciates a sincere skeptic more than an insincere believer. As St. Thomas More taught, "A faint faith is better than a strong heresy."[17] In the Old Testament there are three books that can be categorized as "skeptical books": Ecclesiastes, Habakkuk, and Job. These skeptical books are so named because of the tone and method each author employs. We learn from them that if a person's skepticism is truly sincere, it must inevitably initiate an investigation into truth. In point of fact, the very word "skepticism" comes from the Greek word "*skeptikoi*" which translates as "investigator."

As a social scientist, I was trained to never arrive at a conclusion before analyzing the data. However, even objective scientists posit hypotheses. Like them, it is reasonable, in the investigatory stages of faith, to manifest a hypothetical faith. Making the choice to believe is not insincere or fake, but merely purposeful. If you doubt, but live as if you believe, you might actually come to believe, not because of buying into a self-delusion, but like the man who encountered Jesus and said, "I believe; help my unbelief!" (Mark 9:24). There is a fable about a man who was born with horribly disfigured features. His father, the king, had his face encased in a beautiful golden mask. After years of wearing the mask, it finally was removed, and the young man's face had been transformed into the features of the mask, and he was now beautiful. Saint Cyprian of Carthage made the same point more succinctly when he said, "Let us imitate what we shall one day be."[18]

GIVE FAITH A CHANCE

There is a phenomenon among some church attendees to belong before you believe. That is, while in the past people would be formally initiated into the church community, some who do not fully subscribe to Church teachings nonetheless participate in the life of the Church—though only full members should partake in Communion, as doing so without full membership purports a shared unity, which is lacking.

Jesus told a parable about weeds growing up with wheat, which touches on this point (Matthew 13: 24-30). Weeds of falsehood intermingle with the wheat of truth. But, as this parable teaches, uprooting all the weeds might damage the wheat. George MacDonald states "That no keeping but a perfect one will satisfy God, I hold with all my heart and strength; but that there is none else he cares for, is one of the lies of the enemy. What father is not pleased with the first tottering attempt of his little one to walk? What father would be satisfied with anything but the manly step of the full-grown son?"[19]

To think about it another way, consider what happens when you cook with fresh ingredients, like basil just picked from the garden. The scent of the herb lingers and even rubs off. Similarly, the fragrances of the people with whom we associate can rub off on us and infuse our lives. "But thanks be to God, who in Christ always leads us in triumphal procession, and through us spreads the fragrance of the knowledge of him everywhere" (2 Corinthians 2:14 ESV). We all touch and influence one another, and so too do our thoughts and ideas. Saint Francis of Assisi said, "Sanctify yourself, and you will sanctify society."[20]

The Church continues to insist that reason cannot contradict the truth of divine revelation, nor vice versa. Nonetheless, apparent contradictions do occur all the time. Saint Albert Magnus and his greatest student, St. Thomas Aquinas, explored the benefits of compartmentalizing knowledge, but to admit distinction is not the same as acknowledging incompatibility. Science and faith are distinct disciplines and ought to be studied separately. Reason is learned and grounded in both evidence and experience. Faith is both a gift and a decision to accept the gift. Faith has both a subjective and objective element. Faith is both a personal encounter with the divine and conjointly a new openness to one's neighbor. And in a special way, the Church is a community of fellow believers who not only serve as fellow witnesses but bestowers of sacraments. Faith is closely tied to repentance and conversion (Greek: *Metanoia*). Faith is trust in God and loyalty to him. (Some formulas of faith break the concept into three precepts: Latin: *Notitia*—know, *Assensus*—assent, *Fiducia*—trust.)

Despite these distinctions, faith and reason are necessarily united. Writing on the related topics of nature and grace, David Hart wrote,

> These divisions are illusory. What we call 'nature' is merely one mode of the disclosure of the 'supernatural,' and natural reason merely one mode of revelation, and philosophy merely one (feeble) mode of reason's ascent into the light of God. Nowhere, not even in the sciences, does there exist a 'purely natural' realm of knowledge. To encounter the world is to encounter its being, which is gratuitously imparted to it from beyond the sphere of natural causes, known within the medium of an intentional consciousness, irreducible to immanent processes, that grasps finite reality only by being oriented toward a horizon of transcendental ends (or, better, 'divine names'). There is a seamless continuity between the sight of a rose and the mystic's vision of God; the latter is in fact implicit in the former, and saturates it, and but for this supernatural surfeit nothing natural could come into thought.[21]

It is worth noting that one of the most original of thinkers in history, the atheistic philosopher Friedrich Nietzsche, knew that both for believers and unbelievers alike, faith cannot be divorced from reason. He wrote, "Strictly speaking, there is no such thing as science without presuppositions . . . a philosophy, a 'faith' must always be there first, so that science can acquire from it a direction, a meaning, a limit, a method, a right to exist. . . . It is still a metaphysical faith that underlies our faith in science." [22]

Reason and faith are not enemies, and it may come as a surprise that the Catholic Church is a champion of both. In the wake of the fall of Rome, it was the Christian monasteries that preserved much of Western civilization's great literary works by rescuing many ancient texts from destruction.[23] Monks painstakingly transcribed not only the Bible but countless other works by ancient Greeks, Romans, and other non-Christians. Why? Simply, the Church recognized the importance of secular knowledge. Actually, it was the Catholic Church that gave us the very first universities. "The University was an utterly new phenomenon in European history. Nothing like it had existed in ancient Greece or Rome. The institution that we recognize today, with its faculties, courses of study, examinations and degrees, as well as the distinction between undergraduate and graduate study, comes to us directly from the medieval world. The Church developed the university system, because, according to historian Lowrie J. Daly, it was "the only institution in Europe that showed consistent interest in the preservation and the cultivation of knowledge."[24]

While other belief systems—certain expressions of Gnosticism, for example—saw the world as vile and base, the Church rejected such an extremist view. Catholics are unashamedly sensory and tactile. We baptize with water, anoint with oil,[25] light churches with candle-fire, and burn fragrant incense. Catholics decorate with sacred imagery such as icons, painting, stained-glass, statuary, and colorful vestments. We use the symbols of acronyms, monograms, and illuminated manuscripts. We play music, ring bells, sing, stand, and kneel. Most importantly, we receive the Eucharist (the Body, Blood, Soul, and Divinity of Our Lord) under the appearance of bread and wine.

Additionally, the Catholic Church also uses sacramentals, sacred signs such as wordless expressions we can employ, publicly or privately. Making the sign of the cross and reciting "In the name of the Father, and of the Son, and of the Holy Spirit," is one such sacramental. (The Sign of the Cross derives from the baptismal formula found in Matthew 28:19.[26]) Lighting a devotional candle is another example of a sacramental, an act of devotion that focuses our attention on God. In a very real sense, the entire world is sacramental from the Catholic perspective. In other words, the natural and supernatural realities collide, overlap, and infuse one another. This interaction is, at times, flawed and disfigured, but Christians are called to heal and normalize it. The Catholic ideal is to recognize every legitimate human passion and appetite as a good gift coming from a good and loving God.

Catholic thought and practice move beyond religious observances. The Church understands the entire created order to be worthy of serious attention. Both the natural and social sciences owe a great debt to the esteem with which these topics were treated at Catholic universities in the Middle Ages. To provide even a small sampling of the contributions Catholic clergy and laypersons have contributed to the natural sciences, the social sciences, and the arts, would be a massive undertaking. It is hard to exaggerate the Catholic Church's influence on civilization as a whole and Western culture in particular. The few samples cited below are not about men and women who just happen to be

Catholic and also have contributed to the development of science and culture. No, the effect these people had on society is often inextricably tied to their Catholic identity.

The development of Gregorian chant, for example, influenced music even into modern times, and the construction of medieval cathedrals affected modern architecture. Church law, (canon law) profoundly influenced the development of secular law and justice.[27] In imitation of Jesus' practices, the Church expounded the dignity of each and every human and raised the status of those who were previously marginalized: women, orphans, the poor, and the sick. Certainly, the Hebrew Scriptures alluded to similar concerns, but it is irrefutable that Jesus emphasized the co-equal status and innate worth of these individuals.

This care for others, many of whom were neglected in pagan cultures, was paradigm altering! Medieval hospitals, run by monks and nuns, changed the face of medicine. The preservation and transmission of numerous medical corpuses from antiquity are due exclusively to the tireless efforts of committed Catholic monks copying ancient manuscripts in monastery scriptoriums.

Space here does not allow for a more detailed accounting of Catholic contributions, but I recommend taking a moment to research how Catholics influenced our calendar (Pope Gregory XIII), the use of Hindu-Arabic numerals instead of the clunky Roman numerals (Pope Sylvester II), literature (Dante Alighieri, J. R. R. Tolkien), contributions to Egyptology (Father Athanasius Kircher), and possibly even the invention of the pretzel by a medieval Italian monk.[28]

Historically, Catholics are numbered among the most important scientists of all time, including René Descartes, who discovered analytic geometry and the laws of refraction; Blaise Pascal, inventor of the adding machine, hydraulic press, and the mathematical theory of probabilities; Augustinian priest Gregor Mendel, who founded modern genetics; Louis Pasteur, founder of microbiology and creator of the first vaccine for rabies and anthrax; and cleric Nicolaus Copernicus, who first developed scientifically the view that the earth rotated around the sun. Jesuit priests in particular have a long history of scientific achievement; they contributed to the development of pendulum clocks, pantographs, barometers, reflecting telescopes and microscopes, as well as to scientific fields as various as magnetism, optics, and electricity. They observed, in some cases before anyone else, the colored bands on Jupiter's surface, the Andromeda nebula, and Saturn's rings. They theorized about the circulation of the blood (independently of Harvey), the theoretical possibility of flight, the way the moon affects the tides, and the wavelike nature of light. Star maps of the southern hemisphere, symbolic logic, flood-control measures on the Po and Adige rivers, introducing plus and minus signs into Italian mathematics—all were typical Jesuit achievements, and scientists as influential as Fermat, Huygens, Leibniz, and Newton were not alone in counting Jesuits among their most-prized correspondents.

The scientist credited with proposing in the 1930s what came to be known as the "Big Bang theory" of the origin of the universe was Georges Lemaitre, a Belgian physicist and Roman Catholic priest. Alexander Fleming, the inventor of penicillin, shared his faith. More recently, Catholics constitute a good number of Nobel Laureates in physics, medicine, and physiology, including Erwin Schrodinger, John Eccles, and Alexis Carrel.[29]

If we expand our analysis in two ways, to include not just Catholics but all Christians, and not just scientific contributions but all kinds of progress, then we find that Christianity's contribution to our world is unparalleled. The Church lauds reason, praises the sciences, and promotes rational and logical thought—and has since her inception—though without question there have been some extreme exceptions to this rule.

The Galileo affair comes to mind as an example. Galileo's astronomical calculations led him to believe the earth moved; the Bible seemed to say the earth was fixed. So, a controversy erupted, not so much over geocentrism as over the topic of authority. Under threat of torture and execution, by being burned at the stake, Galileo was required to cease his promotion of Copernicanism. Though history does not record that Galileo was ever actually tortured, there is a famous account of Galileo being shown the instruments of torture to persuade him to recant. Galileo did recant, but prior to this his defense was that he was not promoting Copernicus' heliocentrism but only studying these claims. Nonetheless, he was required to abjure the Copernican model. Even after his recantation, Galileo was sentenced to house arrest, where he continued his scientific studies. History records that Galileo defiantly uttered the words, "and yet it moves," sometime after his repudiation. The Church, eventually, after many years and much anguish, sided with Galileo's point by concluding that biblical authors used phenomenological language much as we do today. In 1992, Pope St. John Paul II addressed the Pontifical Academy of Sciences and confirmed that the theologians and officials of the Church were wrong to have condemned Galileo in 1633.

The sun does not actually rise and set, but we say it does, because that language fits our perspective; we are using phenomenological language. Galileo himself discussed this in his famous letter to Grand Duchess Christina:

> . . . the holy Bible can never speak untruth—whenever its true meaning is understood. But, I believe nobody will deny that it is often very abstruse, and may say things which are quite different from what its bare words signify. Hence in expounding the Bible if one were always to confine oneself to the unadorned grammatical meaning, one might fall into error. Not only contradictions and propositions far from true might thus be made to appear in the Bible, but even grave heresies and follies.
>
> . . . But, I do not feel obliged to believe that that same God who has endowed us with senses, reason, and intellect has intended to forgo their use and by some other means to give us knowledge which we can attain by them.[30]

Especially after the Galileo scandal had long since passed and in the days prior to the Reformation, a new age of camaraderie between faith and science was born. This symbiotic relationship would prove to be short lived, as science began raising serious challenges to certain biblical teachings.

Science is very good at describing the natural phenomena in a certain, distinct, data-oriented sense; however, it breaks down entirely in capturing unique, non-physical qualities—the "meaning of it all," if you will. What's more, faith can provide grounding for a moral life in the context of a God-created universe, a perspective that reason alone cannot offer. A good example of how faith and reason offer two distinct ways of knowing is provided by evolutionary biologist Stephen Jay Gould. He discusses the famous event after the Resurrection when Jesus appears to his followers. Thomas was not present for this visit and proclaimed that he would not believe that Jesus rose from the dead until he actually saw Jesus and touched his wounds (John 20:24-29).

Gould talks about the realms (he uses the word "magisteriums") of faith and science and points out that Thomas was acting like a good scientist but a poor disciple.

. . . I cannot think of a statement more foreign to the norms of science—indeed more unethical under this magisterium—than Jesus' celebrated chastisement of Thomas: 'blessed are they that have not seen, and yet have believed.' A skeptical attitude toward appeals based only on authority, combined with a demand for direct evidence (especially to support unusual claims), represents the first commandment of proper scientific procedure.

Poor Doubting Thomas.[31] At his crucial and eponymous moment, he acted in the most admirable way for one style of inquiry—but in the wrong magisterium. He espoused the key principle of science while operating within the different magisterium of faith.[32]

So, keeping faith and science separate is one technique for reconciling competing truth claims, but the fact is that the claims of science and faith overlap and clash in messy ways, and it is not always possible or even desirable to compartmentalize them. As Cardinal John Henry Newman stated, "There may be momentary collisions, awkward appearances, and many forebodings and prophecies of contrariety"[33] when such clashes occur. However, a strong argument can be made that the empirical sciences thrived throughout much of Europe, especially during the Middle Ages, precisely due to the influence of the Catholic Church,[34] which taught that all of creation is governed by certain identifiable laws.

One of those historical myths that enjoy popular currency, even though they cannot survive the scrutiny of serious historical study, is that, at the dawn of the Christian era, there was a thriving Hellenistic scientific culture that Christianity—through some supposed hostility to learning and reason—methodically destroyed; and that this Christian antagonism to science persisted into the early modern period—as is evident from Galileo's trial in Rome—until the power of the Church was at last broken, and secular faculties of science began to appear.

This story is impossible to reconcile with the historical evidence, ancient, Medieval, or modern. It misrepresents the characters both of Hellenistic science and of early Christianity, as well as that of Medieval intellectual culture; and it entirely belies the fascinating reality that, in the 16th and 17th centuries, Christian scientists educated in Christian universities and following

a Christian tradition of scientific and mathematical speculation
overturned a pagan cosmology and physics unchallenged since
the days of Aristotle.[35]

Later in history, great Western thinkers such as Sir Isaac
Newton and René Descartes worked diligently to connect God to
the natural world. This "natural theology" insisted that creation
reveals a creator, and if we look hard enough at both the macro
pictures (e.g. the planets and the stars) and the micro pictures
(e.g. slides under a microscope) we will find out that this creator
is orderly and rational.

This order was called into question when, in 1755, an enormous earthquake devastated Lisbon, Portugal. The destruction
wrought by this natural disaster was so profound that it may even
have been one of the sparks that ignited the Enlightenment.[36]
Questions about God's providence, his mercy, his very existence
began to find their way into popular culture. Voltaire, a professed
deist who believed in a distant and removed god, wrote about the
Lisbon quake in *Candide*, challenging Leibniz's claim that we live
in the "the best of all possible worlds"[37] and rejecting the idea that
a benevolent deity watches over us with a tender love. There are
variations of this position. Deism posits a god who is remote from
creation and who rarely, if ever, intervenes. It was not such an
intellectual leap for society to move from belief in a remote and
disconnected god to belief in no god.[38]

Enlightenment and post-Enlightenment scientists and philosophers contributed greatly to how we think and behave in the
modern world. Although much positive progress was made, this
radical change in ways of seeing and understanding the world did
not bring about the hoped-for Utopia that some Enlightenment
thinkers had expected. The 1500s brought us the Reformation.
The 1600s and 1700s brought about revolutions in science (Newton) and philosophy (Kant). The 1800s and 1900s came with new
ideas about how we understand our biological origins (Darwin),
our psychological predilections (Freud), our social relations (Dur-
kheim), and our political and economic systems (Marx). These
innovations challenged the Church to do what she always has
done, what she has been commanded to do: to preach the Gospel
in word and deed in a way that is consistent with Jesus' message
but also meaningful to the contemporary world.

Christians sometimes wrestled with the new ideas and technologies that were born out of different ages. It is, for example, no coincidence that the Reformation began around the time when Gutenberg invented the printing press, making Bibles and tracts more widely available.[39]

The same phenomena played out on a considerably larger scale after World War II, when many in Western civilization began to experience sweeping changes in how they perceived and experienced the world. With the popularization of television and the introduction of rock-n-roll, radical social change became the norm. It was not uncommon for individuals, especially young people, to see a message on TV or hear the lyrics of a song and react, "Hey, I think just like that, but I thought I was alone in such beliefs." By sharing these experiences with others, groups formed, and voilà: movements such as Civil Rights sprang forth. But, it was not just the secular world that experienced radical changes. The Church, too, with the onset of Vatican II reforms, experienced a paradigm shift.

What we see, time and again, is that it is not enough to simply adopt the formulaic faith passed on by others. As Christians, we are called to conform to Christ and his Church. This is not, however, a servile, uncritical endeavor on the part of the believer. Each generation appropriates the Catholic faith to a specific time, place, and culture. We cannot be lazy and hope to arrive at truth. Rather, we must continually journey along our own path, accepting—sometimes cheerfully, sometimes solemnly—the mystery of the faith. Happily, not only is God our companion on this journey of faith, but in the Eucharist, we are given living bread to nourish us for the journey. So, God is our companion as well as our destination, and therefore, in a sense, to begin the journey is to arrive.

†

CHAPTER TWO

FREEDOM AND RESPONSIBILITY

LASTING JOY

According to C. S. Lewis, "Whatever we desire is either what God is trying to give us as quickly as He can, or else a false picture of what He is trying to give us—a false picture which would not attract us for a moment if we saw the real thing."[1]

We are pilgrims seeking joy at the end of our pilgrimage. This is not a fanciful or marginal desire, but a yearning that emanates from the very cores of our beings. The book of Ecclesiastes reveals that "He [God] has also set eternity in their hearts" (3:11 NASB). Saints, poets, musicians, artists, and lovers: They may be more vocal about—even more aware of—this longing, but we all share in it. We all have an innate longing for which there is no earthly satisfaction. Philosopher Blaise Pascal once wrote: "The heart has reasons unknown to reason."[2]

We can find reports of a yearning for perfect joy from cultures around the world, going back to the very dawn of civilization. The ancient myth of Pandora unleashing chaos into an innocent world and the Genesis account of the fall of Adam and Eve are two examples of the sorts of stories that recount our innate longing for joy. The details may vary, but the theme of searching for joy, often a lost joy, is widespread. In its most primal form, this universal desire finds its roots in stories that tell about a time when humans lived in idyllic, even blissful conditions that were somehow lost, but which we all yearn to regain. "The best and most beautiful things in the world cannot be seen nor even touched, but just felt in the heart."[3]

Everyone wishes to be ravished by beauty. Actually, every pleasure we've ever felt, every joy we've ever known, is a pale foreshadowing of the divine beauty we are invited to encounter. C. S. Lewis expresses it in an address called, "The Weight of Glory": "We do not want merely to *see* beauty. . . . We want something else which can hardly be put into words—to be united with the beauty we see, to pass into it, to receive it into ourselves, to bathe in it, to become part of it."[4] In another work, he writes: "All the things that have ever deeply possessed your soul have been but hints of it—tantalising glimpses, promises never quite fulfilled, echoes that died away just as they caught your ear. . . . We cannot tell each other about it. It is the secret signature of each soul, the incommunicable and unappeasable want."[5] Most of us spend the majority of our lives on this search for this lost joy. We often get distracted, however, and mistake pleasure or power or some other substitute for joy.

In Oscar Wilde's novel, *The Picture of Dorian Gray*, one of the main characters, the pleasure-seeking Lord Henry Wotton, says, "The only way to get rid of a temptation is to yield to it. Resist it, and your soul grows sick with longing for the things it has forbidden to itself, with desire for what its monstrous laws have made monstrous and unlawful."[6] Virtue seems boring and sin seems exciting. That is why, personally, I love a first-rate villain over and above a boring, saccharine hero. Give me Byron's Lucifer, Shelley's Prometheus, Stoker's Dracula, Lucas' Darth Vader, or Chase's Tony Soprano any day. These villains just seem so much more interesting because, in good Nietzschean manner, they are indomitable: They freely engage in any behavior they choose—or, so it appears.

These characters remind us that life is short and death is certain. In imitation of them, should we not experience and absorb every delight we can? Strangely enough, the answer is "no"—but, not for the reasons you may think. Any pleasure, if we pursue it hedonistically, sooner or later will disappoint. The first time is great, but the second requires twice as much supply to get half as much pleasure. This addictive pattern can play out in drugs, sex, alcohol, riches—any pleasure that is sought after as an end in and of itself.

A life of pure self-interest leads inevitably to despair. To use the language of Søren Kierkegaard:

Eternity asks you . . . about only one thing: whether you have
lived in despair or not, whether you have despaired in such a
way that you did not realize that you were in despair, or in such
a way that you covertly carried this sickness inside of you as
your gnawing secret, as a fruit of a sinful love under your heart,
or in such a way that you, a terror to others, raged in despair.
And if so, if you have lived in despair, then, regardless of whatever else you won or lost, everything is lost for you, eternity does
not acknowledge you, it never knew you—or, still more terrible,
it knows you as you are known and it binds you to yourself in
despair.[7]

In place of the despair that accompanies vice, the Psalmist
tells us to, "Take delight in the LORD, and he will give you the
desires of your heart" (Psalms 37:4). But those heart's desires are
more profound than we might suspect. As C. S. Lewis explains:
"Our Lord finds our desires not too strong, but too weak. We are
half-hearted creatures, fooling about with drink and sex and am-
bition when infinite joy is offered us."[8] We enter into this joy by
entering into the delight of the saints.

As G. K. Chesterton puts it:

Joy . . . is the gigantic secret of the Christian. . . . The tremendous figure which fills the Gospels towers in this respect, as in
every other, above all the thinkers who ever thought themselves
tall. His pathos was natural, almost casual. The Stoics, ancient
and modern, were proud of concealing their tears. He never concealed His tears; He showed them plainly on His open face at
any daily sight, such as the far sight of His native city. Yet He
concealed something. Solemn supermen and imperial diploma-
tists are proud of restraining their anger. He never restrained
His anger. He flung furniture down the front steps of the Temple,
and asked men how they expected to escape the damnation of
Hell. Yet He restrained something. . . . There was some one thing
that was too great for God to show us when He walked upon our
earth; and I have sometimes fancied that it was His mirth.[9]

We are drawn to the joyful lives of the saints: their holiness
and their example of living out the Gospel. Their joy is deeper and
more lasting than any sinful pleasure you can conjure. As mystic

Simone Weil noted, "Imaginary evil is romantic and varied; real evil is gloomy, monotonous, barren, boring. Imaginary good is boring; real good is always new, marvelous, intoxicating."[10] We seem to know this disquieting truth deep down. We simply do not love historical villains the way we love fictional ones.

Who but the most psychotic among us would idolize the tyrants and villains of history? Consider, for example, the very first "Caesar" of Rome. Although he surely was not one of history's greatest villains—he wasn't even among the worst of Rome's emperors—he certainly could be brutal. But, I choose him as my example for a reason: Prior to becoming Rome's *de facto* emperor, Julius Caesar was once kidnapped by pirates. He warned his captors that they would pay with their lives for this outrage. The pirates demanded a ransom; and, when Julius heard of the paltry sum they were asking for his safe return, he insisted they increase the amount to reflect his great worth. Eventually, Julius Caesar was freed. True to his word, he later hunted down the pirates who had kidnapped him and had them all crucified.[11]

This is mere anecdotal evidence. But, during one of my trips to Italy, I visited the grave of Julius Caesar. He and I were alone, for, although there were some fresh flowers on his purported grave site, there weren't many visitors. However, on that same trip, I traveled to the town of Assisi to visit the tomb of the great St. Francis. As so often happens, the line of people who were waiting to get in wrapped around the great basilica dedicated to his memory. Why are so many drawn to the incredible virtue of St. Francis, while so few pay homage to the great pride of Caesar? There are a thousand reasons, I suppose. But, chief among them is the reality that authentic virtue is alluring and ever new. Unlike the monotony of sin, goodness can be practiced in an infinite variety—and, anyone who argues differently is promoting a small-minded homogeneity in lieu of a kaleidoscopic expression of the good. We would all do well to remember St. Vincent de Paul's insight: "Love is infinitely inventive."[12]

So, the directive of Christianity is not to cast off our desires in the name of uniform dullness or a puritanical distaste for pleasure but to free them from enslavement to mere appetites and passions. God does not command us to feel a certain way but to have faith in him regardless of any feelings.

Discipline is an unpopular word in our "live-for-the-moment" culture, but it is key to living a joyful life. The spiritually mature

person knows that the more she disciplines herself, the less she'll
be disciplined by others. Admittedly, some strains of Christian
thought may have taken this point about discipline and self-
control to an extreme. Discipline is paradoxical, because, while
we use it to direct our wills and to maintain control, it is only
when control is necessary—and, always with regard to ourselves.
We ought never try to control another. It may seem ironic that
our self-discipline, to be useful at all, must be restrained, but
as M. Scott Peck wisely pointed out, "The fact that a feeling is
uncontrolled is no indication whatsoever that it is any deeper
than a feeling that is disciplined."[13] Elsewhere he expands on this
theme: ". . . To live wisely, we must daily delay gratification and
keep an eye on the future; yet to live joyously we must also possess the capacity, when it is not destructive, to live in the present
and act spontaneously. In other words, discipline itself must be
disciplined."[14]

In a "Reflection" in his edition of stories of the fabulist Aesop,
Sir Roger L'Estrange writes: "It is with our Passions, as it is with
Fire and Water, they are Good Servants, but Bad Masters."[15] Fire
and water serve us, unless they get out of control—so, too, with
our emotions, our feelings, our passions. Alfred, Lord Tennyson
made a good point when he wrote, "The happiness of a man in
this life does not consist in the absence but in the mastery of his
passions."[16]

One reason we seek such mastery is that only when we control ourselves can we truly and fully give of ourselves, since we
cannot give that which we do not already possess. The Bible is
replete with examples of God's self-giving character, which we are
called to imitate. This truth is repeated time and again in numerous Old Testament stories and passages. For example, in Exodus
33, God identifies himself as "undeserved mercy" and "undreamt
of compassion." This truth is reinforced in the New Testament in
the parables and (more importantly) the actions of Jesus. At the
wedding feast of Cana, for example, Jesus not only turns water
into wine, but he turns over a hundred gallons of water into over
a hundred gallons of really fine-tasting wine. Jesus miraculously
feeds large, hungry crowds with just a few loaves and fishes—
and, in his bountiful generosity, when all had had their fill, the
leftovers were collected in multiple large baskets. God calls upon
us all to display the same kind of generosity: "Give, and it will be
given to you. A good measure, pressed down, shaken together,

running over, will be put into your lap; for the measure you give will be the measure you get back" (Luke 6:38).

I offer the following sublime insight: "No one is really happy merely because he has what he wants, but only if he wants things he ought to want."[17] When we read that word "ought," most of us reject it as unwelcome authoritarianism: an oppressive hegemony. However, I think the insight brings out two points. First, there is an order to the desires in life. The person who puts sex, money, or whatever, at the center of their life not only misses out on other aspects of life but eventually corrupts the legitimate joys of those things which they have idolatrously made central to their existence. ". . . Every preference of a small good to a great, or partial good to a total good, involves the loss of the small or partial good for which the sacrifice is made. . . . You can't get second things by putting them first. You get second things only by putting first things first."[18] This insight is not an endorsement of an "if-you-can't-get-what-you-want-then-change-what-you-want" philosophy, but a recognition that being good and being joyful are two sides of the same coin.[19]

Saint Thomas Aquinas distinguishes between "*beatitudo*"—the happiness one finds in God—and "*felicitas*"—the happiness a person finds in the world. It is possible to possess beatitudo without fully realizing it.

> We are all of us more mystics than we believe or choose to believe. . . . We have seen more than we let on, even to ourselves. Through some moment of beauty or pain, some subtle turning of our lives, we catch glimmers at least of what the saints are blinded by; only then, unlike the saints, we go on as though nothing has happened. To go on as though something has happened, even though we are not sure what it was or just where we are supposed to go with it, is to enter the dimension of life that religion is a word for.[20]

That is partly why, sometimes, especially during the penitential season of Lent, Christians intentionally deny themselves certain pleasures or goods of the felicitas variety. One way to become more aware of the already-present beatitudo in our lives is to purposefully limit, for a time, some experiences of pleasure. Extremes of gloomy asceticism and unreasonable mortifications do not a saint make. How counterintuitive this seems; but, even Bertrand

Russell, that famous atheist, knew that "To be without some of the things you want is an indispensable part of happiness."[21]

The earliest Christians were known for belonging "to the Way" (Acts 9:2). The new faith was about a joyful way of life, a habit of being, and a transformation into a new self—not about an old self following a new set of rules. There is a story, most likely fictional, about St. Augustine's encounter with a prostitute whom he had known before his conversion to Christianity. Seeing her, he ignored her. Believing he had not seen her, she cried out to him: "It is I!" He replied, "Yes, but it is not I." It is not just the saint's intellect that had been converted but, rather, his entire personality. The longer we delay conversion to a new life, the more we are forced to discard of the old life. This new life of grace cannot be added to the old; it must replace the old. The *bios* must be replaced with *zōē*. "Bios" and "zōē" are Greek words for the word, "life." "Bios" is the Greek word from which we derive the word "biology." It refers to a manner of life. "Zōē" references existential life. Jesus says: "I came that [my followers] may have life [*zōēn*], and have it abundantly" (John 10:10b).

At the heart of the Church's evangelism is a simple message: an invitation to be transformed by the startlingly personal love of God. Love, in its most intimate form, unites the lover with the beloved; when the lover's time, resources, and very self are offered to the beloved. This union of love is expressed in many ways, but sex is a great example. An indulgent, egocentric understanding of sex is quite different from what the great romantics describe in their songs and poetry. They speak of a love that is about self-abandonment and mutual joy. The Christian mystics use similar language when discussing experiences or foretastes of heaven, of temporary ecstasy that will be forever eternalized in the new creation. Read the Old Testament book Song of Solomon (also called Song of Songs). There you will find deliberate sexual and sensual imagery used to describe God's relationship with his beloved creation; that is, us. Or, read St. Teresa of Avila's autobiographical account of her ecstatic encounter with an angel of peerless beauty, who pierced her heart with a flaming spear (an event called, the "transverberation").[22]

In both of these examples we encounter analogies for the intimate relationship between God and the human soul. Although other kinds of loving relationships have also been used to describe this "God-to-soul" bond, the closeness of two lovers is apt.

Nowhere is this more telling than in the Eucharist: the giving of Jesus' flesh and blood. The very word "communion," comes from two Latin words: "*cum*," meaning "with," and, "*unio*," meaning "oneness." In a very real way, Communion is about two becoming one. More than just flesh joining with flesh, communicants unite with the God who is the vivifying force for all life.

Torn between love for us and a desire to return to his father, Jesus gave us the gift of his Eucharistic presence, creating a way to be simultaneously in heaven and on earth. The Church, most often, uses the term transubstantiation to identify the change, at the moment of consecration, from bread and wine to the Body, Blood, Soul, and Divinity of Jesus Christ.

The doctrine that Jesus is really, though sacramentally, present in the Eucharist[23] can be traced back to the earliest days of the Church.[24] The word "Eucharist" comes from the Greek, "*eucharistia*" for thanksgiving or gratitude. It (the proper pronoun used to refer to the Eucharist is "it," not "he") is what St. Thomas Aquinas called the Sacrament of sacraments. God manifests himself in countless ways. He is present in his word—the Bible. He is present wherever two or more are gathered in his name. He is present throughout all of creation. In the Eucharist, however, God is with us in a unique way.

By partaking in his Body and Blood we participate in deification,[25] the process of becoming united with the Trinity. Saint Athanasius of Alexandria summarized this by proclaiming, "He became man so that we might be made God." The Mass of the Latin Rite includes a short rite of pouring water into the wine, which will be consecrated. The prayer uttered during this ritual by the priest or deacon is "By the mystery of this water and wine may we come to share in the divinity of Christ who humbled himself to share in our humanity."[26] The commingling of the water and wine signifies this unity.

In the New Testament, St. Peter[27] discusses the mystery of partaking in God's nature. (See 2 Peter 1:3,4). Later in Church history, St. Thomas Aquinas and other theologians, especially those from the Eastern Orthodox traditions, developed more fully how God's abundant grace actually transforms and glorifies us through deification (also, known as "divinization" and by other terms).[28] This grace does not blur the line between human and divine. Christians do not, for example, accept the teaching of Vedantic Hinduism that *atman* (or, each human being's permanent

Self) is *brahman* (or, the eternal Absolute underlying all visible reality). Neither does this participation in the divine nature mean that we become God by way of a purported apotheosis like the Pharaohs of ancient Egypt.

As Karl Adam writes:

> This one God is a God of life and of love. So great, so superabundant is this love, that it not only raises man to its own image and likeness by the natural gifts of reason and will, but also, by the precious gift of sanctifying grace, summons him from his state of isolation to an unparalleled participation in the Divine Nature and in Its blessings, to a sort of active co-operation in the work of God. . . . It is the profoundest meaning and the amazing generosity of the redemption, that it raises the rational creature from the infinite remoteness of its impotence and from the abysmal ruin of its sins into the Divine Life.[29]

Counterintuitively, at the very core of the mission of the Church is the promotion and fostering of ultimate joy and the recognition of the wonderful insight of St. Irenaeus of Lyons: "The glory of God is man fully alive."[30] Today, many people associate being "fully alive" with unfettered freedom. Yet, such radical independence can easily become toxic and oppressive if we do not incorporate the quintessential freedom to obey the God who made us.

Christianity does not understand freedom as "anything-goes" autonomy. Rather, it is the capacity to fulfill one's nature—not the choice to choose one's nature (as if such a thing were even possible). More profoundly, part of the good news of the Gospel is not just that we are free to be ourselves, but, paradoxically, that we are free to be free from ourselves as well.

Many of the greatest teachers the world has ever known—Moses, the Buddha, Jesus, etc.—attest to the lesson that hedonism, materialism, and egotism—and all of their derivative philosophies (e.g., relativism)—may feel good for a season, but quickly and inevitably become toxic to us, body and soul. But, we are not called to retreat into a disinterested Stoicism. Although self-control is seen by many as an endorsement to suppress one's emotions, it is a false Christianity that teaches that God is pleased by an attitude of stoic indifference. As the last book of the New Testament reveals, God is not interested in apathy: "Because you are lukewarm, and neither cold nor hot, I am about to spit you out of my mouth" (Revelation 3:16).

The Gospels are filled with stories of people who were rewarded for boldly expressing their faith by violating societal conventions. The woman with the issuance of blood touched Jesus and was healed. According to Mosaic law, a woman who was bleeding was ritually unclean and should not have been mulling about in a crowd; she could have been stoned for doing so.[31] Yet, she broke with convention and boldly reached out to touch Jesus and was healed. Or, consider the intrepid men who actually climbed up on someone's roof and cut a hole through it in order to lower their friend to meet Jesus. In another story, Jesus healed ten lepers and commanded them to present themselves to the temple priests. Only one of those ten lepers, a Samaritan, whom Jesus healed came back to thank him. But, Jesus commanded them to go to the priests. However, the Samaritan returned to Jesus; this makes sense: As a Samaritan, he was not a Jew; he had no relationship with the Jerusalem temple where the priests offered sacrifices. Jesus rewards him for coming back to say thank you.

Some have drawn the erroneous conclusion that God wants us to be disinterested in life from a particular—perhaps, misinterpreted—strain of piety. Saint Francis de Sales, for example, asked: "What matters it to a truly loving soul whether [God] be served by this means or by another?"[32] There are Bible passages that evoke similar notions, such as Philippians 4:11–12, where St. Paul expresses this apparent indifference toward life, writing: "Not that I am referring to being in need; for I have learned to be content with whatever I have. I know what it is to have little, and I know what it is to have plenty. In any and all circumstances I have learned the secret of being well-fed and of going hungry, of having plenty and of being in need" (vv. 11–12). But, read the very next verse: "I can do all things through him who strengthens me" (v. 13). Saints Paul and Francis de Sales are not merely indifferent; rather, it is just that they both so loved God that they found joy in serving him in any way God chose. Put another way, the great saints are freer than the rest of us because their lives were truer.

CONTRASTS NOT CONTRADICTIONS

On trial in the Roman Praetorium, Jesus was famously asked the question: "What is truth?" (John 18:38; Latin: "*Quid est veritas?*"). Pontius Pilate, the Roman prefect of Judea, may have asked this question rhetorically—perhaps, even mockingly.

Pilate, a noble Roman, would not actually have cared much for the opinion of a fanatical Jewish rebel. From Pilate's perspective, he was the authority figure; he was the judge. But, Jesus must have piqued his curiosity for Pilate to have deigned to have even seen him. Actually, Pilate may have been more than merely curious: There are hints in the narrative that Pilate suspected a fearful truth about Jesus. Perhaps it was a look or a word. Pilate might have sensed he was in the presence of overwhelming holiness—and that likely terrified him.

In response to Pilate's question to Jesus, asking him if he was the king of the Jews, Jesus responded, "Do you ask this on your own, or did others tell you about me?" (John 18:34). Jesus was not merely asking out of idle curiosity but wanted to Pilate to clarify his question. It is as if Jesus were saying, "Pilate, if you want to know if I am the king and messiah of my people then yes; but my kingdom is not of this world. However, if you are asking for yourself and you want to know if I am claiming a kingship in the geopolitical sense then the answer is no; such a kingship is much too insignificant for God's plan."

As a prefect, the agent of Rome, Pilate had no authority in and of himself but acted in the name of the empire. Jesus, however, spoke by his own authority—a fact that must have staggered the mind of that irascible bureaucrat, Pilate. Any eyewitness who saw the interaction between Pilate and Jesus would have described a scene of a powerful judge questioning a defenseless man. History would prove this interaction to be a reverse of what we expect. It was Pilate who was impotent; it was Rome and all corruption in the world that was being judged.

What, then, is the answer to Pilate's question: "What is truth?" Jesus' answer is clear:

> Pilate asked him, "So you are a king?" Jesus answered, "You say that I am a king. For this I was born, and for this I came into the world, to testify to the truth. Everyone who belongs to the truth listens to my voice." (John 18:37)

It is an interesting curiosity that an anagram of Pilate's question in Latin (viz., *Quid est veritas?*) produces the statement in Latin: "*Est vir qui adest,*" which translates to read, "He stands before you." Jesus says, "I am the way, the truth, and the life" (John 14:6). Jesus himself is the answer to Pilate's question.

Sometimes, I will ask my college students a version of Pilate's question: "How do you know what is true or good or just?" Their answers vary.

Some say they learn what is true or good from their parents, their peers, or their teachers. They believe in a "social-contract" sort of truth: We all decide together. So, I ask: "You say that society teaches you what is right and wrong. Tell me, if you were raised in Nazi Germany in the midst of radical anti-Semitism— would that have made such practices right, because many of your fellow community members accepted that ideology?"

Others say they just intuitively know what is true.

More advanced students sometimes reference the works of philosophers, such as David Hume's investigation into "what is" versus "what ought to be."

Other more scientifically-minded students mention tests for truth-claims, discussing things such as the Scientific Method (i.e., observe; hypothesize; experiment; repeat) or Karl Popper's "Falsifiability Principle" (viz., a claim is falsifiable if an argument can be proposed to prove the claim false).

Some of my more naïve students are unconcerned with objective truth and believe that ignorance is bliss. Actually, this is an unfair assessment. Many students express a strong interest in being able to differentiate between true and false information. In the cacophony of competing truth claims they want tools for evaluating various ideas. However, many seem to suffer from a form of cognitive dissonance—a condition of believing or acting in two mutually exclusive or contradictory ways at the same time. The New Testament specifically warns about when our beliefs and actions do not match up. The book of James cautions that we should not be double-minded (James 1:6-8). Inevitably though, we all struggle with contradictory thoughts and behaviors.

Let me give you the quintessential example I encounter. Most of my students believe that the entire universe and they themselves are insignificant cosmic accidents; yet they also believe all life is precious and the earth should be well cared for. They see themselves as inhabitants of the third planet orbiting a medium-sized star in a rather common galaxy. Their life is but one among billions; their planet is one among unknown numbers; their sun is one among countless other stars. While they may feel loved by family and friends, they see both the ultimate origin of all things and the eventual end of it all as nothingness. They believe they exist not because of the providential gift from a benevolent God but because they were the unintended result of a series of natural selection successes—a Darwinian survival of the fittest. Essentially, some students buy into the philosopher Hobbes' dark summary of human life as essentially "solitary, poor, nasty, brutish, and short."

Now, these very same students, when asked, are almost always kind and thoughtful individuals who abhor bullying and domination of any sort. I could list a hundred other examples of dissonant thinking, but the result is often a hearty skepticism about all ideas. Jean Paul Sartre wrote about a would-be atheist: "She believed in nothing; only her skepticism kept her from being an atheist."[33] While a healthy sense of skepticism can be valuable, we should not be too cynical. We should be skeptical about our skepticism.

Secular ideas about our place in the universe need not inevitably lead to the conclusion that one's own existence is random, meaningless, and ultimately of Sisyphean futility. A whole host of reactions can be plotted along a spectrum: At one extreme, despondency and the attendant existential nausea; at the opposite extreme, an emboldening "will-to-power."

Worse than this sort of apathy, some of my more cynical students subscribe to the motto from George Orwell's novel *1984*, namely: "Ignorance is strength."[34] I counter these hermeneutics of skepticism with the argument that either we trust someone else—some authority figure—or, we decide for ourselves based on personal understanding and our analytical skills what is good and what is true. But, whom do we trust? Who exercises legitimate authority in the realms of faith and morals? The question of authority is really a quintessential issue. Erasmus and Luther knew this single point was the hinge upon which the entire Reformation swung.

So, I continue the exercise, hoping to put students (safely) into a space of intellectual discomfort: to introduce them to ways of thinking that they might not have previously contemplated. Moments of discomfort can serve as catalysts for new and fresh ways of thinking and acting. Jesus began his ministry after 40 days of fasting. When we are safe, healthy, contented, and our bellies are full, our perspective may be quite different than if we are in dire need. How easy it is to fall prey to the idea that we have done all that God wants us to do.

Exposure to the "new" and to the "other" can have profound consequences. We come to learn there are things we know that are incorrect. Then, there are things we simply do not even know. And, perhaps, most humbling of all, there are things we don't know that we didn't know. Accepting even one major new idea that was previously unknown to you or previously rejected can be difficult. No idea exists in isolation. Certain beliefs necessarily connect with other beliefs: They go hand in hand, so to speak. Think of a spider's web, which is constructed so that a small quiver in one section sends vibrations throughout the rest of the web.

With this analogy in mind we can think of the Catholic faith as a web of interconnected and interdependent beliefs. The Deposit of Faith, what the Church believes, is derived from divine revelation,[35] communicated via two channels: the Bible and sacred Tradition. The Deposit of Faith is preserved, interpreted, and transmitted via the Church's Magisterium. The Magisterium's teachings fall into the two distinct categories of infallible (or dogmatic) teachings and non-infallible teachings. (Notice the word used is "non-infallible" and not "fallible." The reason for this is that the Magisterium communicates definite truth as related to infallible teachings and communicates legitimate truth as it relates to non-infallible teachings.)

Catholics are expected to intellectually assent and volitionally adhere to the full Deposit of Faith. Full and uncompromising assent, called "sacred assent," is obligatory with respect to all infallible teachings, while mere "ordinary assent" is required for non-infallible teachings.

Of these two categories, infallible teachings are the rarest and probably among the most misunderstood. Whenever a pope speaks on a matter of faith or morals "*ex cathedra,*" that is, in his capacity as leader of the Church and successor of St. Peter, his pronouncement is infallible and binding. For a teaching to be infallible it must have been "always taught" by the Church. However, some matters that were "always taught" are not infallible. What is important to remember about the charism of infallibility[36] is that it works negatively to protect the Church from teaching error. This is not the same kind of infallible inspiration that God used to positively inspire the authors of the Bible. Moreover, even infallible teachings are not all-inclusive statements of faith. "Absolute infallibility (in all respects, without dependence on another) is proper to God. . . . All other infallibility is derivative and limited in scope."[37]

Church teaching is not always popular, but objective moral truth is not always fashionable. The mind cannot easily ignore that which it knows to be true. It can bury it. It can hide it away. It can twist and malign the truth until it is hardly recognizable. But, in those quiet moments of our lives, when circumstances force us into a moment of introspection, the truths we have come to know will be there still. They will be whispering to us, confronting us. They can never be annihilated.

The Book of Ecclesiastes points out: "For in much wisdom is much vexation, and those who increase knowledge increase sorrow" (1:18). But, Ecclesiastes is skeptical—even pessimistic—in its examination of everything "under the sun." The repeated use of that phrase throughout the book indicates to the reader that the critique of "vanity of vanities," for which Ecclesiastes if famous, is an analysis of the purely secular and not the sacred. In other words, everything under the sun is vanity. So, turn your attention elsewhere.

It is worth recalling that much of the pain and suffering we cause in this world is due to ignorance rather than malice. Does intent make a difference? Ignorance may be blissful in certain circumstances. But, we are invited—Catholics would go so far as to say: We are divinely commanded—to overcome our ignorance. When we do, there is no going back.

Catholic tradition divides ignorance into two primary categories.[38] First, "vincible ignorance" is a lack of knowledge that can be overcome by reasonable efforts. Second, there is "invincible ignorance," which cannot be overcome by the average person employing reasonable efforts. According to St. Thomas Aquinas, if a person's conscience is guided by invincible error, then that person is bound to follow where that error leads even when doing so violates God's moral law. In other words, the objective error is present, but the subjective guilt is ameliorated by a person's invincible error.

We have an obligation to educate ourselves and inform our consciences. The word "education" comes from the Latin "educo," meaning "to draw out." The result should be better critical-thinking skills and heightened self-awareness. That is an important part of education: to encourage students to bring out their own excellence. For Christians to become educated in the faith they must not just adopt a formulaic set of beliefs, but, in the words of Bernard Lonergan, "Be attentive, be intelligent, be responsible, be loving, and, if necessary, change."[39]

According to the Bible, every person possesses a conscience: an ability to think about moral issues. Saint Paul explains, "When Gentiles, who do not possess the law, do instinctively what the law requires, these, though not having the law, are a law to themselves" (Romans 2:14). Although it is true that above all else we are all bound by our own individual consciences, as Blessed John Henry Newman forcefully put it, "Conscience has rights, because it has duties."[40] Our conscience is not, or should not be, our god because this adherence to some inner voice too easily turns into a self-idolatry. But, Cardinal John Henry Newman went even further when he was once asked to give a toast at a dinner; as a renowned Catholic, one might have expected him to pay homage to the Church or the pope, but instead he spoke these words, "I shall drink to the Pope, if you please, still to conscience first, and to the Pope afterwards."[41]

Like good soldiers, we should follow the orders of our consciences. But, there is a saying in the military about the two worst kinds of soldiers: First, there is the one who cannot follow an order; second, there is the one who can do nothing other than follow an order. The point is that unfettered freedom disconnected from moral truth inevitably leads to rule of the weak by the strong. Alternately, of course, those in possession of the "moral truth" can lord it over others. This recognition guided Pope St. John Paul II's papacy:

> That is why John Paul relentlessly preached genuine tolerance: not the tolerance of indifference, as if differences over the good didn't matter, but the real tolerance of differences engaged, explored, and debated within the bond of a profound respect for the humanity of the other. Many were puzzled that this Pope, so vigorous in defending the truths of Catholic faith, could become, over a quarter-century, the world's premier icon of religious freedom and inter-religious civility. But here, too, John Paul II was teaching a crucial lesson about the future of freedom: universal empathy comes through, not around, particular convictions. There is no Rawlsian veil of ignorance behind which the world can withdraw, to subsequently emerge with decency in its pocket.[42]

We don't all judge according to the same criteria. Again, the point is not that there is no objective "good" and "evil," but only shades of gray; the point is that moral decision-making in a complicated world requires the balancing of many virtues. The Old Testament book of Maccabees records the conflict between Jews and Syrian-Greeks. Originally, the Maccabees, zealous for God's law, refused to fight on the Jewish Sabbath. The Syrian-Greeks noticed this, and so they would attack on the Sabbath, resulting in massacres (1 Maccabees 2:35-38). After seeing so many fellow Jews being slaughtered Sabbath after Sabbath, the remaining forces resolved to continue to honor the Sabbath by not attacking the enemy of their own accord, but they began defending themselves against these Sabbath attacks (1 Maccabees 2:40-41), and consequently they won battles against their enemy (2 Maccabees 8:26-27). What seemed like a no-win situation became resolvable after much discernment.

The book of Proverbs provides the sobering reminder that, "All deeds are right in the sight of the doer, but the Lord weighs the heart" (21:2). The old saying, "The road to hell is paved with good intentions," an aphorism attributed to Samuel Johnson, is also sobering, because if good intentions can lead to hell, and bad ones do as well, then what are we left with?

A strong argument can be made that Catholicism teaches the opposite: It is the road to heaven that is paved with good intentions. Catholics believe that God, in his mercy, can take our intentions into consideration when he judges our actions. Jesus taught that bad thoughts are equivalent to bad deeds; look at a person in hatred and you have committed murder. How much does God take our good desires as equivalent to good acts? Consider the story of how Zacharias, the father of John the Baptist, was a childless old man when an angel visited him and announced that he and his elderly wife were going to give birth to a son. Zacharias questioned the angel and was struck mute for his insolence.

> 'How will I know that this is so? For I am an old man, and my wife is getting on in years.' The angel replied, 'I am Gabriel. I stand in the presence of God, and I have been sent to speak to you and to bring you this good news. But, now, because you did not believe my words, which will be fulfilled in their time, you will become mute, unable to speak, until the day these things occur.' (Luke 1:18-20)

The same angel, Gabriel, visited the Virgin Mary and announced that God chose her to be the mother of Jesus.

> Mary said to the angel, 'How can this be, since I am a virgin?' The angel said to her, 'The Holy Spirit will come upon you, and the power of the Most High will overshadow you; therefore the child to be born will be holy; he will be called Son of God.' (Luke 1:34-35)

So, Mary asked a question almost identical to Zacharias, but he was temporarily struck mute for his disbelief. Why was Zacharias denied the ability to speak when Mary was simply given a response? The answer may lie in the intentions of Zacharias and Mary. We could infer that Zacharias was disrespectfully incredulous, while Mary was merely sincerely perplexed. According to some ancient accounts, Mary had consecrated herself to God as lifelong virgin, so she simply was genuinely curious how she could honor her vow while also bearing a child. Mary's attitude of reverence and openness to God's will is revealed a few verses after she questions Gabriel, when she utters, "'Here am I, the servant of the Lord; let it be with me according to your word'" (Luke 1:38).

A second point to ponder regarding this story is this: It seems Zacharias was being punished by an angry God. However, it is possible that his inability to speak was a gift, a call, in the tradition of Psalm 46:10, to "Be still and see that I am God." Maybe Zacharias needed the gift of some quiet time.

But, there is a caveat that has to be considered here. Even though intentions matter, they do not matter so much that good intentions can make a bad act morally acceptable. "There is a certain asymmetry to morality. Bad intentions can corrupt good actions, but good intentions cannot rehabilitate bad action. . . . What fundamentally makes an act bad or good is its conformity with moral truth, not with subjective moral perception of that truth."[43] We are never free to do evil or even help, encourage, command, or praise another person's sin. Saint Augustine admonished that, "We may not sin in order to prevent someone else from sinning." To argue that we ought to be free to violate objective moral norms, to be free to sin, is like saying fish should be free to fly. Flying is foreign to a fish's nature like sin is, or should be, to ours.

Although morality is objective and uniformly binding on us all, sin, the failure to fully inform one's conscience, being poorly educated, subscribing to prejudices, and numerous other factors may cause us to act immorally without the full knowledge we are doing so.

Most of us believe we should do good and avoid evil, but how does one identify what is "good"? Is something good if it feels good (Hedonism)? Is goodness tied to certain self-evident virtues (Aristotle's eudaimonia)? Am I to use my reason to discern my duty to differentiate good from evil (Kant's deontological ethics)? Should moral decisions be based solely on outcomes (Bentham and Mill's utilitarianism)? Is the ultimate good an exertion of my will (Nietzsche)? Or are good and evil mere social constructs (Postmodernism)?

Consider how in the Old Testament we read about God commanding Israel to send spies into neighboring countries. Presumably, they had to lie to keep their identities a secret. Did they sin in doing so? Or, think about how during World War II, Pope Pius XII authorized the production of counterfeit baptismal certificates in order to save some Jewish people from the Nazis.

The rubric of "double effect" is a tool to evaluate moral problems. The principle requires first: a moral dilemma. Second, any act being contemplated must be either good or neutral. Third, any evil consequence resulting from the good or neutral act must not be intended. Fourth, the good arrived at must not be a direct result of the evil consequence—if one would exist. This is a useful tool but can lead, in practice if not theory, to the employment of a means-to-ends consequentialism.

A constant guide comes from the Church's traditional list of virtues. These are divided into two categories: theological virtues and natural virtues. There are three theological virtues: faith, hope, and love. There are many natural virtues, but four of them are primary. They are the "Cardinal Virtues." They are named "cardinal," because the word derives from the Latin "cardo," which means "hinge." The four virtues upon which all other human virtues hinge are fortitude, justice, prudence, and temperance.[44] (As a counter to these virtues there is a custom of listing seven deadly sins:[45] sloth, envy, covetousness, pride, gluttony, lust, and anger.)

The gifts[46] and the fruits[47] of the Holy Spirit aid us in practicing these virtues. Sometimes the Church systematizes certain virtuous practices in recognition of the common good—while avoiding the slippery slope of utilitarianism. Specifically, there is a long and deep history of Catholic social thought that includes the principles of: the inestimable worth of every human person; the value of God's creation; the importance of marriage and care of children within a family; care for the sick, the elderly, and the poor; and the dignity of work.

Saint Francis is often attributed as the source of the wonderful quote that we should "preach the gospel every day and if necessary use words." That is, we should live out the Gospel each and every day instead of merely talking about it. "To bear with patience wrongs done to oneself is a mark of perfection, but to bear with patience wrongs done to someone else is a mark of imperfection and even of actual sin,"[48] taught St. Thomas Aquinas.

Trying to convince another person to live virtuously is not usually effective. "To try too hard to make people good, is one way to make them worse; that the only way to make them good is to be good—remembering well the beam and the mote; that the time for speaking comes rarely, the time for being never departs."[49]

To better understand how to inform or educate our consciences, we have to know what is meant by the word, "conscience."

> When we know we have done wrong we often feel guilty, but guilt and conscience are two separate things. Conscience may make us aware of our guilt, which in turn can make us feel guilty, but conscience is not guilt. Conscience is an act of reason rather than a feeling. In fact, it is a part of reason itself, not a distinct faculty. Conscience is the mind thinking morally, evaluating the goodness or badness of our actions. The judgments of conscience are not isolated moral intuitions, but *reasoned conclusions*, even when they happen instantaneously. Sometimes these judgments emerge so spontaneously that they seem more like instincts or feelings than rational judgments. But if we look more closely, we realize such judgments are the result of habits of human reason.[50]

Given that our conscience is the mind thinking morally—weighing, judging, and evaluating what is right and what is wrong—the next step in the process of acting morally is to employ the will to decide whether to follow the judgments of the conscience. We should regularly reflect on these judgments and whether we correctly followed them. This self-examination should not be confused with scrupulousness, but there is a Christian tradition of examining our consciences. The pious St. John Vianney made an interesting point about how the failure to subject our actions to scrutiny can result in vice masking as virtue. He said that a farmer who fasts all day and prays all night, but then is too weak to work his farm, sins. The farmer's intentions may have been good, but his actions were not. Saint Francis de Sales used a variation on this example, explaining, "A man given to fasting thinks himself very devout if he fasts, although his heart may be filled with hatred. Much concerned with sobriety, he does not dare wet his tongue with wine or even water, but won't hesitate to drink deep of his neighbor's blood by detraction and calumny."[51]

What these saints are warning against is a form of hypocrisy. In 2 Samuel 12, we read of how the prophet Nathan told King David the story of an avaricious shepherd who, although having many sheep, stole a poor man's only lamb. King David was enraged at the injustice of the wealthy man's behavior and said that that thief should be put to death. "You are the man!" Nathan then told him. Just as the man in the parable had stolen a lamb, David had stolen another man's wife. Nathan knew that telling the king of his sin outright would have been of no use, because like so many of us he would have been blind to his own greed. He would have found a rationale or justification for his behavior. By forcing King David to step outside himself for a moment and evaluate his actions objectively, David could see how wrong he had been.

Many times, the fault you find objectionable in another person is secretly known by you to be present in yourself. As Carl Jung expressed it, "Everything that irritates us about others can lead us to an understanding of ourselves."[52] Once we admit to our faults, we must take action. Saint Francis de Sales writes: "Let us not, then, afflict ourselves with our imperfections, for our perfection consists in resisting them; and we cannot resist them without seeing them, nor vanquish them without encountering them."[53] One practical way to begin evaluating your hidden faults is to start thinking about what you dislike most in others. G. K. Chesterton pointed out that, "The Bible tells us to love our neighbors, and also to love our enemies; probably, because generally they are the same people."[54]

The Church not only acknowledges individual consciences, but she also teaches that there is a "Natural Law" to which we are all bound. Servant of God Rev. Fr. John A. Hardon writes: "Catholic morality presumes there are objective norms of conduct. Certain actions are good and others bad, certain forms of behavior are virtuous and others sinful, always and everywhere and for everyone who knows what he is doing and does so with sufficient reflection and freedom of assent."[55] A person's conscience testifies to the law written on the heart: the Natural Law.[56]

Not all Christians—not even all Catholics—identify Natural Law identically. Individually, we all have our own set of assumptions, which inform our personal beliefs and values. We have to examine those assumptions whenever exploring questions about truth and goodness. Such an exploration can lead in many directions (e.g., to metaphysics; the logic of inductive, deductive or abductive reasoning; ethics), but all are tied closely to an individual's assumptions or acceptance of first principles.

There is a Latin maxim that offers a caution to those who reject this fundamental idea: "*Non est disputandum contra principia negantem*," or "You cannot dispute against a man who denies first principles." In other words, it simply is not possible to argue about the color of the sky with someone who refuses to admit that such things as color or sky even exist. To try to argue in this way is to engage in an obdurate sophistry: a conversation devoid of its subject matter. Admitting to certain presuppositions, then, does not equate with an inability to be open-minded, but it is a necessary prerequisite to engaging in any meaningful inquiry.

Saint Thomas Aquinas held that the self-evident first principle of the Natural Law is: *Bonum est faciendum et prosequendum et malum vitandum*, which translates from the Latin to mean, "The good is to be done and pursued, and evil avoided."[57] This insight is self-evident, because in order for a person to evaluate it as good or bad requires the investigator to actually employ the principle. He or she must already accept the principle of good versus bad.

Talk of a Natural Law was accepted in the time of Thomas, but the topic does not have much currency in modern philosophy. Jeremy Bentham described the concept of "natural rights" (a subset of Natural Law) as: "simple nonsense: natural and imprescriptible rights, rhetorical nonsense,—nonsense upon stilts."[58] It would be easy to blame this skepticism on overtly secular metaphysics, but even some thoroughly orthodox Christian thinkers take issue with Natural Law—or, at least, attempts to systematize its premises. What is more, though the Natural Law is inviolable, it can and often has been misunderstood or abused. Natural Law arguments have been improperly used to justify slavery, to condone the mistreatment of women, and to condemn the loaning

of money at even a reasonable interest rate. Similarly, history
is replete with examples of people doing very bad things in the
name of God. Mahatma Gandhi purportedly stated, "I like your
Christ, I do not like your Christians. Your Christians are so unlike your Christ," and he declared, "I'd be a Christian if it were
not for the Christians!"[59] Recognizing each one of us as part of
the problem of evil is humbling. G. K. Chesterton purportedly was
once sent a letter by a prominent newspaper asking him, simply,
"What is wrong with the world?" Chesterton could have sent back
a lengthy and thought-provoking essay, but simply wrote back, "I
am."[60] Every Christian could honestly answer the same.

Sometimes, we willfully commit evil and avoid what we know
to be good, but it is not always easy to discern between right
and wrong. Consider how sometimes Jesus' words seem to be
contradictory. Some of his sayings sound as if they disagree with
other sayings. At other times, Jesus appears to directly contradict
the clear teachings of the Hebrew Scriptures, which he says he
has come to fulfill, and not abolish. For example, throughout the
Gospels we see Jesus repeatedly encouraging his followers not to
be afraid. Yet, the book of Proverbs says: "The fear of the Lord is
the beginning of knowledge . . ." (1:7). How can both these sentiments exist simultaneously?

In the musical *Fiddler on the Roof*, the main character, Tevye,
comes upon two men arguing. "You're right," he says to the first
man in the squabble. The argument continues. "You're right," Tevye says to the second man. A passerby hears all this and tells
Tevye that both men cannot be right . . . to which Tevye says,
"You know, you are also right."[61]

We must dig deeper into the subtle nuances of seemingly contradictory statements in order to distinguish them. We actually
do this sort of distinguishing all the time in day-to-day life. For
example, if someone you just met declares that she is a daughter
and a mother, then automatically you reason that she is probably not simultaneously a mother and a daughter in the same
relationship, at the same time.

In the previous example about fear, Jesus uses the word,
"afraid," as in: "Do not be alarmed!" The author of Proverbs, however, uses "fear" to mean "awe" or "wonder." Understood in this
context, the statements express two distinct, complementary notions, rather than two rival, contradictory ideas. We see this same

pattern with common folk wisdom.[62] Just think about a few time-honored aphorisms that seem to contradict one another.

- "Look before you leap" versus "He who hesitates is lost."
- "Opposites attract" versus "Birds of a feather flock together."
- "Absence makes the heart grow fonder" versus "Out of sight, out of mind."

Can both maxims in each set be true? Yes—just not at the same time, in the same relationship. They can be true in one sense, but not necessarily in every possible sense. Consider the last pair of statements about absence and love: On the one hand, it is true that absence can make us long for someone we love; on the other hand, absence can also make us forget about someone we once cared for. An aphorism penned by French author François de La Rochefoucauld explains how these phenomena can be reconciled: "Absence cools moderate Passions, and inflames violent ones; just as the Wind blows out Candles, but kindles Fires."[63]

Christianity is replete with examples of paradoxes: the first shall be last and the last shall be first; true freedom is found in service to others; authentic strength comes from humility and meekness not pride and arrogance; to live you must die. Jesus' conflicting sayings can be understood by applying the same type of analysis.

Here are three examples:

- "Even if I testify on my own behalf, my testimony is valid because I know where I have come from and where I am going, but you do not know where I come from or where I am going" (John 8:14), versus "If I testify about myself, my testimony is not true" (5:31).
- "Do not think that I have come to bring peace to the earth; I have not come to bring peace, but a sword" (Matthew 10:34), versus "Put your sword back into its place; for all who take the sword will perish by the sword" (26:52).
- "In the same way, let your light shine before others, so that they may see your good works and give glory to your Father in heaven" (Matthew 5:16), versus "Beware of practicing

your piety before others in order to be seen by them; for then
you have no reward from your Father in heaven" (6:1).

Other examples of Jesus apparently contradicting himself
could be cited, but the most perplexing incongruity is Jesus' relationship to the Jewish law. Karl Adam explained:

> Our Lord's attitude towards the Mosaic Law, which compre-
> hended both moral regulations and an abundance of liturgical
> ordinances, was by no means one of indifference, or one of un-
> willing tolerance. He is come for this purpose, and regards it as
> an essential part of His task, not to destroy the Law, but to fulfil
> it, down to its last iota. He explains in what sense He conceived
> this fulfillment in the verses which follow immediately, in which
> He presses for a fully spiritual interpretation of the command-
> ments of the Law. . . . Nothing whatsoever, He teaches, should
> be done in a merely external fashion, just because it is the Law.
> Everything should be done on interior principle, under the inspi-
> ration of the love of God and of one's neighbour.[64]

Time and again we find allusions in the Bible to the inade-
quacy of the old law. Moses wandered in the desert for forty years
before arriving at the Promised Land. However, because of an
offense against God, he was forbidden to enter. The symbolism is
clear; Moses, the deliverer of the Ten Commandments, represents
the law, and the Promised Land represents salvation or heaven.
That Moses did not enter the Promised Land symbolizes that the
law cannot get anyone into heaven. This same theme plays out
throughout the Gospels. In John 3:1-21, we read about Nicodemus, an important Pharisee and member of the Sanhedrin, who
visits Jesus under the cover of night. Jesus tells Nicodemus he
must be born again. He may very well have been talking about
Nicodemus individually, but the text is pregnant with meaning.
Nicodemus represents the old religious orthodoxy, which Jesus
criticized as being insufficient and in need of rebirth.

Jesus' attitude toward those laws was neither total acceptance
nor absolute rejection. Jesus, who with divine authority reinter-
preted the old law, sometimes pointed out the deeper meaning of
God's commands. For example, the Old Testament had a system
of justice that demanded "an eye for an eye" and "a tooth for a
tooth." Contrary to what is often thought, this *lex talionis* (Latin:

"the law of *talio*") not only enforced strict justice, but it was also a limit on retribution. In the ancient world, it was not uncommon to mete out harsh draconian punishments for crimes. The Old Testament standard of justice to have "an eye for an eye" was so unique because it set a limit on the extent of punishments. It was "an eye for an eye" not "a life for an eye."

That is the way with God's commands: There are both literal and symbolic meanings. The Christian call to fasting need not apply to food only. We can fast from participating in popular culture or from gossip or from any number of other activities. The commands to "feed the hungry" and "clothe the naked" can take the form of feeding people with encouragement, and clothing them with compassion—though, never to the sole exclusion of the more literal commands.

Sins too take on various manifestations. Gluttony is a sin usually associated with excessive eating, overly fast consumption of food, or being overly fussy about which foods one eats. But, one can be a glutton regarding so many other appetites as well. Avoiding problems can be a variation of the sin of sloth—as when a person avoids necessary problems because of laziness.

In a sense, Jesus personalized the commandments of God, helping us to recognize that the language of "thou shalt not" can be understood to mean: "Trust God, for evil will befall you and others if you do the following."

Actually, the Ten Commandments, in addition to their literal meaning, can have a figurative meaning as well. According to Jesus, anyone who is angry with another person has broken the commandment against murder (cf. Matthew 5:21–22). In light of Jesus' teachings, we can understand God's commands as promises. So, the command, "You shall have no other gods before me" (Exodus 20:3; Deuteronomy 5:7), becomes a promise that God will be our "one and only." The command not to desire one's neighbor's goods (cf. Exodus 20:17; Deuteronomy 5:21b) becomes a promise that we won't want anything someone else has: We will be joyful at the plenitude of our own blessings.

Christianity's tedious list of all those "thou shalt"—and "thou shalt not"—commands are not merely about behavior modification. What's more, there is a reason why there are only ten and not, say, one hundred commandments. In reality, there are few laws that bind Christians. As G. K. Chesterton writes: "The truth is, of course, that the curtness of the [Ten] Commandments is an evidence, not of the gloom and narrowness of a religion, but, on the contrary, of its liberality and humanity. It is shorter to state the things forbidden than the things permitted; precisely because most things are permitted, and only a few things are forbidden."[65]

These laws come from God's intellect.[66] They are not arbitrary but purposefully crafted by an omniscient and omnipotent God in a way that couples freedom with responsibility. Even in the secular realm I am only free to live as I choose until my freedom affects the freedom of others. Or, put another way: I want to live freely, but (as Oliver Wendell Holmes once said) I am prohibited from "falsely shouting fire in a theater and causing a panic."[67]

What we find is a necessary balance between two heretical extreme views: antinomianism and legalism. The first, antinomianism, posits that the moral law is not meaningful if one is a Christian: We can pretty much do as we please. The second, legalism, in this context, means that we must obey each and every one of the moral laws perfectly. Jesus said, "For truly I tell you, until heaven and earth pass away, not one letter, not one stroke of a letter, will pass from the law until all is accomplished" (Matthew 5:18). But repeatedly he distinguished between the letter and the spirit of the law.

Saint Paul made the point that the Mosaic law revealed to us the disease of our sinful ways, but it did not provide a cure. According to Talmudic tradition, there are 613 *mitzvot*, or "commandments," in the Torah.[68] Many of those commandments are directly related to the religious practices and ceremonies of Judaism.

In the Hebrew Scriptures, at least three different kinds of laws are identified: *mishpatim*, which are moral laws (e.g., "Thou shalt not steal"); *edot*, which are ritual laws (e.g., touching a corpse makes one unclean); and, *chukim*, which are commandments from God having no apparent reason (e.g., prohibition against eating pork). It is not always easy to decipher which biblical directives fall into which category. As sinners, it simply is not possible to follow all the laws of the Torah. However, by grace it is possible to follow Jesus, who has fulfilled the law. Saint Thomas Aquinas explained that laws come in four varieties: Eternal Laws (known to God—the inner life of the Trinity); Divine Laws (revealed by God to humans—the Ten Commandments); Natural Laws (discernible by humans—to protect and provide for loved ones); and Human Laws (created by sovereigns—the Constitution of the United States).

Jesus commanded that we give unto Caesar what is Caesar's and unto God what is God's (Matthew 22:15). Jesus knew full well that giving unto Caesar meant funding the Roman government and all its endeavors, many of which ran counter to Jesus' teaching. But, what was the alternative? The use of force against Rome was self-defeating. Shrewd compromise, even provisional accommodation with Roman authorities too easily turned into full cooperation and even assimilation. Self-imposed exile could work for some, but not all of Israel. Instead of these options, Jesus counseled people to worry more about the kingdom of God and less about the kingdoms of the world. His counsel proved wise. Within less than four hundred years, Christianity became the official religion of Rome. Love won the day.

The foundation of the Christian message is that God is love, and we are called to love him and our neighbor. St. Augustine counseled to "Love and do what you want" (*Ama et quod vis fac*). Elsewhere he wrote, "Love God and do what you want" (*Ama Deum et fac quod vis*). The first version of this quote curiously leaves out the word "God," and I think that is because St. Augustine knew that any authentic expression of love, accomplished with sincerity and openness, inevitably draws one closer to the God, who is love (1 John 4:8). However, we are called to be disciples and not merely admirers of Christ. Christianity is not a philosophy or even a chosen way of life but instead is an interpersonal relationship with God.

I was friends with an older gentleman with whom I worked. He told me about a heart attack he suffered. He was rushed to the hospital but was fully conscious. He said the nurses could hear him crying from his hospital bed, "Jesus help me," "Moses help me," "Buddha help me," "Mohammed help me." His story was kind of funny after the fact, but at the time he was terrified, and he said he wanted to cover all his bases. But, there's an old saying, "Unless you stand for something, you'll fall for anything."

Every decision we make and every act we perform starts with a conscious or unconscious attraction. We do what we do because either it appears to be the good and right thing for us, or because we think it will bring us some happiness or satisfaction. The Church counsels us to distinguish between what feels good and what is morally good; though often they are one in the same. As a way of meditating upon how to be good, some find it helpful to ask the question, "What would Jesus do?" A more correct version is: "What would Jesus want me to do?" One of the attributes so many find attractive about Jesus is that he was an authentic and sincere person. So, when we seek to imitate him, we shouldn't just duplicate his behavior, but we too should seek to emulate his authenticity and sincerity; to allow his love to transform us into individuals.

God gives us ample opportunities. "Oh what remorse we shall feel at the end of our lives, when we look back upon the great number of instructions and examples afforded by God and the Saints for our perfection, and so carelessly received by us! If this end were to come to you today, how would you be pleased with the life you have led this year?"[69] I had a spiritual advisor whose advice to me was to "love more and think less." Perhaps he was paraphrasing St. Thomas Aquinas, who proclaimed that, "Love takes up where knowledge leaves off."[70] God's love is transformative and freeing.

†

CHAPTER THREE

WORK AND PRAYER

CALLING

Most of us spend the majority of our adult lives working or looking for work. Ideally, our work should take the form of a vocation and not just a job. The original meaning of the word "vocation" can be traced to the Latin words "*vox*" ("voice") and "*vocare*" ("to call"). This leaves us with the meaning, "being called by a voice."

How do we know what we are called to be? A great desire could be a clue, but it isn't always indicative of God's will. King David strongly desired to build God a temple. But, because he had offended God, his desire was refused. (See 1 Chronicles 22:6–10.) Temple-building was not David's vocation; it was not his responsibility. After discerning this difficult truth, David needed to move onto what he was called to do.

The Catholic monk Thomas Merton observed:

> If you can never make up your mind what God wills for you, but are always veering from one opinion to another, from one practice to another, from one method to another, it may be an indication that you are trying to get around God's will and do your own with a quiet conscience . . .
>
> Your whole existence will be a patchwork of confused desires and daydreams . . . in which you do nothing except defeat the work of grace: for all this is an elaborate subconscious device of your nature to resist God, Whose work in your soul demands the sacrifice of all that you desire and delight in, and, indeed, of all that you are.[1]

The question, "What am I called to do," is absurd to many people today. For, consciously or otherwise, they see their work as a Sisyphean exercise in futility.[2] But, from the Christian perspective, the work we do—the vocation to which we are authentically called—can be salvific, not only for ourselves, but also for those whom we serve through our work. That service can be immediate and direct; or we work for the good of successive generations. Quaker philosopher Elton Trueblood writes: "A man has made at least a start on discovering the meaning of human life when he plants shade trees under which he knows full well he will never sit."[3]

Following our vocation is inevitably rewarding but also requires a generosity of spirit and willingness for self-sacrifice. God will not do for us what he wishes for us to do for ourselves. In the book of Exodus (17:11-13) we read about a battle between Israel and the Amalekites and how Moses interceded with God on behalf of Israel. Whenever Moses held up his hands in prayer the Israelites triumphed in combat, but when Moses grew weary and let his hands fall, the tide of battle turned against them. So, others, Aaron and Hur, helped to hold up Moses' hands until the battle was won. Aaron and Hur could not intercede in the way Moses could, so they helped in the only way they could.

This story reminds me of a scene in J. R. R. Tolkien's *The Return of the King*, where Samwise Gamgee, the loyal friend, wishes to carry an extremely heavy burden borne by his friend, Frodo. Unable to do so, he does the next best thing and actually carries Frodo himself. "'Come, Mr. Frodo!' he cried. 'I can't carry it for you, but I can carry you.'"[4] Jesus may not always carry our burdens, but he carries us as we carry our burdens. Mary Stevenson's "Footprints" poem, perhaps a bit sentimental, tells the story of man who dreamt he was walking on the sand, side by side with Jesus. The footprints correspond to scenes in the man's life. The poem goes on to reveal that during the really difficult times there was only one set of footprints, and the man questioned why the Lord would leave during those hard times. Jesus' response was that there were footprints of only one man because Jesus himself was carrying the man during those difficulties.

We influence most everyone with whom we interact and leave a mark on everyone we brush up against. One of the founders of the Methodist community, John Wesley, goes so far as to counsel: "Neither is love content with barely working no evil to our neighbour. It continually incites us to do good, as we have time and opportunity; to do good, in every possible kind, and in every possible degree, to all men."[5] This is noble advice. But, Brother Thomas Merton offers a prudential caution: "To allow oneself to be carried away by a multitude of conflicting concerns, to surrender to too many demands, to commit oneself to too many projects, to want to help everyone in everything is to succumb to violence."[6]

Jesus himself did not engage in every good act he possibly could take on. In the Acts of the Apostles (3:1–11), we read how Jesus' disciples, Peter and John, encountered a lame man begging at an entrance to the temple. This main entrance, known as the "Beautiful Gate," was one that Jesus must have passed many times. We learn that the crippled man had been carried to the spot in order to beg. He had probably been begging at that gate for years, given that the lame man was known to the crowd and, therefore, not an imposter. Jesus very likely passed by him many times. But, it was only later, after Jesus' ascension, that Peter healed the man, commanding him to take up his mat and walk. (See v. 6.)

Knowing when to step in and help or when to walk by or (more generally) knowing what is too little or too much in each circumstance is not easy. The balance can be tipped in one of two directions: We can blame too much on ourselves or we blame too much on others.

The Roman poet Horace commands: "*Sapere aude*," or "Dare to know!"[7] Coming to know what we must take responsibility for and what is out of our control is a large part of truly daring to know. Often, it is not a question of: "Is some task my job or someone else's job?" But, it is a question of: "Where does my role begin and end in the process?" In the Gospels we see that Jesus often carried out his ministry though he was weary and exhausted, but he did so out of love. Many of us are harried and anxious about our schedules, doing more and more out of a perceived pressure to keep up with our peers, or based on some other fear or desire. This type of agitated labor can never be synonymous with our true calling.

Questions of degree can often confound us: How much must I love? How much must I give? How much must I do? When does a virtue like courage become excessive to the point of rashness, or deficient to the point of cowardice? Is it possible to be too patient or too humble? Should we adopt another Aristotelian exhortation by following the "Golden Mean," which counsels us to practice all things in moderation? This last line of thinking can be found in Christian teachings. For Aristotle, good behavior was often understood as a mean between two extremes. For example, courage is a virtue. Too little courage equals cowardice; too much courage leads to rash behavior. (This is an oversimplification, since one cannot be *too* courageous. Rashness is not merely lots and lots of courage, but an excess of courage that is not coupled with the virtue of prudence.)

Many Christian writers down the centuries have extolled the virtue of moderation. In one of his classic works, *The City of God*, St. Augustine describes what it will be like in the resurrection of the flesh: that each person will neither be more nor less than what he or she ought to be.[8] However, moderation does not mean we should be tepid or timid in what we affirm or in what we desire. A person who is passionless, who doesn't stand for anything, is a fool. But, a person who is dogmatic about everything, who is possessed of such hubris, is arrogant. It is tempting to find truth by finding the balance between two extremes. Yet, there is nothing intrinsically holy about being passionless. As Christ says: "Because you are lukewarm, and neither cold nor hot, I am about to spit you out of my mouth" (Revelation 3:16).

For Simone Weil, the solution comes not through a mediocre practice of virtues, but through grace. She writes: "We cannot by suggestion obtain things which are incompatible. Only grace can do that. A sensitive person who by suggestion becomes courageous hardens himself; often he may even, by a sort of savage pleasure, amputate his own sensitivity. Grace alone can give courage while leaving the sensitivity intact, or sensitivity while leaving the courage intact."[9]

Nonetheless, most of us still struggle with degrees of behavior. In the novella *Billy Budd*, Herman Melville writes, "Who in the rainbow can draw the line where the violet tint ends and the orange tint begins? Distinctly we see the difference of the colors, but where exactly does the one first blendingly enter into the other?"[10]

Melville's insight rings true for many aspects of our lives. Modern life, for all its amenities, has created a lifestyle of continual demands and conflicting stresses. Many see their work not as the fulfillment of a vocation, but as a burdensome obligation for survival. One palliative for this dissatisfaction is the practice of living prayerfully in what some Catholics refer to as "the sacrament of the present moment."

Buddhist monk Thich Nhat Hanh tells the story of his novi-
tiate, when he was responsible for washing the dishes. He hated
the job, because there were a lot of dishes and it was hard work.
You would think that washing dishes would be an instrumental
or pragmatic good; that is, an act that led to something good
(i.e., clean dishes). But, Thich Nhat Hanh explains how doing the
dishes became a good just in itself:

> While washing the dishes one should be completely aware of the
> fact that one is washing the dishes. At first glance, that might
> seem a little silly: why put so much stress on a simple thing? But
> that's precisely the point. The fact that I am standing there and
> washing these bowls is a wondrous reality. I'm being completely
> myself, following my breath, conscious of my presence, and con-
> scious of my thoughts and actions.[11]

Admittedly, the Buddhist practice of mindfulness is different
from living prayerfully in the sacrament of the present moment,
but at least some of the underlying goals are similar. From the
Christian perspective, living in the moment helps us avoid boredom with routine. In C. S. Lewis' *The Screwtape Letters*, the demon, Screwtape, observes in a letter to his protégé, Wormwood:

> The horror of the Same Old Thing is . . . an endless source of
> heresies in religion, folly in counsel, infidelity in marriage, and
> inconstancy in friendship.
> . . . [God] has balanced the love of change in them by a love
> of permanence. He has contrived to gratify both tastes together
> in the very world He has made, by that union of change and
> permanence which we call Rhythm. He gives them the seasons,
> each season different yet every year the same, so that spring is
> always felt as a novelty yet always as the recurrence of an im-
> memorial theme.[12]

This theme plays out in the liturgical calendar of the Church.
In the West, the Church year begins with the season of Advent,
which is a time of penance, reflection, and joyful anticipation occurring several weeks before Christmas. The calendar then moves
into the Christmas season, which is followed by a brief interven-
ing period, called "Ordinary Time." Ordinary Time is followed by
the season of Lent, which prepares us for the Paschal Triduum,

that is, the three-day commemoration of Christ's suffering, death, and resurrection. This leads into the 50 days of Easter, ending in the feast of Pentecost. Then, a longer span of Ordinary Time intervenes until the beginning of the next liturgical year at Advent. In addition to this yearly cycle the Church celebrates the Sanctoral Cycle; special days of remembrance. These holy days are ranked by importance into three categories with Solemnities being the highest, then feasts, and lastly memorials.

We may desire stability and familiarity, but we loathe monotony. Monotony is unheavenly. Søren Kierkegaard declares, "As it is said of the eternal life, that there is neither sighing nor weeping, so we might add that there is also no habit."[13] Thinking about our deaths and the afterlife that awaits can lead to the lament that we will miss the joys that life has to offer: sunrises, mountains, friends—those kinds of things. Our lists may differ. Still, whatever is loveable in this human life will be present in heaven after death and in the new heavens and new earth promised at the end of time in Isaiah 65:17 and Revelation 21:1 (albeit, perhaps, in a different form). Are there sunrises and mountains in paradise? If not, then whatever draws us to love sunrises and mountains, whatever the secret ingredient is in all of our loves, will certainly be present there.

The Latin phrase "*sub specie aeternitatis*" is associated with the Judeo-Dutch philosopher, Benedict (or Baruch) Spinoza. It translates into English as: "Under the aspect of eternity." It helped him explain how there could still be human freedom in his own deterministic view of nature. Instead of following one's own little desires or emotions, individuals should look toward (one might say) the "big plan" that governs everything. While rejecting Spinoza's determinism, Christians can still interpret his idea. "Every moment comes to us pregnant with a command from God, only to pass on and plunge into eternity, there to remain forever what we have made of it."[14]

The eternal perspective reminds us that every decision we make leads us further toward eternal joy or misery, not just for ourselves, but for those around us too. In his sermon, "The Weight of Glory," C. S. Lewis puts it this way:

> It may be possible for each to think too much of his own potential glory hereafter; it is hardly possible for him to think too

often or too deeply about that of his neighbour . . . It is a serious thing to live in a society of possible gods and goddesses, to remember that the dullest and most uninteresting person you talk to may one day be a creature which, if you saw it now, you would be strongly tempted to worship, or else a horror and a corruption such as you now meet, if at all, only in a nightmare. All day long we are, in some degree, helping each other to one or other of these destinations. . . . There are no *ordinary* people. You have never talked to a mere mortal. Nations, cultures, arts, civilization—these are mortal, and their life is to ours as the life of a gnat. But it is immortals whom we joke with, work with, marry, snub, and exploit—immortal horrors or everlasting splendours.[15]

Our interactions with others have real consequences because God imparts to us what Blaise Pascal calls the "dignity of causality."[16] So, we have to work under the burden of this heavy responsibility. Yet, coupled with this truth is the insight of St. Ignatius of Loyola, who counsels: "So trust God as if the success of things depended entirely on you, not at all on God. Yet so bend every effort as if you [are going to do] nothing and God alone is going to do everything."[17]

This commitment to work hard, balanced with a trust in God's providence, has been abused at times. I'm thinking about those who were taught not to try to rise above their current circumstances; your father was a baker, and you should be happy being a baker because God put you there. History is littered with such exploitation exemplified by the ideas that God made you to be a poor, or put you in an abusive relationship, or allowed sickness into your life, and you must accept your current circumstances without complaint.

Appreciating and living in the present moment is a spiritual discipline that cultivates humility but should not produce meaningless acquiescence. Instead, this attitude should foster the recognition that God is with you regardless of circumstances. To quote St. Teresa of Avila: "Granting that we are always in the presence of God, yet it seems to me that those who pray are in His presence in a very different sense; for they, as it were, see that He is looking upon them, while others may be for days together without even once recollecting that God sees them."[18]

So often, we seek instant gratification. We look for the next "rush" in new and untried ways. But, extreme expressions of this behavior can lead to a kind of circular life; like a dog chasing its tail. We are so easily tricked into believing that there is a shortcut to knowing the delight of the saints. Your delights may not be mine. The sins that tempt us reveal something about who we are and what we desire. What lures me may not interest you, but our individual temptations can teach us about ourselves. All temptation is a lure to find something we believe is missing.

Followers of Christ are free, even encouraged—some would go to far as to say commanded by God—to be ambitious. However, a Christian version of the *carpe-diem,* or "seize the day," mentality is different from a hedonistic, live-for-the-moment philosophy,which is often motivated by a conscious or unconscious fear of death or (less dramatically) a fear of self-examination. Saint Augustine says of our relationship with God: "For You have formed us for Yourself, and our hearts are restless till they find rest in You."[19] The call to find rest in God is more challenging than it may first appear. There are many Christians who ". . . are attached to activities and enterprises that seem to be important. Blinded by their desire for ceaseless motion, for a constant sense of achievement, famished with a crude hunger for results, for visible and tangible success, they work themselves into a state in which they cannot believe that they are pleasing God unless they are busy with a dozen jobs at the same time."[20]

Jesus sent out 70 disciples, commanding them to bring no bag, sack, or sandals, and to greet no one along the way. (See Luke 10:4.) Basically, they were called to rely on God's providence and the hospitality of others. Hospitality is an important virtue espoused throughout the Old Testament. As the author of the book of Hebrews counsels: "Do not neglect to show hospitality to strangers, for by doing that some have entertained angels without knowing it" (13:2).

I used to work with a man whose job took him into many people's homes. Often, they would offer him something to drink or eat. He never said no, because he wanted to allow others the chance to serve. He believed that hospitality is blessed by God and that we should not deny others the pleasure of giving.

Jesus says to his disciples that, if they come to a town and are not welcomed, they should shake the dust of that town from their feet. Jesus meant this as a condemnation of that town. But, this could also be interpreted as not letting a bad experience stay with us, like when a coach tells a player who has a minor injury during the game: "Shake it off and go back to playing!"

One of my law school professors—an atheist who was deeply concerned with moral issues—reminded our class that it was a privilege for us to ponder some of the deep, philosophical issues he set before us. He noted that most of the people in the world needed to spend their time working for their next meal instead of having the leisure time to ponder. History shows that most of the great saints were contemplatives in action; hardworking men and women who still found time to reflect on the mysteries of God. We should emulate their example, recognizing that even the busiest among us can do the same. To do so, we simply need only to spend more time with God. This sounds contradictory, but just as fishes and loaves were multiplied by Jesus, your time with him will be multiplied too.[21]

The philosopher Josef Pieper wrote an extraordinary book on the topic of leisure as the basis of culture. In that book, he discusses the importance of Psalm 46:10: "'Be still, and know that I am God!' That language of 'be still' could be interpreted as: 'Be *at leisure*, and know that I am God.'"[22] Leisure is important to our physical and spiritual lives. Pieper writes: "Man seems to mistrust everything that is effortless; he can only enjoy, with a good conscience, what he has acquired with toil and trouble; he refuses to have anything as a gift."[23] George MacDonald observes: "Certainly, work is not always required of a man. There is such a thing as a sacred idleness, the cultivation of which is now fearfully neglected."[24] Relaxation and calmness are not, however, synonymous with laziness and sloth. As John Lubbock observes, "Rest is not idleness, and to lie sometimes on the grass under the trees on a summer's day, listening to the murmur of water, or watching the clouds float across the blue sky, is by no means waste of time."[25] God calls us to such recreation (or, "re-creation").

Most of the great religious traditions of the world advocate taking quiet reflective time to think about life; self; neighbor; God; creation—and our relationship with each. This is why we have days of rest like the Sabbath each week and holidays, that is, "holy days."[26]

Even more surprisingly, we are not just called to divide our life into work and rest, but we are also invited by God to play. Proverbs 8 reads:

When [God] established the heavens, there was I [Wisdom] . . .
When he fixed the foundations of earth,
    then was I beside him as artisan;
I was his delight day by day,
    playing before him all the while,
Playing over the whole of his earth,
    having my delight with human beings. (27a, 29c–31, NABRE)[27]

In this poem to Wisdom, which the author presents as an aspect of God, there is a remarkable account of God's playfulness. Simultaneously, we are talking about God's work. Reverend Father Hugo Rahner wrote a marvelous book on the subject of play. He points out that there is a long and deep tradition of seriousness and (in cases) dourness in Christianity: Many saints caution against playfulness, fun, and laughter. But, Rahner counters with the teaching of St. Thomas Aquinas, who went against that tradition by allowing for and even defending the legitimacy of— non-sinful, of course—joking and playfulness (cf. ST II-II, q. 168, a. 2 ff.).[28] Unsurprisingly, there is a host of other saints whose joy was effervescent, and who counseled in favor of a holy frivolity. This latter group, perhaps, recognized that work and play are not differentiated in God. Like a child whose job it is to play, the two tasks are united.

Curiously, the Bible never records Jesus as having laughed.[29] However, we do find throughout the four canonical Gospels strong evidence that Jesus had a sense of humor and he appreciated a good joke. Much of Jesus' wit is lost to modern Western readers for the same reason we don't always find the jokes of our grandparents' generation or jokes from other cultures all that funny. Many of Jesus' stories and examples employ good comedic formulas. (For example, he uses absurd extremes.) In Matthew 7:3, Jesus chastises hypocrites for noticing a small splinter in their neighbor's eye while they ignore the wooden beam in their own eye. In another instance, Matthew 23:24, Jesus mocks the Pharisees for straining a gnat out of soup but swallowing an entire camel. These might not strike a modern audience as funny, but it likely got a laugh from Jesus' listeners.

Jesus' use of humor to make an important point is nowhere more profoundly used than in the parable of the Rich Fool.

Then he told them a parable: 'The land of a rich man produced abundantly. And he thought to himself, "What should I do, for I have no place to store my crops?" Then he said, "I will do this: I will pull down my barns and build larger ones, and there I will store all my grains and my goods. And I will say to my soul, 'Soul, you have ample goods laid up for many years; relax, eat, drink, be merry.'" But God said to him, "You fool! This very night your life is being demanded of you. And the things you have prepared, whose will they be?" So it is with those who store up treasures for themselves but are not rich toward God.'
(Luke 12: 16-21)

Jesus told his parables orally to his original audience, and it is not hard to imagine a bit of sarcasm coming into his voice at various times. This parable starts out with the insight that the ground yielded an abundant harvest; it was not through the toil or skill of the rich man in the story. This sets the stage for showing how ungratefully and ridiculously the man behaves. We see this when Jesus gets to the part about the rich man's idea to tear down his old barns and build bigger ones. Why not feed the hungry, Jesus may have mused. We see in the parable that the rich man keeps thinking to himself or talking to himself. The point being made is that the landowner may be rich in material wealth but doesn't seem to have any family or friends around him. Next, we see how the rich man plans to take it easy one day in the future, but that day is not now—the hint being, that day will not ever come for this man since he is too interested in accumulating wealth.

The continual process of becoming a spiritually mature person is an inevitably slow, lifelong dedication, full of difficulties and frustrations. As the Venerable Bede offered, "No one is suddenly made perfect."[30] Then again, Christianity is replete with immediate, life-changing Damascene conversions of the sort Saul experienced when he encountered the risen Jesus on the road to Damascus.

There are those who in their very first seeking of it are nearer the kingdom of Heaven than many who have for years believed themselves to be of it. In the former, there is more of the mind of Jesus, and when He calls them they recognize Him at once and go after Him; while the others examine Him from head to foot

and, finding Him not sufficiently like the Jesus of their conception, turn their backs and go to church or chapel or chamber to
kneel before a vague form mingled of tradition and fancy.[31]

A student who sacrifices leisure for study may miss out on
some pleasure now but hopes to more than make up for it come
graduation day. When it comes to our spiritual life, it's hard to
make these kinds of sacrifices because of that nasty habit of ra-
tionalizing that we are good enough already.

> Many a housewife overdrives herself to please some inner voice
> that demands perfection. The voice may be her own demands or
> the relics of childhood training, but it certainly is not likely to be
> the voice of the power behind the Universe.
>
> On the other hand, the middle-aged business man [sic] who
> has long ago taught his conscience to come to heel may per-
> suade himself that he is a good-living man. He may even say,
> with some pride, that he would never do anything against his
> conscience. But, it is impossible to believe that the feeble voice
> of the half-blind thing which he calls a conscience is in any real
> sense the voice of God.[32]

PRAYER

The quintessential expression of how action pairs with contemplation is St. Benedict's famous dictum: "To work is to pray."
What we believe to be correct, "orthodox," influences how we act,
"orthopraxy." Prayer, which takes the form of meditating on the
mysteries of the faith, as well as study and work, is summed
up in the Benedictine motto, *cruce, libro, et atro* ("cross, book,
and plow"). This adage reflects Benedictine spirituality, but there
are many different methods of prayer. Some people pray in motion, others in stillness. Sometimes, we use words or songs, or
we communicate silently. Prayer can take the form of familiar
formulas and repetitions or be spontaneous and conversational.
We can pray that God will teach us how to pray. More astoundingly, Christians, as temples of the Holy Spirit, can beseech God
to help us to pray, and, audaciously, we can ask him to pray
within us, for us. Through prayer we connect with God, always
mindful of the mystery of our communication, never anxious that
God is distracted by a cacophony of competing pleas. "Prayer: In

this intimate union God and the soul are like two pieces of wax melted together; they cannot be separated." [33]

In a very real sense, Christians are not just acting as God wishes us to act, but God acts in and through each one of us. In the words of St. Teresa of Avila:

> Christ has no body but yours,
> No hands, no feet on earth but yours,
> Yours are the eyes with which he looks
> Compassion on this world,
> Yours are the feet with which he walks to do good,
> Yours are the hands, with which he blesses all the world . . .[34]

Our prayer life can be intimate and personal or sometimes needs to be public and communal. The communities in which we find ourselves, our families, our friends, our places of employment, call us to interact regularly with others for whom we are called to pray. That is why so many great prayers are in the plural. In the Our Father we pray, "give us this day our daily bread," not "give me my daily bread." In the Hail Mary[35] we say, "pray for us sinners" not "pray for me, a sinner." At Mass we ask God to bring "all the departed into the light of Your kingdom," not to bring "me into the kingdom."

Most of us tend to think of prayer as a time when we ask God for assistance. It is a mistake to believe that higher forms of prayer avoid asking God for any favors. When Jesus was asked by his disciples how to pray, he responded with a formula filled with requests: "give us," "forgive us," "lead us." We are not just welcomed and encouraged to come to God with our needs, we are commanded to do so. Jesus was a man of prayer, and he counseled all Christians to follow his example. Through prayer we grow in the strength and wisdom we need to overcome challenges and temptations. A rich prayer life infuses supernatural joys and consolations into the praying person. Prayer is empowering and healing.

Our prayer lives should include:

■ CONFESSION. A daily examination of conscience is a good way to consider how open we have been to God's invitation to grow in holiness and love. We especially need to look at those sins we habitually fall back into over and over again and confess them to God through the sacrament of penance.[36] Confessing one's sins to a priest is a humbling exercise. The practice is grounded in several Gospel passages, especially John 20:23, "If you forgive the sins of any, they are forgiven them; if you retain the sins of any, they are retained." No matter what sickness of body or mind infects us, no matter what evil we might have committed against ourselves or our neighbor, so long as there is a single breath in us, we are not beyond the reach of God's forgiveness. Sorrow for one's sins comes in one of two forms: perfect contrition, which is derived from the love of God; and imperfect contrition, which originates from a fear of punishment.

■ PROFESSION OF FAITH. In my office, I have a great painting of Daniel in the lions' den. The amazing thing about the way the artist has rendered this scene is that Daniel has his back to the lions! I don't think Daniel presumes God would hold them at bay, but simply, he turns his back because he submits to whatever God willed for him in that den.

■ ADORATION. Adoration is due to God alone. Our expression of that adoration, that reverence and love, is manifest in how we live and pray. Fifth-century Pope Celestine had a saying: *lex orandi, lex credendi*—the manner in which we offer worship to God represents our understanding of God. Put another way: how we pray reveals (or shapes) what we believe—not just what we say, but the music we use, the symbols we use, the reverence we show with our bodies when we kneel, stand, bow, or clasp our hands.[37]

■ THANKFULNESS. God has been good to each and every one of us. He created us out of nothing and invites us to share in his infinite love for all eternity. There is nothing that we possess that we have not been given by God, and there is nothing we can offer to him that he did not give us in the first place. But, Scripture tells us (and Tradition confirms) that he delights in our love and finds joy in our gratefulness.

■ OFFERING/SACRIFICE. Sufis tell the story of a disciple on a pilgrimage who met up with a man suffering the worst misery. The pilgrim cried aloud, "Why, God, do you not do something to help this poor man?" The suffering man then replied to the pilgrim, "God did do something. He created you." In a baffling way, love and suffering are sometimes two different sides to the same coin.

■ INTERCESSION. Saint Monica prayed that her son would turn from his wicked ways and become a new man. For years she prayed fervently for his conversion, and eventually her prayers were answered. Monica's son was an infamous sinner, but after his conversion, her son, Augustine, became one of the greatest saints in the history of Christendom. But, what about all those mothers who also prayed ceaselessly, yet their sons continued to be anything but saintly? What can be said other than Jesus himself prayed for Judas until the end? We must never give up and always trust in God.

Not only should we pray for others and with others, but we should ask for their prayers in return. That is exactly what Catholics do when we pray to saints for the souls of the dead. We do not kneel before a statue or an icon thinking that somehow the saint is in the wood or stone—like some pagans believed of their gods. For Catholics, the image of a saint is a means to focus our attention.

Icons in particular are often referred to as windows into heaven. We do not pray to saints as if they were gods, but instead as God's friends to intercede for us. Jesus himself intercedes for us. Robert M'Cheyne's insight is so true: "If I could hear Christ praying for me in the next room, I would not fear a million enemies. Yet the distance makes no difference. He is praying for me!"[38]

■ PETITION. Alfred Tennyson was correct when he wrote, "More things are wrought by prayer than this world dreams of."[39] There are some spiritualities that insist that asking God to grant our requests is somehow unseemly, even unholy. But, Jesus himself commands us to ask Our Father to "give us this day our daily bread." We are encouraged to bring before God our deepest needs and desires, even while we seek to be transformed by grace into beings that need and desire what God wants for us.

■ CONTEMPLATION. This kind of prayer takes us away from the all of the questions, pleadings, and demands of life. The word "contemplation" itself has its roots in the actions one performs in a temple. Contemplative prayer is not merely pondering the wonders of God, within the limits of our capacity, but immersing oneself in God's own ineffable presence.

Contemplation isn't just a time to wrestle with the great mysteries but to simply calm our restlessness and spend time in quiet repose with God. Jesus relaxed with Lazarus and his other friends, escaping from the crowds. Occasionally, we can offer him the same comfort, leaving him free from our harried petitions and requests. Like pausing at an oasis in the desert, he occasionally desires that we rest in him. More deeply, we can enter into the silence in which God dwells.

We should not think of prayer as something to do in between making breakfast and getting to the laundry. Prayer is something both deeper and different from anything else we do, though it can also be part of what we do throughout the day. The greatest kind of prayer, of course, is whichever one we actually practice. "The more we pray, the more we wish to pray,"[40] says St. John Vianney. And we do not have to rely on ourselves alone. Jesus invites us to enter into his heart, most sacred and merciful, and to let him pray on our behalf; for he is a God who possesses a human heart that is tenderly understanding and compassionate to each one of us.

Jesus insists that whatever we ask in his name will be granted to us. Mark 11:23-24:

"Truly I tell you, if you say to this mountain, 'Be taken up and thrown into the sea' and if you do not doubt in your heart, but believe that what you say will come to pass, it will be done for you. So I tell you, whatever you ask for in prayer, believe that you have received it, and it will be yours."

But, this teaching is qualified. "And this is the boldness we have in him, that if we ask anything according to his will, he hears us. And if we know that he hears us in whatever we ask, we know that we have obtained the requests made of him" (1 John 5:14-15).

The key phrase here is, "according to his will." "Thy will be done" is the language from the Lord's Prayer, and it is most difficult to utter with any real degree of conviction. Sometimes our prayers are not answered because God has a better plan for us than we have for ourselves. Isaiah 55:8-9 explains, "For my thoughts are not your thoughts, neither are your ways my ways, declares the LORD. For as the heavens are higher than the earth, so are my ways higher than your ways and my thoughts than your thoughts."

Beyond that, other reasons why prayers are unanswered include,

- Lack of faith (James 1:6)
- Sin (Psalms 66:18)
- Conflict with others (Matthew 5:22)

It may be said of even the greatest sinner that should he keep praying one of two things will occur: either he'll stop sinning, or he'll stop praying. It does not matter if we get the words or formulas correct. "Even such as ask amiss may sometimes have their prayers answered. The Father will never give the child a stone that asks for bread; but I am not sure that he will never give the child a stone that asks for a stone. If the Father says, 'My child, that is a stone; it is not bread,' and the child answer, 'I am sure it is bread; I want it,' may it not be well that he should try his bread?" [41] Such is the humility of God.

Regardless of God's humility, communication with God, as recorded in the Bible, was usually preceded by some awesome scene—storms or fire or wind. In Job, God communicates out of a whirlwind (38:1); in Exodus, an earthquake precedes his coming (19:18); and throughout the Bible, God's voice is likened to thunder (1 Samuel 2:10, Job 37:2, Psalms 104:7, John 12:29). According to biblical accounts, people who glimpse the refulgent glory of God (Abraham in Genesis 22:12; Moses in Exodus 3:6; Daniel in Daniel 10:11; or the Apostles, who witnessed Jesus' transfiguration,[42] specifically Peter, James, and John in Matthew 17:6) experience something akin to a holy terror. It is not only humans who can't bear to look upon the unmediated God; the angels themselves cover their faces (Isaiah 6:2) before the God who dwells in unapproachable light (1 Timothy 6:16). God is at once awesome and terrifying. Yet, "We must fear God out of love, not love him out of fear,"[43] says St. Francis de Sales.

The imagery of this unapproachable deity must be counterbalanced with accounts that God's presence is often sublime and subtle, also tender and welcoming. The Bible explains that when God speaks it is not always in hurricanes and tempests but often in a whisper,[44] or as some translations put it, in "a still small voice."

> He [God] is still here: He still whispers to us. He still makes a sign to us. His voice is so low, and the world's din is so loud, and His signs are so covert, and the world is so restless, that it is difficult to determine when He addresses us, and what He says. Religious men cannot but feel, in various ways, that His Providence is guiding them and blessing them personally, on the whole; yet when they attempt to put their finger upon the times and places, the traces of His presence disappear.[45]

An instance of God's whisper comes from the story of Elijah, an Old Testament prophet who sought God. Elijah traveled to an isolated place, atop Mount Horeb, where he encountered a strong wind, but God was not in the wind; and he encountered an earthquake, but God was not in the earthquake; then the prophet heard a still small voice—a whisper, and God was in the whisper. (See 1 Kings 19: 9-13.)

But, why use a whisper when God could have shouted? One reason may be God whispers to us just as lovers whisper to one another. They don't shout. God was in the whisper, because he invites; he does not force. Yet, admittedly, God does not seem to even whisper to most of us.[46] Why?

> God is the most obvious thing in the world. He is absolutely self-evident—the simplest, clearest and closest reality of life and consciousness. We are only unaware of him, because we are too complicated, for our vision is darkened by the complexity of pride. We seek him beyond the horizon with our noses lifted high in the air, and fail to see that he lies at our very feet. We flatter ourselves in premeditating the long, long journey we are going to take in order to find him, the giddy heights of spiritual progress we are going to scale, and all the time are unaware of the truth that 'God is nearer to us than we are to ourselves.' We are like . . . men with lighted candles searching through the darkness for fire.[47]

A few other thoughts on this topic come to mind.

■ Reading the Bible today, it appears God was talking and interacting with his people regularly. But, such is not the case. We are looking at centuries of history, and the few direct encounters with God that are recorded in Scripture are exceptional in human history. What's more, they are rare. The Old Testament ends, and centuries pass before the New Testament begins. Just like the Jewish people were in slavery to Egypt for hundreds of years, so we can say God has been relatively quiet over the past 2000 years. But this is not unprecedented. Moreover, there is the argument of dispensation: that God deals with humanity in different ways in different times.

■ The Holy Spirit communicates often interiorly. The challenge of God is to communicate his will without forcing anyone to action.

■ In Isaiah 53:7: "He was oppressed, and he was afflicted, yet he did not open his mouth; like a lamb that is led to the slaughter, and like a sheep that before its shearers is silent, so he did not open his mouth." Isaiah is an author from centuries before Jesus walked the earth. This passage is read by many Christians as a prophecy, given that Jesus, when he appeared before his accusers, remained essentially silent. Jesus, the Lamb of God, remains silent, perhaps, because actions speak louder words. Saying "I love you to death" is one thing. Dying out of love, however, is quite another.

■ Jesus is not only the Lamb of God, he is also the eternal Logos. Logos means "word" in Greek. Jesus is identified in the Gospel of John as the Logos of God the Father; in other words, he is the Word of the Father. That's why the Christmas carol "O Come All Ye Faithful" has the verse: "Word of the Father, Now in flesh appearing." God need not say another word to us, as it has already been said in Jesus.

■ "Truly, you are a God who hides himself, O God of Israel, the Savior" (Isaiah 45:15). Years ago, there was a television show, *Kung Fu*. There is a scene where the apprentice talks to his master in this dialog:

Master Po: 'Close your eyes. What do you hear?'
Caine: 'I hear the water, I hear the birds.'
Po: 'Do you hear your own heartbeat?'
Caine: 'No.'
Po: 'Do you hear the grasshopper which is at your feet?'

Caine: 'Old man, how is it that you hear these things?'
Po: 'Young man, how is it that you do not?'[48]

In a sense, we can think of God like the grasshopper; he is not silent, but we have to learn to hear him. Perhaps if we directly saw or communicated with God in his refulgent glory, we might neglect seeing him in each other. God gives us the gift of dignity of faith by veiling his beauty and his power from us so that we learn to love him for his goodness. If comparing God to a grasshopper seems irreverent, think of him like a wealthy, handsome king who wanders about his kingdom disguised as a beggar, revealing his true identity only after he finds a bride who loves him—not for his money, beauty, power, or wealth, but for his goodness. Yet, Jesus tells the parable of the man who finds a treasure hidden in a field and then sells all he owns to go buy that field and retrieve the treasure. The moral of the parable is that, yes, God is hidden, but he is not so secretive that those who strive to seek him can't find him—in fact, he wants to be found. Perhaps we look in the wrong places.

CHAPTER FOUR

Sin and Salvation
(Hamartiology and Soteriology)

SIN

Sin weighs us down. Like Scrooge's business partner, Jacob Marley, in Dickens' novel *A Christmas Carol*, most of us continually add links to the heavy, debt-laden chains that burden our souls. We, like Marley, are willfully blind to the malignancy of sin. So, we go about our lives offending the majesty of an all-holy God and, in the process, burden our souls both here and, perhaps, in a wearisome purgation in the hereafter.

Sin can be defined as an act that is contrary to God's law. This definition is a bit legalistic, and so it may be more helpful to equate sin with alienation from God. This alienation inevitably leads to estrangement from each other and even from one's self. Kierkegaard described sin as ". . . not to will to be oneself."[1] Catholics believe that we are utterly dependent on God. At the heart of all sin is a failure to recognize this dependence. As George MacDonald notes, when we sin we become like "a stream cut off— a stream that cuts itself off from its source and thinks to run on without it."[2] This dependence, properly understood, does not rob us of our freedom or our agency.

In the Catholic tradition, sin is divided into two categories. Mortal sins are the gravest, while venial sins are less serious. Mortal sins and venial sins are different in kind and not just degree. For a person to commit a mortal sin, three conditions must be met: 1. the person must commit a serious offense; 2. with full knowledge that the offense is serious, (willful ignorance does not substitute for unintended ignorance); and 3. the person must commit the offending act with the full consent of his or her will.

To die in the state of unrepentant "mortal sin" means to be eternally separated from God. Some Christians throughout the centuries believed it was quite easy to commit a mortal sin, while others believed it was very difficult indeed, given that the actor must have both "full knowledge" and "full consent" of the wrong committed. How many of us ever engage the fullness of our minds, the fullness of our wills?

The Confiteor[3] prayer said at the beginning of Mass, in the Latin Rite of the Catholic Church, starts with these words: "I confess to almighty God . . . that I have sinned greatly . . . in what I have done and in what I have failed to do . . ."[4] This prayer is reminiscent of the Psalmist: "Let the words of my mouth and the meditation of my heart be acceptable to you, O Lord . . ." (Psalms 19:14). The Confiteor is said each week at Mass by all of those in attendance. It is assumed that everyone has "sinned greatly," not because we are all great reprobates, but because any sin is significant. As far as the Church is concerned, sin, though divisible into mortal and venial varieties, is such an offense to our true calling and an affront to God that, as Cardinal Newman astoundingly pointed out,

> She [The Church] holds that, unless she can, in her own way, do good to souls, it is no use her doing anything; she holds that it were better for sun and moon to drop from heaven, for the earth to fail, and for all the many millions who are upon it to die of starvation in extremest agony, so far as temporal affliction goes, than that one soul, I will not say, should be lost, but should commit one single venial sin, should tell one willful untruth, though it harmed no one . . .[5]

To our ears, this admonition sounds like the ravings of a zealot, but the point he is making is that sin is completely foreign to God's original design. Saint John Vianney compared the effects of sin on the soul to a transformation into the likeness of "a dead beast that has been dragged through streets in the hot sun for a week."[6] Through sin we can mar, but never eradicate, our personal innate dignity. Jesus asked, "What good will it be for someone to gain the whole world, yet forfeit their soul? Or what can anyone give in exchange for their soul?" (Matthew 16:26).

Some translations use the word "life" instead of "soul," because it is our lives we start to lose when we choose sin over good.

Temptation is an inclination to engage in sin; the surge of desire to engage in a thought or an act that violates some virtue. What tempts us can help reveal something about our personality. Temptation is more complicated and subtler than most of us suspect. That is why, in Catholic tradition, even placing oneself in a situation that invites sin is in and of itself sinful (referred to as "the near occasion of sin"). An alcoholic who visits a bar without the intention of having a drink is an example. The question must be asked of ourselves before the temptation comes. Trying to make a moral decision in the moment of trial is setting oneself up for failure.

But, we must not carry this concept too far. There is a big difference between the near occasion of sin and the informal cooperation (properly called "material cooperation") in sin. For example, in the United States, some roads in the southern part of the country were originally built using slave labor. It would not be a sin to benefit by driving on one of these roads even though the original forced labor was a great evil.

There are some who believe sin has permeated our nature so profoundly that we are totally depraved.[7] This overly severe doctrine is a Protestant innovation that purportedly emanates from the writings of Saints Paul and Augustine. Catholic dogma teaches that we are all born in a state of Original Sin. What this means is not fully understood; some argue that we are born with Adam's guilt, while others argue that all we inherit are the consequences of his sin.[8]

In Adam, all have sinned (Romans 5:12). The Church has offered a variety of theories about this observation. The Bible reveals that God sometimes treats humans as individuals, like trees in a forest, and other times treats us as a community, more like interconnected branches of a single tree. With these individualistic and communal relationships in mind, Christians throughout the centuries have produced many theories about what Paul meant.

■ FEDERAL MODEL. This theory of imputation puts Adam in the role of head or representative of the human family. Adam represented all humans before God in a way similar to how elected officials represent the larger population in government.

- ■ SEMINAL/REALISTIC. This theory proposes that every person to ever exist was present, at least seminally,[9] in Adam. Consequently, we all sinned with him.

- ■ PELAGIAN/SEMI-PELAGIAN. These models reject the idea that humans are born with the stain of Adam's sin, but instead we all sin out of our own will and then are imitating Adam and uniting ourselves with his acts. (The Church has rejected this theory.)

The effects of Original Sin include the notion that we are all born with self-centeredness, an overzealous sense of independence inappropriate for mere creatures. It is not that our faculties under original grace were totally eradicated; in fact, in substance they remain, but in function they have been hindered. Among other consequences of Original Sin are our weakened condition in both mind and will, and our propensity toward personal sin. Pope St. John Paul II pointed out, "Sin affects our intellect by exchanging a vision of God as Father to one as master."[10] A simple analogy that describes the effect of sin is that of a person walking erectly: God created us to walk upright, but sin has hunched us over.

This sinfulness is not just individual but can be communal as well. (Gustavo Gutierrez explores how sin can permeate an institution, even an entire culture.[11]) The testimony of history noted above speaks to one of the more nuanced theories about Original Sin. The philosopher-anthropologist René Girard proposed a fascinating theory of covetous mimetic behavior, which can be equated with Original Sin. In short, Girard explores the herd instinct and the toxic power of envy.[12]

The Gospels recount that as Jesus' ministry grew in popularity huge crowds would show up to hear him preach. At one point, to accommodate the large number who came to hear him, Jesus actually preached from a boat on the Sea of Galilee (which is actually a lake). After preaching to the crowds who gathered on the shore of the lake, Jesus did something astounding: he went to preach to the inhabitants of Decapolis across the lake. Decapolis ("ten cities") was reputed to be a realm of great iniquity, and so Jesus' visit was not a casual trip but more like a full-on assault against the powers of evil. According to certain Talmudic writings and early Christian sources, Decapolis was comprised of a group of cities whose pagan inhabitants were traditionally associated with the seven Canaanite nations that previously inhabited the

Promised Land. These "Canaanites" commingled with Romans and Greeks and engaged in numerous practices that were highly offensive to Jewish sensibilities. They worshipped and sacrificed (mostly animals but sometimes children) to false gods and were sexually depraved and capriciously violent. Additionally, they sacrificed and ate pigs—the mere presence of which was offensive to a Torah-observant Jew. A legion of Roman soldiers who were stationed in these lands used the head of a boar as their coat of arms.

When Jesus told his disciples of his intention to go over to the other side, it was not just the other side of the Sea of Galilee he was going to but a reference to an incursion into the heart of enemy territory to declare the good news of his father's kingdom. The threat did not go unnoticed, for as Jesus crossed the Sea of Galilee a great storm arose and threatened his crew and boat. The disciples traveling with Jesus included seasoned fisherman, used to tumultuous waters and tempests. Yet, the Gospels record that they were terrified by this particular storm. One reason may be that this was no ordinary squall, but this storm can be understood as an assault by the powers of evil. However, with a word, Jesus calmed the storm and continued on his journey.

Having calmed the tempest, Jesus landed upon the shores of the other side of the lake. Soon thereafter he encountered a possessed man. With the documentation of this encounter, the Gospel writers give us an indication of just how contaminated with evil this land was. This man was not just passively possessed, but he was distraught and intent on harming himself or others.

Yet, with commanding authority, Jesus demanded his name,[13] and the possessed man responded that his name was "Legion, for we are many" (Matthew 8:28-34). The use of the word "legion" is a not-so-veiled reference to Rome, given their use of the term to designate a company of soldiers. This reference is further supported by the fact that the demons cast out by Jesus begged not to be judged by him but instead to be cast into a herd of pigs. Remember, the boar was the symbol of the Roman legion stationed in these parts. When Jesus cast out the legion of demons, there was no struggle between his power and the demonic forces; there was only immediate unchallenged obedience.

Jesus mercifully allowed the demons to enter the pigs, who then rushed off a cliff and drown. The takeaway from the story is that Jesus has authority over nature, over demons, and over

Rome—and, given that the story ends with the tormented man being fully healed, he is the Lord who offers healing.

Dame Julian of Norwich, a medieval mystic and visionary, wrote a parable about how we need to be healed from our sins. She used the illustration of a servant who rushes off to do the will of his master and falls into a ditch from which he cannot escape. It is a touching story, because it begins by pointing out how much the master and the servant love one another. It is this very love that stimulates the servant to run off in such a rush to do the will of his master.

In this parable, we are meant to see ourselves in the role of the servant and God as the master. Julian goes on to talk about sin in terms of a deprivation of our human nature, a perversion that is devoid of any good. Dame Julian continues to explore the topic of sin and God's mercy by pointing out that God looks on the sinner in the same way the loving master looks upon the beloved servant who fell into the ditch and got hurt. Without justifying sin, we can see from Julian's writings, supported by Scripture, that God pities our folly. He recognizes we are following a false direction. Human life, in all of its manifestations and developments, is tainted by the unmistakable stain of sin. Sin is so woven into the very fabric of our lives, cultures, and institutions that we can scarcely imagine what a world free of sin even begins to look like; the entire point of the coming of God's kingdom is to establish such a world. When we sin, we do not become God's enemy; he hates the sin but not the sinner. Conflicts with each other and with the world are often the fruits of our interior conflicts, which we often hide from or deny but which we must face if we are to overcome them.

Saint Francis de Sales understood that facing them does not equate being tormented by them. "We must not be disturbed at our imperfections, since for us perfection consists in fighting against them. How can we fight against them unless we see them, or overcome them unless we face them?"[14] If we do not face them, if we do not overcome them, or at least strive to do so, we run the risk of growing them. Genesis narrates this point well. The first sin we read about is the disobedience of Adam and Eve; the very next is fratricide—the murder of Abel by his brother, Cain.

In James Goldman's play *The Lion in Winter*, we see the English king Henry II walking with his wife, Eleanor of Aquitaine. When they were younger, Henry and Eleanor were madly in love with each other. Now, they are the bitterest of enemies. In this poignant scene, Eleanor asks Henry how they went from lovers to hated rivals. The king responds, wisely, "Step by step."[15] He knew they did not just go to bed one night in love only to wake up the next morning loathing each other. Instead, little by little, they grew apart, then grew bitter, then atrophied into an uncompromising malice.

We cannot kill our consciences, but we can cripple them in a thousand different ways. A petty criminal does not usually become a murderer overnight, but more likely will devolve from lesser crimes to worse crimes. More perniciously, we can be tempted to practice vague virtues, like loving all of humanity but no individuals in particular. Broad commitments to simply "do better" are essentially useless without a specific pledge to address specific faults.

Temptations come in subtle forms. John Milton's *Paradise Lost* magnificently depicts the tempting serpent as a subtle and clever enemy. When Eve first meets the serpent, she is astounded that he can speak. The serpent lavishes compliments on Eve and explains that he gained the power of speech by eating of the fruit of a particular tree—the one forbidden to Adam and Eve by God. At first, Milton depicts Eve as the faithful servant. Eve tells the serpent that she wants nothing to do with that prohibited fruit. The serpent again compliments Eve and continues to subtly lure her into his trap.

It is easy to imagine how the serpent might have motivated Eve to eat of the fruit that brings promised death. Knowing too well that he couldn't tempt Eve to commit such a grave sin easily, a series of smaller enticements might be effective: Did God say you may not look upon the tree? God did not forbid you to visit the tree, did he? You are not prohibited from touching the fruit, are you? Did God say that you might not smell the fruit you've just plucked? If you think it smells good, you should taste it; imagine the knowledge you'll gain—after all, you've already gone this far. And so, step by little step, smaller temptations can lead to larger ones. Or, looked at another way, we can be tempted to practice virtue in a corrupt manner. Regardless of the way we sin, the results are always the same: "A man who has been killed by one enemy is just as dead as one who has been killed by a whole army. If you are friends with one habit of mortal sin you live in death, even though you may seem to have all the other virtues."[16]

Evil actions have personal consequences, familial consequences, communal, societal, and even global consequences. Over and over again, Jesus told parables meant to encourage his listeners to turn away from sin and to begin living as if the kingdom were now among us, so that by doing so the kingdom would be more manifest. This change, however, is not achieved by a Herculean act of will, but by the cooperation with God's grace. Usually, the change is not instantaneous.

> There are a thousand little acts of virtue, such as bearing with the importunities and imperfections of our neighbors, not resenting an unpleasant word or trifling injury, restraining an emotion of anger, mortifying some little affection, some ill-regulated desire to speak or listen, excusing indiscretion, or yielding to another in trifles. These things are to be done by all; why not practice them? The occasions for great gains come but rarely, but of little gains many can be made each day; and by managing these little gains with judgment, there are some who grow rich.[17]

Consider one of Jesus' most famous stories: the parable of Lazarus and the rich man (Luke 16: 19-25). The wealthy man ignores the suffering of Lazarus, who begged at the rich man's gate. There is a detail in the story that tells us the rich man wore purple. Of all the dye colors available in the ancient world, purple was the most expensive. So, we are being told this rich man was truly wealthy. Eventually, both the rich man and Lazarus die, and the former goes to a place of torment while Lazarus enters "Abraham's Bosom," a place of contentment. We learn that although he never harmed or damaged Lazarus directly, the rich man was punished for his wicked indifference. He was condemned merely for ignoring him! The great Italian poet Dante Alighieri wrote, "The hottest places in hell are reserved for those who, in a period of moral crisis, maintain their neutrality."[18]

Only the poor and sick man, Lazarus, is worthy of a name in this parable. (In all of Jesus' parables, only Lazarus is referred to by a proper name.) The fact that the rich man does not have a name may be important. In Scripture, namelessness can indicate a universal identity; that is, each one of us is in danger of being like the rich man.

The rich man complains and seeks consolation from Abraham, asking him to "send Lazarus" to bring him some cool water. Even in his torment the rich man cannot repent of his unwarranted master-servant mentality; as if Lazarus should serve him instead of vice-versa. But, let's suppose that Lazarus did bring the rich man water. As John Henry Newman points out, even if Lazarus could bring the rich man water, the man would not be refreshed but only tormented all the more.

> . . . God cannot change His nature. Holy He must ever be. But, while He is holy, no unholy soul can be happy in heaven. Fire does not inflame iron, but it inflames straw. It would cease to be fire if it did not. And so heaven itself would be fire to those, who would fain escape across the great gulf from the torments of hell. The finger of Lazarus would but increase their thirst. The very 'heaven that is over their head' will be 'brass' to them.[19]

Like all of Jesus' parables, this story forces us to be introspective and think about our own treatment of others. The story is not, however, an endorsement of pre-Pelagian, earn-your-own salvation theology. The good news is not just that God is holy, but that he is love, and that love is unchanging. In 1 Peter 4:8, we are offered the comforting verse, "Above all, maintain constant love for one another, for love covers a multitude of sins." Not only does love help us overcome sin, but all the virtues are a curative to vice. "There is a reciprocal relationship between virtue and acts, because virtue, as an internal reality, disposes us to act externally in morally good ways. Yet it is through doing good acts in the concrete that the virtue within us is strengthened and grows."[20] Modern culture seems to have watered down a good number of virtues—at best, understanding them all to be synonymous with a vague concept of "being nice," and at worst as mild character flaws.

We are not called to be "nice," but we are called to be gentle. The Greek word "*praus*," meaning "gentle," refers to a wild stallion being bridled. Gentleness is not weakness or frailty, but strength. Jesus said: "Blessed are the meek, for they will inherit the earth" (Matthew 5:5). "Meek" is another word for gentle, but, contrary to popular belief, to be authentically meek is to be indomitably strong. Saint Francis de Sales tells us, "Nothing is so strong as gentleness, nothing so gentle as real strength."[21]

> Gentleness is love when faced with provocation; it is acting toward others with charity and humility, without sharpness,

without contempt and without ever becoming impatient with
their shortcomings. The heritage promised to the gentle is the
land of their own hearts of which they have control, the land of
the hearts of others which they have conquered by their goodness, and the land of heaven.[22]

Gentleness is not synonymous with niceness. Make no mistake—Jesus was not a "nice man." To be nice is to do away with
other meaningful and healthy "negative" characteristics. Jesus
got angry, but he remained humble even when he drove the merchants from his father's temple or when he rebuked the hard-
hearted. Authentic defiance can keep us alert. Still, it is easy to
convince ourselves that our negative and defiant behaviors are
merited since most of us are masters at creating the most elaborate rationalizations. We all suffer from a propensity to put even
our worst behaviors in the best possible light. It is easy to justify
and find excuses for our bad behavior, even to convince ourselves
that our vices are actually virtues. C. S. Lewis provides a pointed
illustration of a woman possessed of the "All-I-want" state of
mind. All she wants is a cup of tea properly made, or an egg properly boiled, or a slice of bread properly toasted. But, she never
finds anyone who can do these simple things "properly." Why?
Because her "properly" conceals an insatiable demand for the exact and almost impossible palatal pleasures, which she imagines
she remembers from the past. "The past" is described by her as
"the days when you could get good servants," but is known to us
as the days when her senses were more easily pleased, and she
had pleasures of other kinds that made her less dependent upon
those of the table.[23]

We can evaluate the behaviors of others, but not their mo-
tivations. In 1521, Martin Luther was summoned to the Diet of
Worms by Holy Roman Emperor Charles V. He was expected to
recant his teachings but instead purportedly uttered these famous words, "Here I stand; I can do no other. God help me."
Luther's conscience would not allow him to retract his teachings.

SALVATION

Questions such as: Are you saved? Have you accepted Jesus into
your heart? Are you born again? All are typical of certain strains
of Christianity but are not usually representative of the Catholic

mindset. Certainly, salvation is one of the quintessential issues addressed by the Bible, and the New Testament's prescription for salvation is simple: One must repent, believe, and be baptized. After this initial conversion, this *metanoia* (Greek: "conversion") experience and participation in the sacrament, a person is justified before God.

In the words of Reformed theologian R. C. Sproul: "The question of being saved is the supreme question of the Bible. The subject matter of the sacred Scriptures is the subject of salvation. Jesus, at His conception in the womb of Mary, is announced as the Savior. Saviorhood and salvation go together. It is the role of the Savior to save. . . . The Bible uses the term salvation not only in many senses, but in many tenses. The verb to save appears in virtually every possible tense of the Greek language. There is a sense in which we were saved (from the foundation of the world); we are saved (by being in a justified state); and we will be saved (experience the consummation of our redemption in heaven)."[24]

Catholicism does not offer a single teaching on the subject of salvation, but it does provide certain fixed guidelines. First, God desires the salvation of everyone (1 Timothy 2:4). Second, Jesus' sacrifice is sufficient to save all. These guidelines have informed a number of soteriologies, or theories of salvation, over the centuries. Theological investigations into the efficacy of Jesus' sacrifice can lead to discussions about propitiation, which means seeking to placate an offended party; and expiation, which means seeking to make amends for a sinful act; and a host of related topics. In brief summary, Catholics understand Jesus having atoned for or expiated our sins, whereas Protestants believe that God the Father poured out his wrath upon Jesus.

The only way to become unjustified is by committing a mortal sin, after which the healing sacrament of reconciliation restores a person to the justified state. Our salvation is offered to us by the grace of God, but God gives our participation—our actions—real consequences. God's universal and unfailing love does not equate with an "anything goes" philosophy. The Church teaches that humans are responsible for their actions, and there are rewards and penalties for both good and bad behaviors. Balancing this truth with the reality of God's sovereignty has created a rich body of theology on the topics of grace and free will.

When we do good for a righteous reason, we merit God's reward. When we do good for the wrong reason, say, to be seen and praised by others, no reward is merited. When we do evil, then punishment is merited, though this could be mitigated by our motivation. Catholic theologians recognize that supernatural merit belongs to Christ alone, as he is the only one capable of performing a truly meritorious act. However, subject to this caveat, we can still differentiate between three types of merit.

- CONGRUENT MERIT refers to acts that are worthy of a reward but that God has not obligated himself to reward.

- CONDIGN MERIT refers to acts that are worthy of a reward and that God has obligated himself to reward.

- STRICT MERIT refers to acts that are worthy of a reward and that God has obligated himself to reward in such a way that the significance of the act is equal to the significance of the reward.

Catholics refer to "initial justification," which is a transformative event normatively brought about by the sacrament of baptism. Thereafter, a person's lifelong journey to grow in holiness is called "progressive justification."

A simple analogy might help. Imagine a parent who has a small child. It is the parent's birthday, and the child has no money with which to buy a gift. So, the parent gives the child money, and the child buys a birthday present. Now, in actuality, the parent bought the gift; the child was totally incapable of doing so. The parent is no richer for having received the gift but still accepts the gift as if it came from the child. This is a poor but candid parallel of the concept of God's covenantal love and the merit he offers to us.

Although God does all the work in saving his people, we are not merely passive recipients of his grace. Instead, his grace affects us by rekindling that love for him, which would naturally be present had we not been tainted by sin. We are completely powerless to justly claim any grace from God, but in his unmerited mercy he forgives us, he sanctifies us, and he justifies us. He does not do these things by merely declaring something untrue—we are holy—to suddenly be true, nor does he merely impute to us the holiness of his son by way of some legal contract. Instead, we are transformed by grace. God changes us inwardly so that his love empowers us to live lives of holiness and virtue. These graces all come from God, but at the same time we can declare them as our own because they come from our innermost being, which has been animated by the Holy Spirit.

Although faith is a gift of God's grace, it is one that acknowledges our own free will. The interplay between the two is complex since God, the object of faith, is not usually immediately conspicuous. Few of us encounter burning bushes, like Moses did, or are blinded by a Christophany, like Paul was when he encountered the risen Jesus on the road to Damascus. It is misleading to suggest there is just one understanding and experience of faith, however, it is always God who reaches out for us, who invites us into a relationship. We can never claim to have initiated the relationship. There are many ways to understand this, but one of the most beautiful and empowering explanations comes from a sermon by George MacDonald titled: "Mirrors of the Lord."

> Thus the Lord, the spirit, becomes the soul of our souls . . . as our spirit informs, gives shape to our bodies, in like manner his soul informs, gives shape to our souls. In this there is nothing unnatural, nothing at conflict with our being. It is but that the deeper soul that willed and wills our souls, rises up, the infinite Life, into the Self we call *I* and *me*, but which lives immediately from him, and is his very own property and nature—unspeakably more his than ours: this deeper creative soul, working on and with his creation upon higher levels, makes the *I* and *me* more and more his, and himself more and more ours . . . and [we] know ourselves alive with an infinite life, even the life of the Father.[25]

This is not a uniquely Christian idea. A famous Indian guru leader went into battle with gold-tipped arrows. "He used to shoot a gold-tipped arrow in war so that the person aimed [at], if wounded, could pay for his medical expenses, and if killed, would be compensated for his funeral expenses . . ."[26] We are called to "bear no malice or evil will to any man living. For either the man is good or wicked. If he is good and I hate him, then I am wicked. If he is wicked, either he will amend and die good and go to God, or live wickedly and die wickedly and go to the devil . . . And why should I now, then, hate one for this while who shall hereafter love me forever, and why should I be now, then, an enemy with whom I shall in time be coupled in eternal friendship? And on the other side, if he will continue to be wicked and be damned, then is there such outrageous eternal sorrow before him that I may well think myself a deadly cruel wretch if I would not now rather pity his pain than malign his person."[27]

Always on the lookout for new exercises in my classes, I read about a professor who created an assignment that demonstrated this idea about loving even our enemies for the love of God. He placed a sheet of paper in front of each of his students, blank side up, with a firm warning not to turn it over. He then asked them to use the blank side of the paper to draw an image of someone they really hated, someone who has caused them great pain and suffering, someone they wanted to hurt. When the students had finished, the professor then told the students to tear into their sketch with their pens, to rip it, to cut it, to stab at it. Their fury vented, the students were invited to see what was on the other side of the page. Turning their papers over, they found an image of Jesus. The point of the exercise was to demonstrate Jesus' teaching: "Truly, I say to you, as you did it to one of the least of these my brethren, you did it to me" (Matthew 25:40).

The professor could have put a reflective surface on the other side of the page, because what we do unto others, in a sense, we do unto ourselves as well. This law of reciprocity applies not only to those we injure but to those who have injured us and whom we refuse to forgive. We, on the other hand, forgive grudgingly and with great difficulty.

> There is no use in talking as if forgiveness were easy. We all know the joke, 'you've given up smoking once; I've given it up a dozen times'. In the same way I could say of a certain man, 'Have I forgiven him for what he did that day? I've forgiven him more times than I can count'. For we find that the work of forgiveness has to be done over and over again. We forgive, we mortify our resentment; a week later some chain of thought carries us back to the original offense and we discover the old resentment blazing away as if nothing had been done about it at all. We need to forgive our brother seventy times seven not for 490 offenses but for one offense.[28]

Forgiveness is personal; it is a one-way street, something we do; not to be confused with reconciliation, which is interpersonal and reciprocal. So, we can forgive someone who does not forgive us, does not want to be forgiven, or even someone who is dead.

We must endeavor to cultivate a forgiving attitude—recognizing that in forgiving, we are forgiven by God.

The topic of salvation begs the question: "Saved from what?" The answer to this question varies, depending on who is asking. Some boldly proclaim our salvation is from hell, damnation, and God's wrath. While true at some level, this is a rather anemic view of salvation. Other Christians take a less-superficial view and instead see salvation in terms of both a present tense and future hope of restoration—healing, freeing, ransoming, empowering, and transforming the entire person, not just the immortal soul. Other soteriologies identify with a salvation where we are saved *for* something, not merely saved *from* something. For example, St. Irenaeus' theology of recapitulation is an example of the latter. This understanding of salvation emphasizes the recovery of a beauty and condition that was lost, which Christ has reclaimed for us. We are therefore saved not just interiorly by God, but he acts with and through us to save and restore that which was lost.

We do not come into this world as enemies of God, but we are born beleaguered by the consequences of Original Sin.[29] We can envision Original Sin as a disease that began with Adam and Eve and was then passed down to all of us. The symptoms of this disease are common to everyone: fear, laziness, weakness, separation of reason and passion, and the curse of being disunited from the rest of creation. "Man's religious and moral faculties are not impaired in their natural substance, but weakened in their operation, inasmuch as original sin deflects them from their supernatural course and gives them therefore a false direction."[30]

These theories of salvation can get quite complicated and tie into all sorts of related concepts such as redemption, sanctification, justification, predestination, divine foreknowledge, and related controversies (e.g. infralapsarianism vs. supralapsarianism, the efficacy of baptism[31]). However, in short, the word "salvation" signifies a method whereby a person is somehow brought into a right relationship with God through Jesus Christ. We need not get into the theological minutia but will explore a few of the theories here by considering the following admittedly crude analogy of the human soul as being like an individual trapped at the bottom of a deep well and needing to escape or inevitably dying. This analogy is borrowed from these words of St. Thomas More: "If a man lowers a rope into a well and pulls someone out who could not escape by himself, wouldn't it be true that the man in the well did not climb out by his own power? And yet he still contributed something of his own to the process by hanging onto the rope and not letting it get away. The freedom of the will is like that: It can do nothing without grace."[32] Here, then, is a brief list of some of the more prominent Christian theories, including some that the Church has officially rejected.

- **MONERGISM.** This theory, most often associated with the Reformation theology of John Calvin and Martin Luther (who in turn trace their arguments in favor of monergism back to a particular reading of St. Augustine and the Bible, especially the Epistles of St. Paul), teaches that the trapped person, regardless of how hard he or she tries, will simply be unable to get out.

  So, God does all the work to save the individual. The person in the well contributes absolutely nothing to his or her own rescue. According to some monergist theologies, the person stubbornly denies being trapped in a well in the first place. Most monergists are not universalists, meaning they don't believe God will save everyone. This means God predestines only some, the elect, to heaven, while he chooses not to save the rest. For brevity, this is a broad oversimplification of a rich and nuanced doctrine. However, if you take this position to its logical extreme, as in Hyper-Calvinism, the result is the heresy of pantheism; God is all, and all is God.

- **SYNERGISM.** Synergism can also start out with the person in the well denying he is trapped, but God then comes and offers a ladder. The person, then realizing his plight, will have to cooperate with God's efforts and climb up the ladder of his own choosing. There are numerous monergistic and synergistic theories, too many to list, but here are a few of the more famous:

  ◆ ARMINIANISM is a Protestant theory of salvation that posits a relationship where God invites, and the individual accepts or rejects God's invitation. Returning to the well analogy, God would call down to offer help to the person trapped in the well.

  ◆ MOLINISM. A Catholic theory of salvation named for its originator, the Jesuit priest Luis de Molina, that affirms God's sovereignty to place individuals into circumstances where they will employ their free will to embrace salvation. The prisoner in the well may find a ladder embedded in the rock wall, but its discovery only came about because God made the sun shine down in such a way to show it—otherwise this means of escape would have remained unknown and inaccessible.

- THOMISM. Named after St. Thomas Aquinas, this theory was advanced by Domingo Báñez. The emphasis is on God's free and unmerited choice to save certain individuals. So, in the well example, a rescue mission would be launched, and the trapped individual would be carried out to safety. Only not all who are trapped are rescued; some are left to their own devices and eventually die. Those who are rescued did not do anything to merit their escape; it was merely an act of mercy. The reason why the others were not rescued is known only to God.[33]

- DOUBLE AGENCY. God's grace frees us and is not in competition with human freedom. Humans make real choices with real consequences, but God's grace simultaneously informs, inspires, and guides those choices. God's grace heals our wounded nature. God's sovereignty includes human freedom. To act against God's will is to act against freedom since his will dynamically endorses our freedom, not to act arbitrarily, but to act according to our true nature. We make the choice to leave the well, but only because we are empowered and guided by God's grace.

- PELAGIANISM. Named after the monk, Pelagius (355-425), who first advocated this theory of salvation. The position argues that the person knows he is trapped at the bottom of a well and needs to get out but believes he can climb out of the well on his own, though it will be very difficult.

- SEMI-PELAGIANISM. As the name indicates, a variation of Pelagianism, in watered-down form, which teaches that the person in the well knows he is trapped and wants to climb out but can't quite do it, so he calls out to God for help, who then sends a ladder.

(Both Pelagianism and semi-Pelagianism were condemned by the Church at the Council of Orange in 529 AD.)

- GNOSTICISM. A complicated form of early Christianity that taught that Jesus revealed a secret knowledge ("*gnosis*"

in Greek) to his followers. For them, the way out of the well
is a secret, and when the secret is learned—maybe a hidden
door, for example—the person can escape. More importantly,
many Gnostics believed in a duality between the evil physical
world and good spiritual world. Meaning, for our example,
the person escapes the well by escaping the body, releasing
the soul.

These are simple analogies for complex systems of thought,
so many nuances are therefore lost. For example, if we think of
the well as the person's environment, then some theologies would
teach that the walls are slick with slime and mud that keep us
trapped, indicating the corruption of the world in which we live
and the social structure of sin. More importantly, this simple
analogy is very individualistic. The thought of a single person
caught in a well fails to communicate the reality that God is in a
covenant with an entire people, not just with individuals.

In a sense, we do not sin alone, and we are not saved alone.
God entered into a covenant with all of Israel; Jesus' new covenant is with the entire Church. While we are all personally ac-
countable before God, Christianity is a family, and we need to
reclaim our sense of group identity. Our interconnectedness is
not merely with those we see in Church; it is membership in a
covenantal community that extends throughout the world and
even beyond the grave.

Both the old covenant between God and his chosen people
and the new covenant between God and the entire world, were
not mere legal contracts, nor are they quid pro quo agreements
between an aloof God and his creation. What God did, and continues to do, is to establish a family. So, by grace, we are elevated
to be his sons and daughters. Jesus taught us to pray "Our Father,"[34] not "My Father," implying we are all brothers and sisters.

From the very beginning, in Genesis, when God declared that it
was not good for man to be alone, we see a call to communion with
him. God enters into a covenant with Adam and Eve. Later in that
same book, we see God's covenant with Noah and his family, then
with Abraham and his people. Genesis shows us God's expanding
covenantal relationship, first with a couple (Adam and Eve), then
with a family (Noah and his kin), then with a tribe (Abraham and
the Hebrews). As we move into the book of Exodus, we read again
and again about God wanting to establish a community, a family.

The command that the Passover Lamb be entirely consumed and not discarded intimates that the meal must be shared and never eaten alone. The book of Exodus reveals the next stage of God's plan to expand his covenant to the entire nation of Israel. Later, that nation, under King David, would receive a further covenant, expanding God's outreach even farther. Finally, all of these promises come together in Jesus' inauguration of his father's kingdom and his announcing of the good news that God is our father too.

But, whether we talk about salvation individually or within a community, many questions still abound that simple analogies don't satisfy. Specifically, Christians throughout the centuries have talked about justification, sanctification, regeneration, and a host of other related features of our relationship with God through Jesus. There are multiple orthodox understandings of these issues, but one Catholic expression is nuanced. In summary, it posits the concept of merit, meaning that God does all the work, but in his goodness, he accounts our actions as meritorious.

God has expressed a universal salvific will (1 Timothy 2:4), and his covenantal invitation extends to all the people of the world.[35] How then is it applied? Traditionally, the Catholic Church has employed the phrase "*extra ecclesiam nulla salus*," meaning "outside the Church there is no salvation." This teaching on salvation has been promulgated for millennia and has been officially declared numerous times. In other words, Catholic teaching explicitly rejects the all-religions-are-equally-valid argument, insisting instead that Jesus is the sole, unique, true, savior of the world, and his Church is essential in the salvific work of God.[36] However, in its most radical form, proponents of "exclusivism" understand all non-Christian religions as idolatrous, utterly false, and at odds with Christ and his Church.

My dad was the executor of his aunt's estate. He administered the estate as best he could, but that aunt's sisters disagreed with how my dad was handling things and they wanted to sue him. These other aunts were poor Italian immigrants who could not afford a lawyer, so my dad paid for them to get an attorney to sue him! You see, he loved his aunts, and even though they were involved in a disagreement, he wanted them to be empowered.

I mention this story because it seems to me like a good analogy for salvation. There are those who, wrongly but nonetheless, with a clear conscience, disparage and even seek to destroy the Church. Yet, even the most rabid enemy of Catholicism, acting in good faith and seeking what is good and true, will benefit, albeit unwillingly, from the Church's prayers and graces. Moreover, such souls, though apparently separated from the visible Church, are, by God's mercy, beloved and connected to the body of Christ. God's grace meets individuals wherever they may be, even in sin or error. His limitless love manifests by the bestowal of graces to everyone, even those who do not know him and those who work against him.

The Vatican II document *Nostra Aetate*, which addresses the subject of truth in other religions, emphatically states that Christianity does not have an absolute monopoly on all truth. "The Catholic Church rejects nothing that is true and holy in these religions. She regards with sincere reverence those ways of conduct and of life, those precepts and teachings which, though differing in many aspects from the ones she holds and sets forth, nonetheless often reflect a ray of that Truth which enlightens all men."[37]

God's revelation came into focus more clearly when he chose to reveal himself to Abraham and his ancestors through the nation of Israel. Many scholars have rightly pointed out that God, apparently, if indirectly, revealed something about himself and his laws to other nations and cultures as well. This is evidenced by the commonality of myths and traditions among various ancient civilizations and the transmission of memes. However, Catholic Christians believe the full Deposit of Faith is found in the Tradition and Scriptures of the Church.

This insight that non-Christian philosophies can help prepare people for the gospel can be found in the works of many patristic authors, specifically Justin Martyr's use of the term *"logos spermatikos"* and Eusebius' work on *"praeparatio evangelica."* That is, the truth claims of various faiths are valuable and even, perhaps, salvific, at least to the extent that they correspond with truth.

> In any event, developed Christian theology rejected nothing good in the metaphysics, ethics, or method of ancient philosophy, but—with a kind of omnivorous glee—assimilated such elements as served its ends, and always improved them in the process. Stoic morality, Plato's language of the Good, Aristotle's metaphysics of act and potency—all became richer and more coherent when emancipated from the morbid myths of sacrificial economy and tragic necessity. In truth, Christian theology nowhere more wantonly celebrated its triumph over the old gods than . . . by

despoiling pagan philosophy of its most splendid achievements and integrating them into a vision of reality more complete than philosophy could attain on its own, theology took to itself irrevocably all the intellectual glories of antiquity.[38]

In ancient Greece, worshipers would make offerings to *Agnostos Theos*, or the "Unknown god," to ensure no gods were denied their right. In Acts 17:22-31, St. Paul identifies the unknown god as the One true God. "If he was only the God of the good people, what was to become of the rest when they were lost on mountains? . . . But, every honest cry, even if sent into the deaf ear of an idol, passes on to the ears of the unknown God, the heart of the unknown Father."[39] It is in light of this position that we can better appreciate the concepts of "righteous Gentiles" and "virtuous pagans." In the Old Testament we encounter righteous Gentiles who merited God's favor; in the New Testament we come across virtuous pagans.

The Old Testament labels Cyrus as a "messiah" of God. The Gospel of Matthew's infancy narrative tells of three pagan wise men who followed the star. They used what knowledge and grace they had to seek God. The pagan Greek philosophers who lived before the time of Jesus (e.g., Aristotle and Plato) offered insights that were so valuable as to be incorporated into some of Christendom's greatest theologies (Thomism and Augustinianism). Later in history, Jesuit missionaries to Asia would find a similar connection between Christian revelation and certain teachings the Taoist and Confucian traditions. We must be careful not to drift into a pluralism, positing a many-paths-lead-to-one-truth philosophy. Instead, the argument simply recognizes that God's grace is not bound to the visible sacraments, nor is God even bound by the visible Church.

The Church specifically condemns both de facto and de jure claims that Jesus is but one among many saviors.[40] So, reading philosophy or comparative religion are not salvific in and of themselves, but these and countless other good activities can be "propaedeutic," meaning they can aid in preparing a person for something greater; they can soften our hearts and predispose us to receive God's grace.

Karl Rahner posited the idea of individuals who are followers of Christ unbeknownst to themselves. He wrote about people who seek God and follow their consciences but do not know Jesus:

". . . if I hold if everyone depends upon Jesus Christ for salvation, and if at the same time I hold that many live in the world who have not expressly recognized Jesus Christ, then there remains in my opinion nothing else but to take up this postulate of an anonymous Christianity."[41]

Some contemporary Christians avoid using the term "anonymous Christians," because it smacks of a kind of arrogance. After all, other faiths don't normally go around labeling people as secret Buddhists or unidentified Hindus. Some talk in terms of a high Pneumatology (the study of the divine person and work of the Holy Spirit). For them, Jesus' ministry was a continuation, perhaps, a culmination, in his death and resurrection, of the ongoing work the Holy Spirit has been doing since creation and whose work continues outside the visible Church.

Christians of different denominations understand Jesus' death and resurrection, his work of atonement, in various ways. Some see it as a ransom[42] for slaves to sin; others see it as payment due for the debt of sin, which had offended the dignity of a righteous and Holy God. Some understand this reestablishment to be based in Jesus' "vicarious atonement," or payment of a debt we all owed to God. Others equate Christ's sacrifice with a conquering of evil and death. Still others understand Jesus' sacrifice in terms of medicine for a critically ill patient. A popular understanding of Jesus' death is that God the Father poured his just and furious wrath out on his son; a righteous anger that rightly belonged to each one of us. This theory, commonly called penal substitution, is a distinctly Protestant idea that dates back only to the 1500s.Catholicism offers a variety of theories, one of which ("vicarious satisfaction") is somewhat similar to penal substitution. Under this representation of Jesus' death, it is believed that Christ went to the cross of his own free will. He not only consented to his death but allowed his executioners to take hold of him, torture him, and eventually crucify him. In this view, humans, not God, orchestrated his execution. God never punishes his son, but instead accepts the infinite merit of Jesus' free-will sacrifice as recompense for the sins of every person. Jesus never ceases to be innocent. Jesus never ceases to be holy, because he is God incarnate, and God is ever holy.

Undeniably, Jesus is our brother and our friend, but he is foremost our God. I laugh when people tell me that when they meet Jesus they will give him a piece of their mind. More likely, an encounter with Jesus will be like St. John's.[43] John, the beloved disciple, who was close friends with Jesus during his ministry, fell prostrate in abject terror before the glorified presence of Jesus.

> I saw one like the Son of Man, clothed with a long robe and with a golden sash across his chest. His head and his hair were white as white wool, white as snow; his eyes were like a flame of fire, his feet were like burnished bronze, refined as in a furnace, and his voice was like the sound of many waters. In his right hand he held seven stars, and from his mouth came a sharp, two-edged sword, and his face was like the sun shining with full force.
>
> When I saw him, I fell at his feet as though dead. But he placed his right hand on me, saying, 'Do not be afraid; I am the first and the last, and the living one. I was dead, and see, I am alive forever and ever; and I have the keys of Death and of Hades.' (Revelation 1:13-18)

John of Patmos had an encounter with the holiness of Christ, and it terrified him. "On a handful of occasions the Bible repeats something to the third degree. To mention something three times in succession is to elevate it to the superlative degree. Only once in Scripture is an attribute of God elevated to the third degree. The Bible says that God is holy, holy, holy . . ."[44]

Saint John of Patmos' experience was not unique; in fact, for some, a casual disregard of God's holiness cost them their lives. There is a story in the Old Testament (2 Samuel 6:1-15) of a man named Uzzah, who drove a cart carrying the sacred Ark of the Covenant. Uzzah reached out his hand to steady the ark, and upon touching the sacred vessel God struck him dead. Though Uzzah's instinct was to protect the ark from falling, he became too comfortable with this holy object. God wasn't being unpredictable when he struck down Uzzah because the consequence for touching this sacred vessel was clearly set forth in Numbers 4:16-20.

Elsewhere, in the New Testament (Acts 5: 1-11), we read about a husband and wife, Ananias and Sapphira, who were struck dead by the Holy Spirit after lying about a donation they claimed to make to the early Church.

Nonetheless, God is love (1 John 4:8). So, we can rejoice in the anticipation of seeing Jesus face to face; we need not fear. But we can't help but be reverential.

We are wounded creatures, yet God gives us strength in the sacraments (*ex opere operato*[45]) and through other graces. Unlike some Christians who teach a "once saved, always saved"[46] soteriology, the Catholic Church teaches that, in this life, absent a special private revelation, we are not assured of salvation. (That is the sin of presumption and an affront to free will.) But, we ought to maintain a deep and abiding trust in God.

✝

CHAPTER FIVE

SUFFERING AND LOVE

SUFFERING

Consider that, as you read these words, countless people (and animals) are being tormented by the ravages of disease and injury. Numerous others, including innocent children, suffer from poverty, starvation, and all sorts of misery. Even if only one person were suffering, instead many millions, the problem would be the same. In a sense, one starving child is no less grotesque than a thousand. We do not properly measure suffering by the number of people who are experiencing pain at any given moment; that is utilitarianism.

If God is infinitely good and infinitely powerful, then why do pain and evil exist? If God cannot help us, or if God simply won't help us, then he just doesn't seem all that godly. Or, put another way, if God is the greatest being possible and so wants what is best and has the power to create what is best, then why doesn't he do so?

Why do some cries to God for help get no response? How are we to make sense of his inscrutable silence? Heartache, pain, and afflictions of every variety are probably not unfamiliar to you. Maybe your suffering came with the sudden loss of a loved one, the onset of some disease, or in the infliction of some injustice. "All suffering is unique—and all suffering is common. I have to be reminded of the latter truth when I am suffering myself—and the former when I see others suffering."[1]

My Italian great-grandmother used to tell the parable of the cross and the field. According to the story, there was a field in which a person may bring his cross and lay it down, but then he must pick up another cross to carry. Inevitably, everyone who went to the field ended up returning to pick up their own crosses again, finding the suffering others too much for them to bear. While this story may seem heartening because it means our suffering is custom-made and God providentially determines just what each person will have to endure, there is a cost for this sort of thinking.

The Easter liturgy refers to the first sin as a *"felix culpa"* (Latin: "happy fault"). The phrase highlights the fact that the sin led to the coming of our redeemer, Jesus. Taken to a heretical extreme, this phrase posits that we are all better off because of sin, or equally absurd, that God needed evil and sin in order to bring about some greater good. It is one thing to say God can bring about good in the presence of evil, but that is very different than saying God needed the evil; that without it he could not have brought about some good. Clearly the Bible does not teach a dualism of the Zoroastrian sort that we encounter in the heresy of Manichaeism,[2] where there is a god of light and a god of darkness or single God with both properties. Nonetheless, a central theme in the Christian message is that our world is not as God intended; it is fallen, broken, and in need of healing.

Life's universal testimony documents suffering in one form or another for all of us. The first of Buddha's Four Noble Truths (*dukkha*) teaches that life is suffering. The father of psychoanalysis, Sigmund Freud, proffered a similar diagnosis of our common condition, offering out as his best curative for overwhelmed patients merely the possibility of exchanging hysterical misery for the more ubiquitous general unhappiness.[3] We all search for answers and meaning in the tragedies of life. (We would do better to search for them also when the pain of tragedy is far removed, because psychologists tell us that a phenomenon labeled mood-dependent memory can cause us to only remember misery and pain when we are in the midst of suffering.) These hauntingly somber outlooks have been echoed by philosophers (e.g., Schopenhauer's "Never a rose without a thorn; yet many a thorn without a rose") and authors (e.g., Melville's ". . . one grief outweighs ten thousand joys . . ."[4]) and poets (e.g., Shelley's "We look before and after/And pine for what is not:/Our sincerest laughter/With some pain is fraught . . ."[5]) and countless others.

The Bible offers us numerous passages that point to the fact that we live in a world filled with sorrows and suffering. Some verses go so far as to hint that joy is not something we can fully experience in this life. Proverbs 14:13 cautions, "Even in laughter the heart is sad, and the end of joy is grief." Inundated with temptations and distractions, drained from the endless search for lasting joy, we settle for temporary fixes, pretending that life will finally get better—after I graduate, or after I get married, or after I get that promotion, or when I retire, etc. When lasting joy never comes, some demand that God justify himself to a broken and suffering world. "To some people the mental image of God is a kind of blur of disappointment. The years by no means dim the tragic details of the Prayer that was Unanswered or the Disaster that was Undeserved. . . . Any suggestion of obeying or following God can be more than countered by another glance at the perennial Grievance."[6]

But by focusing our attention solely on the cause of suffering we become distracted from remedying the situation. Jesus was an expert at focusing on what counts. In one New Testament account, Jesus' disciples ask him about the cause of a particular man's blindness. They want to know if he is blind because he had committed some sin, or because his parents somehow offended God. Rather than answering them, Jesus simply restores the man's sight (John 9:1-12).

This story is analogous to the story of the poisoned arrow. The Buddha told the story about a man who was shot in the leg with a poisoned arrow. Off he went in search of help, asking questions of each person he met along the way. "Did you see who shot this arrow?" "What kind of poison was used?" The poison killed him before he got any answers. Had he just focused his attention on getting the arrow removed from his leg, he might have lived to find out the answers he sought. In both stories, it was more meaningful to focus on a solution to a problem instead of fixating on its cause.

This is expressed well in the famous prayer of St. Francis:

> Lord, make me an instrument of your peace.
> Where there is hatred, let me sow love.
> Where there is injury, pardon.
> Where there is doubt, faith.
> Where there is despair, hope.
> Where there is sadness, joy.

Divine Master, grant that I may not so much seek to be consoled,
    as to console;
To be understood, as to understand;
To be loved, as to love;
For it is in giving that we receive,
It is in pardoning that we are pardoned.
It is in dying that we are born to eternal life.[7]

The point is not that we have to avoid asking difficult questions but that we should simultaneously become part of the answer. In the great prayer Jesus taught us, the *Pater Noster*[8] (Our Father), we petition God for his kingdom to come. It is not merely a request for him to do something outside of us, but a petition to God asking him to use us in manifesting his kingdom in our world.

> Our faith is in a God who has come to rescue His creation from the absurdity of sin and the emptiness of death, and so we are permitted to hate these things with a perfect hatred . . . As for comfort, when we seek it, I can imagine none greater than the happy knowledge that when I see the death of a child, I do not see the face of God, but the face of his enemy. It is . . . a faith that . . . has set us free from optimism, and taught us hope instead.[9]

Recall the story of the blind man whose sight was restored by Jesus. There was a presumption that the blindness was a form of punishment. Jesus corrected this false notion, explaining the man was not blinded in retribution for some offense; and then he restored the man's sight. What a heavy weight must have been lifted from the shoulders of those who thought their sufferings resulted solely from some personal or inherited sin.

In the Gospel of Luke (13:4), Jesus talks about a tower that fell in the nearby community of Siloam. Eighteen people were killed. Jesus explained that those who died in the collapse of the tower were no greater sinners than anyone else. Presumably, his listeners thought the eighteen deaths were punishment for some sin, and it was perfectly reasonable for Jesus' listeners to believe this. The Torah is filled with examples of God punishing sin and blessing righteousness.

How do we connect these two biblical truths? One explanation is that the Old Testament stories of God's chastisements are arbitrary punishments inflicted by an angry deity, but they are better understood as the inevitable consequences that naturally flow from bad choices. A component of the good news Jesus preached is that God loves sinners; he loves the people who make bad choices and engage in bad behavior. Jesus went a step further. He chastises some who saw themselves as holy and righteous by saying, "Truly I tell you, the tax collectors and the prostitutes are going into the kingdom of God ahead of you" (Matthew 21:31).

Jesus was not ignorant of the problem of suffering and evil; what's more, he provided a radical solution. He came personally to address, and in the resurrection, overcome the problem of evil. In his resurrection, we find the victory over evil, the recognition that not even the evil of death can conquer God's redeeming love. Moreover, to emphasize God's intimacy with his people, after Jesus' resurrection he said he would leave this world to return to the Father. But, he would not leave us alone.

I once heard a sermon preached about a man who was dying and needed help, so he asked his closest friend to send aid. The close friend did not send money or provisions, but, because of his great love, he went personally to help his sick friend. There is no one closer to Jesus than the Holy Spirit, so that is who he sent to be with us. The Holy Spirit is the third person of the Trinity. Now, Jesus could have delegated the work of continuing his ministry to angels or to some chosen apostles, or he could have merely left with some encouraging words, but, like the friends in the example, love compelled Jesus to ensure that the continuation of the Father's work was handled by the one whom he personally loved and trusted.

And is it by the empowerment of the Holy Spirit that we experience glimpses of the way things ought to be; manifestation of God's kingdom, which is both now and not yet. Christians are ". . . transformed by the renewing of [our] mind" (Romans 12:2). And with this transformed mind we "strive for the greater gifts." Saint Paul says, "And I will show you a still more excellent way" (1 Corinthians 12:31) to move from deception to truth, from doubt to faith, and from ordinary human unhappiness to real, sometimes even overwhelming joy.

Saint Paul tells us that one of the fruits of the Holy Spirit is joy: "By contrast, the fruit of the Spirit is love, joy, peace, patience, kindness, generosity, faithfulness, gentleness, and self-control" (Galatians 5:22). How do we balance the reality of sorrow in our life with Jesus' invitation to share in his joy? St. Thomas Aquinas offers us the hint of an answer by distinguishing between *beatitudo* and *felicitas*. Beatitudo is the happiness one finds in heaven, the beatific vision. Felicitas is the happiness we find in the world. Yet, the two are not fully separated. In part, our happiness here is tied to how we think and how we act. When we act virtuously we are rewarded with joy. Jesus is a man of Joy.[10]

Actually, the book of Genesis is a rich resource for information about suffering and evil. There are clues about how we can reconcile the conundrum of evil and suffering existing in creation, which was brought into being by the omni-amorous (all-loving) and omnipotent (all-powerful) God. Genesis uses imagery suggesting that God created a world where darkness and disorder already existed. The Genesis account of the Earth's origins tells of God bringing order to the "void," to the "darkness," to the "unformed world," and to the "deep." (See Genesis 1:2.) These words are not used haphazardly, but for the ancient author they are rich in the symbolism of chaos and evil. Moreover, the use of this language is not a denial of creation ex nihilo[11] but simply recognition of how the narrative reads. God himself called into the being the formless void, the chaotic material from which creation was ordered. There was no preexistent substance God used to create. There was no struggle, no effort, just a sovereign command from an infinitely powerful God.

It follows logically that if God created the world from nothing, he did not create it tainted. We read in Genesis that God created the world and declared that it was "good," and later, "very good." How do we reconcile this good world with one that is contaminated with suffering and evil? Knowing that God is not the author of any evil, what are we to make of the negative implications of the "void" the "darkness" the "deep"? Some speculate that there are agents and forces within God's good creation with whom he has bestowed a contingent agency. "For we wrestle not against flesh and blood, but against principalities, against powers, against the rulers of the darkness of this world, against spiritual wickedness in high places" (Ephesians 6:12, KJV).

Certain scholars have suggested that angels, both the holy ones and the reprobate ones, had a role to play in creation. But more mundane explanations can be posited. "God not only makes

the world, he makes it make itself or rather, he causes his innumerable constituents to make it."[12] So we needn't ascribe rules
of physics such as Maxwell's equations, Lorentz force, and Fara-
day's law of induction to supernatural origins.

The negative forces referenced in the creation account of
Genesis, and the principalities and powers referenced in Ephesians, are a necessary consequence of living in a finite, contingent
world. This theory would suggest that what some of what we label
as "evil" could be pre-moral or amoral events, inevitable in the
universe in which we find ourselves. In Catholic theology, this
topic is associated with the study of ontic evil. Ontic evil posits,
in part, that some of the pain we all experience as sensitive beings
in this world is necessary, not because we are corrupted or the
world we live in is corrupted, but simply because we cannot be
both sensitive and not sensitive simultaneously.

If we love, we risk the pain of losing that love.

> To love at all is to be vulnerable. Love anything, and your heart
> will certainly be wrung and possibly broken. If you want to make
> sure of keeping it intact, you must give your heart to no one,
> not even to an animal. Wrap it carefully round with hobbies and
> little luxuries; avoid all entanglements; lock it up safe in the cas-
> ket or coffin of your selfishness. But, in that casket-safe, dark,
> motionless, airless—it will change. It will not be broken; it will
> become unbreakable, impenetrable, irredeemable.[13]

Along the same line of thinking, we can recognize that while
living in Eden, in the state of original innocence, Adam and Eve
were subject even then to a kind of privation of good. In Genesis
2:20-25, God declares that it is not good for man to be alone. This
"not good" exists before the fall.[14] Adam is charged with tending
the garden and naming the animals, and so he works before the
fall (though his work was likely joyful and not laborious). Death
too may have been a part of the original pre-fall good creation,
though then it would have not been such a horror.[15]

In Genesis 2:17, we read that God warns Adam and Eve ". . .
you must not eat from the tree of the knowledge of good and evil, for
when you eat of it you will surely die." Obviously, they did not die
immediately after eating the fruit; so, the concept of "death" in the
garden is nuanced. At first glance, this command may seem un-
just. Humans are inquisitive. Yet, Adam and Eve are admonished

not to eat of the forbidden tree of the knowledge of good and evil. This language about "good" and "evil" is likely a merism, a literary device that uses opposites as shorthand for an entire range. For example, if I said I looked "high and low" for a lost item I would mean that I looked everywhere, not just up high and down low.

Beyond the fact that this is likely a merism, the episode communicates the idea that in eating of the forbidden fruit the first couple would exchange God's wisdom for their own judgment.[16] Dietrich Bonhoeffer posits that the first sin of Adam and Eve, of all of us, is to put our understanding of good and of evil ahead of our knowledge of God. They eat of the fruit (the Bible does not use the word "apple" but the word "fruit") of the forbidden tree to become their own masters, and instead, as is always the case, they become enslaved. That's the serpent's temptation, *sicut deus* (Latin: "be like God.") There are some theologians who argued that the devil would not freely have chosen a serpent shape. "Satan would have liked to have worn a handsome and appealing shape when he appeared to Adam and Eve, but God would not let him, lest the temptation he offered be irresistible; neither did God allow him to take his own grotesque shape, which would have been too repellent . . ."[17] It's ironic that Adam and Eve succumbed to the temptation when, in fact, they were already made in God's image and likeness.

Of course, they do eat of the tree of the knowledge of good and evil, but they do not instantly die. What does happen is devastating. They lose their relationship with creation; where once they were stewards over the land and the animals, now they are subject to the snake and the thorns of the field. They lose their relationship with each other, where before they were faithful companions. Adam turns on Eve, blaming her for eating the fruit. In short, the Edenic order is turned on its head. After the fall, the Genesis story indicates that God casts Adam and Eve out of the garden. Actually, Genesis specifies that God drives them out. Being forced to leave the happiness of Eden seems like a harsh punishment. Adam and Eve undoubtedly yearn to return to the delights of the blissful Garden of Eden, but an angel(s) with a fiery sword blocks their way. However, reading the narrative closely reveals that in the Garden of Eden there are two trees: the Tree of Life and the Tree of the Knowledge of Good and Evil. God banished Adam and Eve from the Garden of Eden after the couple eats of the fruit of the Tree of the Knowledge of Good and

Evil and before they could eat of the fruit of the Tree of Life. The story is telling the reader that if the couple were left in the garden then they might eventually have eaten from the Tree of Life, which would have sealed their immortality on this earth. Immortality in isolation from God, whose friendship they lost by disobedience, would have been a hellish existence.

> It is a safety-device, because, once Man has fallen, natural immortality would be the one utterly hopeless destiny for him. Aided to the surrender that he must make by no external necessity of Death, free (if you call it freedom) to rivet faster and faster about himself through unending centuries the chains of his own pride and lust and of the nightmare civilizations which these build up in ever-increasing power and complication, he would progress from being merely a fallen man to being a fiend, possibly beyond all modes of redemption.[18]

So, God's curse after the fall was not arbitrary, where the punishment does not fit the crime, but a "severe mercy."[19] In the Genesis narrative, we need not see a vengeful God punishing a wicked Adam and Eve, but a loving father who had warned of the inevitable results of overstepping the mark; a God who then intervenes not to curse but to limit the curse that surely had to follow. At the serpent's first appearance he was presumably ambulatory; he must have had legs and feet. Now, in order to limit the power of this creature, God takes those limbs away, having him crawl on his belly, eating the dust of the earth.

Consider how Genesis reveals that God gave two commands or blessings. He said that Adam and Eve should will have dominion over the earth (Genesis 1:3), and they should be fruitful and multiply (Genesis 1:28). After the fall, these two blessings were transformed into a curse. Humans would not dominate the land but would struggle now with thistles and thorns (Genesis 3:18) and multiplying now comes through pain (Genesis 3:16).

Some have seen these curses as the just punishment of a wrathful God on his sinful people. Others offer an alternative by suggesting the curse is not directly from God as punishment but an inevitable consequence of violating the relationships and rules that govern the inherent makeup of creation. Although God does not actively will evil, that does not mean he does not allow free choices to bring about results he does not desire.

Nonetheless, there are theological debates about God's omni-causality, his undeterred will. In their extreme form we come face-to-face with heresy because it means that God is the primary and secondary cause of everything—evil included. Really, this sort of thinking cannot help but devolve into pantheism, where everything is determined by God for everything is an expression or manifestation of him.

God's will can be categorized into his hidden will, which is both unknown and unknowable to us; and his revealed will, which can be known but may not be fully understood. Additionally, we can distinguish between God's permissive will and his active will. Distinguishing between his permissive will (in contrast to his active will) allows us to begin to plumb the depths of the mystery of suffering.[20] Jesus, anxious about his impending torture and execution, pled with God in the garden of Gethsemane: "Father, if you are willing, remove this cup from me; yet, not my will but yours be done" (Luke 22:42). We know the rest of the story. Jesus, who was a wholly innocent man, was not spared but voluntarily went on to face his tormentors who killed him after inflicting the most horrible suffering. After being scourged and nailed to a cross, Jesus offered yet another prayer to his father. Only this time he didn't include the words "if you are willing." Amid the pain of the crucifixion, Jesus simply asked that his executioners be forgiven. He said, "Father, forgive them; for they do not know what they are doing" (Luke 23:34). Jesus' Gethsemane prayer included a qualification: God please grant this, but only if it is your will. On the cross, however, Jesus did not say, "God if it is your will please forgive my persecutors." The lesson here is that God is always willing to forgive, but he is not always willing to prevent suffering. The quintessential example of this comes from the life of Jesus. He prayed fervently to be spared the suffering of crucifixion, if that was his father's will (Matthew 26:39). But, he was not delivered from this cruel death. It was only with the resurrection that Jesus was fully and finally vindicated.[21] In light of this recognition, Catholics have a ready response to the many explanations that have been offered about our suffering. Here are a few, along with some Catholic reactions:

■ Suffering is not part of God's original design. The world has been subjected to powers and principalities that are at enmity with God. This argument has its roots in the Bible but must be framed within the larger proposition concerning God's omnipotence, God's omnibenevolence, and his permissive—not active—will.

■ Suffering does not exist; it is just an illusion. This is just a variation of Plato's cave scenario, which asks the metaphysical question, "How do we know what is real?" One Catholic answer is to point out the self-contradictory nature of that position. If you insist the world is illusory, isn't that very insistence its own type of illusion?

■ God does not care about our problems and pain. At best, this is the heresy of deism; at worst, this is blasphemy. God is love and cares more for us than we do for ourselves.

■ God is incapable of helping us because he doesn't have the power. Classical Christian theology labels this argument as heresy. God is omnipotent and can do anything.

■ We deserve to suffer. Perhaps this is true sometimes; but, the wicked often prosper and the good often suffer.

■ God, in Jesus, suffered with us. God invites us to offer our sufferings to him; to express our trust and love for him by staying faithful in bad times. By doing so, we can participate in our redemption and the redemption of others.

■ Better to suffer a little now than a great deal later. To uproot a small sapling is hard but not impossible. To pull up a full-grown tree is another matter entirely.

■ Our suffering is customized for us in some way. Recall the story I shared, which my great-grandmother used to tell, explaining that if we had the chance to lay down our crosses (our suffering) and exchange them for the crosses of anyone else, we'd find anyone else's cross too hard to carry, and no matter how many different crosses we tried out, we'd eventually return to our own.

■ Suffering is a necessary consequence of our existence. If we want to enjoy the heat of the sun, we risk sunburn. Life in a free universe comes with inevitable risks.

Professor John Haught explained,

> According to a biblically inspired theology of nature, beneath life's diversity, descent, and flawed design, stirs an evolutionary

drama that has been aroused, though not coercively driven, by
a God of infinite love. The cosmos is called continually into being by a Creator who wills, but does not force, truly interesting
outcomes to emerge in surprising new ways. God, as scripture
suggests, is the one who 'makes all things new.' The drama of life
and its evolution is a response to this invitation.[22]

Whenever we see what appears to be evil perpetrated by God,
we must, if we are to maintain our orthodoxy, seek another explanation. For instance, God's wrath is really justice—a justice that
is curative, not vengeful. More astonishing, St. Thomas Aquinas
taught that mercy is the fulfillment, not the disregard or elimina-
tion, of justice. By this, he meant that for mercy to be dispensed
it must be predicated by the just act of acknowledging that an
offense took place. Of course, our greatest example of the commingling of justice and mercy comes from Jesus himself.

You may, at times, face the incomprehensibility of the God
who commanded Abraham to sacrifice his son and who tested
Job to the point where he was counseled to simply "curse God
and die." You may face the apprehensive terror of the sort Martin
Luther experienced while contemplating the thrice-holy God or
the despondency of the apparent absence of God during a dark
night of the soul.[23]

If we insist that God is love, and he wills for us love, then by
irrefutable logic we must concede that the allowance of evil is loving. The logic here doesn't lead us to state that evil is good, but
only that the good and loving God allows evil, because doing so is
good and loving. So there is no misunderstanding: Unquestionably, sin and evil are deplorable to God and were not directly of
his making. God does not have a dark side; *Lux Umbra Dei* (Latin:
"light is the shadow of God").

In the Bible, we find numerous examples of how suffering
purges and refines a person, or in the case of Israel, an entire
people (e.g., Malachi 3:3 compares God to a refiner's fire that
purifies silver and gold). The Bible addresses God's remedy for sin
and suffering more than it addresses its initial causes.[24] Specifically, we learn, in the words of Paul Claudel, that "Jesus did not
come to explain away suffering or remove it. He came to fill it with
his presence."[25]

However, some thoughts about why we suffer, offered by various biblical authors, include:

- We live in a fallen world (Romans 8:22)
- Our own bad choices (Galatians 6:7)
- A test (James 1:2, 1 Peter 1: 6-7)
- A punishment for sin (Hebrews 12: 3-11)
- Malevolent forces (2 Corinthians: 12:7)

Of course, it is exactly these kinds of arguments that trouble so many skeptics, as some of them appear to depict God to be like an abusive parent who beats and bullies the children, allegedly for their own good. Growing up nurtured by benevolent, supportive parents helps to form an adult concept of a benevolent and loving God. On the other hand, growing up distressed by harsh, critical authority figures can predispose one to see God as an oppressor who is to be feared and resented. Such fear is often accompanied by guilt for feeling resentful toward God. To divorce oneself from one's early influences and begin to authentically understand God takes a lot of work, but rejecting these sorts of false impressions helps us grow in a relationship with him.

A friend of mine shared with me the not-uncommon story of his upbringing. He and his father had a violent relationship. As a boy, there was little he could do to defend himself against the onslaught of his father's rage. Then one day, in his teens, his father was older and weaker, and he was stronger, and he'd had enough. His father raised his hand to strike my friend but was shocked when his son blocked the blow and warned: This ends now! The father, deeply satisfied at what he had created, never laid a hand on his son again. It may be that the father actually wanted his abuse to have a transforming effect on his son, changing him from a "fearful boy" into a "strong man."

I mention this troubling story because many see God like the father in this story. They agree with Captain Ahab, who, in *Moby Dick*, railed against God as an "unearthly . . . hidden lord and master, and cruel, remorseless emperor."[26] Nothing can be further from the truth. People like my friend's dad are often pitiless and vulgar; their sycophantic life choices continue to chill their already cold hearts.

The Christian understanding of God cannot be further from this caricature. Instead of thinking about God as a parent who bullies his wayward children, Jesus came to show us his loving father who desires to heal and transform the world. The world, with all its evil and filth, could not simply be let alone by its creator. The God of the deists may be able to abandon his work to its own self-destruction, but the Lord revealed by the prophets of the Judeo-Christian tradition is an intimate lover of his creation. God is not like the abusive father; God revealed his willingness to step in and take the place of the battered son. In the person of Jesus, God willingly took on all the evil this world had to offer. He freely occupied the space that terrorizes us. The cross declares the gravity of sin while simultaneously proclaiming the immense love of God.

To make progress in our understanding, we need to do the hard work of distinguishing and compartmentalizing concepts. While we often lump suffering and evil together in the same category, they really are distinct. Moreover, both can be bifurcated into natural and moral categories (e.g., earthquakes can fall into the category of natural evil while murder would fall into the category of moral evil). At some level, these distinctions break down, given that an earthquake is caused by natural forces and a murder committed by one human against another, but both are "natural" in that the murder, too, is part of nature. My point here is simply to recognize that both natural and human-willed suffering and evil point to a universe that is off the mark.

In the book of Habakkuk, we read about a period of time between the reign of King Manasseh, known for his wickedness, and the reign of Josiah, Manasseh's righteous grandson. The prophet Habakkuk asks questions about the good God of Israel allowing great evil to continue among his people. While the more familiar book of Job focuses on the suffering of one man, Habakkuk focuses on the broader question of suffering within a community. The answer given is that God is fully aware of all the complaints Habakkuk raises, and more. God insists that, despite the many evils in the world, he will fulfill his will, and, he counsels Habakkuk, and all of Israel, to live by faith.

The more famous book of Job, which is among the most sublime in the entire history of world literature, tells a similar tale. Job presents the story of a righteous and holy man, renowned for his wealth and piety; yet he loses his family, his property, and his health—but not his faith. The very name "Job" means "persecuted or hated." Interestingly, Job is said to have lived in the land of Uz. It is possible, therefore, that Job was not identified as a Jew, so, perhaps the biblical author was equating Job's plight with everyone in the world, not just God's chosen people. More cautiously, we can speculate that the land of Uz is a fabled land. The word "*uts*" in Hebrew translates to "advice," and so Job may live in the metaphorical land of advice. Since the opening lines of the story are oddly worded in Hebrew—typically, we would expect "there was a man," but instead we read "a man there was"—we may be dealing with a fable since we see this same type of wording in other fables in the Hebrew Scriptures.

A troubling aspect of this story is that God was not merely passively allowing bad things to happen to Job, but minimally, God consented to the evil perpetrated on Job by the Accuser. We read about mythological gods recklessly playing with the lives of mortals but hardly expect the God of Israel to parlay with Satan (Job 1:6). Yet, Job does not respond like some Greek hero wronged by a capricious god; Job remains faithful. More importantly, a closer reading of the text shows that God is not behaving like the gods of myth. His absolute sovereignty over Satan is revealed in that Satan must give an account to God. (Elsewhere in the Bible we read of Jesus warning Peter and his other disciples that "Satan has asked permission to sift all of you like wheat," Luke 22:31, ISV.)

As the story unfolds, we read that Job suffers deeply, but still he remains faithful to his Lord. His own wife advises him to "curse God and die," but Job remains resolute. Job's friends insist that he is being punished by God for some sins he must have committed, but they are wrong. Most of us like to associate most often with people who encourage and validate us, so it is a testament to Job's character that he has friends who criticize him. The irony here is that Job's friends were welcome, but they were flat out wrong.

God himself calls Job "blameless" and makes the point that God is not the source of evil—yet, neither is Job. Job's sufferings are remarkable and extraordinarily confounding because the story does not give us a good reason for his plight. Reflecting on the conventional theodicy that Job is being punished for some personal sin proves inadequate. As G. K. Chesterton said, Job was "tormented not because he was the worst of men, but, because he was the best."[27]

What is the reason behind this? As Robert Frost poetically put it, is the moral that we must "submit to unreason"[28]? Eventually, God speaks directly to Job, and while we don't get a direct answer in the text, we are provided with some important guidance. First,

God speaks to Job out of a whirlwind or storm. These conjure images of chaos and destruction, but God is found therein. The chaos is not outside God's sovereignty. Second, God speaks to Job not about Job's own suffering but about the bigger picture of creation as if to try to put Job's plight into a larger perspective. God's goodness and care is directed toward all of his creation.

The concluding chapter of Job moves us from the dialog and multi-sided debate of the earlier chapters and features a monologue in which God reprimands Job's friends. Although they appeared pious and wise and may have sounded like they knew what they were talking about, they were very wrong in the things they said about God and about Job. It is interesting to note that, in some translations, Job intimately refers to God as "Yahweh," God's revealed name, but his friends, Eliphaz, Bildad, and Zophar, continually refer to God more distantly as "Elohim," which means "Creator," or "El Shaddai," which means, "Almighty One." When God speaks later in the book he refers to himself as Yahweh, suggesting first that Job knew God on a more personal level, and second, that having such a personal relationship with God does not insulate a person from great tribulations and suffering—in fact, such trials can be a direct result of such a relationship.

Interestingly, while God scolds the friends for being incorrect, God never gives a clear justification for Job's suffering. Instead, God asks Job a series of humbling rhetorical questions. Where was Job when the sun was formed and the foundations of the earth were laid? Where was Job when the waters were divided? What does Job know of the mysteries of life? Who can instruct God? Who can discern God's judgments? These questions are rhetorical, and they do not resolve into neatly contrived answers. The book of Job is not written like a logician's argument but is exploratory and inconclusive. The book does not even hint at the idea that Job's suffering was necessary for God to achieve some end he would not otherwise have been able to achieve absent that suffering.

Still, Job remains a puzzling yet sublime book. G. K. Chesterton said of Job: "The riddles of God are more satisfying than the solutions of man."[29] So, God does not give us a complete or even satisfying answer to the mystery of suffering. But, what God does give us is something far greater than an explanation: ". . . he gives up a Son. Such is the spirit of the angel's message to the shepherds: 'Peace upon Earth, good will to men . . .' A Son is better than an explanation. The explanation of our death leaves us no less dead than we were; but a Son gives us life, in which to live." [30]

Mystic Simone Weil proposed, "The extreme greatness of Christianity lies in the fact that it does not seek a supernatural remedy for suffering, but a supernatural use for it."[31] We are not free from suffering, but in Jesus, suffering can have a new teleology or meaning. Perhaps you have heard someone tell you to offer up your sufferings to God. This offering is an express intention to unite one's suffering to the suffering of Jesus. Catholics sometimes use the language of "co-redemptive suffering," which is a participation in the sacrificial love that Jesus Christ offers to the world.[32] Saint Paul writes about how we can "complete what is lacking in [Jesus'] sufferings" (Colossians 1:24). As Pope St. John Paul II explained:

> Does this mean that the Redemption achieved by Christ is not complete? No. It only means that the Redemption, accomplished through satisfactory love, remains always open to all love expressed in human suffering. In this dimension—the dimension of love—the Redemption which has already been completely accomplished is, in a certain sense, constantly being accomplished. Christ achieved the Redemption completely and to the very limits but at the same time he did not bring it to a close.[33]

Maybe you have experienced an inconsolable grief; a sorrow so penetrating that you cannot conceive of how any redemptive use of your suffering or any potential future joy, either here or in the afterlife, could possibly heal your broken heart. Consider Augustine's lament over the loss of his friend.

> My heart was black with grief. Whatever I looked on had the air of death. My native place was a prison-house and my home a strange unhappiness. The things we had done together became sheer torment without him. My eyes were restless looking for him, but he was not there. I hated all places, because he was not in them. They could not say: 'He will come soon,' as they would in his life when he was absent. I became a great enigma to myself and I was forever asking my soul why it was sad and why it disquieted me so sorely. And my soul did not know what to

answer me . . . I had no delight but in tears, for tears had taken the place my friend had had in the love of my heart.

I was at once utterly weary of life and in great fear of death. It may be that the more I loved him the more I hated and feared, as the cruelest enemy, that death which had taken him from me; and I was filled with the thought that it might snatch away any man as suddenly as it had snatched him . . . I wondered that other mortals should live when he was dead whom I had loved as if he would never die; and I marveled still more that he would be dead and I his other self living still. Rightly has a friend been called 'the half of my soul'. For I thought of my soul and his soul as one soul in two bodies, and my life was a horror to me, because I would not live halved.[34]

The message of Christ is that, despite such grief, he is a God who not only wipes away every tear but restores multiple times over all that was lost, including the lost years and experiences that seem to us as irretrievable. We should not languish in the hope that one day God will explain the necessity of our suffering, showing the purpose it served or the good that it brought about. Instead, we hope God will pass judgment and declare every unholy cause of misery and pain as utterly profane. And, in response to all of this, we can imagine Jesus speaking something like these words, "Behold I do what cannot be done. I restore the years that the locusts and worms have eaten. I restore the years which you have dropped away upon your crutches and in your wheel-chair. I restore the symphonies and the operas which your deaf ears have never heard, and the snowy massif your blind eyes have never seen, and the freedom lost to you through plunder, and the identity lost to you, because of calumny and the failure of justice; and I restore the good which your own foolish mistakes have cheated you of. And I bring you to the Love which all other loves speak, the Love which is joy and beauty, and which you have sought in a thousand streets and for which you have wept and clawed your pillow."[35]

Although we have not arrived at a satisfactory explanation for why an all-good and all-powerful God allows suffering, as long as we draw breath we have hope in God's unfailing and joyful love. The prophet Zephaniah declared that, "God will exult with joy over you . . . he will renew you by his love. He will dance with shouts of joy over you . . ." (Zephaniah 3:17 Jerusalem Bible).

LOVE

This chapter discusses the dual topics of suffering and love, and I was disappointed to realize that in my final draft was page after page of material I'd written about pain and loss, but comparatively little on the much more important topic of love. After giving the matter some thought, it occurred to me: The entire book really addresses the subject of love; God's love for us or our love for him and for each other. With that in mind, here are a few points worth considering.

God loves each and every one of us, even at our worst. He can count every step you've taken since your initial unsteady toddle. He can number every breath you've drawn since your very first. We never fully understand what this heavenly, undiminished love is like, but going back to the original Greek of the New Testament can help. The Greek language has multiple words for love: *eros* (erotic love—not just between a man and a woman, but also the kind of passionate love one feels for great food, music, or art); *philos* (love between close friends); and, *agape* (selflessness; willing the good for the beloved). All three terms rightly describe God's love, although—if we were limited to one, agape might capture divine love most completely.

The statement "God is love" describes God's character and essence. Love involves three ingredients: a person who loves, a person who is loved, and a relationship between the two. "Lover, beloved, and the love they share" is, according to St. Augustine, an apt definition of the Triune God. God is love. He loves with an infinite, personal, and incompressible love that cannot be earned. The Greek god Eros is a god of love, and he is often pictured as being blindfolded, indicating love is blind. However, God's love is not blind. That is an astonishing teaching central to Christianity. Even the vilest sinner is loved by God—not because God is blind to sin but because he loves unconditionally.

As an observant Jew, Jesus followed the precepts of the law perfectly, but often at a level deeper than the expected superficial ritualism. For example, it was ritually unclean to touch a menstruating woman, a leper, or a corpse. When we read that Jesus came into contact with a woman who had a bleeding condition (symbolic of menstruation), it was not Jesus that became unclean but the woman who was healed. When Jesus touched lepers, it was not he who was contaminated but the lepers who were cured. And when Jesus touched a corpse, again he was not made unclean; instead, he restored the dead to life.

As another example of Jesus rising above the law we read in the Gospels that Jesus used spit in three of his miracles. Once, he brought hearing back to a deaf man (Mark 7:33). Then, on two other occasions, he used his own saliva[36] to heal two different blind men (Mark 8:23). In Jewish tradition it was a great insult, akin to cursing someone, to spit on them (Deuteronomy 25:8, Numbers 12:13). Yet Jesus overcomes the curse, transforming it into a blessing.

We see Jesus transforming curses into blessings elsewhere. The Christmas carol "Joy to the World" includes a verse:

> No more let sins and sorrows grow,
> Nor thorns infest the ground;
> He comes to make His blessings flow
> Far as the curse is found,
> Far as the curse is found,
> Far as, far as, the curse is found.[37]

Jesus' blessings flowed through his teachings and the miracles of physical and spiritual healing, through his command over nature, through his merciful forgiveness of sinners, through his confounding interactions with Jewish and Roman leaders, through his gracious implementation of the sacraments, and ultimately in the establishment of God's kingdom. The rapid expanse of the kingdom, from a handful of disciples in an unimportant Roman province to a multi-million-member faith, in just a few centuries, is the greatest response to suffering the world has ever known. We are called to continue in this work.

✝

CHAPTER SIX

GOD
(THEOLOGY)

APOLOGETICS

All we know about God or can know about him[1] is derived either from human reason or via supernatural revelation. Montesquieu once quipped: "It has been very well said, that if triangles were to make to themselves gods, they would give them three sides."[2] We tend to anthropomorphize God, making him more like us. Voltaire once said: "If God has made us in His image, well have we repaid Him the compliment."[3]

One of the first things we must acknowledge is that God is God: "*Ego sum Deus*," "I am God," says the Lord. God is uncreated and essential, while we are created and contingent. We are totally dependent on him for our very existence, while he is Existence and Being itself. "Between the Creator and the creature there cannot be a likeness so great that the unlikeness is not greater."[4]

God is incomprehensible to us and will remain ever so—even in heaven.[5] Catholic theology distinguishes between absolute mysteries (which we will never fully understand) and relative mysteries (which will be understood in the beatific vision). As St. John Chrysostom teaches: "We therefore call God Himself the indescribable, the unfathomable, the invisible, the incomprehensible, the one who surpasses the power of the human tongue, who exceeds the comprehension of the mortal mind, who is inscrutable even to the angels."[6]

Kant's *Critique of Pure Reason* inaugurated a strong rebuke of rational arguments that purported to evidence God's existence. He argued that God belongs to that "noumenal world," which we humans cannot access by logic, sensory perception, or most other means. Saint Thomas Aquinas, that superior doctor of the church who wrote astute volumes of theology,[7] after having a vision of God, said that all he had written about God now looked like so much straw.

I could cite a hundred other examples that show that God is simply bigger than we can imagine, greater than our limited concepts and language allow for. Yet, God is accessible. While no one can prove the existence of God, the following arguments—some classical proofs[8]; others less well-known—as Iago says in Shakespeare's *Othello*, ". . . may help to thicken other proofs that do demonstrate thinly."[9] These synopses do not do justice to the nuances of some of these arguments,[10]and not all the arguments are of equal strength. What is important to remember is that if we could satisfactorily prove God's existence using nothing but rational arguments, then all we would end up really proving is that the God of orthodox Christianity is nonexistent; he is not provable via rational arguments.

ONTOLOGICAL ARGUMENT. Attributed to St. Anselm of Canterbury (1033-1109 AD), this is a philosophical argument in five steps:
1. If God exists then God would be the greatest, most perfect possible being.
2. We can imagine a perfect being like God in our minds.
3. The greatest kind of God would be one that exists not only in our minds but in reality, too.
4. So, the God we imagine to exist in our minds isn't the greatest of all possible Gods because God might be greater by simply existing in reality.
5. Since we can imagine a god as a being in which a greater is impossible, God must, therefore, exist.

CAUSALITY ARGUMENT. This is one of five "proofs" ("*Quinque viae*," or "Five ways") made famous by St. Thomas Aquinas in his *Summa Theologiae*. Since there is creation, there must be a creator. Critics of the causality argument counter that there is no Creator, or First Cause, but only an infinite set of effects. Causality argument critics have then been countered with logical analogies such as positing that there is an infinite set of cars to a train with no engine.

UNMOVED MOVER ARGUMENT. This is another of Aquinas' arguments. It is similar to the causality argument but focuses on the issue of motion. Anything that is in motion must have been moved by some other force. Since an infinite regression is impossible (an infinite number of train cars without an engine still will not move along the tracks), a "primary mover" must exist. God is that primary mover.

COSMOLOGICAL ARGUMENT. This Thomistic proof begins with the premise that all of creation, plants, animals, earth, the universe, are all unnecessary. That is, they all came into existence at a point in time. Consequently, there was a time when nothing existed. However, if nothing existed at some time, nothing would exist at all times unless an "outside necessary force" intervened. This outside necessary force is God.

ARGUMENT FROM DESIGN. According to yet another of Thomas Aquinas' proofs, our world could not have come into existence spontaneously. It must be the work of a creator. This "creator" is God. This is a nuanced and often misunderstood argument. Aquinas is not arguing the position of modern "Intelligent Design" proponents but instead is making a metaphysical argument. In summary, God not only created the universe out of nothing, but imparted agency, the power of self-determination, to all of nature. This agency coexists with God's sovereign and providential love for creation. Thus, God is not the divine watch-maker of the deists, a god who created the world with certain potency and then left the scene, perhaps occasionally tinkering with the world to set things right. Nor, however, is God the immediate cause of every occurrence in the universe, as some pantheists and hyper-Calvinists might argue.

ARGUMENT FROM INTELLIGENT DESIGN. Intelligent Design is a popular position among certain Protestant fundamentalists and is not usually associated with Catholic theology. The argument is really a material version of Aquinas' metaphysical argument from design (and thus a much weaker argument), which usually focuses on the topics of irreducible complexity and the narrow parameters for the existence of life. We see that, within the universe, there exists a constellation of conditions that are so fine-tuned that if they differed even by an incomprehensibly miniscule amount, human life would not exist (e.g., nuclear forces, gravity, expansion rate of the universe, speed of light, density of the universe, tilt of earth's axis, distance of the sun from earth, distance of the moon from earth, atmospheric pressure, thickness of the earth's crust, etc.). While these parameters are indeed extraordinary, science has reasonable responses that charge Intelligent Design proponents with succumbing to a form of anthropocentrism that relies heavily on gaps in scientific understanding.

ARGUMENT FROM GOODNESS. Everything that exists is good to a greater or lesser degree—but in reference to what? Everything is measured against the standard of the "greatest good." This greatest good is God.

PASCAL'S WAGER. In his book, *Pensées*, mathematician Blaise Pascal argues that if you don't know whether God exists, it is better to live as if he does and chance eternal joy, than to live as if he doesn't and chance unending sorrow.

ARGUMENT FROM COMMON EXPERIENCE. All cultures have traditionally had disproportionately more believers than nonbelievers.

ARGUMENTS FROM WITNESSES. A number of otherwise credible men and women have claimed to experience a vision of God.

ARGUMENT FROM MIRACLES. It is a mistake to conceive of God as being regularly distant and disinterested in our lives but occasionally involving himself in our affairs. The Trinity is always intimately present and continually working in this world, yet in a way that allows for genuine freedom to be expressed.

The history of religious experience is replete with inexplicable phenomena that can only be explained by the intercession of a God not bound by the laws of nature. Certainly, the God of Abraham, as depicted in the Old Testament, and testified to in the New Testament, is a miracle-working God.

ARGUMENT FROM DESIRE. All of our natural desires have corresponding satisfactions—we thirst and there is water, we hunger and there is food, we tire and there is sleep, we all get lonely and so we enter into relationships. However, whether we are rich, poor, young, old, famous, or ordinary—each of us longs for something more, something beyond what this world can provide. We all desire to live forever and to find perfect love. Given these unfulfilled yet universal longings, there must be forever life and an infinite lover and joy-giver. Since all other universal desires have corresponding satisfactions, this desire intimates that there must be a God.

These are some of the most common arguments for the existence of God. But, we must remember St. Augustine's words, "For, if what you wanted to say, you then grasped it, it would not be God."[11] That we will never fully be able to understand God might stir up some anxiety for believers who had hoped that his mystery would be solved once they encountered him face-to-face.

THEOLOGY

God's unfathomable greatness should be a point of hope—not despair. After all, "if the scheme of Revelation were small enough for our intellectual capacity, it would not be great enough for our spiritual need."[12] And there is simply none greater than God. In Genesis 22:15-19, God made an oath to himself[13] that he would bless Abraham and his descendants. The author of the book of Hebrews explains: "When God made a promise to Abraham, because he had no one greater by whom to swear, he swore by himself" (6:13).

God's greatness, his incomprehensibility, is expressed in an experience of St. Augustine of Hippo. One day, while walking by the sea and contemplating the Trinity, St. Augustine encountered a small boy on the seashore. Having dug a hole in the sand, the boy took a spoon and went to the sea. He scooped some water out of it, and then, going back to the hole, dumped the water from his spoon into the hole. When the saint asked the boy his intent, the boy responded that he was trying to empty the ocean into the hole he had dug in the sand. The saint protested that such a task was impossible. The boy responded that he would sooner empty out the ocean into his hole than St. Augustine would be able to exhaust the mystery of God.[14]

To some, the language of the mystery of God seems to employ the use of meaningless and nonsensical combinations of words: God is one and also three; Jesus is fully man and yet fully God;

God is all-loving but wrathful. Some may object to what they view as intrinsic impossibilities or the irrational blending of words to describe certain theological principles. Yet, these objections fail to appreciate the nuanced distinctions employed by the use of precise theological and philosophical terms.

We tend to anthropomorphize God, that is, many of us think of him as another one of us—only bigger and more powerful. We are stupefied when his behaviors do not fit our preconceived expectations. God does not fit completely into our categories and descriptions. But, we try to categorize and describe him nonetheless. It is not that our categories and descriptions are false—only, that they are limited.

For example, what do we really mean when we say God is all-powerful or omnipotent? Only that he can do anything that is consistent with his nature and is not an intrinsic contradiction. Although we use logic and reason when discussing God, we do well to remember that the God of whom we speak is not fully conceivable using our own human faculties. The God of Abraham, Isaac, and Jacob (cf. Exodus 3:6), the God who revealed himself in Jesus Christ, is wholly unique. If we were to think of a pyramid, with lesser beings—maybe, single-celled organisms—at the bottom, and God as the Ultimate Being at the top, then we would be misunderstanding who God is. God is not the Supreme Being in that way. Instead, as St. Thomas Aquinas teaches, God is the act of existence subsisting in and of itself.[15]

Overemphasizing God's "otherness," his infinite transcendence, can lead to difficulties. Teilhard de Chardin said, "We imagine [the Divine] as distant and inaccessible, whereas in fact we live steeped in its burning layers."[16] The God Jesus came to reveal is not the distant god of Epicureans (deists), but the God of the Bible, who is sovereign over and active within his creation. The deist notion of a god who set the laws of nature into motion and then simply stepped away, perhaps only to intervene now and again, is anathema to Christians. (Though, admittedly, this is an opinion alive and thriving today.)

> His action in the world is not to be thought of as invasive, intrusive or (still less) 'interventionist'. All of those words imply . . . the divinity is normally outside the process of the world, and occasionally reaches in, does something, and then goes away again. But in biblical thought heaven and earth—God's sphere and our

sphere—are not thought of as detached or separate. They overlap and interlock. God is always at work in the world, and God is always at work in, and addressing, human beings, not only through one faculty such as the soul or spirit but through every fibre of our beings, not least our bodies.[17]

Conjoining the notions of this intimate presence (immanence) with God's transcendence can be challenging. Focus too much on immanence and risk straying into the false idea that God is indistinguishable from creation (pantheism). (The Stoics thought of the divine as being embodied in or indistinguishable from the world around us. Christians, however, firmly reject this idea, insisting that God is not part of creation; he is wholly other.) Focus too much on transcendence and risk faith in a distant and disinterested God.

The tension between God's presence and his distance is not unique to Christianity but is addressed in other monotheistic religions. Christians are neither deist, like the Epicureans, nor pantheists, like the Stoics, but represent a third belief system that holds in balance both God's immanence and his transcendence. God can be revealed in the world he created, but at the same time he can be hidden, and in either case he is certainly separate from his creation.

God is ever-present in time and space but occupies neither. There is no past or future for him. He is fully present in all places at once, so that all that is—from rocks and slugs to humans and angels—live and move and have being in God.

There is an old Negro spiritual, "My God Is So High," which goes:

> O, [God]'s so high, you can't get over Him;
> He's so low, you can't get under Him;
> He's so wide, you can't get around Him—
> You must come in, by, and through the Lamb.[18]

It is through the sending of his "Lamb," Jesus Christ, that the transcendent God truly has become immanent for us.

God is: infinite; unchanging; uncreated; eternal; sovereign; omnipotent; omniscient; omnipresent. God's attributes are so far removed from our own that, in a sense, we can say that God does not exist—at least, not as you and I exist. In one of her ecstasies, the "Seraphic Virgin" St. Catherine of Siena declared to God: "I am she who is not, and if I spoke as being anything of myself, I should be lying . . . because Thou alone art He who is. And my being and every further grace that Thou hast bestowed upon me, I have from Thee, who givest them to me through love, and not as my due."[19] God is the ultimate being: the Source of Being. Each one of us exists only because God willed to create us and wills to sustain our existence. Although perhaps just quoting a stock phrase from Ancient Greek culture, St. Paul nevertheless declared to his pagan audience at the Areopagus that in God, "we live and move and have our being" (Acts 17:28).

And—perhaps, surprisingly—God is simple; meaning he is not made up of separate parts. His simplicity is absolute: "In him there is no composition of any kind, of substance and accidents, of essence and existence, of nature and person, of power and activity, of genus and specific difference."[20] The reason for this is that God is pure act (*actus purus*). In other words, there is no potentiality in Him. We who are creatures, however, are not like this. We are acorns that have the potential to grow into great trees. Yes, the power is within us, albeit not absolutely; it has been put there by Another.

There is no potentiality in God that is not realized. He is not on his way to becoming more loving, or wiser. On earth, we experience time in a way that shows what was—say an acorn; what is—a tree; and what will be—decomposing wood. God, being outside of time, does not suffer change; he is immutable and impassible. No outside influence can affect him since he is infinite and totally self-sufficient.

Some theologians argue that early Christian ideas concerning God's immutability were influenced by Greek ideas of perfection as well as Stoic and Platonic philosophies. However, the Bible is on record declaring God's "unchangeableness." ("For I the LORD do not change," Malachi 3:6.) Yet, the Bible also teaches us that God exhibits behaviors we associate with changing emotions. He is jealous and angry on occasion and welcoming and joyful at other times. One means for understanding how God can be both unchangeable and yet can also display feelings is by distinguishing between the terms "passions" and "affection." A passion comes from within and can be physical (a desire to eat) or emotional (the sentiment of pity). God's mercy, jealousy, anger, joy, etc. are all choices he makes based on right judgment.

Although, the attraction toward a changeable God is undeniable; we want a Lord who empathizes with us. However, the metaphysical implications of such an anthropomorphic deity are profound. A God who can be affected by anything outside himself is less than perfect and more like an enhanced version of a human being[21] or one of the capricious ancient pagan gods, subject to passing emotions.

A God who is not subject to emotion is not a stoic, uncaring, abstract metaphysical concept. "God is love itself, feeling is the dribs and drabs of love received into the medium of passivity. God cannot fall in love . . . for the same reason water cannot get wet: it is wet. Love itself cannot receive love as a passivity, only spread it as an activity."[22]

Some Christians throughout the centuries have discussed God's existence in terms of what he is *not*. This is called Apophatic Theology. According to *The New Dictionary of Theology*, it is:

> Negative theology, that is, theology which is so conscious that God transcends all created conceptions that it limits itself to statements about what God is not rather than making any claims to know God in himself.[23]

To declare what God is not, in this context, is not a denial of his existence; rather, it is an admission that God is wholly "Other" than what we are or what anything in the created world is. Apophatic descriptions of God are useful. But, as the Bible itself shows, there is much to affirm about God as well. (This affirmative, or "positive," theology is called "kataphatic."[24]) God is merciful, gracious, faithful, forgiving, and loving.

What we never find anywhere in the Bible or in sacred Tradition is an origin story for God. Unlike so many pagan myths that give a "theogony," or origin for the gods, the God of Abraham is without beginning. Indeed, from the opening verse of the Bible, he simply and already *is*: "In the beginning when God created . . ." (Genesis 1:1). Rather, *Theogony*, written around 700 BC by the Greek poet Hesiod, describes the origins of the Greek gods. The first book of the Bible is named "Genesis," which comes from the Greek word for birth. But, the text is not about the birth of God; rather, it is the story of God's masterful creation of the world and of his covenantal love for Abraham and his descendants.[25] This is a unique aspect of a creation story as opposed to other ancient

Near Eastern creation stories. The *Enuma Elish*, a Babylonian creation epic dating from the second millennium BC, tells the story of those gods' own creation of the world and of humankind—not out of love, but in order to have someone to worship them and take care of their needs.

God possesses "aseity," that is, uncreated existence.[26] His self-existence does not mean he is self-created. This would be contrary to reason, for: *Ex nihilo nihil fit* (Latin: "Nothing comes from nothing"). Rather, God is uncreated and eternal. Moreover, at no moment did God move from a state of unconsciousness to consciousness. He is perfectly and eternally aware of himself. What is more, he is a dynamic—not a static—reality: an infinite "Act of Existence."

We shall never know how to express the infinite abyss of the Trinity's self-giving love. As C. S. Lewis observes: "For in self-giving, if anywhere, we touch a rhythm not only of all creation but of all being. For the Eternal Word also gives Himself in sacrifice; and that not only on Calvary. . . . From before the foundation of the world He surrenders begotten Deity back to begetting Deity in obedience. And as the Son glorifies the Father, so also the Father glorifies the Son [*John 17:1, 4, 5*]."[27]

Christians are monotheists. We believe in only one God; that is, the divine nature is wholly unitary and singular. Yet, Christians also believe that this one and only God exists as three persons: God the Father, God the Son, and God the Holy Spirit. There is only one God, one Substance, but a trinity of persons; the unbegotten Father, the begotten Son, and the Holy Spirit, who proceeds from the Father and the Son.

The word, "Trinity," does not appear in the Bible. It comes from two Latin words: "*tria*" ("three"), and "*unitas*" ("unity, oneness"), referring to the three persons who are one God.[28] That there is only one God is clear from the Hebrew Scriptures. (See Isaiah 45:20–21; see also v. 5 and 46:9).[29] Sometimes, however, the Hebrew Scriptures intimate that this one and only God exists in a kind of plurality. For instance, when God creates humanity in the book of Genesis, we read:

Then God said, "Let us make humankind in our image, according to our likeness" (Genesis 1:26).[30] This use of the word "us" may simply be an example of the majestic plural that was occasionally employed by the ancient Hebrews but could also be a clue to God as Trinity.

Moreover, Jesus reveals that he and his father do not exist as a solitary dyad, for they are a community. During their last Passover together, Jesus tells his followers about the "Advocate" and "Spirit of truth" whom he will ask his father to give to them. This "Holy Spirit," whom the Father will send them in Jesus' name, will remind them of Jesus' teachings. (See John 14:15–17, 26; see also 15:26.)

To say that God is Trinity is to say that he is one nature made up of three persons. This formulation may seem confusing to some readers who identify the words, "nature," and, "person," with casual understandings of the terms. But, these words have formal, philosophical definitions. A "nature" is that which makes something what it is and without which it would not be what it is. Generally speaking, it addresses the question of "what" something is. A "person" is the individuation of a rational or intellectual substance, which exists properly and perfectly unto itself. It addresses "who" someone is.[31] Although completely identical with the divine nature, what distinguishes each person of the Trinity is his relation to the others (cf. *CCC*, para. 252).

Yet, the mystery of the Trinity does not mean there are three gods.[32] Nor does it mean that there is simultaneously one God and three gods. Rather, it means that there is one divine nature or essence that is possessed equally and fully by three distinct persons. As the *Catechism of the Catholic Church* explains, "*The Trinity is One.* We do not confess three Gods, but one God in three persons . . . The divine persons do not share the one divinity among themselves but each of them is God whole and entire" (para. 253; italics in original). To say that the Father, the Son, and the Holy Spirit are of one and the same substance means that each one is "consubstantial" with the other. This has been described using the Greek term "*homoousios*" ("of the same substance"). Adopted at the Council of Nicaea (325 AD), it was meant to combat any denial of Christ's divinity; that he was of the same substance as the Father.[33] The Father is in the Son and in the Holy Spirit; the Son and Holy Spirit are both in the Father and in each other. Yet, the Son is not the Father, the Holy Spirit is not the Son, etc. So, it would therefore be incorrect to assert a notion such as "God the Father died on the cross."[34] It would be correct, however, to say that the cross expresses the infinite love of the Trinity, with God the Father offering his Son in love, the Son freely taking on this sacrifice in obedient love of his Father and love of his creation, and with the Holy Spirit offering and applying this sacrificial gift.

In regard to the Trinity, one category of heresies overstresses God as one, typically called "Monarchianism" or "Modalism." In its various forms, which start appearing as early as the 200s AD, Monarchianism tries to reconcile the profound monotheism of the Bible with the Church's developed instinct that Jesus also is God (and, later, the same for the Holy Spirit).[35]

But, as Fr. Hardon also describes, there is a form of Monarchianism that declares that only God the Father matters. It is he alone who truly can be called "God;" and, Jesus and the Holy Spirit are either lesser "gods," or not God at all. This view is called: "Subordinationism."[36]

There is also the view of "Tritheism," namely, the belief that the Godhead is divided amongst three different gods. This view is as old as John Philoponus (+ ca. 570 AD), the philosopher and theologian who taught that the unity of nature in the Father, Son, and Spirit was simply a mental abstraction; rather, each person was an individual with his own divine nature and properties.[37]

Of the three divine persons, we can often identify with the Father and the Son, since we have earthly analogies. But, the Holy Spirit is, for many, more enigmatic. This enigma is not helped by the fact that the other divine persons of the Trinity are also "holy" and "spirit." In theology, Pneumatology is the study of God the Holy Spirit. The word "*pneuma*," means "breath" in Greek. The Holy Spirit is a divine person—not an "it" or some cosmic or (even) divine force. He is God: the third person of the Holy Trinity. He is God, uncreated, coeternal and coequal in power, majesty, and glory with the Father and the Son. He is no more and no less God than the Father and the Son, either singly or in unison.

The symbol of fire is one of the images associated sometimes in the New Testament with the Holy Spirit (cf. e.g. Matthew 3:11; Luke 3:16; also, Acts ch. 2). We might do well to use the analogy of light as well. We do not actually see light, but light illuminates our world and allows us to see. I think this is a good, albeit imperfect, analogy for the work of the Holy Spirit. Yet, it is the Holy Spirit's grace that prepares us to accept his presence in the first place. That is his gift. As the Reverend Maurice Boyd pointed out, "To look for the Holy Spirit and complain that we can't find Him is like a man complaining that he can't find his glasses, having forgotten that he is already wearing them. The presence of the

Holy Spirit is the power of our seeing. It is by the Spirit that we seek the Spirit."[38]

What distinguishes the one divine nature of the persons of the Trinity is their relationship to each other: The Father generates the Son; the Son is generated, or begotten; the Holy Spirit proceeds (see *CCC* paras. 254–55). The three divine persons are in a relationship that is dynamic and communal—not static. As per the *Catechism of the Catholic Church* (para. 236), sometimes theologians distinguish between the Trinity's internal reality (i.e., the "immanent" or "theological" Trinity) and the Trinity's activity *ad extra* in the created world (i.e., the "economic" Trinity).

A famous analogy for the Trinity is attributed to St. Patrick. According to legend, he used the three-leaf clover to show how one plant had three distinct leaves, while still remaining just one plant. So, while each of the three persons—or, "leaves"—of the Trinity is distinct, they are not separate; rather, they are united by the divine nature—or, "plant." Such an analogy goes only so far, however; and this clover symbol can easily drift into heresy if taken to the extreme or too literally.

Another—admittedly faulty—analogy is that of a dance. In other words, the relationship amongst the persons of the Trinity may be imagined as a sort of eternal dance. Christian theology uses the Greek term *"perichōrēsis,"* which means "dancing around something," to describe "the manner in which the three persons . . . dynamically share the self-same nature of Godhead and enjoy dynamic intercommunion in the most intense unity imaginable through the distinct relations, within common being, of Father, Son, and Holy Spirit."[39]

There is a legitimate criticism that these sorts of distinctions rely on categories that are, at times, at variance with more mystical expressions of the faith.[40] In the end, we should remember the caution of Pope St. Gregory I, who wrote: "Well nigh every thing [sic] that is spoken touching God, is by this alone . . . unworthy, that it admitted of being spoken."[41]

A standard objection that arises to God's infinitude goes something like this: "If God can do anything, can he create a rock so big that he cannot move it?" Or, "Can God create an argument so complex that he cannot solve it?" At first glance, this conundrum seems to raise a real and interesting no-win situation. However, once we insist on more clearly defining our terms, the apparent difficulty disappears. The answer to either of the questions posed above is "No," but not because God is limited in any way; his power is limitless. But, limitless power only means the ability to do anything that can be done. While it is true that when talking about God we inevitably must employ symbols, paradoxes, and analogies to express mysteries beyond our understanding, that is not the same as simply accepting logical contradictions.

If this appeal to logic is unconvincing and someone still insists God should be able to do anything at all, even if it involves a contradiction, then one need merely point out that if God purportedly has such a power, the conundrum about creating rocks so big they can't be moved is useless because that proposition itself presumes a logical coherence. In other words, either God's power is understood logically, or it isn't. If it is, the explanation above suffices to overcome the objection. If logic is irrelevant in reference to God, well then there is no use of posing logical puzzles about immovably big rocks since those sorts of questions are grounded in logic.

If we say God cannot do anything that does not conform to his nature—for example, he cannot lie—then we are saying there is something about God's nature, not his will, that prevents him from lying. But, from where did this nature originate? There is no force outside of God that governs him, no laws he himself did not author. Voluntarist models posit that God is unfettered power and can perform any act without regard to its morality or his immutable goodness. Yet, if we abandon belief in God's nature then we say God can will anything he wishes. William of Ockham believed God could have redeemed humanity by becoming a donkey, a tree, or stone, instead of becoming Incarnate as Jesus. Martin Luther and René Descartes, among others, intimate that God's sovereignty and omnipotence are not bound by logic. Square circles, married bachelors, and the like make no sense to us, but they could be possible for a limitless God. Non-voluntarist, or realist models posit that God acts only in ways that are consistent with his good nature.

On a similar note, Plato, in his work *Euthyphro*, has Socrates explore the question: Is goodness commanded by God because it is good, or should anything commanded by God automatically be deemed good? The first option suggests that there is a law outside of God; a moral code to which God is bound. This position is inconsistent with the Judeo-Christian understanding that God is infinite and omnipotent. The second option, that anything God commands is automatically "good" (Divine Command Theory) also has its own set of problems, as this would mean that if God willed murder or theft, those acts would become good simply because God commanded them.

Christians resolve the dichotomy by recognizing that in God there is no distinction between his freedom and his nature. God does not just act in a way that is good; he is goodness itself. He is not bound by some outside standard but is in himself ultimate goodness; thus, anything he commands is necessarily good, and it would be incorrect to talk about him commanding any sort of evil. When any command of God appears to be morally wrong—such as the command given to Abraham to sacrifice his son, Isaac—we have to examine the matter further in the hope of resolving the difficulty.

Some Christians, after examining troubling passages, misrepresented God and came up with heretical resolutions to such difficulties. By the second half of the first century after Christ, such mischaracterizations of the God revealed in the Old Testament led to the heresies of Marcionism and various strains of Gnosticism. The teaching of Marcion (declared heretical by orthodox Christians), was that the God revealed in the Old Testament was some lesser being, an evil demiurge.

Such distortions continued throughout Christian history. Many Christians throughout the ages understood God to be angry, vengeful, and enraged at sinners. Both the Old Testament and the New Testament are filled with promises and assurances of the Father's love. (Read the book of Hosea and see how God's love continues despite the disloyalty of his chosen people.)

Reformed preacher Jonathan Edwards' sermon, "Sinners in the Hands of an Angry God," preached in colonial Massachusetts, is a prototypical hellfire and brimstone sermon. This classic of American literature is characteristic of a sermon from the Great Awakening. There are many Catholic parallels that mirror Edwards' sermon. However, unlike the Reformed theology of God's anger, which Edwards so eloquently represented, Catholic theology is rich in alternate understandings of God's purported wrath. For example, Dame Julian of Norwich explored God's mercy in a way that could be titled "Sinners in the Hands of a Merciful God." In her famous mystical visions, or "shewings," Julian revealed, "All shall be well, and all shall be well, and all manner of things shall be well,"[42] and, more specifically, with respect to God's anger she wrote, "I saw truthfully that our Lord was never angry, nor ever shall be, for He is God: He is good, He is life, He is truth, He is love, He is peace; and His power, His wisdom, His Love, and His Unity do not allow Him to be angry. . . . God is the goodness that cannot be angry, for He is nothing but goodness."[43]

But, there is a radical difference between our concept of goodness and God's infinite goodness. The prophet Isaiah wrote, "'For my thoughts are not your thoughts, neither are your ways my ways,' declares the LORD. 'As the heavens are higher than the earth, so are my ways above your ways'" (55:8-9). God's goodness is not so different from ours that we are unable to even comprehend what it means to be good. To put it to a simple analogy: His goodness is to ours like a sphere is to a circle, and not like a triangle is to a square. They are similar, but not identical.

†

CHAPTER SEVEN

JESUS
(CHRISTOLOGY)

THE FULLNESS OF TIME

After over two thousand years' investigation into and meditation upon his life, the biography of Jesus is perhaps the most well-known in all of recorded time. It is no surprise then that more books, songs, and works of art have been devoted to him than any other individual in history.

His image is among the most reproduced in the entire world; though art that depicts Jesus always does so in a stylized manner. There is no genuine representation of Jesus because we do not know what he precisely looked like. Although neither the Bible nor any ancient text records Jesus' height, weight, physical features, eye color, etc.—it would not be all that difficult to locate people who are convinced that Jesus was a six-foot tall, blonde-haired, blue-eyed Caucasian man possibly with a slight British accent.

This false picture of Jesus' physical form is pretty tame compared to some very curious biographical theories that have been posited about his life.[1] For example, Albert Camus, in his novel *The Fall*, has the main character, Jean-Baptiste Clamence, speculate that Jesus wished to be crucified to allay his guilt over the babies Herod killed in an attempt to murder Jesus as a child.[2] Other novel ideas that have been put forth include: Jesus was the illegitimate son of a Roman soldier named "Panthera" (or Pandera or Pantera); Jesus was married to Mary Magdalene and fathered a child; Jesus was merely a magician; Jesus never existed but rather is a composite of earlier mythological figures, and so on.[3] The list of oddball Jesus-theories is extensive.

Even so-called Jesus experts fall into the trap:

> The same can be said of the Jesus-searchers of every era: the de-
> ists found a deist, the Romantics a Romantic, the existentialists
> an existentialist, and the liberationists a Jesus of class struggle.
> Supposedly equipped with the latest critical and historical tools,
> the "scientific" quest for the historical Jesus has nearly always
> devolved into theology, ideology, and even autobiography.[4]

Descriptions of Jesus' personality and mission often fail because of their one-dimensionality and their simplicity. I'm told
that there is a bridge somewhere in Europe that is lined with
statues of Jesus in his various roles: Jesus the Healer, Jesus the
Teacher, Jesus the Storyteller, etc. People who cross this bridge
will stop to pray at the statue that they can best relate to. Hundreds of different statues could adorn such a bridge, each statue
depicting an authentic aspect of Jesus. But, we shouldn't carry
this too far. If some have fallen into the trap of making Jesus too
simple, others have mistaken his universal appeal to mean he
was protean, even omni-talented.

Yes, he was a prophet. Yes, he was a revolutionary. Yes, he
was God's Anointed. But, a misplaced piety would have us believe
that Jesus was the greatest of all athletes or the finest among history's musicians or had the ability to effortlessly achieve any goal,
and that is simply not the case.

The complex personality presented by the modern Church is
not the result of centuries of religious ornamentation added to the
simpler Jesus of history. In fact, "The contrary of that premise is
true. If we could get back to the 'original', that is, if we could work
our way back to the picture of Christ as it existed before it had
been turned over in the apostles' minds or elaborated by their
preaching, before it had been assimilated by the corporate life of
the faithful, we could find a figure of Christ even more colossal
and incomprehensible . . ."[5]

So, who is Jesus? Eduard Schweizer called him, "Jesus: the
man who fits no formula."[6] Looking at his name is a good starting
point for better understanding him. During Jesus' time, people
were acknowledged by an appellation or identifier. So, in the New
Testament, we encounter more than one Simon. We have "Simon,
son of Jonah" (Matthew 16:17), and we have "Simon the tanner"
(Acts 10:6). The identifier can change over time. Jesus was called

Jesus of Nazareth, because Nazareth was his hometown. Later, Jesus accumulated numerous identifiers, the most common being "Jesus the Christ," which simply became "Jesus Christ." The word "Christ" translates from the Greek word "*Christos*," which means "anointed" or "chosen one." The word "Christ" was a title, not a formal name, but since Jesus was so closely identified with his role as God's chosen one, his name transformed into Jesus Christ.[7]

Jesus' status as God's chosen was established before the foundations of the world. He was not a human who took on a divine nature but a divine person who took on a human nature. The earliest written testimonies attesting to Jesus' divinity come from Christian hymns, such as those found in the letters of Paul of Tarsus (+ ca. 66 AD). Such hymns likely pre-date the earliest Gospel, Mark, perhaps by 20 years. These hymns are even prior to the Pauline witness; and, Paul drew on them.

The Gospel of John poetically describes the preincarnate Son of God in these words: "In the beginning was the Word, and the Word was with God, and the Word was God" (John 1:1). While his incarnation was unique and unprecedented, some theologians see this event as the culmination of a long history of God's presence among us.[8] (Genesis recounts how God walked with Adam in Eden; the Old Testament is replete with examples of God's presence, as in the Torah, in the temple, and in the Shekinah, etc.)

Jesus is both fully God and fully human. He is, however, a single divine person with two natures that are hypostatically united. According to the Council of Chalcedon:

> . . . the only begotten Son, must be acknowledged in two natures, without confusion or change, without division or separation. The distinction between the natures was never abolished by their union, but rather the character proper to each of the two natures was preserved as they came together in one Person and one hypostasis. He is not split or divided into two Persons, but he is one and the same only begotten Son, God the Word, the Lord Jesus Christ.

Saint Gregory of Nazianzus taught: "For that which [God the Son] has not assumed He has not healed; but that which is united to His Godhead is also saved."[9] In other words, Jesus had to be divine to fulfil his vocation, because only God can save, but he also had to become a mortal man so as to be an authentic representative of the human race. How easy it would have been for God to have taken on a stoic attitude, even a royal indifference to our human situation. Yet, as Jesus, he neither ignored nor merely tolerated the human condition—he made it his own. The idea that the infinite God would walk among us as a finite man was, "Scandal to the Jew and folly to the Greek" (1 Corinthians 1:23 -24). For different reasons, it was truly unthinkable to Jewish and Greek minds that such an event could ever take place.[10]

One of the consequences of the union of a human nature to the divine person of the Son is that all of his human activities as Jesus, albeit remaining properly human, nevertheless have a divine quality conferred upon them. Since the proper subject of Christ's earthly life is the person of God the Son, everything about his life and ministry can and must be attributed as accomplished by God. Christ's human nature was assumed—not absorbed. Admittedly, we can become confused in this teaching, especially if we are casual in our use of technical language. He is the only begotten Son of God. To borrow useful imagery from the Church Father Tertullian, (an image that found its way into the Nicene-Constantinopolitan Creed) the Father is like the sun, while the Logos, the Son, is like the light that emanates from the sun. We see here unity and distinction. (This analogy must be carefully parsed so as to avoid the heresy of modalism, which posits that God is not a trinity of persons but one person who presents in different modes.)

Put more technically, both divine and human natures subsist in the Person of Jesus. This means that there is one Son. Prior to assuming a human nature, he is divine; after having assumed a human nature, he is still divine. This is so because he remains the same divine person, namely, God the Son. This means that Jesus is not a human person, but a divine person with a human nature. The two terms, "person," and "nature," are not synonymous. The word "person" (as described above) defines who someone is. The word "nature" defines what someone or something is. The word "relation" defines what a being does or can do.

The subject can get a bit more complex. Consider that Jesus' two distinct natures are hypostatically united in one person. One might think, then, that he also must have just one will and natural operation, namely, the divine. On the contrary, Jesus has two wills and two natural operations: one divine, and one human (cf.

CCC, para. 475).[11] Also, given that Jesus was fully human, he too had both a fleshly body and a spiritual soul.[12]

The Hebrew Scriptures attest over and over again to God's intention to send a Messiah. This hope was never more acutely desired than at the time of the incarnation. Jesus, the Messiah, came when the circumstances were suitable. Saint Paul wrote "But when the fullness of time had come, God sent his Son" (Galatians 4:4).

"The fullness of time" arrived at the culmination of theological and historical conditions that had finally come to fruition. Various Christian writers throughout the centuries have written about how the Son of God longed to come to earth but patiently waited for such things as prophecies to be fulfilled and for his mother, Mary, to be born. Moreover, it is no accident that Jesus came after the time the Roman Empire had formed and expanded. Infrastructure that made travel easier, and a common culture and language (Greek was the *lingua franca* of the region and much of the Roman Empire) that united most of the Mediterranean world and beyond, allowed for the spread of the gospel. Jesus' timing did not just allow for his message to spread across much of the Western hemisphere but also exposed a great number of people to his ministry. Unlike Judaism, which was an exclusivist religion, Christianity is universal; and so, Jesus came at an opportune time—for at no other date prior to his coming could his message have been easily spread globally.

> It's not the number of years but the levels of human population that are the issue here. The Population Reference Bureau estimates that the number of people who have ever been born is approximately 105 billion. Of this number, about 2 percent were born in the 100,000 years before Christ came to earth. . . . He showed up just before the exponential explosion in the world's population, so even though 98 percent of humanity's timeline had passed, only 2 percent of humanity had previously been born, so 98 percent of us have walked the earth since the Redemption.[13]

One of the theological reasons he came when he did is hinted at with the words Jesus used toward the beginning of his public ministry. The Gospel of Luke recounts how Jesus followed his customary habit of visiting the synagogue on the Sabbath. He read from the Scriptures these words: "The Spirit of the Lord is upon me, because he has anointed me to bring good news to the poor. He has sent me to proclaim release to the captives and recovering of sight to the blind, to let the oppressed go free, to proclaim the year of the Lord's favor" (Luke 4:18-19).

The verses Jesus read come from chapter 61:1-2 of the book of Isaiah. It was no accident that he read these particular verses to inaugurate his ministry. Look at what is being claimed. Jesus is telling his audience—many of whom were filled with a great Messianic expectation—that he is the anointed, the chosen One of God. He will come to set free those who are in bondage and to heal those who are sick.

But, there is more. The last line Jesus read, ". . . to proclaim the year of the Lord's favor," refers to something called the Jubilee year. The Jews had a custom[14] of celebrating a Jubilee year every 50 years. (See Leviticus 25:10.) This was a year when all debts were forgiven, and all slaves were freed. Scholars tell us that Jesus was crucified in a Jubilee year. The second point worth noting is that Jesus did not quote all of Isaiah 61:1-2.[15] Jesus cuts short his quote of verse two, which mentions "the day of vengeance of our God . . ." The cross is about mercy, not vengeance.

Jesus is the subject of hundreds of prophecies of the Old Testament, some written millennia before his birth. Jesus testified that the Hebrew Bible foretold details about himself. "You search the Scriptures, because you think that in them you have eternal life; and it is they that bear witness about me . . ." (John 5:39). Jesus fulfilled prophecies[16] and was himself the final and supreme prophet of God. Here are five among numerous examples:

- Jesus was born of a virgin
  - Prophecy: Isaiah 7:14
  - Fulfillment: Luke 1:34-35
- Jesus taught in parables
  - Prophecy: Psalms 78:2-4
  - Fulfillment: Matthew 13:34-35
- Jesus was crucified
  - Prophecy: Psalms 22:16
  - Fulfillment: Matthew 27:35
- Jesus interceded for his executioners
  - Prophecy: Isaiah 53:12
  - Fulfillment: Luke 23:34

- Jesus rose from the dead
  - Prophecy: Hosea 6:2
  - Fulfillment: Luke 24:6-7

Our primary written sources[17] about Jesus' life and ministry are the three synoptic (or "eyewitness") Gospels[18]—Matthew, Mark, and Luke—along with the Gospel of John. These Gospels serve as the *locus classicus*, that is, the most authoritative source of information, for Jesus' life and ministry. Indeed, John the Evangelist tells us that he wrote his Gospel, "so that you may come to believe that Jesus is the Messiah, the Son of God, and that through believing you may have life in his name" (20:31).

Each of the synoptic Gospels recounts many of the same stories in similar sequences. They focus on Jesus' preaching and teaching and are descriptive in nature. The Gospel of John excludes some material found in the synoptic books and includes information the others do not. John's Gospel has been described as reflective rather than descriptive.

All four Gospels provide biographical information about Jesus—though, they are not biographies. They give us accurate historical details—though, they are not books of history. Instead, the Gospels are testimonies written to share the good news that God has sent his son, who is Lord and Messiah. (See Acts 2:36.)

The authors of the Gospels drew heavily from the Hebrew Scriptures, appropriating the language used to describe God—language of mystery and of the inexpressible—in reference to Jesus. This testimony, while true and at times even precise, still falls short. Jesus tells his Apostles: "'I still have many things to say to you, but you cannot bear them now'" (John 16:12).

These accounts of his life are filled with rich symbols and hidden ironies. As St. Augustine observed: "Life came down, to be killed; bread came down, to go hungry; the way came down, to grow weary on a journey; the fountain came down, to experience thirst . . ."[19]

Many surprising incongruities can be found throughout Jesus' life.

- He was born in the humblest of circumstances, yet his birth was heralded by angels.

- His birth foretold his death, and his death brought forth a new birth. He was wrapped in swaddling clothes and laid in a manger. In Jesus' day, it was customary to wrap the corpse in the swaddling cloth (not unlike a mummy) and to place it in a grave; as an infant, Jesus was wrapped in this burial cloth, foreshadowing his future death.

- When Jesus was born, a great light, the Star of Bethlehem, shone brightly in the sky, leading both Jews and Gentiles to him, because he would be a light to all; when he died there was great darkness—an eclipse.

Even unbelievers are fascinated by Jesus. Those who categorically deny the existence of the supernatural and the possibility of miracles cannot help but read the Gospels with a sense of bewilderment. Albert Einstein, a famous skeptic, among other things, once said in an interview: "As a child, I received instruction both in the Bible and in the Talmud. I am a Jew, but I am enthralled by the luminous figure of the Nazarene."[20] Asked whether he accepted Jesus' historical existence, Einstein replied: "Unquestionably. No one can read the Gospels without feeling the actual presence of Jesus. His personality pulsates in every word. No myth is filled with such life."[21]

Jesus' life is so far from myth that his story could be called an "anti-myth." While there may appear to be parallels between the life of Jesus and certain pagan traditions—the virgin birth, the dying and rising god—a closer inspection of these similarities often reveals them to be superficial, asynchronous, or counterfeit.[22] Moreover, Jesus is a real historical person, which differentiates him from some vague mythological character.

Also, simply because two similar rituals coexist does not necessarily mean there is a connection between them. Many religious traditions rely on the cycles of nature and the seasons of the year, and they use common objects such as candles and ceremonial clothing.

As a specific example, we can point to the fact that many pagan religions employ ceremonial washings, but that alone is not evidence of an affiliation between Christian baptism and these cleansings.[23] It would be disingenuous to label a non-Christian ceremonial washing, such as pagan lustrations, as a "baptism," since baptisms are specifically Christian acts that symbolize profound and rich theologies. Insisting they are the same is to fall prey to the fallacy of reductionism.[24]

Nonetheless, both Judaism and Christianity were affected by outside influences. When the Persians ruled Jerusalem (539 BC), Jews began to use Aramaic, the language of the Persian Empire, in place of Hebrew. (Jesus spoke Aramaic.) Not only did language change, but certain Persian philosophies and practices may have influenced the Judaism of this time. The Greeks then conquered Persia with Alexander the Great taking control of Jerusalem in 331 BC. So, once again, Jewish culture had to adapt. It is no co-incidence that the New Testament, written by Jews, was written in Greek.

After the Greeks came the Romans. In 63 BC, Pompey captured Jerusalem. Roman rule then lasted up to and after the time of Jesus. Through all these changes, Jews struggled both externally with the occupying power and internally among themselves about how best to live as God's chosen people amidst foreign rule. Rome, more likely for practical reasons rather than out of beneficence, exempted Jews from the requirement to worship the Roman pagan deities (including the mandate that everyone in the empire must confess Caesar to be a god). The imperial government recognized Judaism's ancient roots and therefore allowed for this and at least one other important accommodation: exempting Jews from serving in the Roman army. Despite these considerations, the Jews of Jesus' time were an oppressed and subjugated people.

To further appreciate the originality of Jesus and his ministry, we must step away from certain modern mindsets. The men and women of New Testament times knew nothing of germs or helio-centricity or other contemporary ideas about science, history, or even self-identity. Since Jesus was truly human, not just play-acting (belief in the latter being the heresy of Docetism), we can say without risk of heresy that God though he was, Jesus was not planing wood in Joseph's carpentry shop, musing about quantum mechanics. He was truly human and truly grew in wisdom (Luke 2:52), and he wrestled with discerning God's will in his life—though he never faltered in his commitment to follow that will.

Christ claimed authority over sin and the interpretation of the Scriptures. Remarkably, he did not qualify his teachings with "God says," but instead assumed an authority reserved for God alone by daring to utter the words: "I say to you." "Now when Jesus had finished saying these things, the crowds were astounded at his teaching, for he taught them as one having authority, and not as their scribes" (Matthew 7:28-29). Jesus' self-proclaimed authority would have made him a blasphemer if he were not God incarnate. Throughout his ministry, Jesus invoked his authority in a manner that no patriarch or prophet would have ever dared. Neither the authoritative Abraham, the emboldened Moses, the chastising Ezekiel, the wise Solomon, nor the visionary Daniel claimed to act out of a self-possessed authority.

The Gospels lay out a narrative that begins with Jesus' miraculous conception. By the power of God, the Holy Spirit, and through the cooperation of Mary, Jesus was born of a virgin. The story of a god–man being born of a virgin is not uncommon in ancient myths and folklore, but Jesus' conception and birth is quite different. In many of those stories, a god, such as Zeus, would come in the form of a man or animal and ravish a young maiden, not always with her consent. Jesus was conceived by the power of the Holy Spirit only after Mary agreed to become his mother. And the miraculous process, correctly called the incarnation but often mistakenly named "the immaculate conception," occurred when God the Holy Spirit came upon Mary and overshadowed her (Luke 1:35). This is not unlike God's life-giving Spirit hovering[25] over the waters at creation (Genesis 1:2).

Jesus' ancestral lineage is recounted in Matthew 1 and Luke 3. These genealogies connect Jesus with important figures in Jewish history, specifically linking him to Israel's history of faith and redemption. Interestingly, not all of those listed were paragons of virtue. In fact, some were notorious sinners, like the Judahite king Manasseh (cf. 2 Kings 21), and the harlot Rahab (cf. Josh 2 and 6). One of the points being made by including these unexpected ancestors in Jesus' lineage is to show how Jesus came to us as a sheer gift of the Father, rather than as a reward earned by the virtue of others.

Among the most prominent of Jesus' ancestors are members of Israel's royal family, including King David (who reigned ca. 1000–961 BC).[26] Jesus' connection to David[27] was either a biological one through matrilineage or a legal one in terms of Jesus' foster-father, Joseph. The Gospels of Matthew and Luke each provide a long genealogy for Jesus, in which we read that Joseph was Jesus' legal father, although he was not his biological father. The point of Jesus not being Joseph's biological son is reinforced by the use of a feminine Greek pronoun for the word, "whom," in the following: "[There was] Joseph the husband of Mary, of whom [*ex hēs*] Jesus was born, who is called the Messiah" (Matthew 1:16).

Jesus was born in first-century Judea (modern Israel) and was given the name Joshua—the Hebrew word is "Yeshua"; in Greek, "Iesous"—which means God saves. Historians tell us that this was a very common name at the time; an everyman sort of name. Like Adam, he represented everyman, so the widespread use of "Joshua" was appropriate. Raised as an observant Jew, he was like us in all ways except sin.

His conception was announced by an angel. After he was born, wise men[28] (Magi) brought him gifts of gold, symbolizing royalty; frankincense, symbolizing divinity; and myrrh, a burial spice, symbolizing mortality.[29] They paid him homage. After Jesus' birth, a nativity scene that portended great events for the babe in the manger, the next event in his life as described in the Gospels was that of Jesus fulfilling the requirements of law. He shed his blood for the first time at his circumcision, and then we read about a scant few of his childhood experiences.

Jesus lived in a Roman-occupied part of the Ancient Near East. He was born Yeshua Bar Yoseph in the village of Bethlehem[30] circa 6–4 BC during the reign of Emperor Caesar Augustus (r. 27 BC–14 AD). He lived the rest of his life under the rule of the Emperor Caesar Tiberius, who died in 37 AD.

Jesus' life so profoundly affected history that we actually measure time by his birth.[31]

> He is the centerpiece of the human race and the leader of the column of progress. I am far within the mark when I say that all the armies that ever marched, and all the navies that ever were built, and all the parliaments that ever sat, all the kings that ever reigned, put together have not affected the life of man upon this earth as powerfully as has that One Solitary Life.[32]

The exact date of Jesus' birth is a matter of some debate. We know that he was not born on December 25 in the year 1 AD. More likely, based on various biblical stories and historical markers, and taking into account that change from the old Julian calendar to the Gregorian calendar, Jesus was born sometime between 6 BC and 4 BC. The New Testament provides events we can date that clearly identify points in Jesus' life and ministry.

Israel was in the period of Second Temple Judaism when Rome (under the reigns of Emperor Caesar Augustus, 27 BC–14 AD, and Emperor Caesar Tiberius, 14–37 AD) controlled the realm of Judea. This rule was localized under the authority of Quirinius, the governor of Syria, and the overlapping jurisdiction of the Jewish "king" Herod the Great,[33] who ruled as a "client king" with limited authority and independence granted to him by Rome.

No other biographical information about his childhood[34] is presented in the Gospels until he is twelve years old. It was then that his family visited Jerusalem for Passover, and on the journey back home, Mary and Joseph realized Jesus had been separated from them. Jesus lived in a communal society, and it would not have been uncommon for Jesus to have traveled with other kin in a large caravan of pilgrims. But, realizing he was not traveling with any other fellow pilgrims, Mary and Joseph were distraught. They returned to Jerusalem to look for Jesus, and after three days of searching finally found him in the temple, amazing those he spoke with. His parents were exasperated, but the boy Jesus was confounded, asking them why they were so surprised to find him in his own father's house, about his father's business.

> The recorded experience itself cannot be explained as an irruption [sic] into his consciousness of his belonging to the Father; as though the child, who had lived hitherto in the manner of any other pious child of his age and environment, now suddenly discovers his relationship to God, being impressed and moved by the Temple and its worship, by the sight of the capital and its history, by the piety of his parents and the great crowds of people; as though he should become aware of himself as God's child and at the same moment become what he knows himself to be. There is not the slightest hint that this is what took place.[35]

There is very little else recorded in the Bible about Jesus' early years. The primary narrative begins approximately 30 years later, when Jesus began a public ministry centered on preaching about his father's kingdom and going about performing miracles. The first three or so decades of Jesus' life were pretty typical for a first-century Jewish man. He worked, prayed, and likely longed for freedom from Roman rule; to reestablish the Davidic monarchy. He grew up in the countryside in the company of farmers, shepherds, and laborers—not amongst the sophisticates of

Jerusalem. However, as a carpenter, Jesus likely went from place to place, meeting people from different classes and backgrounds. He lived amidst powerful religious-political tensions between the Jews and the Romans and among an assortment of diverse Jewish sects—each with their own theology and beliefs about how to be good Jews while living under Roman rule.

By the time of Jesus' birth, the Jewish culture had amassed almost two millennia of history filled with theological insights as well as rich rituals and traditions—not to mention frustration over their oppression (for example, in Egypt) and frequent subjugation to foreign powers (e.g., Assyria; Babylon; Persia; Rome).[36] Jesus would have been familiar with the Jews' sacred writings and with the figures recounted in them, like Abraham, Jacob/Israel, and Moses.

According to the Gospels, around the age of 30, Jesus began a public ministry. He prepared with the profoundly symbolic gesture of being baptized by his cousin, John the Baptist. John protested at first, saying that Jesus should be baptizing him (Matthew 3:14). John knew he was not his cousin's equal and even told his followers: "The one who is more powerful than I is coming after me; I am not worthy to stoop down and untie the thong of his sandals" (Mark 1:7-9).

However, in humility and obedience, John consented to Jesus' wishes and baptized him. Then ". . . a voice from heaven said, 'This is my Son, the Beloved with whom I am well pleased'" (Matthew 3:17). After his baptism, Jesus retreated into the wilderness to fast and pray. The Gospel of Mark tells us that the Holy Spirit actually "drove" him into the wilderness (1:12). Imagine the aridity of the surroundings, the oppressive heat by day, the stabbing cold at night, and the cries of wild animals. During Jesus' time, the skies weren't polluted by light like they are today; the stars would have been clearly visible to the naked eye. The barren desert would have allowed for an unimpeded horizon in all directions, and wandering away from the comfort of a campfire would have been to enter into a vast, terrifying blackness.

Although these sensory experiences brought about clarity of mind, the time Jesus spent in the solitude of the wilderness was not a peaceful isolation where he discovered who he really was; that he always knew. Unlike other great religious figures of history, Jesus never had an epiphany, an "Aha!" moment, when he grasped his uniqueness and accepted his vocation. The Gospels do not present to us a figure who gradually comes to know God or who suddenly has a life-altering conversion experience. Moses was unwillingly called upon by God to lead the Hebrew people. The Buddha found enlightenment in the form of the Four Noble Truths and the Eightfold Path under the Bodhi tree. Mohammed began work on the Quran in 610 AD at the age of 40. Jesus, though, is never converted but always possessed an intimate relationship with God, an untainted desire to do God's will.

Still, Jesus had to decide what form his mission would take. Would he align himself with a particular individual or faction? In Jesus' time, there were numerous different expressions of Judaism. The Gospels most frequently refer to two main Jewish groups: Pharisees and Sadducees. Each claimed to represent authentic Judaism, and membership in any of these groups was exclusive; one could not be a Pharisee and a Sadducee simultaneously. The differences between the Pharisees and Sadducees are complex, but in general, Pharisees accepted oral traditions in addition to the Hebrew Scripture and believed in the resurrection of the dead, while Sadducees did not. There were also Zealots, who chose to fight, often unsuccessfully, as well as a mass of common folk, whose beliefs and loyalties were not always well defined. These people were grounded in Jewish beliefs and practices as set down in the wisdom of the Prophets and the instructions of the Psalms.

Jesus chose neither to be like one of the zealous prophets of the Old Testament nor an ascetic like the Essenes. He rejected the philosophy of the Pharisees,[37] who were anti-Roman to their core, both to the empire's political rule and cultural influences. Jesus also dismissed the ways of the Sadducees, who were religiously conservative but accommodated their Roman overseers and accepted and even welcomed the Hellenization of Jewish culture. Jesus rejected all these tactics and instead set out on his own course of reform—the most original the world has ever seen.

Jesus fasted for 40 days in the wilderness, harkening back to Israel's 40 years of wandering in the desert. There he resided with the wild beasts of the desert and eventually was tempted by Satan himself. Jesus, being untainted by the stain of Original Sin that burdens the rest of us, was subjected to temptations of a more elevated variety. These temptations were subtle, inviting Jesus not to blatantly abandon his ministry but to simply alter it. For example, in tempting Jesus to turn stone to bread, it is as if

Satan were saying, "Go ahead and feed the hungry; it's enough to be a social minister."

Furthermore, Jesus' temptation in the desert was not a *fait accompli*. Although as God incarnate he could have effortlessly banished Satan with a single glance, in his humanity Jesus was subjected to real temptation. The temptations he faced recall the serpent's tempting of Adam and Eve in the garden. But we know that Jesus is the new Adam[38] from the many parallels between his life and the life of Adam, as recorded in Genesis. The Genesis story tells how the serpent offered three temptations to Adam and Eve (3:1-6). First, he tempted them to put God to the test by claiming that the forbidden fruit would not cause death. Second, he argued that the fruit was good to eat, and so Adam and Eve should disobey God. Third, the serpent claimed that if they ate the fruit it would make them like God. They were tempted—not wanting for food or drink or company, surrounded by plenty and peaceful creatures—and they failed. When Jesus was tempted in the desert, the devil tried the same three appeals[39] (Luke 4:1-13). He tried to convince Jesus to turn a stone into bread—just like the fruit, it would be good to eat. He tried to convince Jesus to throw himself off the temple roof, trusting that God wouldn't let him die—just like he tempted Adam and Eve to put God to the test by claiming that eating the fruit would not cause death. He tempted Jesus by offering him all the kingdoms of the world if Jesus would but worship him, so he would become like God—just as he tempted Adam and Eve with the false promise that through disobedience they would become like God.

Jesus, however, was greater than Adam. He overcame his temptation in a fallen world when he was hungry from his fast, thirsty in the dry desert, and alone in the dangerous wilderness, home of wild beasts. Adam gave in to temptation in a world prior to the curse when his belly was full, his thirst was quenched, and he was in the company of Eve in the safe and paradisiacal splendor of Eden, home to tame beasts.

Although the undertaking was immense, Jesus did not display anxiousness or indecisiveness during his ministry. Nor do we have a record of him avoiding anything due to irritation, exhaustion, or sickness. We can infer from the stories in the Gospels that Jesus was often weary but continued to carry out his ministry.

This weariness was undoubtedly both physical and mental. After all, he did experience the full range of human emotions.

In anger, Jesus overturned the tables of the money-changers in his father's temple. In his mercy, he saved a woman caught in adultery. With heartfelt compassion, he multiplied a few loaves of bread and some fish to feed a hungry crowd. In frustration, he chastised his "slow-to-learn" disciples and Apostles. With stinging wit and a sense of humor he mocked the hypocritical temple priests. In sorrow, he wept at the grave of his friend, Lazarus.[40] With unfathomable anguish, he sweat blood in the Garden of Gethsemane. Out of love for us, he bore the weight of the wood of the cross, the intense pain from the scourging that tore into his flesh, and the final agony of crucifixion.

His devotion to his father's plan was unreserved. He was delighted to carry out his task, and he never shirked his calling nor sought to escape his vocation. His only hesitation, if that is even the right word, was that he never demonstrated his full power. His actions were always restrained. He always could have opted to demonstrate additional, grander displays of his supremacy. "We sense the terrifyingly mighty stream of this self-realization flowing unseen beneath all we see and perceive. His words and gestures rise up out of this. It is this from which his actions and his destiny spring. On occasion we are allowed a glimpse into this abyss."[41]

The New Testament book of Philippians addresses the subject by taking up the issue of Jesus' kenosis, his self-emptying. (The word "kenosis" is a transliteration of the Greek word "kénōsis" which means "emptying.") In Philippians 2:6, we read: ". . . who, though he was in the form of God, did not regard equality with God as something to be exploited." Jesus did not use his divinity to his own benefit, but instead, out of a perfect and obedient love for the Father, submitted himself to certain limitations. Jesus did not just choose a life of self-imposed limits but a life of service. Legend tells that upon being cast out from heaven, Lucifer cried out, "I will not serve" (non serviam). He, a mere creature, was unwilling to serve God, which led him into damnable misery. Jesus, the Son of God, declared that he, ". . . came not to be served but to serve" (Matthew 20:28). His abdication to the Father's will led to his infinite glory.

The tension between kenosis and fullness can be reconciled by realizing Jesus that did not divest himself of his power but merely veiled his power; he refused to invoke his power as God except in accordance with the will of his father.

The language of this passage in Philippians, "something to be used to his own advantage," is very telling. Jesus did not impose himself on others but respected the freedom of even the most sinful person. Enforced conformity is antithetical to God's way, which is never compulsory or coercive but gentle and invitational. Most of us can scarcely understand when mortals say no to power, let alone when omnipotence chooses limitation. Consider that Jesus revealed that all power had been given to him both in heaven and on earth (cf. Matthew 28:18). Yet, despite this, Jesus was more likely to be found in the company of prostitutes, tax collectors, and beggars rather than learned priests, wealthy patrons, or powerful dignitaries. With the former, he shared in their plight, respected their autonomy, and served them with love. He loved his neighbor like no man before him, not just with a zeal and intensity that had never been expressed but with a goal that no one dared before to attempt: He came to save the lost.

MAY THE PEACE OF CHRIST DISTURB YOU

Jesus was a charismatic figure who, soon after his ministry began, earned a reputation as a teacher and miracle-worker. He was enlightening but also could be confounding. Even his closest Apostles, Peter, James, and John, were often baffled as they pondered and quarreled amongst themselves about what Jesus meant. Why would Jesus hide truth from the crowd? Jesus spoke in parables not to keep truth from the crowd, but to force them to look for it. His teachings are deep and sublime, and simple expressions of them are not always as useful as parables and stories. Jesus' use of parables made his words more timeless; his use of metaphors provided a new way of understanding mysterious truths. Jesus' parables were unlike any other literary convention of the time. "At its simplest, the parable is a metaphor or simile drawn from nature or common life, arresting the hearer by its vividness or strangeness, and leaving the mind in sufficient doubt to its precise application to tease the mind into active thought."[42]

Both Jesus' words and his very identity puzzled many people, even those who he grew up with. One reason Jesus was so reluctant to identify himself as the Messiah[43] may be that the title of "Messiah" was so laden with political expectation. Jesus was quite apolitical, and yet he would disconcert all the political systems and upset the governing authorities by circumventing their power and attracting massive crowds from among the common folk. Actually, Jesus purposely sought out those most ostracized by society. He welcomed sinners and publicly associated with those who were deemed ritually unclean. This heretofore unseen love and compassion lavished on these outcasts of society made Jesus quite popular among the less-respectable citizenry while simultaneously provoking the ire of the authority figures. While on a visit to Nazareth, Matthew the Evangelist recorded the following episode:

> [Jesus] came to his hometown and began to teach the people in their synagogue, so that they were astounded and said, 'Where did this man get this wisdom and these deeds of power? Is not this the carpenter's son? Is not his mother called Mary? And are not his brothers James and Joseph and Simon and Judas? And are not all his sisters with us? Where then did this man get all this?' And they took offense at him (Matthew 13:54–57).

We tend to sentimentalize his life, but undoubtedly Jesus offended many. He forgave adulterers, though he himself was accused of being a bastard. He exorcised the demon-possessed but was himself accused of being in league with the devil or being the devil in disguise. He healed the mentally ill but was thought to be insane—even by members of his own family. He broke with tradition and befriended the sick, the unclean, and the unworthy. He counted women among his followers, a taboo in his culture during his lifetime. He rejected the "children ought to be seen and not heard" mentality of his peers and welcomed them with love. He ministered to those in league with Rome: tax collectors, soldiers, and collaborators. He preached to the semi-pagan Samaritans, reviled by most in his society. Yet, even his enemies must have come away from encountering him with the impression that he was possessed of some preternatural power.

He loved the fickle crowd. More accurately, he loved individuals who made up the crowd, and he tended to their needs; but, he sought the solace of privacy when he could. He fasted in the wilderness, prayed atop mountains, beseeched God alone in a garden. It is not that Jesus was a loner seeking to escape the wearisome crowd, but "he was reserved towards men, even towards his closest friends. He always remained peculiarly detached. . . . And the only time he did look for comfort of human companionship, he did not find it: 'Could you not watch one hour with me?' (Matt. 26:40)."[44]

Though he likely maintained a house in Capernaum (cf. e.g. Matthew 4:13 and Mark 9:33), Jesus had no permanent home; rather, he relied on others to provide lodging for him as he moved around from place to place. Jesus himself once described his vagabond existence: ". . . 'Foxes have holes, and birds of the air have nests; but the Son of Man has nowhere to lay his head'" (Matthew 8:20).

Jesus had family with whom he could have undoubtedly stayed, but his preaching took him far from home. The Gospels clearly identify some who befriended Jesus (e.g., Lazarus and his kin; Mary of Magdala), with whom, too, he could have presumably lived. Certainly, his followers and admirers contributed to his ministry (cf. Luke 8:1–3). Yet, Jesus and his disciples apparently had very little in terms of material possessions. The Gospels tell us that Jesus borrowed from others: To travel across the Sea of Galilee and to teach the crowds along the shoreline, he seems to have borrowed someone else's boat (cf. Matthew 9:1 and 13:2 paras.); to ride into Jerusalem, he borrowed a colt (cf. Mark 11:1–6). Even his tomb was borrowed (cf. Matthew 27:59)!

Why would the Creator of the Universe deign to be dependent on others, even living to the point of virtual homelessness? The answer is not that he shunned all earthly pleasures. In fact, we see him at parties, feasts, and celebrations.

He was virtually homeless, because by being itinerant he could better facilitate the work of inaugurating God's kingdom. If living in a palace would have been more efficacious for his mission, he undoubtedly would have done so. There are indications in the Bible that Jesus was quite familiar with the behaviors and expected codes of conduct of the well-to-do. In Luke (7:44), we read that Jesus chides his host for not offering him any water to wash his feet before dinner. Jesus thoroughly understood and appreciated social mores and courtesies.

Jesus had many followers, but there were twelve core disciples who traveled with him and learned from him with a depth of understanding. Jesus did not choose his followers haphazardly but prayed through the night before he made his choices (cf. Luke 6:12-16):

> The small inner circle, called 'the Twelve' for short (Luke 8:1, etc.), are especially close to him. We may recall the intimate bond which existed in ancient times between the philosopher or religious teacher and his disciples. The Twelve are always about

him. Wherever he is invited, they go too. He shares food and lodging with them. After he has spoken they cluster around inquiring into the meaning of what he has said. And he tells them expressly that all is made clear to them, whereas the multitude will have to be content with parables (Mat. 13:11 ff.). He sends them out to test their strength; he tells them what to preach, what to take with them, and how to conduct themselves on their journey; and he gives them power to perform signs. On their return he calls for their report, and the whole scene reveals how deeply he was involved in their activities (Mark 6:7-13, 30-1; and cf. Mat. 10-11:6, 25-9; Luke 10:1-22).[45]

Given Jesus' willingness to circumvent the conventions of his time, it may seem curious that he chose twelve disciples who were all Jewish men. After all, women and Gentiles were among the most influential early Christians. Women were instrumental in expanding the primitive Church. As pagan mothers and spouses began to convert to Christianity they brought their new faith into the home.

Certainly, Jesus desired to bring the kingdom of God to all peoples, yet he recognized the biases of the culture in which he lived. Judaism was both patriarchal and exclusivist, and although Jesus was unhesitatingly countercultural regarding other social norms, he chose to work within these limits.

There were also symbolic reasons why Jesus chose twelve Jewish men. Genesis recounts how God entered into a covenant with Abraham, whose grandson Jacob had twelve sons. Those twelve sons inaugurated the twelve tribes of Israel. Clearly, then, the twelve disciples of Christ were representative of the new Israel. This is further evidenced by the fact that Jesus commanded the twelve to minister only to fellow Jews and to avoid proselytizing Gentiles. It was not until after the resurrection that Jesus issued the great commission, commanding his disciples to evangelize all people.

The first named of the twelve is Peter, who, along with James and John formed an inner circle of three close followers, and they were witnesses to Jesus' most significant miracles including healings, exorcisms, raising the dead, and his own transfiguration. These three closest Apostles were not intellectual or influential men but were simple fishermen.

Peter and John are recognized as "uneducated and ordinary men"[46] by the leaders of the Sanhedrin in Acts 4:13. How could Jesus rely on these inexpert followers and their successors to record and spread his message? The Holy Spirit informed and guided them. ". . . We speak of these things in words not taught by human wisdom but taught by the Spirit, interpreting spiritual things to those who are spiritual" (1 Corinthians 2:12).

Unlike other famous teachers of his era, Jesus did not establish a school or academy where seekers could come for instructions. Jesus did not write even a single verse of the New Testament. Most of the material about him was authored by his disciples or other early followers. He traveled among the people, teaching, preaching, and healing—and he instructed his disciples to do the same. Given the limits of the time, Jesus covered an impressive geographic area. At its start, his ministry was localized in and around the region of Galilee, which was part of the tetrarchy of Herod Antipas, who was one of the sons of Herod the Great (ca. 73–4 BC). To the south lay the Roman province of Judea. The Mediterranean Sea lay to the west, and the River Jordan marked its eastern boundary. Across the river was the region of the Decapolis (or "Ten Cities"). To the north was the Province of Syria:

> [Jesus] . . . moved about from place to place. . . . this way of life was not a manifestation of wanderlust. The instructions he gave the disciples he sent out may safely be taken to reflect, with certain limitations, the kind of life he himself led and the experiences he had gained by it . . . He taught wherever opportunity arose—in the synagogues, where, moreover, every adult Jew had a right to speak . . . in the porticos and courts of the temple . . . in market-place [sic] and street . . . in houses . . . at the well where people came to draw water . . . by the seashore . . . on hill-slopes like the one that has given its name to the Sermon on the Mount . . . in the fields . . . in the "wilderness", that is, in uncultivated places . . . and so on.[47]

He often moved about in order to spread his message, but his itinerant style also allowed him to evade those who wished him harm. Jesus had many opponents whose attacks against him came both openly and secretively. Those loyal to Rome saw him as a threat to the empire. The legalistic Pharisees feared he would undermine the established authority of their interpretation of Mosaic law. The list of adversaries also included the Herodians, the Sadducees, etc. These antagonists were not allies with one another, but their shared hostility toward Jesus united them in a common cause.

Despite his numerous enemies, Jesus was ever at peace. We see his serenity displayed again and again throughout the Gospels. Yet, imperturbable peace continually emanated from the very core of his being. This tranquility did not mean, however, that everyone who encountered Jesus was comforted. He healed some and cursed others; he comforted the afflicted and afflicted the comforted. Those who met with Jesus were on unequal footing, for Jesus is always the greater individual. Many who met Jesus went away deeply troubled; "We find that he is spiritually examining us. The roles are reversed between us . . . We study Aristotle and are intellectually edified thereby; we study Jesus and are, in the profoundest way, spiritually disturbed."[48]

Jesus' challenging message brought some to repentance and faith but antagonized many of those in power and those who mistakenly believed themselves to be holy and blameless, and he regularly pointed out their hypocrisy.

> They could, perhaps, tolerate a saintly other-worldly figure, who never sees any harm in anyone, claiming to be God in human form; but for a real man, who seems to be the embodiment of all that is truly human, as well as being quite plainly en rapport with the hidden meaning of life, to claim to be God is a very shocking thing. Eyes that penetrate life's little disguises, a tongue that expresses truth in a peculiarly undiluted and memorable form, a personality without the slightest fear and yet quite obviously filled with the highest kind of love—these are formidable things to meet, even for the best of men.[49]

Jesus regularly warned against certain damnable behaviors, such as hypocrisy, blasphemy, and the love of money. In Matthew 19:25, he says that it is easier for a camel to pass through the eye of a needle than for a rich man to enter the kingdom of God. (Jesus could have been talking about a literal needle or he could have been referencing a narrow-gated entrance within Jerusalem named "The Eye of the Needle Gate" which was a tight fit for a camel.)

Elsewhere we find a rich young man approach Jesus, calling him "good" and asking Jesus what he needs to do to inherit eternal life. (See Matthew 19:16–30.) Some call this the story of the "Apostle Who Said No." The rich man was invited to give away his wealth and to follow Jesus, but he chose to keep his material wealth instead. (It is worth noting that most of us likely have more wealth than the rich young man in this story.)

Jesus did not accuse the rich young man. He did not have to.

> Jesus did not go about constantly denouncing men as 'miserable sinners.' Indeed, there would be no need of that. Insincerity always feels uncomfortable in the presence of sincerity, unreality in the presence of reality and selfishness in the presence of love. We may expect then that in the presence of a morally complete man, a good deal of spiritual discomfort will be spontaneously aroused, sometimes dully and sometimes acutely. Some men would be stimulated to an intense hunger for wholeness, but some would be angered and resentful and determined either to get out of range of the cause of their discomfort or to get rid of it.[50]

In one story, Jesus is confronted by an angry crowd asking him what they should do with a woman they claimed had been caught in the act of committing adultery. His enemies thought they had caught Jesus in a trap. It was the law of Moses that adulterers be stoned to death. Jesus, however, was a preacher of mercy; he told them, "Let he who is without sin cast the first stone." What a clever answer. Who in the crowd would dare to throw a rock at this poor woman? But, what is particularly interesting is that, while Jesus gave the crowd time to respond to what he just said, he wrote in the sand. The story doesn't tell us what Jesus wrote, but some of the early Christians thought he may have been recording the sins of the crowd. (This event may be the fulfillment of an Old Testament prophecy, recorded in the book of Jeremiah 17:11-15.) Regardless of what he wrote, Jesus forgave the woman without condoning her behavior.

The story also tells us something about God's timing. Jesus appeared on the scene just as the woman was about to be stoned. There is a saying that God may not come when you expect, but he's always on time. We see this sense of timing elsewhere. When Jesus' friend Lazarus died, Mary, Lazarus' sister, chided Jesus for being late in coming to see him. She protested that if Jesus had been at Lazarus' side when he was merely ill then he would not have died. But, Jesus did the unexpected and raised him from the dead.[51]

Jesus spent his ministry announcing the kingdom of God (sometimes called by other names like the kingdom of heaven). His mission, through words and examples, was to bear witness to the truth of God's love and mercy. Jesus summarized for us the way in which we ought to participate in the work of the kingdom by repeating the famous Hebrew prayer the Shema:[52] "One of the scribes came near and heard them disputing with one another, and seeing that he answered them well, he asked him, 'Which commandment is the first of all?' Jesus answered, 'The first is, "Hear, O Israel: the Lord our God, the Lord is one; you shall love the Lord your God with all your heart, and with all your soul, and with all your mind, and with all your strength." The second is this, "You shall love your neighbor as yourself." There is no other commandment greater than these.' Then the scribe said to him, 'You are right, Teacher; you have truly said that "he is one, and besides him there is no other"; and "to love him with all the heart, and with all the understanding, and with all the strength," and "to love one's neighbor as oneself,"—this is much more important than all whole burnt offerings and sacrifices.' When Jesus saw that he answered wisely, he said to him, 'You are not far from the kingdom of God.' After that no one dared to ask him any question" (Mark 12:28-34).

We are told that the kingdom of God is within us (Luke 17:21), but it is also beyond us; that the kingdom of heaven is near (Matthew 4:17), but it is also distant; that we should pray for the kingdom to come (Matthew 6:9-13), and that it will be manifest at some future date (Matthew 13:40-43), but that it is here already in some ways. These references suggest a rich and complex reality. The kingdom is both a realm and state of being.

Jesus taught us to pray the Our Father,[53] but God is not our father in the same way he is Jesus'. (After teaching this prayer to his disciples, there is no record of Jesus praying the Our Father, also known as the Lord's prayer, alone or with others. He could not have sincerely uttered the words "forgive us our trespasses," for he was without fault. Moreover, his relationship to the Father was qualitatively different than ours.)

PASSION

No death in all of history has been more studied and meditated upon than Jesus Christ's. As the events of his Passion unfolded, there was no way for the witnesses to comprehend the central importance of what was transpiring. The final hours of his life have been the subject of innumerable narratives, theological reflections, personal devotions, artistic inspirations and prayerful meditations. Each of the four Gospels devotes more attention to Jesus' Passion than to any other topic in his life.

Jesus' life, the life of every Jewish person at the time, was steeped in religious ceremony and significance. During the first century, three of the primary foci for most of Jesus' contemporaries were the temple, the Messianic expectation of the people, and the Torah—especially the central story of God, through Moses, leading his chosen people out of bondage. At Passover, Jews sing a song called "Dayenu," which means, "It would have been enough." It recounts the many blessings God showered on his people:

> If God had only allowed us to leave Egypt, it would have been enough.
> If God had only given us the Sabbath, it would have been enough.
> If God had only given us Torah, it would have been enough.

It would have been enough for Jesus to simply walk among us, but, following his father's example, Jesus gave more than what could have possibly been expected. A single sigh from his holy lips would have been of enough value to appease his father and make reparations for an infinite number of sins. But, he chose to do the most he could do by utterly giving of himself. Father John Hardon explains:

> . . . Christ chose to save the human race by enduring poverty, rejection, opposition, and finally, the disgrace of crucifixion although, absolutely speaking, the Redemption might have been accomplished without pain. That Christ preferred this method of saving the world shows his wisdom in proving how much he loves us and how much we mean to him; it also invites us to follow his example and prove our love for him in return.[54]

The Gospels differ a bit on the chronology, but the story of Jesus' bold entry into the temple of Jerusalem to clear out the merchants and money changers appears in all four. There is deep symbolism to Jesus' action at the temple, but he also enacted a very practical reform.[55] The temple had become a very lucrative endeavor for certain high-ranking Jewish officials, and Jesus' cleansing disrupted their business. It is no coincidence that soon after this event Jesus was arrested and brought to trial.[56]

The temple[57] was central to the lives of all practicing Jews and to the economy of the city of Jerusalem. Some scholars estimate that 99 percent of the total economy of Jerusalem was tied to the temple sacrifices. A number of festivals are scattered throughout the Jewish calendar. Many of these holy days would have involved the sacrifice of an animal. The copious flow of blood, the massive quantity of roasted animal flesh, fragrant clouds of incense, and the profusion of coins were impressive. The requirements for an acceptable sacrifice were precise in terms of the animals used (e.g. lambs) and the coins offered (e.g. the half-shekel).

The catalyst, the temple cleansing, was more than just an act of purification; it was a challenge to the Jewish hierarchy—or, perhaps, a signal to Roman authorities of more trouble to come. Jesus' repeated allusions to the kingdom of God would alarm some in the community. After all, a new kingdom necessarily implies a new sovereign. This threat was formidably met, and decisive action was taken.

The short period of time between the cleansing of the temple and Jesus' death sentence is packed full of events with weighty theological significance. After the temple cleansing, Jesus rode into Jerusalem and the crowds placed their cloaks and palm fronds[58] on the ground before him and called out praises to him. This harkens back to the time the revolutionary Maccabeus brought hopes of freedom to Jerusalem and was greeted "with a chorus of praise and the waving of palm branches" (1 Maccabees 13:51). And how did Jesus respond to the shouts of "Hosanna" and the crowd greeting him like a political revolutionary? He wept (Luke 19:41) because the crowd still did not comprehend his mission.

Knowing that his life was nearly at an end, Jesus took the opportunity to share a final meal with his disciples. He washed the feet of his followers and then offered a prayer of thanksgiving to his father. (In the high-priestly prayer found in the Gospel of John, Jesus not only thanks the Father but restates his complete and utter dependence on him.) Then, after singing Hallel psalms, Jesus shared a Passover meal in the upper room with his followers, where he announced that he would be giving his life for many. (To the Semitic listener, the word "many" could be substituted for the word "all.") That meal marked the establishment of the sacrament of the Eucharist[59] and the establishment of holy orders.[60] Jesus instructed his followers to offer this meal in remembrance of him (Luke 22:19). The Greek word used for "remembrance" is *"anamnesis,"* a term that expresses not just remembering but participation.

This Passover meal is packed with theological symbolism. The festival of holy days,[61] Passover, and the feast of Unleavened Bread, recounts how God freed the Israelites from Egyptian slavery. This holiday is at the very center of Jewish identity and belief. Passover has been celebrated for thousands of years and is the oldest continuously observed holiday in all of history.

Though the events of Passover occurred twelve-to-fourteen centuries before the birth of Jesus, both he and his followers would have been able to relate to the oppression the Jews suffered under the Egyptians because they suffered similarly under Roman rule. The Passover story foreshadows and typifies Jesus' own story in many ways. Saint Paul referred to Jesus as "our Passover Lamb" (1 Corinthians 5:7), and the Gospel of John provides a rich comparison.

> There's no mistaking the fact that St. John, the beloved disciple, understood our Lord's sacrifice as the culmination, the fulfillment of the Old Testament Passover. For instance, why is it that Jesus happened to be wearing a seamless linen garment at the cross, when just coincidentally that's what the priest was legislated to wear when he sacrificed the Passover? Here is the true priest, as well as the true victim. And when he was crucified, unlike the two thieves whose legs had to be broken to expedite death, his bones were not broken. Why? To fulfill the scripture where it says, 'None of his bones shall be broken.' What's that talking about where it says, 'None of his bones shall be broken'? One of the things is that if you took a lamb to sacrifice for the Passover and you discovered that it had a broken bone, you had to throw him out and get another one. The only fit sacrifice was a lamb without broken bones.[62]

This is only a sampling of the connections between Christ and the Passover. Consider how at the Seder feast, matzo (unleavened bread) is broken, wrapped in cloth, and then hidden. Later, it is returned to the meal. Jesus, the bread of life, broken in death, was hidden in a tomb but later revealed in the resurrection. Here are a few other striking similarities:

1. The Passover meal must consist of a lamb or possibly a goat (Exodus 12:5). Jesus is referred as the Lamb of God (John 1:29).

2. The lamb used at the Passover meal must be an unblemished male (Exodus 12:5). It was examined to ensure its worthiness. Jesus is described in the New Testament as an unblemished lamb (1 Peter 1:18-19). He was examined at trial and found innocent by Pontius Pilate.

3. The lamb for the Passover meal was picked out four days before being slaughtered on the fifth day (Exodus 12:3-6). The lambs were brought to Jerusalem on the day Christians refer to as Palm Sunday. Jesus arrived in Jerusalem on Palm Sunday, on the tenth of Nisan, four days before his crucifixion; he was executed on the fifth day (John 12:12).

4. At three o'clock p.m. (the ninth hour of the day by Jewish reckoning), the Shofar (a ram's horn) is blown to signify the death of the Paschal lamb (Leviticus 23:5). Jesus died at three o'clock p.m. (Matthew 27:45).

5. The Passover lamb was killed without any of its bones being broken (Exodus 12:46). It was consumed the same day it was killed. When Jesus was tortured and crucified, his bones were not broken (John 12:33). Jesus offered his flesh in the Eucharist within 24 hours of being killed (John 6:52-55).

7. Passover commemorates God freeing his people from Egyptian slavery. The blood of the lamb on the wood saved God's people from death (Exodus 12:23). Jesus' sacrifice frees us from the slavery of sin. The blood of Jesus on the wood of the cross saves God's people from death (1 John 1:7).

8. The Passover lamb's blood was brushed on the doorway with a hyssop branch (Exodus 12:22). Jesus drank wine from a sponge, raised to his lips on a hyssop branch (John 19:29). At the Last Supper, Jesus consecrated the wine into his blood, further establishing the blood-wine connection here.

Just before dying on the cross, Jesus spoke the words "It is finished" (John 19:30). The phrase is translated from a single Greek word "*tetelestai*" and echoes the work of God as recorded in

Genesis. God spoke these words on the sixth day of creation—the first Friday; Jesus spoke them on the sixth day of the week—Good Friday—from the cross, to inaugurate the new creation.

A deeper look into the etymology of "tetelestai" reveals that the term was written on receipts to indicate that a debt had been paid in full. Oftentimes, the word is associated with a document nailed to the cell door in a debtor's prison. Those who were incarcerated for an inability to pay were locked away with a debt notice attached to their jail door. If someone paid their debt, the notice would be marked with the word "tetelestai." The analogy here is clear. We all had a debt we could not pay, and Jesus used this word to denote that payment had been made on our behalf.

The Gospel of John is quite astute in its presentation of Jesus in connection with Judaism. For instance, during Chanukah, Festival of Lights, Jesus declared himself to be the light of the world (John 8:12). Elsewhere, we find John's Gospel paralleling Jesus' final hours with the Jewish religious services. In the Jewish synagogues the services followed a lectionary, or sequence of passages, which were read at appointed times. By comparing John's Gospel with that lectionary, we find numerous similarities. John is telling us that Jesus was intimately connected to and refashioning Israel.

> So, in his washing of the disciples' feet, Jesus echoes the Synagogue Lections for Passover from the Book of Numbers in which the Israelites are told to sprinkle the Levites, the sacerdotal class, with water, 'that they may do the service of the Lord'. (Numbers 8:1 ff.)
>
> Such Scriptural echoes may be discovered in all the final chapters of the gospel. The readings for the Jewish New Year, for example, conclude with Deuteronomy 2:13: 'Now then, arise'; and Exodus 33:1: 'Depart—go up hence!' In the middle of his last great discourse, the Fourth Gospel Jesus makes the contextually baffling comment, 'Arise, let us go hence'. If we see that he has here come to the end of his 'New Year discourse', then these words of Jesus make sense. In ordinary narrative terms, they are incomprehensible, since the disciples do not, at this juncture, arise or go hence. Similarly, in the readings for Tebeth, we find I Kings 2:37: "On the day thou passest over the brook Kidron, know thou for certain that thou shalt surely die." In the apparently 'straight' narrative of John 18:1, we read "When Jesus had

spoken these words, he went forth with his disciples over the brook Kidron."[63]

The imagery continues as we read on that Jesus went to the Mount of Olives and off to the Garden of Gethsemane ("Gethsemane" in Hebrew: "oil press") to pray. Adam and Eve fell into sin in a garden, and now Jesus, the new Adam, would begin our redemption in a garden. Jesus was tempted by Satan in the desert; and in the Garden of Gethsemane, temptation of a different sort plagued him. Earlier that same night, per John 14:30, Jesus declared, "I will not say much more to you, for the prince of this world is coming. He has no hold over me." The devil did not come in person as he did in the desert. This is an important point.[64]

We are told that it is night. This darkness is rich with symbolism. Jesus brought with him his three closest followers, the inner circle of his Apostles—Peter, James, and John—but while he agonized in prayer, time and again, they fell asleep (Matthew 26:40).[65] Jesus' struggle was not that of two opposing wills; a meek Messiah crushed by the incomprehensible demands of his bloodthirsty and justice-obsessed father. The will of the Father is identical to the will of the Son. Jesus was simultaneously perfectly obedient and perfectly free. Jesus totally abandoned himself to the providence of his father. He knew the Father had a plan and a purpose. Both the Father and Son desire to show mercy to the world; to express the unfathomable, divine love that God has for his creation.

With his Passion forthcoming, Jesus knew what he was about to do was incomprehensible. He would take upon himself the burden of the entire world's sin, not simply as a token gesture but as an investiture. Jesus did not merely observe these horrors, but, accepting the full weight of their disgrace, he would nonetheless present himself to God, seeking mercy on behalf of all before his infinitely holy and righteous father. This undertaking was so agonizing that (according to the Gospel of Luke, written by a physician) Jesus sweat drops of blood.[66]

At one point during the night, Judas came to him and betrayed him with a kiss. Judas was in charge of the community's money because he was so trusted by Jesus and the others, and so his treachery was all the more bitter.

During this terrible despondency Jesus was eventually arrested. His sleepy friends made ready to fight the soldiers off with swords, but in Matthew 26:53, Jesus announced that if he so chose he could call upon his father to send twelve legions of angels to come to his aid in that garden. A Roman legion was comprised of as many as six thousand soldiers, so seventy-two thousand angels would have been an imposing retinue.

Instead of making such an appeal, Jesus allowed himself to be arrested and taken into custody. Picture this scene: Jesus is facing a group of soldiers that came to bind him. Jesus asked who they wanted, and the soldiers said they were looking for Jesus of Nazareth. Then Jesus responded, "I am he." (See John 18:2-6.)

These men were armed, trained soldiers; yet, when Jesus spoke the words

> "I am he," they drew back and fell. The words "I Am"[67] recall God's name, which was revealed by God to Moses[68] centuries earlier: "God said to Moses, 'I AM WHO I AM.' He said further, 'Thus you shall say to the Israelites, 'I AM has sent me to you.' God also said to Moses, 'Thus you shall say to the Israelites, "The LORD the God of your ancestors, the God of Abraham, the God of Isaac, and the God of Jacob, has sent me to you":
> This is my name forever,
> and this my title for all generations.'" (Exodus 3:14-15)

So, Jesus revealed to the soldiers that he is the great I Am—and at that utterance of the sacred tetragrammaton they fell back. The shocked soldiers composed themselves, and eventually Jesus was arrested and subjected to a series of sham trials with the testimony of perjurers; he, the Judge of the entire world, would be falsely accused and judged. A careful reading of the Gospel accounts reveals that Jesus was tried six times, suggesting that a sentence of execution was not easily won even by the lax standards that applied at the time.

1. Before Annas, Caiaphas' father-in-law (John 18:12-24)
2. Before Caiaphas, in Caiaphas' home (John 18:19-24)
3. Before the Sanhedrin—a court of ecclesial jurisdiction (Matthew 26:57)
4. Before Pontius Pilate (John 18:23; Luke 23:6-12)
5. Before Herod (Luke 23:7)
6. Before Pontius Pilate yet again (Luke 23:11-12), where he was sentenced to death.

Under Roman law, jurisdiction over capital cases rested solely in the hands of Roman officials. Although we read in the Gospel that John the Baptist was beheaded by King Herod, and the angry crowd was ready to stone the adulteress and even tried to push Jesus off a cliff, these are rouge actions outside the law of Rome (though Herod may have had limited power to murder John).

What went through the mind of Jesus as he appeared before Caiaphas the high priest, along with members of the supreme council of the Sanhedrin? These were the elders and scribes who longed for the Messiah, yet they accused Jesus of blasphemy.

Herod seemed unwilling to involve himself too deeply in the trial, and so, in an act of cowardice, he passed the case to Pilate, who had no love for the Jews he governed. As a political calculation, Pilate grudgingly issued the order to have Jesus, a purported king, crucified, despite the fact Pilate publicly proclaimed Jesus to be without fault (Luke 23:4).

Jesus was not merely executed but was brutalized and humiliated. First, he was stripped[69] down and secured to a whipping post. Then a soldier, or perhaps more than one, flogged him with a whip with sharp, flesh-piercing shards attached to the end. After this agonizing whipping, which would have left his body torn and his flesh shredded, Jesus was crowned with a circlet of thorns. He was then made to carry his own cross, or the crossbeam to which his hands would be nailed. The weight of this wood could easily exceed one hundred pounds.

And all this ignominy was prior to the crucifixion itself, where Jesus also underwent a spiritual misery no mortal can fathom. Jesus, nailed to that tree, hearing the jeers and insults of each passerby, had yet another suffering added to his misery as he had to see the pain of his beloved mother as she stood at the foot of the cross, enduring anguish beyond what any mother can bear. As mystic Simone Weil pointed out, "The cross is infinitely more than martyrdom. It is the most purely bitter suffering . . ."[70]

Jesus hung in agony for possibly six or more hours. There he faced not only the worst cruelty Rome had to offer but he had faced that ancient adversary who has plagued humanity since the beginning:

> . . . the real enemy, to be met head-on by the power and love of God, was the anti-creation power, the power of death and destruction, the force of accusation, the Accuser who lays a

charge against the whole human race and the world itself that all are corrupt and decaying, that all humans have contributed to this by their own idolatry and sin. The terrible thing is that this charge is true. . . . Accusations come rushing together from all sides, as the leaders accuse Jesus before Pilate; and Pilate finally does what all the accusations throughout the gospel have been demanding and has him crucified. Jesus, in other words, has taken the accusations that were outstanding against the world and against the whole human race and has borne them in himself.[71]

There are many ironies in the story of Jesus' crucifixion. That he, the living water, thirsts; that he, the truth and the life, was convicted on lies and sentenced to death—these are all cruel ironies.[72] Another is that a murderer named Barabbas, who was scheduled to be executed with Jesus, was set free.[73] The same crowd, made up of at least some of the people who just days before praised him as Messiah and sang "Hosanna" in exaltation of him, chose to save the murdering rebel Barabbas[74] and instead execute the Lord of life.

The crowd was given the option to release one man and preferred Barabbas to Jesus. On the face of it, this seems like a mere injustice: Barabbas was guilty of his accused crime but went free; Jesus was innocent and was executed. At one level, we can appreciate the symbolism of Jesus dying and Barabbas[75] going free; it is the story of our own individual salvation, of Jesus dying in our place.

I'm confident that there were voices in the crowd that called out for Jesus to be freed; perhaps his mother or some of his followers called out. But, the louder voices crying out for his execution drowned out these pleas.

The story of Jesus' crucifixion is recounted in all four Gospels: Matthew, Mark, Luke, and John. Jesus was taken outside the city limits of Jerusalem. The Jewish practice to atone for sin was to sacrifice an unblemished lamb but to first symbolically place the sins of the people on a goat (called the scapegoat) and set it free in the wilderness outside of Jerusalem. Jesus was both the unblemished sacrificial lamb[76] and the scapegoat who bore the sins of the people, and he was cast out into the wilderness.

He never lost his compassion, even in his own misery. But, on the way to his crucifixion Jesus encountered women[77] who were crying and wailing. One would expect a man in such suffering as his to pass by the cacophony of the crowd, or to despise every one of them whom he looked upon, but in tender warning he turned to them saying, "Daughters of Jerusalem, do not weep for me, but weep for yourselves and for your children" (Luke 23:28).

His care for others remained prominent even during his own torment. On the cross he saw his mother. What unspoken emotion passed between their gazes? He also saw John, his beloved disciple. Dying on the cross, Jesus was concerned with who would care for Mary after he was gone, Joseph likely having long since died. So, he commended Mary to the care of John (John 19:26-27).

Yet another example of Jesus' kindness was to the good thief (whom tradition names Dismas): "Truly I tell you, today you will be with me in Paradise" (Luke 23:43).

Passersby taunted him, saying, "If you are the Son of God, come down from the cross," (Matthew 27:40) an echo of the temptation with which Satan tempted Jesus in the desert (to invoke divine prerogatives).

Jesus was not only deluged by a flood of visible hate, but he suffered unseen miseries as he bore the sins of the world upon himself—each of which he could identify specifically. We all have experienced physical and mental anguish, but the kind of intense suffering Jesus went through is beyond conception. His suffering was different from ours, not just in degree, but in type: Jesus utterly emptied himself on the cross. "Jesus, the Crucified, endures our inner darkness and estrangement from God, and he does so in our place. It is all the more painful for him, the less he has merited it . . . Indeed, he suffers more deeply than an ordinary man is capable of suffering, even were he condemned and rejected by God, because only the incarnate Son knows who the Father really is and what it means to be deprived of him, to have lost him (to all appearances) forever."[78]

Imagine the full range of human emotions that Jesus felt at being betrayed by Judas; denied by Peter; abandoned by his disciples; mocked by the authorities; scorned by the crowds; and heartbroken at the suffering of his beloved mother, who witnessed this cruelty. He was beaten, crowned with piercing thorns (see in this crown a reference to the curse in Genesis, where the land would be entangled with thorns), and nailed to the wood of a cross (symbolic in that Adam and Eve ate the fruit of the forbid-den tree and Jesus brought salvation through a tree.)

The place where Jesus was executed is called "Golgotha" in Aramaic and means "the place of the skull." The hill where Jesus was crucified may have been shaped like a skull, or there were so many executions there that many skulls may have been strewn about the area. Some scholars posit that Golgotha was once a quarry that was no longer being used by the time of Jesus' cruci-fixion. Psalm 118:22, written centuries before the birth of Jesus, reads "The stone that the builders rejected has become the chief cornerstone." There is a metaphorical meaning to this Messianic prophecy, but, if in fact Golgotha was an abandoned quarry, it is likely that Jesus' cross was anchored into a stone that was rejected by the masons, so there may be a literal fulfillment of this prophecy too.

Jesus' pain on the cross is indescribable. The word "excruci-ating" comes from the Latin root for "crucify." Not only did he suf-fer excruciating physical pain, but Scripture hints at and mystics corroborate that his mental and spiritual torment were inconceiv-able. Theologians refer to Jesus' Cry of Dereliction. The Gospels of Matthew and Mark are almost identical in these details: "At three o'clock Jesus cried out with a loud voice, '*Eloi, Eloi, lema sabach-thani?*' which means, 'My God, my God, why have you forsaken me?'" Was Jesus in despair? Did God disconnect from God in an incomprehensible (and incidentally ontologically impossible) separation? This Cry of Dereliction is actually a quote used by Jesus and taken directly from Psalm 22:1-2.

Saint Faustina Kowalska's description of her own soul's an-guish gives us an inadequate glimpse into Jesus' experience.

> God has hidden himself from it, and it can find no consolation in creatures, nor can any of these creatures find a way of consoling it. . . . The soul is drawn to God, but feels repulsed. All other sufferings and tortures in the world are as nothing compared with this sensation into which it has been plunged; namely, that of being rejected by God. . . . This thought is torture beyond all description. . . . If God wishes to keep the soul in such darkness, no one will be able to give it light. It experiences rejection by God in a vivid and terrifying manner. From its heart burst forth pain-ful moans, so painful that no priest will comprehend it, unless

he himself has been through these trials. . . . The ordeal reaches its climax. The soul no longer looks for help anywhere. It shrinks into itself and loses sight of everything; it is as though it has accepted the torture of being abandoned. This is a moment for which I have no words. This is the agony of the soul.[79]

Jesus never abandoned his perfect trust and complete submission to the will of his father, and in Luke's Gospel we read a final confident utterance of Jesus commending his spirit into his father's hands. Nonetheless,

> . . . Jesus feels abandoned by the Father, He knows, however that that is not really so. He Himself said: 'I and the Father are one.' (Jn 10:30), and speaking of His future Passion He said: 'I am not alone, for the Father is with me' (Jn 16:32). Dominant in His mind Jesus has the clear vision of God and the certainty of His union with the Father. But in the sphere bordering on the senses, and therefore more subject to the impressions, emotions, and influences of the internal and external experiences of pain, Jesus' human soul is reduced to a wasteland, and He no longer feels the presence of the Father.[80]

After hours of agony, Jesus died on the cross. We know he really died, because his executioners were Romans, and they were experts at killing. A soldier risked his own life if he were given an order to execute a criminal and failed to do so. "Now when the centurion, who stood facing him, saw that in this way he breathed his last, he said, 'Truly this man was God's Son!'" (Mark 15:39).

According to the Gospel accounts, Pilate had ordered those being crucified to have their legs broken to quicken their deaths. However, when the time came to break Jesus' legs the soldiers saw he was already dead. To ensure this, a soldier pierced Jesus' chest with a spear, and from that post-mortem wound flowed blood and water.

> This blood and water wash human sin and create the New Testament Church, with its grace-bestowing mysterious gifts: baptismal water and Eucharistic blood. Out of the side of the old Adam was created woman, who tempted him to fall. But, the wound delivered to humankind from Adam's side is healed by the spear wound in Jesus' side. The blood and water that flowed into the

world—abide in the world. They sanctify this world as the pledge of its future transfiguration.[81]

The momentousness of Jesus' death was marked by wondrous signs both in the heavens and on earth; the earth quaked, stones broke, and an eclipse darkened the sky. Perhaps most significantly, the Gospels record that upon Jesus' death, "the curtain of the temple was torn in two, from the top to the bottom" (Mark 15:38). This is the great curtain that separated the Holy of Holies from the rest of the Jewish temple. It hung from the ceiling to the floor, and scholars estimate that it was approximately three feet thick. Behind this curtain sat the Ark of the Covenant—a holy vessel, a representation of God on earth. Ordinarily, no one was allowed to enter this special section of the temple. Only once a year the high priest of the Levitical priesthood would appear before the ark to make a sacrifice to God. This priest wore bells on his garments and he was tied with a rope. If God disapproved of his offering and he were struck dead, the bells would stop ringing and he could be pulled out by the rope, as no one else would dare enter the Holy of Holies. The rending of this curtain and the fracture of the temple at the moment of Jesus' death represents the demolition of the wall between humans and God; the replacement of the Levitical priesthood with Christ's. From that moment on, God's Holy Spirit would reside in the new temple—the hearts of all the faithful.

In this final torment, his kenosis, Jesus did once and for all what the Jewish priests used to repeatedly perform.

> It was 'for us' that the Son came down from heaven, 'for us' that he was crucified, died and was buried. And this means not only 'for our benefit' but also 'in our place,' taking over what was our due. If this is watered down, the fundamental tenet of the New Testament disappears and it looks as if God is always reconciled, sin is always forgiven and overcome, irrespective of Christ's self-surrender, then the Cross becomes merely a particularly eloquent symbol of God's unchanging kindness, only a symbol, indicating something but not effecting anything. . . . Without noticing it, we have become like the men of the Enlightenment aware of God's kindly disposition but refusing to countenance his anger over sin, of which Scripture speaks so insistently, because it does not fit in with our enlightened concept

of God, in the end we make it all into an anemic, transparent philosophy. . . . And the high price becomes a cheap price, costly grace becomes cheap grace.[82]

The cross was such a disgraceful symbol that the early church used a fish[83] as a sign for Christianity. As time passed, however, the cross was embraced as the quintessential emblem of Christian identity. What once was reprehensible became the true sign of hope. The cross, once reserved for the worst of criminals, turned into a symbol used by emperors and kings.

The only possible way such a sacrifice could be salvific would be if the one doing the saving has no need of salvation himself. Peace and salvation come through Jesus' blood. In Genesis, Abel's blood "cried out for vengeance" (4:10), but Jesus' blood cries out for mercy.

While the deplorable tradition of blaming the Jews for Christ's execution became a standard explanation that arose in the early Church, the learned leadership of early Christianity was more concerned with understanding the theological implications of the crucifixion than they were with legal questions surrounding it.

Saint Catherine of Siena observed that "nails were not enough to hold God-and-man nailed and fastened on the Cross, had not love held Him there."[84] Salvador Dali communicated the same truth with his painting, *The Crucifixion*, which portrays Jesus on the cross, only there are no nails in his hands or feet. Jesus is suspended instead by his own loving choice. "God loves each of us as if there were only one of us."[85]

Such suffering could bring any person to a state of despair or fury, but Jesus willingly plunged into an ocean of suffering so that we could be submerged in the flood of God's grace. Jesus not only offers a sacrifice like the high priests of the temple did, he is himself both the high priest and the sacrifice. There are theologies that purport to explain Jesus' sacrifice in terms of appeasement of an angry God. The best of such theological explanations focus on God's absolute holiness. The worst of these approaches merely echo the wicked practice of human-sacrifice-to-appease-the-gods, perpetrated by some pagan cultures.

The mystery of Jesus' atoning work on the cross does not end with his death. The limitlessness of his love has inspired speculation that Jesus' salvific work continued beyond his death. In the book of 1 Peter, we find two passages that Jesus' mission extended to those who have previously died (1 Peter 3:19–20 and 1 Peter 4:6). These passages, when read in connection with other verses from both the Old and New Testaments, gave rise to the teaching that Jesus went to preach to the dead. Up to the time of Jesus' death, the Scriptures refer to various realms for the dead including Sheol and Abraham's Bosom. However, the term for Jesus' descent was previously known as the "Harrowing of Hell." Both the Apostles' Creed and the Athanasian Creed reference this event.

The passages in Peter likely refer to Jesus' entry into the realm inhabited by the righteous dead, announcing the good news that the gates of heaven have been opened through his work. Theologians differ as to what exactly the Bible refers to by noting that Jesus descended to the dead. However, some argue Jesus' descent was even more profound and his sufferings continued in the realm of the dead. There, he endured the absence of the Father, with whom he previously reigned in infinite bliss as the pre-Incarnate Word.

> His descent into the underworld is part of this sign: he does not just pass fleetingly through these areas unknown to us; he stays there for three days. He therefore takes the entire accumulation of his strength into the sacrifice that led to his death, beyond death and into the underworld . . . the world that he brought with him is his heavenly world, the world of the Father and of the Spirit, a world that infinitely surpasses our own.[86]

THE RESURRECTION EVENT AND BEYOND

The resurrection is the most unprecedented event ever known in recorded history.[87] Here, we encounter God's ultimate victory over death and sin. It is, for me, easy to imagine Jesus on Easter morning, stepping out of his tomb, (probably hewn out of rock) after experiencing the torment of his Passion, all the evil that could be poured out upon him, and essentially announcing, "Is that all you got?" The resurrection of Jesus Christ is the fulcrum of all of time.

There were other would-be messiahs, some of whom we know, some who are lost to history, but Jesus' story has withstood the test of time. Why? What power drew thousands of early followers? What message transformed men like Peter and Paul and millions of others throughout the centuries? Saint Paul declared, ". . . if Christ has not been raised, then your faith is useless . . ." (1 Corinthians 15:17).

Jesus often referred to his own death by linking it to his resurrection.[88] When Jesus stood trial before the high priest he remained silent in the face of false accusations. "But Jesus was silent. Then the high priest said to him, 'I put you under oath before the living God, tell us if you are the Messiah, the Son of God'" (Matthew 26:63). Then, Jesus was taken to be questioned by Governor Pontius Pilate; "But when he was accused by the chief priests and elders, he did not answer. Then Pilate said to him, 'Do you not hear how many accusations they make against you?' But he gave him no answer, not even to a single charge, so that the governor was greatly amazed" (Matthew 27:12-14). Jesus was so unified with the will of his father that no promise or threat could possibly distract him. Christ's silence was only temporary. His resurrection was the ultimate answer to their probing questions.

While other religions have taught there is a life after death, the good news of Jesus' resurrection is that we are not called to some shadowy existence in the hereafter. Jesus is the only figure in history to make the credible claim of having not just returned from the dead, but of actually conquering death and resurrecting to new life. He did not just rise from the dead; he is the source of resurrection life itself. Jesus said to Martha, Lazarus' sister: "I am the resurrection and the life. Those who believe in me, even though they die, will live" (John 11:25).

The Gospel of John tells us that the Son of God the Word became flesh (John 1:14). The resurrection confirms that the Word did not become flesh temporarily but eternally. The resurrection tells that we are not merely spiritually imperishable but that our bodies and our souls unite again to live forevermore.

Throughout his ministry, Jesus possessed the power over life, all life, including his own. "No one takes it from me, but I lay it down of my own accord. I have power to lay it down, and I have power to take it up again. I have received this command from my Father" (John 10:18). So, his resurrection was not the reward of a life well lived but the expression of a power that was always present in himself that so often lay hidden—though not dormant—below the surface of his actions. That first Easter morning gloriously revealed this power, which was ever present in him and which, when unleashed, no earthy force could possibly thwart.

In the Gospel of John (20:15), we learn some details about Jesus' resurrection. Jesus' disciple, Mary, came to his tomb and saw that it was empty. She began to cry and turned to talk with a man whom she mistook as a gardener. He was not a gardener but was the resurrected Jesus. Earlier, John tells the reader that Jesus' tomb was located in a garden—not a mere cemetery, but a garden. The parallels are clear: the garden, with Jesus as gardener, refers to Genesis, to Adam in the garden. John is cluing us in to a multi-layered truth about Jesus' resurrection undoing the curse brought on by Adam. Jesus is renewing all of creation. He is the foremost gardener. As God walked with Adam and Eve in the Garden of Eden, he now returns to walk again in the garden of the new creation.

There is a reason why Easter, not Christmas, is the holiest day of the Christian calendar. Jesus' resurrection is not just the story of Jesus coming back to life. If Jesus merely came back to life, he could die again. Resurrection is not mere resuscitation or coming back from the dead temporarily, only to die yet again at a later date. He was still the same man. He looked much the same. He still carried the wounds of his crucifixion. He still ate with his followers. But, he passed through locked doors. He entered into a new and radically different existence. Jesus won't ever die again because to be resurrected means to be transformed—not merely brought back to the old life but renewed in a way that restores and exceeds the original human nature prior to the fall. More than that, the resurrection is the inauguration of the new creation. The gates of heaven are now open; the kingdom of God is now launched. After his resurrection there is not even a hint that he regretted his sacrifice.

The Gospel accounts of Jesus' resurrection differ in some details, but the fact that women are listed as the first witnesses to Jesus' resurrection is incredible given that they were not even allowed to testify in a Jewish court during this time period. Any person wishing to perpetrate a hoax would surely have been cleverer. The four Gospels agree Jesus rose from the dead, but they differ in certain key details. If the story were made up it would have been an easy task to simply edit the texts so that all the narratives were reconciled in every detail. Ask any lawyer: When all the witnesses agree on every detail then suspicions should be raised.

In John 19, we read how Jesus was laid in a new tomb, one that had never before been used. "At the place where Jesus was crucified, there was a garden, and in the garden a new tomb, in which no one had ever been laid" (John 19:41). Why an unused tomb? He was poor, after all. But, once again, we have the hint of Jesus' true status as a king.

"Joseph arranged for the Lord's body to be laid in a new tomb that belonged to him, a tomb in which no one had yet been buried (Mt 27:60; Lk 23;53; Jn 19:41). Here we see a mark of respect for this dead person. Just as on 'Palm Sunday' Jesus availed himself of a donkey on which no one had yet ridden (Mk 11:2), so now he is laid to rest in a new tomb."[89] The newness of the donkey may also allude to a connection to when King David moved the Ark of the Covenant—he built a new cart for the holy relic to travel upon (1 Chronicles 13:1-8).

This one verse provides much insight into the Gospel writer's mindset. Jesus, having been born in a virgin's womb, was now laid to rest in a "virgin tomb." We can envision Joseph of Arimathea, Nicodemus, and perhaps some of Jesus' female disciples reverently taking Jesus down from the cross. Overcoming their revulsion at the brutality of his execution, they pulled the nails from his palms and feet, then cleaned his body and wrapped it with balm and linen. "John tells us that Nicodemus brought a mixture of myrrh and aloes, 'about a hundred pounds weight.' . . . The quantity of balm is extraordinary and exceeds all normal proportions: this is a royal burial."[90] In a normal burial, 20 pounds would have been customary, and 50 pounds would be extraordinary—so a hundred would be extravagant beyond expectation and reflects God's lavishness.

How can this show of respect increase? Angels were present at and announced Jesus' birth, and angels were present, too, at his resurrection. When the visitors to Jesus' tomb encountered an empty sepulcher, they were greeted by angels (Matthew 28:6). In some translations, the angels invited Jesus' followers to come see where "Our Lord" had lain. The term "Our Lord" signifies Jesus is Lord of both mortals and angels.

Jesus' entire ministry was devoted to promoting the kingdom of God, and Jesus himself is the great king. He holds this office by right in his divinity, but he also can claim the title in his humanity by right of conquest.

We read that Jesus' burial shroud was neatly folded and left in the tomb. "The Jews said robbers had abstracted the body; but if so, surely they would have stolen the clothes; they would never have thought of wrapping them up and laying them down so carefully; they would be too much in haste to think of it. . . . Jesus Christ leisurely awoke, took off his cerements, left them all behind him, and came forth in his pure and naked innocence, perhaps, to show us that as clothes were the offspring of sin . . ."[91]

The resurrection event was so profound that it transformed fearful Apostles into fearless martyrs. (With the exception of Judas, who killed himself, all of the original Apostles were violently killed for their faith. All except John were martyred, and according to Tertullian, John was plunged into boiling oil but suffered no harm and was then banished.) Saint Paul's encounter with the risen Lord was so profound he went by a new name[92] (from Saul, his Hebrew name, to Paul, his Roman name) and spent the rest of his life proclaiming the good news about Jesus Christ. The resurrection convinced the early church, made up mostly of Jews, to observe the Sabbath on Sundays instead of Saturdays. Given the importance of Sabbath observance to a Jew, this is an extraordinary occurrence.

After his resurrection, Jesus occasionally appeared to his disciples. (Curiously, there is no biblical report of Jesus appearing to Mary, his mother, but there is a tradition among various Church fathers that such a meeting took place.) He talked with them, walked alongside them, and even shared the occasional meal. The Gospel of Luke (24:13-35) tells how Jesus walked with his disciples on the road to Emmaus without them realizing who he was.[93] Then we read that in the breaking of the bread (a clear reference to the Eucharist since Jesus' followers referred to "breaking bread" for Communion) their eyes were opened. In the book of Genesis, we read about how Adam and Eve ate the forbidden fruit and *their eyes were opened*. That is, they became aware of their sin and were ashamed. Luke uses the same language as that which was used in Genesis when Adam and Eve's eyes were opened—only they brought the great curse into the world by eating forbidden fruit; in consuming the Eucharist, the disciples begin the great renewal.

But, after a short time (40 days), Jesus ascended to his father. Too often we think of his ascension into heaven as if Jesus were some Greek god leaving this earth to dwell physically on Mount Olympus. Carl Sagan once commented on the ascension of Jesus, saying that, even if he were traveling at the speed of light, Jesus would still not have reached the end of our own Milky Way galaxy, let alone heaven. Sagan's point would be well taken if Jesus' ascension were just a physical phenomenon, but Jesus transcends the physical.[94]

The New Testament is replete with verses about Christ's return. For example, sacred Scripture records that Jesus will come again in the same way he departed—in a cloud of glory (Acts 1:10-11). However, there is no mention of Jesus' "second coming." What's the difference? Well, perhaps, since he is already among us in the Church, in the Eucharist, and elsewhere, his return may simply be a sort of disclosure of that which already exists yet remains hidden.

Both the Bible, in Ephesians 1:20 and Hebrews 8:1-2; and the Creed, mention that Jesus, after his resurrection, ascended into heaven and is seated at the right hand of God. God the Father is pure spirit and technically has no right hand; he has no body whatsoever. So, the imagery of Jesus being seated at the Father's right hand is not to be taken literally, but it is important symbolically. To be seated is indicative of a job being completed. In the Jewish temple, there were no seats for the priests, as sacrifices were offered continually. Jesus, as the great high priest, did what no other high priest could do: He sat down because the work of atonement was finally completed.[95]

We might expect that at Jesus' ascension his followers would become overcome with sorrow. The master had gone and now they were left to continue without him. Luke 24:52 tells us, however, that the disciples were filled with joy.

> . . . The joy of the disciples after the 'Ascension' corrects our image of this event. 'Ascension' does not mean departure into a remote region of the cosmos but, rather, the continuing closeness that the disciples experience so strongly that it becomes a source of lasting joy.
> . . . The cloud reminds us of the hour of the Transfiguration, in which the bright cloud falls on Jesus and the disciples (cf. Mt 17:5; Mk 9:7; Lk 9:34-35). It reminds us of the hour of Mary's encounter with God's messenger, Gabriel, who announces to her the 'overshadowing' with the power of the Most High (cf. Lk I:35). It reminds us of the holy tent of God in the Old Covenant, where the cloud signified the Lord's presence (cf. Ex 40:34-35), the same Lord who, in the form of a cloud, led the people of Israel during their journey through the desert (cf. Ex 13 :21-22). This

reference to the cloud is unambiguously theological language. It presents Jesus' departure, not as a journey to the stars, but as his entry into the mystery of God. It evokes an entirely different order of magnitude, a different dimension of being.

. . . Hence he has not 'gone away,' but now and forever by God's own power he is present with us and for us. In the farewell discourses of St. John's Gospel, this is exactly what Jesus says to his disciples: 'I go away, and I will come to you' (14:28).[96]

Not only did Jesus come, but he sent the Holy Spirit, who transformed the despondency of Jesus' followers into joy.

†

CHAPTER EIGHT

MARY
(MARIOLOGY)

In Marian tradition, the relationship between Mary and Jesus is sometimes analogized to that of the sun and moon. This symbolism is drawn from the Marian passage of the book of Revelation: "And a great portent appeared in heaven, a woman clothed with the sun, with the moon under her feet, and on her head a crown of twelve stars; and she was with child and she cried out in her pangs of birth, in anguish for delivery" (Revelation 12: 1-2). This is a fitting analogy, as, "There are two ways of spreading light, to be the candle or the mirror that reflects it."[1] Jesus is the light of the world, and Mary is the flawless reflection of that light.

The Bible tells us relatively little about Mary's life. Surprisingly, more is written about Mary in the Muslim Quran than in the Christian Bible. Actually, Mary, "Maryam" in Arabic, is the only woman mentioned by name in the entire Quran.[2] The Gospels attribute not a single miracle to her. She is not recognized as having died a martyr's death. Much of what we know about her is derived either directly from the Bible or from hints and allusions that the Bible provides, and which the early Church fathers and later Christians eventually ascertained. Her life was foreshadowed in several persons of the Old Testament (e.g. Eve), typified in various Hebrew religious symbols (e.g. the Ark of the Covenant), and foretold in the words of prophets of the Old Testament (e.g. the writings of Isaiah).

In addition to the Bible, there are many oral traditions and non-canonical writings about the mother of Jesus. There are also volumes of material provided by saints, scholars, popes, and mystics who offer great insights concerning her life. Reflecting on these rich sources offers us a somewhat detailed portrait of Mary's life and her vocation. Since the details of Mary's life are not well documented in Scripture it can be painfully difficult to separate authentic historical information from mere hagiography or pious speculation.

I once heard of a priest who had a particular devotion to Mary and would preach about her regularly. He gave details to his congregation that I think St. Joseph himself wouldn't know. Where'd he get the information? Probably from various apocryphal sources, the writing of saints, the speculation of theologians, maybe even from his own reflections. However, the historical details of Mary's actual life may be different—but we shouldn't be surprised.

Her biography begins, not as most biographies do, with a date of birth, but with her conception. Mary was not merely chosen by God but created to be the mother of his son, Jesus. The difference, as I once heard it banally explained, is analogous to choosing a car off a lot or a suit off a rack as opposed to having one custom-made. Mary was tailor-made by God to bear his son. One of the most important aspects of her unique design is that ". . . the Blessed Virgin Mary, from the first moment of her conception, by a singular grace and privilege of almighty God, and in view of the merits of Jesus Christ, Saviour of the human race, was preserved free from every stain of original sin . . ."[3]

To better understand her special identity, an analogy may prove helpful. Suppose you and some others are waiting for a bus, when a passing car drives into a dirty puddle, splashing and staining your clothes. The second person, too, would have been splashed, but a friend moved her out of harm's way. This friend helps you out by cleaning you up and giving you the clothes off his back. This is a crude analogy, but you were saved by the friend, after the damage; the other person was saved too, but before the damage.

This grace, no matter how extraordinary, does not remove Mary from the human race. She, too, was created; she, too, is finite. The term used to describe this "singular grace" is "immaculate conception." The words "immaculate conception" are often misapplied to Jesus' incarnation,[4] however they actually describe not only the formation of Mary, but more profoundly they describe Mary's very essence. She is the Immaculate Conception,[5] the flawless creation envisioned by God her maker. She is the *sine qua non* (Latin: "without which there is none") of God's good creation.

Think about it as an artist conceiving his greatest painting or an author envisioning her greatest novel, then creating these masterpieces. The poet William Wordsworth described Mary as "Our tainted nature's solitary boast."[6]

Despite this singular grace, Mary can and must legitimately refer to God as her savior. Mary is human, fully human, a creature of God, born of parents Tradition names Joachim and Anne. She is neither divine nor is she some sort of demigoddess. She is a mortal, like all other humans, but was graced to be the daughter of God the Father, the mother of God the Son and the spouse of God the Holy Spirit. These graces, while appropriate to Mary, should not be taken to irreverent extremes. (Think about it, if we call Mary our mother and she is called daughter of God the Father, using the analogy of a human relationship, God the Father becomes our grandfather.)

There is a substantial body of literature that purports to catalog Mary's life from infancy, through adolescence, and finally until adulthood and the end of her life. Although the New Testament provides no details about her early years, there is a rich tradition of devotional material and extra-biblical literature that purports to share details about her conception, infancy, and childhood. The Church has long celebrated the feast of her conception (December 8); her birth nine months later (September 8); and her purported consecration to God and service in the temple (November 21), an occurrence related in apocryphal works, not in the Bible. The Church similarly celebrates a feast day commemorating her assumption into heaven (August 15), the oldest Marian feast day dating back to the first centuries of the Church. Sources for the biographical material of Mary's early years originate in non-canonical writings, early oral traditions, and other sources. Perhaps the most influential non-canonical source is the book *Protoevangelium of James* (written circa 120 AD), which provides a wealth of purported Marian biographical material.

The Bible, however, introduces us to Mary when she was likely a young teenager. We learn that it is then that she was visited by the angel Gabriel, who announced to her God's favor and his incredible plan (Luke 1:27-30).

The angel shows Mary her situation; he does not create it. Through the greeting she achieves possession of self-knowledge; but she herself seems in this to be standing already in the service of heaven. The salutation sounds like a retrospect of her entire attitude until now, and we are not told when her mission had begun. The greeting promises a coming event; she is going to conceive the Son, she does not yet have him physically in her. But, her mission she possesses already; it is much older than the conception (of Jesus). And so the promise of the Lord who is to come is the verification of the Lord who is already there in the mission which she received at the beginning (the immaculate conception).[7]

This biblical account is very different from pagan stories of gods impregnating virgins.[8] In the Bible, Mary is asked for her consent, while in pagan myths we usually encounter gods raping or seducing morals.[9] She humbly and fully agrees to the invitation Gabriel brings, and she consents to becoming the mother of Jesus, the mother of God. Her fiat echoes through the millennia as a statement of unconditional faith, "And Mary said, 'Here am I, the servant of the Lord; let it be with me according to your word'" (Luke 1:38).

Mary's acquiescence is without reservation.

> When a person who has been tainted with original sin places himself, body and soul, at God's disposal, it never happens without a certain calculation. He sees and feels the renunciation of a great many natural gifts to which his nature seems to have a certain right, and what he has renounced is always reflected in his surrender. He cannot perfectly free himself from an attachment to what he has given away. The Mother (Mary) does not know this compromise. She does not weigh what she is giving and what she will receive for it. She knows no other use for her soul and body than being a servant.[10]

The Bible makes no mention of intercourse between Mary and God, but instead the language of Luke 1:35 parallels Exodus 40:34-35, which describes God's Spirit as "overshadowing" the temple in Jerusalem. Thus, Mary is a virgin prior to the conception of Jesus, continues her virginity during her pregnancy, and remains a virgin after giving birth. The Church insists on her perpetual virginity,[11] pointing out that scriptural references to Jesus' brothers were likely cousins or step-brothers from a previous marriage by Joseph.

Mary consented to becoming Jesus' mother in her Magnificat, her statement of trust and faith. However, she was confused about how she could become a mother since she was a virgin. And, with her consent, "The angel answered, 'The Holy Spirit will come upon you, and the power of the Most High will overshadow you. So the holy one to be born will be called the Son of God'" (Luke 1:35). The language used here in Luke's Gospel is not accidental. In Greek, the word "*episkiasei*" was used for the term "overshadowed." The word references the Shekinah, or the earthly glory of God that was present in the temple of Jerusalem in connection with the Ark of the Covenant. (See, for example, Exodus 40: 34-38.)

The Ark of the Covenant was a visible sign of God's relationship with the people of Israel. Luke, who would have known the stories about the Ark from the Old Testament, our Old Testament, purposefully uses the same language in his story to identify Mary as the new living Ark, the bearer of God.[12] Here then is an excellent example of how a teaching about Mary might not be found directly in the Bible but can be, must be, inferred. Saints Athanasius, Gregory, and others referred to Mary under the title the Ark of the Covenant. Mary is never addressed by this title in the Bible, but look at the parallels between Mary's life and the verses in the Bible that discuss the Ark of the Covenant.

In Luke's Gospel, the Evangelist describes how Mary goes on a trip to visit her cousin, Elizabeth. Compare her journey with the journey of the Ark recorded in the book of 2 Samuel.

- "At that time Mary got ready and hurried to a town in the hill country of Judea" (Luke 1: 39).

    - "They set the ark of God on a new cart and brought it from the house of Abinadab, which was on the hill. Uzzah and Ahio, sons of Abinadab, were guiding the new cart" (2 Samuel 6: 3).

- Elizabeth says of Mary: "But why am I so favored, that the mother of my Lord should come to me?" (Luke 1:43).

    - David asks: "How can the ark of the LORD come to me?" (2 Samuel 6:9).

- John the Baptist leaped (danced) in the presence of Mary. "As soon as the sound of your greeting reached my ears, the baby in my womb leaped for joy" (Luke 1:44).

- ◆ "David danced before the Lord with all his might;
  David was girded with a linen ephod." (2 Samuel 6:14).

- ■ "Mary stayed with Elizabeth for about three months and
  then returned home" (Luke 1:56).

  - ◆ "The ark of the LORD remained in the house of
    Obed-Edom the Gittite for three months, and the LORD
    blessed him and his entire household" (2 Samuel 6:11).

The comparisons could continue,[13] and not only between Mary and the Ark, but between Mary and Eve, Mary and the temple of God, etc.

Interestingly, while Mary has been held up for many comparisons, she also has a famous contrast, a polar opposite in the figure of Lucifer, God's former great work. It may seem odd to compare Mary to the angel who became Satan, but Lucifer was the greatest among angels, beautiful and proud, and he chose hell; Mary was the greatest among humans, the Immaculate Conception of Almighty God, beautiful and humble, and she chose heaven. She did not look inward and awe at her own supremacy, as did Lucifer, but she looked outside herself to her creator, to the greater mystery of God. Lucifer disobeyed and hated and refused to serve; Mary trusted and loved, and her entire life was service.[14] Lucifer wanted to be like God in power but not goodness, and he lost all; Mary wanted to be like God in goodness but not in power, and she gained all. Lucifer was the highest and fell to the lowest; Mary was the lowest, the humblest, and was raised to the highest glory—higher than Lucifer ever was. Some speculate that Lucifer rejected the idea of God becoming flesh; Mary welcomed the Son of God in flesh. On earth she lowered herself in humility, imitating her son, and God raised her in glory in heaven.

These are but a few examples from a substantial body of scholarship and devotional material known as Mariology, the study of Mary (not to be confused with the heresy of Mariolatry, the worship of Mary). The Eastern Orthodox refer to Mary by the title *Theotokos*, which translates to mean "Mother of God." Similarly, Catholics have numerous titles for her, hundreds that describe her unique relationship with God, some of which may seem unusual at first glance—Our Lady, Queen of Heaven—or her title as the New Eden.[15] Mary's identification with the Garden of Eden may seem strange, but Jesus often analogized himself to inanimate objects (e.g. "I Am the gate," John 10:9), and Bible identifies the faithful as "a well watered garden" (Isaiah 58:11, Jeremiah 31:12). Some other titles are ancient, such as Theotokos, while others are more modern creations (e.g. Our Lady of the Americas).

Some may complain that Catholic and Eastern Orthodox Christians turn Jesus' relationship with his mother on its head. They argue that while Jesus certainly loved Mary, there is no biblical evidence that she was as Christ-like as we make her out to be. Those who are argue this point misunderstand Marian devotion.[16] In honoring Mary, we both follow Jesus' example and fulfill her own prophecy that "henceforth all generations shall call me blessed" (Luke 1:48). What's more, when Catholics refer to Mary as their mother, it is in humble recognition of Jesus' role as our brother. Being our brother's mother makes Mary our mother as well.

After Mary's assent to bear the Son of God, her life became very challenging. She had to cope with the judgments of her family and community, being an unwed pregnant girl in a very conservative culture. In Jesus' day, marriage was a two-stage process within the Jewish community. Stage one consisted of a betrothal, while stage two was the marriage. It would be an error to equate the betrothal period as merely an engagement. Under the custom of the time, a man and woman who were betrothed to one another were considered to be married, though they did not yet live together. To understand the story of Mary and Joseph's relationship, it is essential to understand they were legally married, but had not consummated their marriage, when Mary announced she was with child. She had to bear the scrutiny of Joseph, who is described in the Gospels as a "just man." Joseph was obviously perplexed. Undoubtedly, he knew of Mary's reputation as a devout and virtuous Jew. Joseph, upon learning of Mary's pregnancy, had decided to divorce her quietly, not wishing to shame her. Actually, Joseph's virtue likely went beyond this. He was, according to some (Origen, for example), not suspicious of Mary or reproving of her, but may simply have considered himself unworthy to participate in the great the mystery of the incarnation.

However, the Gospels tell us that God revealed to Joseph that Mary had not illegitimately conceived a baby but was with child by the will of God. Without taking the analogy too far, one could see Mary as typifying the Church, who brings Jesus to the world, and equally Joseph is an exemplar of Israel. His righteousness recollects Israel's righteousness. His trust in God when confronted with the unexpected Messiah is Israel's challenge.

She gave birth in a stable in Bethlehem and began a life as a mother of the world's most unique child. Soon after giving birth, she had to flee to Egypt to avoid King Herod's murderous plans. Eventually returning to Nazareth, Jesus was hers to raise and love for years. As his mother, Mary loved Jesus as a son; but she also adored him as God-Incarnate. She helped to shape how he learned to love others.

> She seldom sees him and has little news of him. She cannot clearly envisage what kind of work he is doing and what his active life is like. The unfamiliar, unknown side of his life has gained the upper hand; no longer, as at home, it is regulated and punctuated by an accustomed order. She hardly knows anything of his surroundings; most of the people he meets are unknown to her; she does not know whether he is among friends or enemies, how he is proclaiming the Father's message to the people . . . She only sees the huge burden he has taken on his shoulders; she feels lonely and knows that the help she can give him now can only be prayer. . . . Whatever she finds hard in her loneliness, forsakenness and insecurity has its place in her prayer. She does not ask for her own load to be lightened: She asks God to send her everything in such a way that others may be helped, but also that God the Son, who is her Son as well, may be helped. . . . The Lord's divinity and the divinity of his undertaking have become more central to her. That which is of the Father, the Spirit and the Son, the impenetrable area to which she has no human access, which moves in her premonitions and hopes, which she has taken over intact and sealed, as it were, from the Son . . . And she prays her way into this transposition, a prayer of love to God, a prayer of discipleship, a prayer which is also shaped by the far-off Son. Often it is pure worship, sometimes only anguish or pain. It is a prayer that is given to her but that she experiences, that takes place in her life . . .[17]

Reading though the few interactions between Jesus and Mary that are recorded in the New Testament, it actually seems like Jesus is overly abrupt, some might say even rude to his mother. Yet, reflection on these abrupt moments then leads to the conclusion that Jesus was preparing Mary to share in his great mission.[18] With each slight, she tasted of the bitter fruit of his Passion, so that what seemed liked cruelty was, in fact, an unparalleled intimacy, an invitation—perhaps puzzling at the time to Mary—by Jesus to contemplate in wonderous awe the depths of his divine mystery. In each instance where Jesus appears to reprimand Mary, she ponders Jesus' words and she patiently defers to her son's wishes despite her lack of understanding. By doing so, Jesus prepared his holy mother to share in the suffering and abandonment he would undergo in his Passion. His entire life with her was characterized not just by the typical mother-son relationship but by the master-disciple relationship. Yet that mother-son relationship was incomparably strong.

Although Mary was a poor girl, her ancestry traces back to King David; therefore, so does Jesus'. This is extremely relevant for a number of reasons, not the least of which has to do with the *gebirah.* The word "gebirah" can be translated as the "Great Lady" or "Queen Mother," and we encounter the term in the book of 1 Kings. Throughout the history of the Davidic line of kings, we find that while a king may have had many wives he had only a single mother, and she was accorded great honors. The quintessential example comes from King Solomon, who afforded his mother, Bathsheba, both a queenly throne and a role as intercessor. "So Bathsheba went to King Solomon, to speak to him on behalf of Adonijah. The king rose to meet her, and bowed down to her; then he sat on his throne, and had a throne brought for the king's mother, and she sat on his right. Then she said, 'I have one small request to make of you; do not refuse me.' And the king said to her, 'Make your request, my mother; for I will not refuse you'" (1 Kings 2:19-20).

Mary, too, makes requests of her son, always with the intent of drawing us to Jesus and drawing Jesus to us, just as at the wedding feast at Cana. Mary and Jesus attended a marriage celebration. The hosts ran out of wine. Mary asked Jesus to help. She interceded for the embarrassed hosts. Jesus' response indicated that he would not have otherwise gotten involved. But, he was a good Jewish son and loved his mother; moreover, he was king, and Mary was his gebirah, so he acquiesced to his mother's wishes and performed his first miracle by turning water into wine. These jugs were used for purposes of ritual cleansing, and the fact that Jesus turned them into wine was not only a miracle, but, perhaps, was a slight against the purification-obsessed religious leaders of his day. And, incidentally, Jesus' comfort with providing wine to the guests speaks volumes about his views on hospitality; while he did not promote a Dionysian revelry, neither did he insist on ascetic denial.

At the feast, Mary told the servants to do whatever Jesus commanded. She practiced this unquestioning obedience throughout her own life. Mary submitted to the will of God even in the most difficult circumstances. This obedience found full expression in her fiat, her consent to become the mother of Jesus. It is hard for contemporary readers of her story to conceive of the great social stigma that would have befallen a pregnant unmarried woman of her time and culture. Her example of obedience to God is inspiring for individuals and for the Church as a whole. Mary's life typifies the Church. She brought Jesus to the world, and so must the Church. She submitted in obedience to God's often mysterious and hard-to-accept will, and so must the Church. She attained heaven after a faithful earthly sojourn, and so, we hope, will the members of the Church.

Yet, we must not take the miraculous events in her life as signs that she did not struggle with the mysteries playing out before her eyes. Although we read in the Gospels about Mary being visited by the angel Gabriel and about her miraculous conception, we should not draw from these events the false idea that Mary had a fully formed understanding of her son's mission. We encounter Mary pondering and seeking understanding about the mysteries she witnessed.

Then, in the years spent with him, she suffered, knowing, though perhaps only in a vague manner, the future torment that he faced. Then, when he grew older and left her side, Mary continued to be formed by Jesus and to cooperate uniquely in his ministry. In this way, he shared with her the great dignity of his kenosis, his full emptying of himself for us all. And in this giving, she suffered greatly. Though close to the Trinity, she was not privy to the mysterious will of God in all things, and so she suffered loneliness, confusion, and anxiety. But, because of her great faith in God, she submitted to his imponderable will by always acquiescing to her son's wishes. Just as she agreed to become the mother of Jesus, this consent to God's will never ended throughout her life. "This single, all-encompassing act accompanies her at every moment of her existence, illuminates every turning point of her life, bestows upon every situation its own particular meaning and in all situations gives May herself the grace of renewed understanding. Her assent gives full meaning to every breath, every movement, every prayer of the Mother of God."[19] In other words, her example, (perhaps even more than the suffering of Job), is a testimony to the importance of remaining steadfast in our faith to God. Mary accepts the will of God—a will she cannot understand or easily reconcile with her own personal suffering—because she trusts in God completely.

Her complete faith and trust remedied the faithlessness of Eve. As the Immaculate Conception, Mary was privileged to be born into this world in the same spiritual state as Adam and Eve before their fall. One of the titles of Mary is "the New Eve." Eve, the archetypical mother of humanity, fell into sin. Mary, as the New Eve, took on the role, actually was given the honor by her Son, of being mother to the whole world (John 19:26-27). From the cross, Jesus, the new Adam, called out to Mary but strangely referred to her as "woman" (John 19:26-27). Why? Jesus was harkening back to the very first woman, Eve, who was referred to as "woman" by Adam in Genesis 2:23. In his lavish kindness, Jesus exchanged our sin for his holiness, our weakness for his strength, our sorrow for his joy, and as if all this were not enough, he not only gives us his very self, but his holy mother as well.

Saint Irenaeus explained, "The knot of Eve's disobedience was untied by Mary's obedience; what the virgin Eve bound through her unbelief, the Virgin Mary loosened by her faith." While adoration ("*Latreia*" in Greek) is due to God alone, and reverence (Greek: "*Dulia*") is due to all saints, only Mary is worthy of extreme reverence (Greek: "*Hyperdulia*"). Mary is holier than any angel by grace, not by nature. She is the greatest of all saints because she is the unblemished reflection of her son, Jesus. The Eastern Orthodox Church reminds us of Mary's connection with Jesus by traditionally never showing her alone in any art; instead she is usually portrayed in the company of Jesus.

On the cross, Jesus said, "Here is your mother" (John 19:27). Giving us everything, including his life, Jesus also gave us his mother as our mother. He brought us his father and then his mother. Pierced with sorrow beyond our imagining, she was faithful to her son to the end. And in that faith, she revealed a strength beyond reckoning. The Gospel of John reveals that Mary stood at the foot of the cross (19:25-27). What mother could bear to stand in the presence of her child's suffering? Yet, she gazed in awe at his unfathomable loving sacrifice.

> She stands before the Lord on the Cross like the embodiment and summation of mankind. When he looks at her, he no longer sees, for a moment, the atrocious sinners for whose sake and at whose hands he is dying; he sees mankind as if transfigured in the form of his Mother. He had redeemed her also, by preserving her from sin. That gives her the capacity to suffer with him, vicariously for all, as an embodiment of the meaning of redemption, in the perfect unity of human nature and divine grace.[20]

By submitting to the ineffable torment of her son's death, by intimately sharing in his suffering, his kenosis (full emptying), and perfectly reflecting his virtues, she merited graces beyond what any other would ever receive. The writings of the Church fathers are replete with references to Mary's special role in God's plan of redemption.

Therefore, it should come as no surprise that Jesus honors his mother in heaven as he did on earth. Catholic Tradition holds that she was blessed with the grace of being God's Immaculate Conception, she was privileged to be chosen as the mother of God, and when her earthly life was finished she was assumed into heaven and continues to cooperate with her son's divine mission.

There is no record in the Bible of the resurrected Jesus having visited with his mother, but theologians have speculated that such an intimate meeting would rightly remain private. And there is other evidence to suggest that Mary lived out the remainder of her life on earth, secure in the joy of her son's resurrection. She stayed with his followers, was present with them in the upper room at Pentecost (Acts 2:3), and after her life came to a close, she was assumed, body and soul, into heaven.

Mary was with Jesus from the first moment of his conception in her womb. She raised him as a boy and accompanied him as an adult. She was a faithful witness to both his cruel execution and his glorious resurrection. At the end of her earthly life Mary was assumed into heaven to be with her son.

This dogma, believed since apostolic times, was formally promulgated *de fide* in 1950 by Pope Pius XII. In simple language the Pope declared, "The Immaculate Mother of God, the ever-virgin Mary, having completed the course of her earthly life, was

assumed body and soul into heaven." The use of the qualifier "Immaculate" is not accidental. Mary was conceived purely and lived
purely; it is only fitting that her death led not to corruption in a
grave but to glory in heaven. (Notice, too, that instead of using
the word "death," the phrase "having completed the course of her
earthly life" is employed. This is because there is a long tradition
known as the Dormition of Mary, the commemoration of which
is still celebrated by the Eastern Orthodox Church to this day.
Some believe Mary was not subject to natural death but merely
entered into a final sleep. This is not a dogmatic teaching, and
many argue that given the fact that Jesus himself was subject to
natural death, Mary, too, died.)

Her son honored her in life and all the more so after death,
with the coronation of Mary as the Queen of Heaven. She is not
just the gebirah, but Mary is the Mediatrix of God's grace. Out
of immeasurable love for her son, Mary shared in his sufferings
and perfectly and submissively cooperates in his work. She is full
of grace and distributes graces. "Mediatrix" does not mean she
controls all grace or channels all grace. She does not channel her
own grace, nor the grace Jesus possessed. In a way, all people
who do good are mediators of God's grace. With this in mind,
Catholics pray for Mary's intercession in the deeply scriptural
prayer of the rosary[21] and in other prayers.[22]

Neither saint nor angel is closer to Jesus than his holy mother, Mary. No martyr loved God more. What Mary did on earth she
perpetuates in heaven. Her objective is to bring Jesus, her son, to
the whole world.

†

CHAPTER NINE

SAINTS AND ANGELS
(HAGIOLOGY AND ANGELOLOGY)

SAINTS

Saints are those who have had a deeply profound and transformative encounter with the divine. Their response to this meeting was one of staunch faith in, loyalty to, and love for the living God. The very word "saint" derives from the Latin word "*sanctus*," which means "holy." Saints remind us that no one has ever regretted loving God too much.

Saints are our models and intercessors. They did not merely assent intellectually to certain teachings and creedal formulas, but instead they experienced a transformation of the total person, body, mind, and spirit; they lived the beatitudes. For the rest of us, we look on their humility, their holiness, their utter sorrow for even minor faults and wonder if they haven't taken things a bit too far.

> Every now and then one meets them. Their very voices and faces are different from ours; stronger, quieter, happier, more radiant. They begin where most of us leave off. They are, I say, recognisable; but you must know what to look for. They will not be very like the idea of 'religious people' which you have formed from your general reading. They do not draw attention to themselves. You tend to think that you are being kind to them when they are really being kind to you. They love you more than other men do, but they need you less. . . . They will usually seem to have a lot of time: you will wonder where it comes from. When you have recognised one of them, you will recognise the next one much more

easily. And I strongly suspect (but how should I know?) that they recognise one another immediately and infallibly, across every barrier of colour, sex, class, age, and even of creeds. In that way, to become holy is rather like joining a secret society. To put it at the very lowest, it must be great fun.[1]

A person who is officially recognized by the Church as a saint is declared to be in heaven and worthy of veneration, though not all that the saints said or did is necessarily sanctioned by the Church. The roads to sainthood are interesting and varied. For many, their biographies start out in manners not dissimilar to their contemporaries—lured by the same joys, burdened with the same worries, pursuing the same ambitions. But, then, suddenly for some and gradually for others, a numinous encounter happened. Maybe the saint encountered another holy person or came face-to-face with suffering or death. Whatever the cause, a passion for God was kindled. Then those same joys and worries seemed like so much dross. What once seemed urgent and essential in life ultimately became trivial.

Each one of the stories[2] of the lives of the saints can be summarized as a journey toward holiness; one that is filled with both suffering and joy. In growing closer to God, each saint moved through various stages in their relationship with the Almighty. Their love for God was purified throughout their lives. Many described this purification as a test in which God stripped away comforts and certainties in order to invite the saint to have total reliance on God. Time and again, we see in the biographies of holy men and women how, during times of great distress, doubt, and suffering, the person's reliance on God brought about a deeper and truer relationship with God and a better understanding of self. All this led to the saint becoming a truer disciple of Christ; a joyful, disciplined follower.

Another theme found throughout the lives of all the saints is that they have all shared an attitude of detachment or holy indifference. Not in the form of hatred for this world but with the perspective of eternity in mind. Saint Teresa counseled:

Let nothing disturb you,
Let nothing frighten you,
All passes away,
God alone will stay,

Patience obtains all things.
Who God possesses, is lacking in nothing;
God alone suffices.[3]

The farther along this new path the saint travels the clearer God's holiness becomes and the more obvious does humanity's calamitous situation manifest itself. Failure followed by mercy is the experience in all our lives. If you read the life stories of great saints throughout the ages, you will see a pattern of growth emerge. Failure and sin are followed by repentance and renewal; fear and doubt are overcome by hope and faith, again and again. One of the truisms of conversion is that, if you have recently overcome some addiction or bad behavior, it is more likely than not that you will return to it a few more times before having given it up for good; so too with the saints.

Often, they learned to see themselves as great sinners as they grew closer to God, but, as with so much of the Christian experience, they simultaneously grew in joy. All human beings are creatures of habit. It is our choice to make those habits help or hinder our spiritual growth. Some of the greatest saints spent years trying to overcome habitual sin. Saint Augustine, one of the fathers of Western culture, was, before his conversion, addicted to sex. His famous prayer, "Lord, make me chaste, but not yet!" is a plea many can recognize. But, Augustine later lamented that he did not leave his licentious lifestyle and follow Christ sooner. He lamented:

> Late have I loved Thee, O Beauty so ancient and so new; late have I loved Thee! For behold Thou were within me, and I outside; and I sought Thee outside and in my unloveliness fell upon those lovely things that Thou hast made. Thou were with me and I was not with Thee. I was kept from Thee by those things, yet had they not been in Thee, they would not have been at all. Thou didst call and cry to me and break open my deafness: and Thou didst send forth Thy beams and shine upon me and chase away my blindness: Thou didst breathe fragrance upon me, and I drew in my breath and do not pant for Thee: I tasted Thee, and now hunger and thirst for Thee: Thou didst touch me, and I have burned for Thy peace.[4]

Saint Augustine finally overcame his habitual sin, and he is in good company because many saints suffered from habitual sins; some committed some very serious offenses. It's true that "Every saint has a past and every sinner has a future."[5] Moses, who killed a man, was the greatest prophet of the Old Covenant; St. Peter, who denied Jesus, was the rock upon which Christ's church was built; King David lusted after a woman, Bathsheba, and murdered her husband in order to have her. But, they all repented and returned to God.

Holiness is not what most of us envision. We liken saints with demigods or some strange and wonderful beings. And why shouldn't we? The biographies of the saints are filled with astounding tales. Saint Simeon the Stylite was famous for spending nearly 40 years living atop a pillar. Saint Christina the Astonishing was incapable of being executed. She was thrown into a fire; that method having failed, she was cast into a lake with a weight tied to her; yet, she survived. Saint Joseph of Cupertino could fly about a room. Saint Pio of Pietrelcina (Padre Pio) was able to bilocate (be in two places at the same time). But, fantastic hagiographies aside, people are not declared as saints simply because wondrous deeds are attributed to them. The saints are canonized because they are holy examples.

Brother Thomas Merton described a saint as being

> . . . capable of loving created things and enjoying the use of them and dealing with them in a perfectly simple, natural manner, making no formal references to God, drawing no attention to his own piety, and acting without any artificial rigidity at all. . . . Hence a saint is capable of talking about the world without any explicit reference to God, in such a way that his statement gives greater glory to God and arouses a greater love of God than the observations of someone less holy, who has to strain himself to make an arbitrary connection between creatures and God through the medium of hackneyed analogies and metaphors that are so feeble that they make you think there is something the matter with religion. The saint knows that the world and everything made by God is good, while those who are not saints either think that created things are unholy, or else they don't bother about the question one way or another, because they are only interested in themselves.[6]

The word "saint" can stir up some confusion. Technically, anyone who makes it to heaven is a saint. No one alive is a saint because the word denotes a person who is forever preserved in the beatific vision. So, the moniker "living saint" is theologically incorrect. Unlike those in certain strains of Protestant Christianity, who teach that any person who receives the gift of sanctifying grace is a saint, Catholicism affirms that saints are those who continue in sanctifying grace until death. The difference has to do with concepts of personal freedom and what is known as the perseverance of the saints. To put it colloquially, some Protestants believe that once a person is saved that person is incapable of losing that salvation. Catholics, on the other hand, believe that even the most pious among us can fall into mortal sin and thus risk alienation from God.

A saint can also be a holy person from within the tradition who is recognized as a model for the rest of us. So, we can refer to the patriarch, Abraham, as a saint, or to Daniel, the visionary, as a saint. But, the moniker of saint, for them, is a consideration given their piety and not a formal title bestowed through canonization. Alternately, there are saints who, either via Tradition or canonization, have been formally recognized by the Church as especially holy and worthy of emulation.

In the earliest days of the Church there was no formal process for recognizing individual saints. Paul occasionally identified other Christians as "saints" in his epistles. Later, a tradition spread whereby Christians who displayed heroic expressions of the faith were honored with the moniker "saint." This is especially true of martyrs who were killed for their faith, and for confessors of the faith—those who suffered but did not necessarily die for their Christian beliefs.

The process by which a person is formally recognized as a saint in the Catholic Church has changed over the centuries, having begun in 1234, with the most recent modification ordered by Pope Saint John Paul II in 1983. In the early days of the Church, martyrs and holy men and women were recognized by the community as being saints. Later, the identification and declaration of sainthood was a function of local bishops. Eventually, the process became a papal responsibility. Church documents reveal that in 993, a man named Ulrich, who was bishop of Augsburg, was the first to be formally made a saint in the process known as canonization, under the auspices of Pope John XV. Today, there is a formal process (which can take a very long time, centuries even, to go through, and which is very expensive to fund), which begins with a declaration of a person as being a "servant of God," then moving to the status of "venerable," then "blessed," and finally being declared a "saint."[7] There are thousands of officially recognized saints. (It's worth noting that there is no such thing as an anti-saint; that is, the Church has infallibly declared many thousands of people to be in heaven, but no single individual has been so declared to be damned.)

The long road to sainthood cannot start until the Catholic in question is deceased. The first step begins with a bishop who had jurisdiction over the holy person conducting an investigation into a purported saint's life in an effort to identify the person's sanctity (heroic virtue) and faith (orthodoxy). Notice, intellectual acumen is not a requirement for sainthood—though they all possessed great wisdom. Interviews are conducted, the writings and other available works of the individual are scrutinized,[8] and eventually the body of the person being investigated is disinterred.[9] The results of this investigation are reviewed by the official Church office dedicated to the task of discerning new saints: the Congregation for Cause of Saints. If a candidate makes it past the evaluation process, which requires all but martyrs to demonstrate at least one bona fide posthumous miracle, then that person is beatified. An officially beatified person can be venerated locally in his or her home diocese. Thereafter, a second miracle is required before the beatified person is officially, infallibly, and irrevocably canonized by the sitting pope. An additional but rare honor has been bestowed on a few saints who so profoundly contributed to the faith of the Church that they bear the title "doctor of the church."

Confusion can stem from the fact that the three archangels listed in the Bible—Gabriel, Michael, and Raphael—are referred to as saints, and each has his own feast day. In addition, there are some who have been previously been venerated as saints, but whose historicity is now called into question.[10] Saint Christopher is, perhaps, the most famous example. The name Christopher, which means "Christ bearer," explains the legend of the saint bearing the infant Christ upon his shoulders. Although the Church never declared St. Christopher as a fiction—quite the contrary; there is little doubt that a Christian named Christopher did in fact exist—his biography contains little historical account of his life due to the lack of verifiable information. Vatican II mandated a reform of the liturgical calendar for the Roman Rite, and Christopher was removed from the officially celebrated feast days.

The Apostles' Creed, a statement of faith from the early Church, includes the phrase, "I believe in . . . the communion of saints." The communion of saints refers to those holy individuals who have already died and are forevermore in God's presence. This experience of being with God is a conscious experience. Although we pray for the dead to "rest in peace," that "rest" is not akin to sleeping. The Bible is clear: "He is God not of the dead, but of the living" (Mark 12:27).

In a sense, we, too, participate in the communion of saints. The Church can be divided into three categories.

1. The Church Militant describes the Christians here on earth.
2. The Church Suffering describes those Christians in purgatory.
3. The Church Triumphant describes those Christians in heaven.

These refer to the bond between Christians who live among us and those who have died. Catholics believe that relationships are not terminated in death. Hebrews 12:1-2 mentions that we are surrounded by "so great a cloud of witnesses." Part of the Catholic tradition includes prayers for those who have died. When I was at my grandmother's wake, a kindly nun entered the room and knelt before the coffin. Afterward, she came to me to pay her respects. I had expected her to console my loss by saying she had offered a prayer, but she surprised me when she said she asked my grandmother, whom she knew as a kind and faithful woman, to intercede in a few matters on the nun's behalf. That nun knew the wonderful secret that St. Francis de Sales formulated in these words, "There is nothing small in the service of God."[11] Holy men and women of God need not be celebrated for their great deeds. "The saint does not have to bring about great temporal achievements," says Cardinal Henri de Lubac; "he is one who succeeds in giving us at least a glimpse of eternity, despite the thick opacity of time."[12]

We ask the saints, or a particular saint, to intercede or pray for us much in the same way we might ask our family or friends for their prayers. We see numerous biblical examples of this. Abraham interceded with God on behalf of Sodom (Genesis 18:22-33), Moses interceded for Israel (Exodus 32:30-33), friends interceded with Jesus to heal a paralyzed man: "When Jesus saw their faith, he said to the paralytic, 'Son, your sins are forgiven'" (Mark 2:5). Jesus healed the man specifically because of "their faith"; the faith of the man's friends, not the paralyzed man's faith. That is the power of intercession.

The Church provides specific prayers to saints and offers a litany of saints at different liturgical celebrations, such as at the Easter Vigil. The liturgical calendar is filled with days dedicated to particular saints. There are so many saints today that numerous saints share certain days. Individual saints are often associated with or even formally identified as patrons. Saint Thomas More is, for example, the patron saint of lawyers.

Adoration is reserved for God alone. Catholics do not worship saints as if they were God but simply venerate or honor them. The Church encourages prayer to the saints but forbids worship of them. The saints have no power independent of God; they are mere creatures. Of course, we can go to God directly in prayer, however, there are numerous biblical precedents as well as a long tradition in both Judaism and Christianity of asking others to intercede with God for us.

Praying to a saint can involve the use of a relic. Relics come in one of three classes. First-class relics are actually body parts from a saint. Second-class relics are pieces of property a saint possessed. Third-class relics are objects that either have been touched by a saint or that have touched another relic. (While extremely rare, there are relics associated with Jesus himself, though having been resurrected, he left no first-class relics.)

Relics may seem odd, even gruesome, but there is biblical precedent for their existence and use. In the Old Testament, 2 Kings 13:20-21, the bones of the prophet Elisha brought a dead man back to life. In the New Testament, Acts 19:11-12, we read how people were healed when touched by pieces of cloth that were previously handled by St. Paul. Later in Church history, we see the use of relics from the early Church as the remains of martyrs were reserved and venerated.

It goes without saying that relics are not enchanted artifacts but objects that simply communicate God's grace. Relics, icons, statuary, any image or symbol that brings to mind a saint is not empowered in the way pagans used to believe their idols were; the saint does not reside within or empower the image. Catholics who have not been well catechized can get muddled on this point.

When I was a college student I used to walk past a statue that stood outside Holy Trinity Church in the Ironbound section of Newark, New Jersey. The statue depicts a nondescript saint; there is no name or symbol to really identify which saint is being represented. Every so often, I used to walk by and see smaller statues of other saints scattered around the feet of the larger statue, only the little statues usually were decapitated. I thought someone vandalized the property, but the parish priest told me that some of his older parishioners get mad when their prayers are not answered, so they decapitate small statues of a saint and leave them outside near the larger statue of the unnamed saint. I thought this was kind of funny, but also surprisingly superstitious.

Faith in God, and in this case, the intercession of his saints, should not be solely based on having our prayers answered in the affirmative or positive—God doing what we want. The saints knew best of all that we are called to do what God wants us to do.

> Our greatest fault is that we wish to serve God in our way, not in His way—according to our will, not according to His will. When He wishes us to be sick, we wish to be well; when He desires us to serve Him by sufferings, we desire to serve Him by works; when He wishes us to exercise charity, we wish to exercise humility; when He seeks from us resignation, we wish for devotion, a spirit of prayer or some other virtue. And this is not because the things we desire may be more pleasing to Him, but because they are more to our taste. This is certainly the greatest obstacle we can raise to our own perfection, for it is beyond doubt that if we were to wish to be Saints according to our own will, we shall never be so at all. To be truly a Saint, it is necessary to be one according to the will of God.[13]

How does the spiritually mature person discern what choice God wants? With a sincere commitment to follow God's will and a firm pledge to specific reforms in our lives instead of a mere vague hope "just to do better in life." This commitment does not equate with a dull conformity. Often saints were men and women of individual virtue coupled with a holy rebelliousness. But, their rebellion is of a very different sort than the world is used to. The worst of earthly rebels and nonconformists, the tyrants of history, were untrusting solitary figures, always looking over their shoulders for an enemy. Saintly nonconformists seem to attract, not repel, those around them. Consider these saintly duos: Mary[14] and Joseph, Perpetua and Felicity, Benedict and Scholastica, Francis and Clare, Francis de Sales and Jane de Chantal, Vincent de Paul and Louise De Marillac, Hans Urs von Balthasar and Adrienne von Speyr; the list goes on, along with the thousands of followers who were inspired by these men and women of faith. There are several married couples who have been declared blessed, and there's even a family of saints. Saint Thérèse of Lisieux, a doctor of the church, was canonized in 1925. Her dad, Louis Martin, and her mom, Marie-Azèlie Guèrin Martin, were canonized in 2015.

These couplings or groupings are not based on some mutual admiration for one another. The lives of these saints crossed paths because their mutual holiness and devotion to God connected them to one another. However, saints, usually, are not concerned with the opinions of others. Consider the story of St. John Vianney, who crossed paths with two people in the same day. The first person he met complimented him and praised his virtues; the second person ridiculed and insulted the saint. John Vianney explained that the first meeting added nothing to his day, and the second person took nothing away.

Some saints were so unconcerned with the opinions of others that they ran afoul of the institutional Church. Saint Francis of Assisi was considered a zealot by many of his contemporaries. Saint John of the Cross was held prisoner by hostile Carmelites. Saint Joan of Arc was executed by rogue churchmen.

There is no single way of being a good person. The wide variety and profuse authenticity of the saints is well attested.

> . . . By the side of the saintly hermit and the ascetic of the desert stands the social saint, the saint of the great city and of the industrial classes. By the side of the foreign missionary stands the saint who gave his life to cripples, or idiots, or to the criminals condemned to the galleys. By the side of the saint who is arrayed in robe of penance and rough girdle, stands the saint of the salon, the refined and saintly man of the world. By the side of the saint of strict enclosure and constant silence stands the joyous friar, who calls the swallow his sister and the moon his brother. By the side of the saint of divine learning stands the saint who despised all knowledge save of Christ. By the side of the contemplative mystic, the world-conquering apostle. By the side of the

saint who does penance in filth and rags, and values ignominy beyond all things else, stands the saint robed in imperial purple and crowned with the glory of the tiara. By the side of the saint who fights and is slain for his faith, stands the saint who suffers and dies for it. By the side of the innocent saint stands the penitent. By the side of the saint of child-like meekness, the saint who must wrestle with God until He bless Him.[15]

ANGELOLOGY

Accounts of angels date back to the ancient Hebrews. Although the early Jewish tradition concerning angels was not as developed or theologically sophisticated as later writings, the Jews provided an indispensable body of literature about these messengers of God. One important lesson garnered from the Hebrew Scriptures is that the Jews were scrupulous about preserving both God's sovereignty and his goodness. The story of angels, specifically the fall of the rebellious angels, helps to address the question of evil without compromising God's limitless goodness (the Luciferian angels were the originators of evil) or God's infinite power (there is no preexistent evil with which God had to wrestle).

Catholic teaching about angels builds on the Jewish traditions and adds centuries of rich theological insights. Angels are free and intelligent creatures of pure spirit made by God to know, love, and serve him, and thereby find their ultimate joy. Importantly, angels should not be confused with God himself, nor with humans who have died. Angels are assigned the mission of being the messengers of heaven. They are actual material beings, just like us, except they are non-corporeal. That is, they don't have physical bodies. It is unclear how many angels are mentioned in the Bible, but there is reason to believe their number is myriad despite the fact that only three are referred to by name: Michael, Gabriel, and Raphael. These three are archangels and the only angels to have individual feast days; they are often referred to as St. Michael, St. Gabriel, and St. Raphael.[16] (Notice that each angelic name ends in "el," which in the original Hebrew refers to being "of God" and is similar to names like Emmanuel and Daniel.)

Tradition has divided angels into nine[17] distinct choirs made up of three separate orders: angels, archangels, and principalities make up the first order; powers, virtues, and dominations make up the second order; thrones, cherubim, and seraphim comprise the third order. Saint Thomas speculated that each of the orders is divided according to the degree to which the angels understand God. Most of the teaching of the Catholic Christian tradition has maintained that angels are ontologically higher than human beings, while strains of Eastern Orthodox Christianity have taught that humans are God's greatest work and that angels are the attendants and servants of humans.

When talking about angels, it is easy to convince ourselves that they exist in a dreamlike world where all is shadows. But, the exact opposite is true. Life in the spiritual realm is more real than it is here. When we pass through the veil we shall then see clearly what is vague to us now. Some speculate that Christians of the past wondered about the nature of angels by asking silly questions like "How many angels can dance on the head of a pin?" Firstly, this question likely did not plague the minds of serious theologians. Second, the answer to this is simple: "As many a wish to." Being creatures of spirit, angels take up no space, and so more than one can occupy the same place at the same time.

The Old Testament story of the prophet Elisha tells how he came to defeat a great army that threatened the kingdom of Israel. Elisha's servant awakened early one morning to the terrifying sight of having been surrounded the night before by the enemy's army of horse-drawn chariots and warriors. Frightened, the servant went back to Elisha to report what he saw.

> 'Alas, master! What shall we do?' He replied, 'Do not be afraid, for there are more with us than there are with them.' Then Elisha prayed: 'O Lord, please open his eyes that he may see.' So the Lord opened the eyes of the servant, and he saw; the mountain was full of horses and chariots of fire all around Elisha.
> (II Kings 6:15-17)

It was then that the servant could see what the prophet Elisha saw—that they were going to win this battle because God had provided a multitude of angelic warriors. Angels again are seen in the book of Joshua, but, surprisingly, they are not aligned with any mortal army. "Once when Joshua was by Jericho, he looked up and saw a man standing before him with a drawn sword in his hand. Joshua went to him and said to him, 'Are you one of us, or one of our adversaries?' He replied, 'Neither; but as commander of the army of the LORD I have now come'" (Joshua 5:13-14).

These invisible hosts show up time and again in Scripture and in the lives of the saints, who counsel us to call on the good angels in time of need and recognize the influence of the bad angels in our times of conflict. They are actively engaged in our lives. Pious convention holds that each one of us has a guardian angel with whom we are encouraged to establish a relationship.

Accounts of angels coming to the aid of mortals can be found throughout the Old Testament. In the story of Joshua leading the Hebrews into the Promised Land, we see parallels back to Eden with the presence of the unnamed angel who is associated, by some scholars, with the very same angel who barred readmittance to the Garden of Eden. Not only is the sword-drawn commander of God's army present again, but there is a reference to the knowledge of good or evil, echoing back to the forbidden fruit of Eden. "And as for your little ones, who you thought would become booty, your children, who today do not yet know right from wrong, they shall enter there; to them I will give it, and they shall take possession of it" (Deuteronomy 1:39).

DEMONOLOGY

We must avoid dualistic caricatures that pit the good God on one side and the evil devil on the other as if they were co-equal but opposite. Satan is, perhaps, as ungodly as a being can possibly be, as opposite God as is ontologically possible. But, neither Satan, nor evil, nor suffering, nor hell is equal to God. Though this dualistic image continues to predominate in our society, it is theologically incorrect on a number of points. God is the infinite goodness, which has no opposite. He is uncreated and limitless. The devil is a finite, created being, wholly dependent on God in order to exist. It is, therefore, a caricature to think of God and Satan, good and evil, as an eternal wrestling match between two equally strong opponents. Satan and his devils are creatures. They exist and operate only because God sovereignly deigns to allow them to.

This then begs the question, why would an all-good God make such horrible fiends? As previously mentioned, God didn't make them to be demons but originally created them to be holy angels—who then chose to rebel against him. In an abuse of their freedom, they chose for themselves to turn away from God. The cause of the fall has been the subject of much speculation over the centuries. Some theologians posit that Lucifer and all the angels were created by God in the midst of heaven, but the Godhead was hidden from the angels. During this time of concealment, the angels were given the opportunity to merit heaven for all eternity. The test of merit (though "test" is really a misnomer) could have been simply a test of gratitude or perhaps one of loyalty where the angels needed to acknowledge their owed, unfettered allegiance to the God who made them from nothing. Lucifer instead became corrupted with a self-love. He was given graces beyond his fellow angels, and instead of being appreciative he became prideful and perhaps envious of those blessings others were given that he was denied.

Other theologians speculate that the Luciferian fall stems from the angel's refusal to acknowledge that God would take the form of a human. Lucifer, a spirit being, was appalled that he must one day worship God in the form of a man of flesh. Psalm 96:7 and Hebrews 1:6, and other passages, allude to this position.[18] This theme is echoed in John Milton's *Paradise Lost*[19]; and in the Quran, too, a similar theme is exhibited, where Iblis (Satan), who was a being made of fire, was offended by the blessings bestowed by Allah on man, made of mere clay. [20]

The origin of sin presents a perplexing problem. Catholics cite Original Sin as a source of our inherited concupiscence, but this merely begs the question of the source of that Original Sin. The Genesis narrative identifies Adam as blaming Eve for his sin, and Eve blaming the serpent for hers, but what we have here is regression, not origination. Why not trace the origin of the serpent's sin then? Well, assuming for purposes of this argument that the serpent is synonymous with Lucifer (Satan), then indeed we do come at last to the primordial sin, the first turning away from God. The mystery of iniquity still remains unsolved, however, as we must then ask, why did Lucifer choose to sin? Many theologians have attributed Satan's free will as his introduction of sin into the created order. But, this vague generalization does not adequately answer questions about why Lucifer had sinful inclinations to begin with—or, if he did, why God's grace was refused in favor of such inclinations?

Also, we have the problem of free will in the heavenly realm.[21] We know that the blessed now are free in heaven, yet they are sealed in their beatitude. The citizens of heaven cannot sin; they do not wish to. For them, God is their all, and nothing outside of him could possibly tempt them. Why was this not the case with Lucifer and his rebellious followers? We turn back to the aforementioned theological speculation that originally the angels were in God's presence, but it was a veiled presence. They were presented with a choice to follow him, and then only after the fall did God fully reveal himself to the loyal angels. Once in God's full and refulgent presence the loyal angels were enraptured and could not possibly be tempted by anything outside of God and his good will; since he is infinite, there really is nothing outside of him that is tempting.

Evil has no being in itself but only exists as a corruption of what was once good. Evil has been described with the Latin phrase "*privatio boni*," meaning "privation of goodness." Evil is not a thing in itself but a corruption or absence of good. This idea of evil as a turning away from good helps to better understand the devil himself, who has completely turned away from God—only since God is everywhere this is an impossible task. So, where can the devil hide? As described above, one hiding place is found by turning in on themselves and cutting themselves off from God. With this disassociation from the source of Life itself, the fallen have devolved into a kind of non-being, a demon, or legion of demons (Luke 8:26-30), devoid of personality and individualism, possessing only hate and malice. There is no mention of the devil or Satan in the Creeds. In this way, we can say Satan and demons do not exist as beings as we know them. If we say that God does not exist as a being we understand it is because he supersedes our ontological categories. If we say that devils don't exist as beings we recognize, it is because they have degraded beyond such classification.

"The devil is not impersonal like stones or bureaucracies; he is a non-person. The Devil has become all that God is not; he is not beyond personality—he is without it. His purpose in creation is not to destroy God; he knows that he cannot do that. He wants to draw us into the vortex of non-personhood that he has become, and the nothingness of non-being that he is becoming. Satan, in short, aims to take as many of us with him as he can."[22] Demons live in a state of self-imposed torment and despair. They coexist in hell and yet are free to interact with creation. "Being spirits, the devils do not need to be chained in one place to undergo their punishment; they bear it whersoever the Creator permits them to be and to act. The good angels who assist us see the face of God, and bear with them everywhere the celestial beatitude. In like manner, the demons everywhere undergo their damnation . . ."[23]

If it were in their power to self-exterminate, they would. But, as fallen *angels*, it is in their nature to exist eternally—this is an example of the natural good left to them—and the impossibility of having their plight ever change just makes them rage all the more. They are still loved by God, though he hates their sin. They experience his love as a burning fire.

Lucifer's choice brings with it a host of imponderable questions. Why would a being choose hell over heaven? If Lucifer harbored so much malice, why did God create him in the first place?

Why would God create any being that chooses to exist as an abomination—this is, perhaps, the simplest to answer. Everything God creates is done out of love. The first fallen angel was made for the sake of loving and being loved. But, for love to be true and real, it must be freely given and accepted. Lucifer and his companions freely chose themselves over God. Lucifer seeks both to be annihilated, to end his torment, and to continue his existence in order to work his evil, thus existing between two desires and becoming all the more contorted. Yet, God does not destroy Lucifer because immortality is essential to an angel's nature—even a fallen angel. God does not bind the devil from working his evil because through that evil, men and women have merited great rewards.

How can the other angels be sure they won't fall at some time in the future? The answers are entwined in mystery. Pride, lust, envy, and the same trials that confront us overcame Lucifer. As an angel with a free will, he was free to choose an eternity of torment as the ruler of hell over an eternity of bliss as a servant in heaven.

Most ancient civilizations believed the world was saturated with divine activity in a way that leaves little or no room for natural contingencies. We see this in the Greek myth of Persephone. The crops would not grow in the winter because Demeter, the goddess of the harvest, did not attend to the harvest in winter because that was when her daughter Persephone was in the realm of Hades. In the spring, when Persephone returned to her mother's side, Demeter was focused on her responsibilities and crops grew.[24]

Christianity rejects such mythological thinking but does recognize that our world struggles "not against enemies of blood and flesh, but against the rulers, against the authorities, against the cosmic powers of this present darkness, against the spiritual forces of evil in the heavenly places" (Ephesians 6:12). These "authorities" and "cosmic powers" can be understood as supernatural realties, but adopting too strong a view about evil powers and principalities operating in our world may cause some to drift dangerously close to superstitious thinking. If there is a drought, we must have offended the powers and principalities governing the rain. If there is a cancer diagnosis, what power or principality brought this on? Many scholars believe that ancient peoples, including some authors of the Bible, operated from the perspective of this sort of undifferentiated consciousness.

Though demonic forces are not the cause of every evil and suffering in the world, these beings should be taken seriously. Certain fallen angels are known by name. Abaddon—which is Hebrew for "destruction" and was originally a section of Gehenna (the place of the dead)—appears to be the name of a fallen angel (Revelations 9:11). Lucifer, who is now Satan, assuredly is the name of another.

We are unsure of the number of demonic beings. Pious tradition posits that one third[25] of all the angels became demons because of a passage in the last book of the Bible ("Then another sign appeared in heaven: an enormous red dragon with seven heads and ten horns and seven crowns on its heads. Its tail swept a third of the stars out of the sky and flung them to the earth . . ." Revelation 12:3-4), but this is mere speculative interpretation. What can be said is their numbers will never grow from the ranks of the holy angels. There simply is no danger of more angels falling from heaven,[26] as the time of testing has passed, and God has long since revealed himself fully to the angelic realm. The loyal angels were rewarded with the beatific vision and can no longer be tempted; they cannot sin. All the loyal angels are now so closely united with their creator that they will what he wills.

Lucifer, the prince of demons, has been described by one saint as a chained mad dog seeking to devour any prey within his reach. The Bible uses similar imagery: "Like a roaring lion your adversary the devil prowls around, looking for someone to devour" (2 Peter 5:8). In order to lure souls closer to him, he takes on the guise of an innocent lamb.

Satan is referred to as the "ruler of the power of the air" (Ephesians 2:2) and the "ruler of this world" (John 12:31). When he tempted Jesus, he showed him all the kingdoms of the world that he would give to him in exchange for Jesus bowing down to worship him (Luke 4:7-8). But this is God's world, not the devil's, and references to him being ruler of the "world" does not mean ruler of the earth; the original Greek refers to an age or an era. Jesus himself claimed to have overcome the world (John 16:33), and he certainly did mean "world" geographically.

Regardless, Satan's influence is limited. "Let the enemy rage at the gate, let him knock, let him push, let him cry, let him howl, let him do worse; we know for certain that he cannot enter save by the door of our consent."[27]

Satan is a single being and as such one wonders how the devil can tempt more than one person simultaneously. There are several different theories, but two prominent conjectures are that while the devil is not omnipresent like God, he, like all angels is not bound by space in the same way we are. Therefore, we can speculate the devil can be not everywhere at once but can be several places at once. (This is a crude physical analogy for a spiritual being.) Another more practical explanation may be that when we attribute some act to the devil we actually mean him directly or one of his many demons.

Lucifer's minions do not serve him out of love. They all suffer; they plot and despair. They have permanently and irrevocably chosen evil, but they can mimic some goodness. For example, Satan's minions can be patient when tempting, but in their damnable state they find no real pleasure in any "good" they do. The kind of "good" fallen angels can do is that which is natural to their state. They are incapable of any supernatural virtue that requires the grace of God, from which they are forever cut off.

While it is improper to find the devil's hand in every evil of this world, the spiritually mature have always admitted to a personified evil that tempts us and seeks our destruction. However, God gives us all enough grace to overcome the influence of the devil. (See 2 Corinthians 2:19.)

✝

CHAPTER TEN

THE CHURCH
(ECCLESIOLOGY)

THE EARLY CHURCH

The New Testament is replete with references to Jesus' objective to gather a people, to form a community, to restore Israel, and to launch a movement. Jesus declared his intention to build a church in Matthew 16:18-19. Later, after his resurrection, he told his disciples to "Go therefore and make disciples of all nations, baptizing them in the name of the Father and of the Son and of the Holy Spirit" (Matthew 28:19).

But just because Jesus wished to gather and unite a community of believers does not mean he had a specific, detailed blueprint for how the Church should develop. His earliest followers were comprised mostly of Jewish believers who were ostracized by their own people and scorned by pagan society. Of the original twelve Apostles only eleven were left, and they gathered together in the company of Jesus' mother and Mary Magdalene, as well as other disciples, to pray and to reflect upon what Jesus had taught them.

By casting lots, the Apostles chose a new member, Matthias, to replace Judas, and along with over a hundred other Christians, they gathered together on the feast of Pentecost. The consensus was that Jesus' death did not end his vision but actually inaugurated a new era. This was not mere wishful thinking but the actual result of deeply personal and profound encounters some of Jesus' followers had with the risen Christ. The testimonies are clear that these meetings were not dreams or fantasies but actual face-to-face interactions with the living Jesus.

The exact moment of the Church's beginning is hard to pin down. Some scholars cite Jesus' Last Supper (when both the Apostles were ordained and the Mass was instituted) as a legitimate point of origin, while others point to Pentecost (the descent of the Holy Spirit on Jesus' followers) as marking the birth of the Church.

The timing of the arrival of Pentecost is not accidental. The day of Pentecost was 50 days after Jesus' resurrection, and 50 days after the second day of the Passover feast, on Shavuot. Shavuot is the festival that commemorates God's bestowal of the Torah, the word of God, to Moses. Pentecost happened on Shavuot, and this time the word of God, under the new covenant, was bestowed by God as "tongues of fire."

The account in the book of Acts describes how a great tumult, like the wind of a storm, came upon those gathered in Jesus' name. Then, flames, which appeared as tongues of fire, came upon each person, and they began to speak in strange and unfamiliar languages. The symbolism is clear: Millennia after the confusion of languages at Babel (Genesis 11:1-9), the miracle of the tongues of fire, Pentecost (Acts 2:1-8), promised to restore, through Jesus, humanity, which was once scattered and confused.

A crowd had gathered outside the place where the followers of Jesus had met, probably drawn there by the sound of the great wind and the ebullient voices of those who had just been filled with the Holy Spirit. Jew and Egyptian, Asian and Cyrenian, they all heard their own native languages being spoken to them.

There are hints of the Holy Spirit's work at Pentecost, reflecting the creation narrative in Genesis. Christians are again animated by the breath of God, this time, born anew, to begin the work of participating in the restoration of creation, the coming of God's kingdom, the establishment of God's Church. The book of Acts records that 3,000 people were converted to Christianity that first Pentecost.

The earliest Christians, their numbers having grown, formed congregations that met in synagogues and private homes. Jesus' disciples were initially considered by many to be a sect of Judaism. (Some early converts to Christianity were neither Jews nor pagans but a hybrid between the two. In Acts 13:50, 17:4, 17:17, and 18:7, and elsewhere in the New Testament, we read about God-fearers. These people were likely Gentiles who respected and, to a limited extent, followed Mosaic law.)

The change from a Jewish faction to a new religion was not immediate, not without controversy, and was not the work of a single, unified group. From the earliest days of the Christian Church, different competing factions struggled to understand and put into practice the teachings of Jesus. Those who had encountered Jesus personally relied on building a Christian community in light of his teachings and ministry from the perspective of his death and resurrection.

When preaching the gospel, evangelists of Jesus Christ found that some listeners were converted but others engaged in passionate debate. Gentiles debated using philosophy and pagan religious doctrine while fellow Jews debated using Scripture, theology, and points of law. Eventually, they were cast from the synagogues. These first believers, too nascent to even be called "Christians," were identified by such monikers as "disciples" or simply as those "who belonged to the Way" (Acts 9:2). As the Church expanded, the various congregations began looking for a structure to keep them unified.

The Apostles held a special authority in the early Christian communities. Peter, who had a deep love for and loyalty to Jesus, was the preeminent Apostle. More biographical details are provided about him than any other of the original twelve followers. The Apostles are listed by name four times in the Bible, and Peter always appears as the first on the list. He was the putative leader of the other eleven Apostles. In recognition of his peerless role he served as the Church's very first pope. (The word "pope" derives from the Greek word "*páppas*," which is a tender moniker for one's dad or papa. Originally, all bishops of the Church could be identified as a pope, but around the fourth century the title became exclusive to the bishop of Rome.)

Jesus had changed Simon's name to Peter, because "Peter" means "rock," whereas Simon means "God has heard." The bestowal of that servant-authority is found in Matthew 16:18-19, wherein Jesus declares, "And I tell you, you are Peter, and on this rock I will build my church, and the gates of Hades will not prevail against it. I will give you the keys of the kingdom of heaven, and whatever you bind on earth will be bound in heaven, and whatever you loose on earth will be loosed in heaven."

Yet, later, this rock denied Jesus three times. This disgraceful betrayal is recounted in all four Gospels. A second passage, John 21:15-17, reads: "When they had finished breakfast, Jesus said to Simon Peter, 'Simon, son of John, do you love me more than these?' He said to him, 'Yes, Lord; you know that I love you.' He said to him, 'Feed my lambs.' He said to him a second time, 'Simon, son of John, do you love me?' He said to him, 'Yes, Lord; you know that I love you.' He said to him, 'Tend my sheep.' He said to him the third time, 'Simon, son of John, do you love me?' Peter was grieved, because he said to him a third time, 'Do you love me?' and he said to him, 'Lord, you know everything; you know that I love you. Jesus said to him, 'Feed my sheep.'"

This exchange takes place on a beach, between the post-resurrected Jesus and Peter, while sitting near a fire. Jesus asks Peter three times, "Do you love me?" The parallel is clear. Jesus' three questions for Peter emphasize and forgive the three denials by Peter, which also occurred near a fire. Thus, Peter renews his faith in Jesus. He does more than just affirm his faith; he lives up to his name as a rock of faith and the preeminent member of the Apostles. According to tradition, and as recorded in the non-canonical book *Acts of Peter*, Peter met the risen Lord one last time before his own death. In an attempt to avoid execution by crucifixion, Peter left Rome and encountered Jesus,[1] asking him "*Quo vadis domine?*" (Latin: "Where are you going, Lord?") Jesus answered that he was going to Rome to be crucified once again. This inspired Peter to return to Rome, where he in fact was arrested and crucified. Yet, in Peter's humility, he declared that he was unworthy to die in the same way as Jesus and requested that he be crucified upside down.

By the time of Peter's martyrdom, the Church's core beliefs and practices had begun to take form. The early Church did not just spring up *sua sponte* but was prefigured in Jewish people, who were called to be an authoritative community of believers serving as an example for the world. It is no exaggeration to say that salvation is from the Jews.

> If there is one theological issue which both Jews and Christians should be able to agree on, it is that 'salvation is from the Jews.' It has been a constant teaching of Judaism from the days of Abraham onwards that the salvation of all mankind is to come from the Jews. That is the primary sense in which the Jews are 'the Chosen People.' And Christians believe that 'salvation is from the Jews,' since those are the very words which Jesus spoke to the Samaritan woman at the well. (John 4:22)[2]

Not only did the early Church adopt and integrate the Jewish Bible as the Christian Old Testament, but they also employed the rich religious heritage of the Jews, including a consecrated priesthood and liturgical rituals, which were transformed and integrated into Christian worship. In the moving encounter between Jesus and the Samaritan woman, Jesus uttered both a prophecy and a command. He said, "God is spirit, and those who worship him must worship in spirit and truth" (John 4:24). This somewhat cryptic saying has many layers of meaning, but a point Jesus is making is that God desires to be worshiped according to certain norms, namely spirit and truth. Now, couple this teaching with what we find in 1 Timothy 3:15, identifying the church as "the pillar and bulwark of the truth." So, the early Christians reasoned that if God wishes to be worshiped in spirit and truth, and the Church is the pillar and foundation of truth, then the Church is the normative means for a relationship with God.

Catholics are Bible-believing Christians. The Mass,[3] the principal form of worship for Catholics, is deeply scriptural through and through. The liturgy celebrated by Christians for over two thousand years is not random or arbitrary but is a conscious reflection of the heavenly liturgy. Look through the book of Revelation and you can find most elements of a Catholic Mass. What's more, the liturgy celebrated here is not just a cheap imitation or poor reenactment of the celestial liturgy but participation therein.

Jesus commanded the celebration of the Mass when at the Last Supper he told his disciples to reenact the meal he shared with them (Luke 22:19). I once knew of a priest who began every Mass with these words: "Welcome to this celebration in which Jesus offers himself once again to the Father for our sake, knowing that he understands our weakness and he will forgive us our sins." This is a pattern of God interacting with himself on our behalf that has played out since God created humans. Moreover, it is God interacting with us and through us.

At the center of Catholic worship is the Eucharist—praise and thanksgiving in commemoration of the sacrifice of Jesus, of God interceding with God for our sake. At his Last Supper, Jesus commanded his followers to "Do this in remembrance of Me" (Luke 22:19; 1 Corinthians 11:24). The Mass is this remembrance, this memorial of Jesus' Eucharistic meal. The word "Mass" evolved from the Latin verb "missa," meaning "to send"—which Jesus did: He sent his disciples out to preach the good news. Catholics refer to the Mass as the "holy sacrifice of the Mass." The word "sacrifice" is used not because the Church teaches that Jesus is slain over and over again. No, Jesus died only once and cannot die again. So, the liturgy makes manifest the "once for all" (Hebrews 10:9-18) sacrifice of Jesus. That is, the Mass is the unbloody re-presentation of Jesus' sacrifice. The bloody sacrifice on the cross, over two thousand years ago, is sacramentally renewed at each Mass. Jesus is physically present in the sacrament, but we must avoid a crude understanding of this presence. Jesus was physically raised from the dead in his resurrection, but his new glorified body is beyond what we understand as physical existence; so too with the Real Presence in the Eucharist.

Jesus established this sacrament at the Last Supper and established the Church (Matthew 16:18) with an ordained priesthood, which began with the Apostles and continues to this day. It is not just that Jesus founded a community over two millennia ago, and today believers who share a belief in him come together. This visible organization is more than a mere assembly of like-minded believers who come together in a common cause. If this were the case, the sacraments would be hollow symbols and the teachings would be arbitrary.

The word "Church" is a translation of the Greek term "ekklesia"—a gathering or assembly. Nowhere was this assemblage more important than at the agape meal; the Lord's table. In many ways, the history of the Eucharistic feast is the history of the Church. Early on, Christians would gather to share a meal, often including others who were less fortunate. This gathering was open in a way quite foreign to the secretive mystery cults of the pagans as well as the exclusivist meetings of the Jews.

Yet, the image of a gathering does not do justice to the reality of the Church, as it conveys a passivity that belies the true nature of the kingdom-advancing people of God. The Church was not created by the followers of Jesus but is a human-and-divine institution formed by God, which he continues to shape, to guide, and to uphold. Membership in this Church is essential from the Catholic perspective. Saint Cyprian of Carthage said, "You cannot have God for your Father if you don't have the Church for your Mother."[4] This does not mean that all members are holy; in fact, the Church is populated by of an assortment of sinners.

Since the time of the very first Christians gathering themselves and struggling to make sense and put into practice Jesus' teachings, the Church became an organization that began with a kerygmatic phase and moved then to a catechetical phase. The Church is an organization. Truly, Catholicism is, in a sense, the quintessential organized religion. The Church is simultaneously the body of Christ[5] and the body of believers, which exists as an eschatological community and witnesses to the world. The Church's goals are promoting conversion to and reconciliation with God and each other. The Church's sole mission is to carry on the work of Jesus Christ. Each Catholic is called, according to his or her vocation, to act *in persona Christi* (Latin for "in the person of Christ"); that is, imitating his goodness, his holiness, and his selfless love.

The Church can be understood in many varied ways, as an organization, as the body of Christ, as a mystical Communion, as a sacrament, as a Herald, as a Servant,[6] as *Mater Et Magistra* (Mother and Teacher),[7] as the bride of Christ, etc. Notice these last two models, "mother" and "bride," are feminine. Therefore, we can legitimately refer to the Church by the pronoun "her" since she is the bride of Christ; sometimes the Church is referred to as "it" since the Church is the body of Christ. The Catholic Church is not simply a human innovation but is a "complex reality which coalesces from a divine and human element."[8]

That human element comes with flaws. Henri Cardinal de Lubac wrote,

> I have been told that a young intelligent priest, full of good qualities, has left the Church and apostatized, declaring he was scandalized by 'certain attitudes on the part of the hierarchy'. I am not interested in what these 'attitudes' were. I am willing to grant, as a hypothesis, with my eyes shut, that these 'attitudes' were in fact regrettable. I am even willing to imagine worse ones. But, what was this young priest's faith, then, before the disaster happened? What was his idea of the Church? . . . Young as he may still be, could he wonder himself at men sharing in the human condition?[9]

Catholics are bearers of a tradition, and in that sense may be called "traditional," however this is often confused with being fundamentalist, which Catholics are usually not. The celebration of the Mass is not possible without an ordained priesthood. Certainly, all baptized Christians are priests by nature of their

baptismal covenant; however, the nature of this universal priesthood is not the same as that of ordained priests. The ordained
priesthood exists only as a share in the unique priesthood of Jesus Christ, who is priest, prophet, and king. Ordained priests are
different in kind, not just degree, from the priesthood held by all
baptized believers. The difference is that the man who is ordained
a priest receives the sacrament of holy orders and undergoes an
ontological change. He is indelibly sealed by the Holy Spirit and
graced with the power to consecrate. In deference to this charism,
Catholics refer to priests as "Father."[10] There is formally only one
sacrament of Holy Orders in Catholicism, but there are multiple
stages, from the permanent deaconate to priesthood, and, for
some, on to the episcopacy (bishopric).

But, surprisingly, Jesus' role of high priest need not be understood solely in terms of the traditional Jewish priesthood. "Jesus'
priesthood is not merely a priesthood of religion, isolated in the
sanctuary from all things ordinary or impure. This priesthood is
carried on in the very midst of ordinary life. . . . Jesus' priesthood
is not Aaronic or Levitical, not a priesthood of religion, based
on sacred shrines and rites. It is the priesthood of Melchizedek,
named for a Gentile king (Genesis 14:17-24) and shared with all
humanity."[11] We can conceive of Jesus' priesthood in terms of the
totus Christus (Latin: "whole Christ"). The one church is united
to the one Christ, unified in the Holy Spirit into a single mystical
Body with Christ as the head and the church as the body. The
apostle Paul notes as much in 1 Corinthians 12:12, "For just as
the body is one and has many members, and all the members of
the body, though many, are one body, so it is with Christ." Saint
Paul did not use the metaphor of a body haphazardly. As a pious
Jew familiar with the Hebrew Scriptures' reverence for the physical form, Paul would have revered the body as the good creation
of God. Coupling this respect with the reverence he had for Jesus
led him to represent Jesus and his Church as a unified head and
body. The message then is one in which the Body, the Church, is
where the Christian community gathers not just to pray to God
but to be transformed into the persons, the images of God, we
were created to be.

The Holy Catholic Church is an authoritative servant-com-
munity, a living body of believers—both lay and ordained, guided
by the Holy Spirit—who profess and live a common faith in Jesus
Christ and who gather together regularly to worship God and

celebrate the sacraments. She is comprised of those who share common beliefs and practices. United by the Holy Spirit, Catholics also share in the seven sacraments of baptism, Eucharist, reconciliation, confirmation, marriage, holy orders, and anointing of the sick; numerous sacramentals; and participate under the auspices of the hierarchical institution of the Church. The Church is not a democracy but a hierarchy with the pope as the leader. Although the pope is the absolute ruler of the Church, he serves as the custodian of truth and not as some sort of living prophet who can arbitrarily change what God has revealed as being true. The pope imparts some of his power and authority to a number of juridical bodies. The Roman curia is a universal governing body of the Church. There are official congregations (e.g. the Congregation for the Doctrine of the Faith); synods; councils; papal encyclicals; and conferences of bishops, cardinals, local bishops, and the *vox populi* ("voice of the people"). The people, not just the clergy, make up God's Church, and the vox populi is an essential element of the faith.

The Church is a reconciling community of believers but not a democracy; she is a monarchy with Christ as her King. The Church is a hierarchy—a sacred order—in which some have authority over others. But, those in authority are called to serve. Even the pope himself is called *Servus Servorum Dei* (Servant of the Servants of God). The premise, then, that the pope is an absolute monarch, is false, given that he is bound to adhere to certain teachings. In theory, he is even bound by canon law, though he has the power to change canon law.

Nonetheless, every person in the Church has a voice, and when those voices are spoken in unison, the vox populi has been immeasurably influential in Church history. Remember, the Church existed before the New Testament was formalized, and this point is critically important. Guided by the Holy Spirit, the oral tradition, and the collective memory of the community of believers, the early Church decided which books to include in the canon of the Bible and which doctrines were included and excluded from various creeds.

The early Church began with controversy. The book of Acts records an example of one of the first disagreements to erupt in the newly formed Christian community. A council in Jerusalem (not formally an ecumenical council) was called to resolve a dispute about the necessity of circumcising new Gentile Christians.

Eventually, this specific issue was resolved, but Christianity continued to wrestle with challenges and controversy.

It is helpful to recall the cultural milieu in which the nascent Church was formed. Rome ruled the known world. That is, the Roman Empire was massive in geographic size, covering much of Europe, the Middle East, and parts of Africa. Within this single empire there existed numerous tribes, races, ethnicities, and cultures. The Greco-Roman influence on these disparate peoples was quite impressive in that certain laws, languages (Greek and Latin), and economic as well as concrete infrastructures united the empire. There was not a single religion in the world into which the Church was launched. However, it is fair to bifurcate into two groups—Jews and pagans[12]—those whom the early Church sought to evangelize. The Roman world was thoroughly Hellenized (influenced by Greek culture), though the Jews remarkably did manage to maintain their way of life—to a large extent due to the Maccabean revolt and the success of the Herodian kings in placating Rome.

In the book of Acts, we find that, when preaching to Jews, the disciples reasoned from the Scriptures (Acts 12: 2-3). However, when preaching to pagans they began from a different starting point: "The God who made the world and everything in it, he who is Lord of heaven and earth, does not live in shrines made by human hands" (Acts 17:24). In both audiences, early Christians found a yearning for a Messiah; the Jewish expectation was grounded in the writings of the prophets, and the pagan expectation was tied to certain mystery cults. But, Jesus transcended Messianic hopes as well as pagan expectations.

The early Church was not just a phenomenon local to Jesus' homeland. Just as Jesus was sent by the Father, so Jesus sent out his followers to continue his mission. In what is called the Great Commission, Christ sends out his disciples. (See Matthew 28:16-20.)

Soon after Jesus' resurrection, the gospel began to spread like wildfire through the missionary zeal of men like Saints Peter and Paul.[13] It is worth noting that, after the crucifixion and resurrection, it was Paul who was a primary builder of the church, and he did so not by amazing people with miracles but by relying on his deep and abiding faith, an unparalleled intellect, and indefatigable commitment to evangelization.[14] Paul was considered to be an Apostle of Jesus, and he both performed and witnessed miracles done through the power of Christ. However, Paul taught that miracles are just one among many spiritual gifts (others include the gift of prophecy and the gift of speaking in tongues). Paul's ministry made him one of the most influential New Testament figures. Prior to his conversion experience, Paul went by the name Saul, and he was a convert to Christianity from Judaism. Paul was not just a casual practitioner of the Jewish faith. He was, instead, a self-described member of the tribe of Benjamin who identified as a Hebrew of the Hebrews and a Pharisee of Pharisees (Philippians 3:5-6). Paul studied in Jerusalem under the famous Gamaliel, who was a member of the Sanhedrin and among the most influential rabbis of the day. Paul thoroughly knew and conscientiously followed both the Hebrew Scriptures and religious traditions of his people.

In addition to his expansive and penetrating knowledge of Judaism, Paul was a Roman citizen who hailed from Tarsus. This means he was quite familiar with the teachings and practices of the Hellenized world. At some point, he learned of and developed a visceral antipathy against Christians. He intensely persecuted other Jews who proclaimed Jesus as the long-awaited Messiah. Undoubtedly, Paul was troubled with the Christian claim that the temple and the law, both central to Paul's theology, were now nonessential.

However, while on the road to Damascus, Jesus, surrounded by a blinding light, appeared to him. After he had this intense transformative encounter with the risen Christ, and at the instruction of the Lord, a blinded Saul went to a nearby city to wait. There, he was found by the Christian Ananias, who healed Saul's blindness, instructed him in the faith, and baptized him, giving him a new name. Paul's conversion was total. His zeal for the God of Israel was transformed and channeled into a devout and fearless love of Jesus.

After Paul's conversion, he became a tireless evangelist for the Lord Jesus Christ. Paul traveled thousands of miles, endured dreadful hardships, and established nearly two dozen churches throughout the Mediterranean and beyond. He was shipwrecked, blinded, beaten, bitten by a poisonous snake, and eventually martyred. Yet, this great saint and missionary clarified some of the most foundational teachings of Christian theology, managing to write nearly a third of the New Testament.

By contemplating "the boundless riches of Christ" (Ephesians 3:8), Paul concluded that not only the Jews, not even all of humanity, but really all of creation had been painfully waiting for the Messiah, Jesus (Romans 8:19-23). There are thirteen epistles, or letters, making up over one quarter of the New Testament, which are attributed to his name.[15] These Pauline books[16] are the earliest New Testament writings, dating between 35 AD and 65 AD. (By way of comparison, the earliest Gospel was authored around 65 AD.)

Interestingly, Paul's writings are quite different than the Gospels. We don't find him recounting Jesus' life, his parables, or his instructions; we don't even hear much about Jesus' miracles. However, Paul repeatedly focuses on the resurrection; the anastasis of Jesus. Additionally, Paul preached and wrote about a number of thorny theological questions that plagued the early Christian community. His insights established foundational principles that quelled certain important controversies and provided a framework for orthodox teachings on a host of issues. Among the most important issues with which Paul wrestled was the question of the role the Old Testament law played in the lives of followers of Jesus. This is an important question because on the one hand, the authority of the Old Testament bears witness to the Messiah. On the other hand, that authority is now non-binding given Jesus' new covenant. Furthermore, while the first followers of Jesus were Jews, it did not take long for Gentiles to become Christians. Paul wrestled with question of whether a Gentile follower of Jesus must first become Jewish and get circumcised and follow Jewish dietary restrictions, etc. This controversy is actually one example of the broader question of how the old and new covenants relate.

Jesus made it clear he did not come to do away with the old law or the teachings of the prophets[17] but to fulfill them (Matthew 5:17). Paul figured out how this truth played out in practical terms. Specifically, he solved the riddle of how the law can be authoritative without being binding, by bifurcating the law into the "letter of the law" and the "spirit of the law." With this incisive insight, Christians came to learn they are bound by the moral code of the Old Testament but not by the obligations to perform certain religious rituals. The letter of the law cannot save because it cannot be perfectly kept by sinners. However, the spirit of the law, including the virtues of faith, hope, and most importantly agape love saves, through God's gracious gift of Jesus. In other words, no observance of the law, no matter how meticulous, can save a person. The chasm between the Holy God and sinful humans is just too great. But, the good news is that while we can't reach God, he can and did, in the person of Jesus, come to us.

A close reading of Paul reveals that his deep interest in Jesus' resurrection, his claim that all of creation groaned in anticipation of the Messiah's coming, and his reconciliation of the old and new law, all tie together brilliantly. Paul realized that Jesus was not merely the Jewish Messiah who came to redeem and restore the Jewish people; instead, he is the universal savior who came to reestablish God's kingdom—a kingdom of love.

The churches founded by St. Paul, along with other early Christian communities, loved in a new and radical way. They displayed mercy heretofore unseen and had a strong commitment to the dignity of women, the poor, and the sick. Moreover, Christians abandoned not just the false gods of pagan culture but also many of the attendant philosophies that were common currency in the ancient world. In their place, they proclaimed the sovereignty of Jesus. His miracles, whether they be over nature—like calming a stormy sea—or over disease—as when he healed lepers and the blind or deaf—all speak to Jesus' authority, and they foreshadow life in the kingdom of God, where sorrow and pain cease to exist. The sacraments that Jesus established—and above all else, Jesus' resurrection and glorification—foretell what awaits all of the faithful.

As mentioned, the converts were not just from the Jewish community but from the Gentile world too. Historically, Jews did not seek to convert non-Jews, as they believed they were God's chosen people—born into that life. Originally a derivative of Judaism, by circa 41 AD, Gentiles too were becoming Christians alongside Jews. The followers of Jesus began to form communities. Circa 70 AD, Jerusalem fell to the Romans and the temple was destroyed. Christianity still expanded beyond the Middle East. Unlike many of the world's other great religions, Christianity did not stay localized for long. The origins of the faith are firmly rooted in the Middle East, but soon Christian Churches were established all over the world. Within a few hundred years, the Roman Empire became "Christianized," and Christianity dominated Europe for centuries. From there, the Church spread out across the globe.

To be sure, this early Church is one and the same with today's Church, but there were some individuals and even entire congregations who held to beliefs considered heretical today.

Contemporary Christianity, diverse and complex as we find it, actually may show more unanimity than the Christian churches of the first and second centuries. For nearly all Christians since that time, Catholics, Protestants, or Eastern Orthodox, have shared three basic premises. First, they accept the canon of the New Testament; second, they confess the Apostolic Creed; and third, they affirm specific forms of church institution. But, every one of these—the canon of Scripture, the creed, and the institutional structure—emerged in its present form only toward the end of the second century.[18]

We should not overemphasize this diversity at the expense of the early Church unity, however. As the Church grew, some of the communities became transcongregational, with one leader over several churches. Thus, they were not completely autonomous. To ensure the passage of the truth about Jesus and his message, Christians began to record their understanding of their faith. The letters of St. Paul became part of the New Testament. In the latter part of the first century, Christians had developed their own unique liturgies, sacraments, and songs of praise. Statements of belief, as recorded in the *Didache*,[19] a second-century recounting of early Christian beliefs and practices, tell us what the early Church believed.

Itinerant missionaries traveled extensively, preaching the gospel message and establishing local congregations. These missions necessitated a formalization of doctrine as individual congregations were formed and began to develop their own practices. For example, some early Christians insisted that new Gentile converts had to be circumcised before becoming Christians. Paul strongly protested against this practice and set forth guidelines regarding circumcision and other disputes. (Many of these guidelines, communicated in the form of letters to local churches, were collected and accepted by the Church as part of the New Testament.)

Because Christianity was so novel, early Christians had to face the challenge of trying to explain new theological concepts and practices. They either had to use old words in new ways or, in some cases, had to create entirely new terms to pass on the richness of Jesus' message. Saint Paul was among the first and the best to do this. Paul's purpose in educating the various churches was not just to enforce some kind of doctrinal conformity but, in the Spirit of Pentecost, to foster a new kind of community.

This community must have rules, but these ordinances must be understood as means and not ends in themselves. The Eastern Orthodox distinguish between rules applied in a strict manner (Greek: *akreveia*), or in a lenient manner (Greek: *economia*). The concept of economia allows for generosity, accommodation, and certain flexibility when following the laws of God and his Church. Economia is not an excuse to break the laws of God but is in itself part of the law of love, which allows one to focus on the reasons for a law instead of the actual law itself. Economia is the antithesis of strict legalism and fundamentalism. Though the word "economia" is not often used in Catholic circles, the concept is regularly applied in pastoral practices.

The experience of the Christian community continued and developed in the forge of Roman persecution. The Imperial government felt threatened by this new religion, and Christianity was outlawed—bringing the penalty of death. The Church began to form its own strong identity, where it could have simply become one more cult in the vast pantheon of Roman religions or one more variation of an already fragmented first-century Judaism. Soon after Pentecost, the Church began to grow by the thousands. There were many choices that had to be made by the members of this new community, not least of which was what they should be called. The New Testament provides several names by which first century Christians identified themselves, including People of "the Way" (Acts 9:2) and "Nazarenes" (Acts 24:5).

The Church of Antioch offered the name "Christian" around 40 AD. This identifier may have been self-chosen or possibly a derogatory label that pagan authorities used to differentiate traditional Jews from those who continually preached about Christ.

Confusingly, the Church has never been called the "Christian Church" but just "the Church." Because the early followers were so unified, there was not a need to qualify a denomination of the Church in the way we do today. There was only one Church, and it was universal—in Greek, "*katholikos*." And it is from this word we derive the name "Catholic." The first written record we have of the Church being identified as the Catholic Church is from St. Ignatius of Antioch in 107 AD.

Living among fellow believers and establishing a group identity was not the choice of all Christians. Some retreated from the world as monasticism began to take hold. Communal life was hard for Christians during the years of persecution of the Church by the Roman government. During the reigns of emperors Nero, Titus, and Diocletian, thousands of Christians were killed, including St. Peter and St. Paul. While one would expect oppression from the governing authorities to stymie the growth of the Church, it was the blood of these many martyrs that helped to grow the early Church. Another reason why Christianity spread so quickly is that Jesus' message reached out to those whom the pagan culture had marginalized: the sick, the elderly, and, perhaps most importantly, women.

Christians were set apart from the rest of the world not only because of what they believed but also how they lived. These men and women treated society's poor, widowed, and sick with dignity, respect, and love. Women, second-class citizens in most of the world at this time in history, were elevated to a new standing in early Christian communities.

> It was a source of scandal for women to travel openly with a rabbi; but 'many' women followed Jesus through Galilee (Lk 8. 2-3).
> . . . Women continued to play a prominent role in the early gatherings. They were prophets (1 Cor 11. 5). Paul addresses them as leaders in the various gatherings he formed- Choe in Corinth, where she speaks for 'her establishment' (1 Cor 1: 11); Phoebe, the manager (diakonos) at Cenchreae (Rom 16:1); Apphia at (probably) Colossae (Phlm 2), where Nympha was also a leader (Col 4:15). At Philippi, Eunoe and Syntyche 'struggled by my side for the gospel' (Phil 4:3). Lydia, the dealer in fabrics, led a whole group of women instructed by Paul (Acts 16:13) Other women are mentioned as partners in missionary activity. Junia is called an emissary (apostolos), Paul's own title for himself. She and her husband shared Paul's imprisonment (Rom 16:7). Prisca and her husband are 'my fellow workers, who risked their own necks to save my life,' so that the whole assembly owes the two of them its gratitude (Rom 16:3-5). Paul refers to four women- Mary, Tryphaena, Tryphosa, Persis- as having 'toiled with effort' (kopiaein, Rom 16:6-12) for the Christians, the same verb he uses of his own activities (Gal 4:11,1 Cor 15:10).[20]

Christianity is often mistakenly portrayed as having European origins. However, this world-spanning religion was birthed in the Middle East. Given the fact that while Jesus walked the earth his message was not well received by the masses, the post-resurrection

Church, empowered by the Holy Spirit, grew with amazing rapidity, despite being persecuted by the Roman Empire. Rome was very adept at conquering and inflicting punishment and mercilessly tried to crush this upstart sect. This cruel maltreatment only served to increase the number of converts to the faith. There is an irony in the fact that the conquering Roman Empire was itself conquered by the faith, which used Rome's own resources to advance Christianity. Christian missionaries traveled on roads built by the Romans; they traveled in relative safety in territories conquered and ruled over by the Romans; they preached in the language common to the empire; and, perhaps, most ironic of all, they courageously accepted death at Roman hands instead of renouncing their faith. Tertullian, the second-century Church father, proclaimed that "the blood of martyrs is the seed of the Church."[21]

Saint Peter himself traveled to Rome within a decade of the crucifixion of Jesus. There, he boldly preached the gospel and eventually was martyred for his faith. Yet, the seeds he and other Christians planted bore a rich harvest in a short time. At the time there were hundreds of different cults of various pagan gods, yet Christianity did not become just another competing sect. We actually have archeological evidence of Christianity's growth from hundreds of thousands of Christians buried in catacombs near Rome. Trying to explain how a small band of the followers of an executed criminal grew into a Church of possibly six million or more by the early 300s is a real challenge. Author Rodney Stark provides some interesting insights into some reasons why Christianity overcame opposing religions.

> Christianity revitalized life in Greco-Roman cities by providing new norms and new kinds of social relationships able to cope with many urgent urban problems. To cities filled with the homeless and the impoverished, Christianity offered charity as well as hope. To cities filled with newcomers and strangers, Christianity offered an immediate basis for attachments. To cities filled with orphans and widows, Christianity provided a new and expanded sense of family. To cities torn by violent ethnic strife, Christianity offered a new basis for social solidarity. And to cities faced with epidemics, fires, and earthquakes, Christianity offered effective nursing services.[22]

In the decades that followed Jesus' resurrection, the original Apostles had passed away by the year 100 AD with the death of John. The Apostles themselves had disciples, some of whom wrote important texts. We have access to historical documents, such as the *Didache*, that first-century Christian text that provides valuable information on liturgical and moral practices and teachings. In the *Didache*, we begin to see the existence of a formalized hierarchical structure within the Church, with bishops playing a central role of unifying authority.

What followed was the sub-Apostolic age, where the Church was led by disciples of the Apostles, alongside other Christian leaders divided into three primary roles of bishops, presbyters, and deacons. The responsibilities of these specific offices became more clearly defined as the Church grew, however, from the earliest days, bishops were closely tied to the celebration of the Eucharist.

As Christianity expanded and developed, statements of faith and uniformed practices were instituted in response to numerous challenges. The Christian community was so united that it gradually began to form a distinct subculture, some would go so far as to say a Christian state, within the larger society. The Church faced persecution from the Roman Empire from without and conflicts of theological disagreements from within. In order to maintain unity and strength, the Church adopted a hierarchical structure based on apostolic succession. Just as Christ gave his Apostles authority, they in turn appointed leaders, bishops, to oversee specific geographic areas. This nascent chain of command became fully developed as early as the start of the second century.

The Patristic Age overlapped with the sub-Apostolic age and generally covers the years 100 AD to about 800 AD. The Patristic Age produced some of Christian history's greatest saints and theologians, starting with Clement of Rome, Ignatius of Antioch, and Polycarp of Smyrna. Early in the Patristic Age, important Christian writings such as the *Didache* and the *Shepherd of Hermas* were authored.

The first two centuries AD saw the spread of Christianity as far as Great Britain, and the world was introduced to the writings of Justin Martyr, Irenaeus of Lyons, Origen, Tertullian, and numerous others whose views still influence Christianity today. As the Church grew, debates ensued over which doctrines were orthodox and which were heresies.[23] Heresy can be defined as, "Anyone who, after receiving baptism, while remaining nominally a Christian, pertinaciously denies or doubts any of the truths that must be believed with divine and Catholic faith."[24]

Ironically, many pagans, who vainly placed their faith in follies such as mythical gods, astrology, magic, and augury (discerning the will of the gods by watching birds fly), saw Christians as superstitious and naïve. The idea that a Jewish peasant's death somehow brought about salvation was nothing less than absurd. To the mind of a pagan, the belief that there was a single God who providentially guides not just individual lives but all of history was simply bizarre.

The early Church suffered then, from persecution from without and controversy from within. As deniers of the Roman Pantheon, Christians were sometimes labeled as atheists (as were Jews). Closely connected to this claim was the charge of treason, for there was no separation of Church and State. To deny the pagan gods of imperial Rome, whose praise and worship was considered essential to the success of the empire, was seen as a betrayal of Rome itself. They were also accused of incest, due to the fact that they greeted each other with a kiss and they referred to each other as "brother" and "sister." The pagan mystery cults were so steeped in sex that Christians were just assumed to be engaging in the same sort of debauchery. They were also accused of cannibalism because of partaking in the Body and Blood of Jesus in the Eucharist. Unlike the Jews—for whom Romans, for political and practical reasons, had a resigned tolerance, due in part to the antiquity of their beliefs—the new upstart Christian insistence on worshiping only one God was not acceptable to Rome. In addition, as Christians became more separated and distinct from their Jewish roots, the Roman Empire became less tolerant of this new religion. One can imagine the hardships faced by those pagans who decided to convert to the Christian faith.

However, pagan Rome was gradually becoming converted. Why? Despite the empire's merciless persecution of Christians, the religion grew rapidly due in large measure to the loving way in which they lived. Christians fed the hungry, cared for the needy, shared common resources, avoided sexual immorality, and lived sober, industrious lives. They were unified, coming together to worship God and commemorate the Last Supper. In short, Christians were good citizens.

By 313 AD, the *Edict of Milan* was issued by Emperor Constantine, putting a stop to Christian persecution, thereby legalizing Christianity. This edict resulted from meetings in Milan between the two emperors of a divided Rome, Licinius, who ruled the eastern empire, and Constantine, who ruled in the western empire. Within ten years of the edict, Christianity had become Rome's official religion. By the early part of the fourth century, scholars estimate there were 6 million Christians. Thereafter, communities of Christians began to flourish and formalize Christian teachings.

In 325 AD, the First Ecumenical Council of Nicaea was convened, which formulated the Nicene Creed.[25] Approximately 150 years later, in the year 476 AD, the Roman Empire fell due to a combination of decadence, incompetence, and invasions by Vandals, Visigoths, and Ostrogoths. With the empire gone, the Church took up the mantle of preserving and circulating the great traditions of the western world, including much of the philosophy and cultural practices of antiquity, which would otherwise have been lost. The absence of a Roman Empire, and later, the founding of Islam, both shifted the focus of Christianity from its origins in the Holy Land to the European world.

As Christian communities grew, and members slowly began to realize that Jesus' second coming was not imminent, the Church adopted a structure of authority that was heavily influenced by the hierarchy of the Roman Empire. Nonetheless, there was a kind of pluralism that manifested in the form of at least three major rites, or traditions, for celebrating the sacraments, which came about within the faith: the Roman, the Antiochian, and the Alexandrian. From these three, numerous others have developed over the centuries. Christian theology was viewed through the lens of Platonic philosophy by Augustine of Hippo (350-428 AD), whose famous books *Confessions* and *City of God* set the foundations for much of subsequent Christian thought in the West, regarding grace, Original Sin, and other topics. It was around this time that Jerome completed his Latin translation of the Bible (404 AD). The Church, in this same era, had to contend with a power vacuum left by the fall of Rome (476 AD).

An important development in the understanding and expression of Christian faith was the institution of ecumenical councils. These councils or official gatherings of bishops and other church members were tasked with defining specific doctrines and verifying orthodox teachings. After some debate, the resultant teachings were formalized into creedal statements or official teachings. The declarations of a council, after being approved by the pope, are authoritative and irreversible.

The first such gathering was an Apostolic Council set in Jerusalem.[26] (See Acts 15:2–35.) The Catholic Church recognizes 21 such councils in her history (along with a plethora of lesser regional gatherings such as provincial councils and plenary councils). The Orthodox Church, however, only recognized the first seven: First Council of Nicaea I (325 AD); First Council of Constantinople I (381 AD); Council of Ephesus (431 AD); Council of Chalcedon (451 AD); Second Council of Constantinople (553 AD); Third Council of Constantinople (680–681 AD); and Second Council of Nicaea (787 AD).

The Creed, or statement of belief, issued by the Council of Nicaea, includes four identifying characteristics of the true Church: Christ's Church is one, holy, catholic, and apostolic. These attributes have come to be known as "the Four Marks of the Church." To be "one" is to be united in essentials of the faith, across space and time—not in the cult-like sense of all members thinking exactly alike about everything, but in the sense of a shared belief in truths of faith. To be "holy" is to be set apart and sanctified by God's Holy Spirit[27] and to continue and pass on the work of Jesus through sacraments, teachings, and good works. To be "catholic" is to be universal,[28] to be worldwide. (The Church is not bound to a particular geographic location or ethnicity). To be "apostolic" means, in part, to be traceable to Christ's first Apostles, in direct succession.

The one holy catholic and apostolic Church is made up of a communion of 24 rites, or churches—the Latin Rite and 23 autonomous Eastern Rites *sui juris* (self-governing) churches—all in communion with the pope but each with a distinct "liturgy, ecclesiastical discipline, and spiritual heritage."[29] While some Christian denominations may be loosely affiliated by certain shared beliefs and practices, each local Catholic parish is not merely connected to the Universal Church by mere affiliation or shared belief but is in itself an expression of the one holy catholic Church.

The Church's history dates back over two thousand years, and an enormously rich and multi-variant tradition has come down to us today. That tradition is based on the Bible, ecumenical councils, creeds, magisterial papal declarations, and a plethora of other sources. Not all of these sources are to be treated with

equal reverence. There is a single source for both Scripture and
Tradition, which is revealed in these two expressions. The word
"tradition" causes some confusion, because there are at least two
uses of the term in Catholicism. Sacred Tradition, with a capital
"T," refers to authoritative teachings of the Church. Sacred Tradition holds the same weight as Scripture within the Catholic
community; however, no Tradition can contradict the teachings
of Scripture. The idea that Tradition is co-authoritative with
Scripture makes sense when one considers two points. First, the
Church existed before the Christian New Testament. It is the
Tradition of the Church that gives us the canon of Scripture.
Second, there is precedent in the Jewish religion for this sort
of Tradition-Scripture symbiotic relationship. As New Testament
scholar Floyd Filson noted: "The scribes, mostly Pharisees, copied, taught, and applied the Mosaic Law and the oral tradition,
which they claimed was an integral part of the Law, received
through a direct succession of teachers going back to Moses.
Moses' seat [was a] synagogue chair which symbolized the origin
and authority of their teaching. Jesus does not challenge their
claim; he seems here to approve it [Mt 23:2]."[30]

The confusion arises when we see that the word "tradition,"
with a lowercase "t," can also refer to certain habits and customs
that are not authoritatively taught by the Church. Jesus condemns these sorts of traditions (Matthew 15:3), while upholding
authentic Tradition, such as those mentioned above.[31] Differenti-
ating between these two types of traditions can sometimes prove
challenging. The catechism expresses the distinction this way:

> The Tradition here in question comes from the apostles and
> hands on what they received from Jesus' teaching and example
> and what they learned from the Holy Spirit. The first generation
> of Christians did not yet have a written New Testament, and
> the New Testament itself demonstrates the process of living Tra-
> dition. Tradition is to be distinguished from the various theo-
> logical, disciplinary, liturgical or devotional traditions, born in
> the local churches over time. These are the particular forms,
> adapted to different places and times, in which the great Tradi-
> tion is expressed. In the light of Tradition, these traditions can
> be retained, modified or even abandoned under the guidance of
> the Church's Magisterium.[32]

It was during this time period that bishops began to take on more responsibility. As mass conversions followed the Christianization of pagan rulers, bishops were responsible for larger congregations and often coupled their teaching function with other ecclesial and juridical roles. Although important theological and jurisdictional controversies often erupted, the Church grew, generally homogeneously, with several major exceptions (e.g. Arianism), until the Great Schism of 1054. In that year, tragically, the Churches of the East and the West split over issues such as the filioque.[33] (The Church in the West focused more on how God acts and behaves while the Eastern Churches concentrated more on God's essence, who he is.)

While the Church was becoming more hierarchical and organizing into more formal structures, there were some Christians who were drawn to a more solitary and contemplative life. This practice of some Christians separating themselves from society to grow closer to God has existed since the inception of Christianity. In the earlier years of the Church, holy men—St. Anthony of the Desert, for example—and women—like Mary of Egypt—sought the isolation of the wilderness. (The very word "hermit" traces its etymological roots to the Greek word "*eremia,*" which means "desert.")

In later centuries, this lifestyle drew so many that the communal life needed to be fused to the solitary life, and so monasticism was born. Monasteries (from the Greek word "*monachos,*" meaning "solitary") sprouted up all over the Christian world, and many adopted the simple yet profound rules authored by the great monk St. Benedict at Monte Cassino. The three pillars of the Rule of St. Benedict are vows of poverty, chastity, and obedience, also known as the "three evangelical counsels." These three vows were not randomly chosen but reflect the poverty of Jesus, the chastity of Jesus, and Jesus' obedience to the Father. In the Gospels, Jesus calls upon his followers to exhibit all sorts of behaviors and traits, such as humility, generosity, holiness, etc. Yet, the Church, reflecting on these commands, finds that some are binding on all Christians while others are binding only on those who seek perfection. Thus, they are formally acts of supererogation.

Notice the big themes of life here; a person pursuing worldly wealth, romantic love, or any personal desire cannot also pursue a life totally dedicated to God. So, the three vows of poverty, chastity, and obedience are a kind of shorthand for living the consecrated religious Christian life.[34] In addition to following these vows, and in some cases others, the consecrated life is measured out according to a preset schedule. Just as the early Christians followed the Jewish practice of praying at specific times, the life of a monk or nun includes the regular recitation of certain official prayers.[35]

In the ensuing centuries, the Church expanded, and by 1095, the first crusade launched, in part to aid Christians being mistreated in lands usurped by Muslim forces. More importantly, the following century brought with it important scholarly advances within the Church:

> . . . it was the twelfth-century innovators who first introduced systematic order into the mass of intellectual materials which they had inherited in a largely uncoordinated form from the ancient world. The general aim of their work was to produce a complete and systematic body of knowledge, clarified by the refinements of criticism, and presented as the consensus of competent judges. Doctrinally the method for achieving this consensus was a progression from commentary to questioning, and from questioning to systematization.[36]

MEDIEVAL TO MODERNITY

This experience of the Church remained generally stable for centuries but changed as secular and ecclesial interests began to amalgamate. "The monasteries became wealthy in the mundane sense by ignoring wealth. The individual monks renounced money, but their labors produced enormous wealth for the monasteries. The wealth grew over generations, because the monks did not have children or the expenses they require. More importantly, their lands were not constantly divided as children inherited the land from their father."[37]

For centuries, the Church would participate in the coronation ceremonies of European kings and queens. Actually, an argument can be made that Church participated in the king-making business, while European royalty was in the pope-making business. This entanglement led some in the Church to become tainted by unwarranted worldly interests.

In the year 1205, an Italian merchant named Francis Bernadone prayed inside the old dilapidated Church of San Damiano.

While in prayer, he heard a voice command him to rebuild God's house, which was near ruin. Francis immediately went about the work of personally renovating the physical structure of the Church of San Damiano. Only later did he realize God's call was not to rehabilitate a building but to renew the entire Catholic Church that was then plagued by corruption.

Francis Bernadone became St. Francis of Assisi, and his contemporary, the holy St. Clare, introduced reforms to recapture the gospel message through a life of simplicity, humility, service to others, and prayer. Once again, the radical vision of Jesus found a voice, and many of the reforms initiated by Francis and Clare remain with us to this day.

Time passed, and new challenges faced the Church. For example, in 1378 AD, we encounter not one but three claimants to the papacy. The Church had one pope and two anti-popes. The matter was not fully resolved until 1417. By that time, the Renaissance was burgeoning in Italy, and the heart of Italy's culture was Florence, birthplace of Dante and Michelangelo.[38]

A century later, advances in science and technology, especially the invention of the printing press and the discovery of the Americas, brought forth other disputes. The year 1517 marked the onset of one of the greatest tribulations in the history of Christendom, occurring with the onset of the Reformation. In the years that followed, Martin Luther, John Calvin, John Wickliffe, John Knox, William Tyndale, and other reformers, promoted a new theology based on:

- SOLA SCRIPTURA ("by Scripture alone")
- SOLA FIDE ("by faith alone")
- SOLA GRATIA ("by grace alone")
- SOLUS CHRISTUS ("Christ alone")
- SOLI DEO GLORIA ("glory to God alone")

These reformers made many legitimate and significant points, and originally Luther simply wished to reform the Church—not begin a new denomination. "The Protestant Reformation began when a Catholic monk, rediscovered a Catholic doctrine in a Catholic book. The monk, of course, was Martin Luther, the doctrine was 'justification by faith' and the book was the Bible."[39] Actually, prior to the formal Reformation, there was a cry throughout Europe, "*reformatio ecclesiae in capite et in membris*" ("reform the church in head and members").

The Reformation Era was a period of turmoil marked in the West by wars and revolutions (both actual and philosophical). The Church responded to the challenges of this Protestant[40] Reformation with a Catholic Counter-Reformation. Soon afterward, the Western world entered into an age that placed science and philosophy over theology. By the late 1600s the Age of Enlightenment had dawned, bringing forth numerous profound insights and advancements in human knowledge and challenging certain paradigms that had dominated Western thought, and which predated the Axial Age.

Among the most profound shifts in thinking was the idea that instead of a king or queen ruling over people by divine right, the Creator gives rights to all who people. The Church's relationship with this new culture was like her relationship with other governments over the centuries: never fully acquiescing nor fully resisting the state.[41]

Too often, we pass by this fact and assume that the paradigm of individualism that is so prevalent in the post-Enlightenment world is universal. I think this is because we confuse "community" with "commonality."

> To differ, even deeply, one from another, is not to be enemies, it is simply to be. To recognize and accept one's own difference is not pride. To recognize and accept the difference of others is not weakness. If union has to be, if union offers any meaning at all, it must be union between different men. And it is above all in the recognition and acceptance of difference that difference is overcome and union achieved.[42]

The struggle to discern which Christian beliefs are orthodox is not new. Early Christians wrestled with understanding and practicing the faith left to us by Jesus. When controversies lingered, the faithful would meet in councils, and the Church would engage with the controversy in question. Just as God gradually revealed himself throughout pre-Christian times to Abraham, Moses, the prophets, and the kings, Jesus' revelation is slowly understood more clearly throughout the centuries. All has been revealed, but not all has been understood. The Church is ever seeking to provide insight into the continuity of the Christian faith, throughout the ages. In one sense, the Church is always reforming. As Karl Barth noted, *"Ecclesia semper reformanda est"* (Latin: "the church is always to be reformed").

Catholic teaching develops over time (though it does not evolve into anything new). Consider how, for the greater part of the Church's history, most Christians were illiterate and looked to heads of local authorities for protection and guidance. The Church recognized that those in power could abuse their positions and therefore advocated for social justice by such innovations as the *Magna Carta Libertatum,* (the Magna Carta 1215). This foundational legal and political document emanated from Catholic moral ideas and was originally authored by the archbishop of Canterbury.[43] Another safeguard the Church developed was the doctrine that "error has no rights." In the past, when the Church had a strong and influential presence in Europe, she taught "error has no rights" as a way to protect people and preserve the Church from potential corruption in a feudal system. According to this principle, while sovereigns did have some legitimate authority, there were limits. For example, it may have been the practice in some parts of Europe for land barons to claim the right of defloration—the right to have sexual intercourse with any betrothed virgin who resided on their land. Although some scholars doubt if such a practice ever took place, abuses of this sort led the Church to formulate the "error has no rights" protection.

To declare that "error has no rights" is not the same thing as saying "people in error have no rights," but, unfortunately, this philosophical distinction was not always recognized or put into practice. There is a Latin proverb used in law, *"Abusus non tollit usum,"* which translates to, "Misuse does not nullify proper use." The "error has no rights" doctrine played an important role for centuries. However, once society advanced to a point where most citizens were literate and consequently more capable of making informed judgments for themselves, the Church began to promote the liberty of individuals to follow the dictates of their own informed consciences.

There is an old Latin saying, *"Ratio est legis anima; mutata legis ratione mutatur et lex,"* which means, "Reason is the spirit of the law; the reason of the law being changed, the law too is changed." Simply put, matters of dogma cannot change. The Trinity, for example, will be a teaching of the Church in perpetuity. But, teachings on non-dogmatic issues can change and sometimes do.

This is the benefit of theological controversies. As Bishop Fulton Sheen taught, the Church can benefit from certain types of controversy:

> The Church loves controversy, and loves it for two reasons: because intellectual conflict is informing and, because she is madly in love with rationalism. The great structure of the Catholic Church has been built up through controversy. It was the attacks of the docetists and the monophysites in the early centuries of the Church that made her clear on the doctrine concerning the nature of Christ; it was the controversy with the Reformers that clarified her teaching on justification.[44]

First and Second Maccabees provide, perhaps, a good biblical example of this challenge—though the example applies to the Jewish faith, as Christianity had not yet been born. When living under the rule of a foreign power, such as the Babylonians or the Romans, faithful Jews had the difficult choice of fighting against their Gentile oppressors or adapting to their new circumstances. When the Persians ruled Jerusalem (539 BC), Jews began to use Aramaic, the language of the Persian Empire, in place of Hebrew. (Thus, Jesus spoke Aramaic.) Not only did language change, but certain Persian philosophies and religious concerns may have informed the Judaism of this time. Eventually, the Persians were replaced by the Greeks when, in 331 BC, Alexander the Great conquered Jerusalem; again, the Jews had to adapt. It is no coincidence that the New Testament, written by Jews, was written in Greek. Then, Greek culture gave way to Roman culture when Pompey captured Jerusalem in 63 BC. Roman rule then lasted up to and after the time of Jesus. Through all these changes, Jews struggled both with the occupying power of Rome and among themselves about how best to live as God's chosen people. Around the time of Jesus, some, like the Zealots, chose to fight; the Essenes chose to separate from the Gentile culture; the Sadducees acquiesced to Roman rule; and the Pharisees maintained Mosaic law. Each claimed to represent authentic Judaism, and, you'll recall, membership in any of these groups was exclusive, so Jews had to select one strict style of practice and worship with that group.

The nascent Christian Church, ideally, should have been free from many of these difficulties, since it was an inclusive religion.

God entered into a covenant with Abraham, which expanded to the people of Israel, and then expanded again with Christ's new covenant to the entire world. It is not just that Jesus' message was preached across the planet but that each and every human being was welcomed into God's egalitarian kingdom.

Christianity is radical, revolutionary, and counter-cultural, but it exists in the world and must, to some degree, acclimate to the world. Therefore, Christians did not always incorporate into pagan cultures, not because of an exclusivist or elitist attitude but due to an uncompromising fidelity to Jesus Christ's teachings. Over the centuries, the Church has learned better how to borrow what is good from other traditions and cultures while rejecting what is incompatible with the faith, balancing the notion that the Church is in the world but not of it.

> The biggest paradox about the Church is that she is at the same time essentially traditional and essentially revolutionary . . . Human traditions all tend toward stagnation and decay. They try to perpetuate things that cannot be perpetuated. . . . Church tradition, supernatural in its source, is something absolutely opposed to human traditionalism.
>
> . . . And yet this tradition must always be a revolution, because by its very nature it denies the values and standards to which human passion is so powerfully attached. To those who love money and pleasure and reputation and power this tradition says: "Be poor, go down into the far end of society, take the last place among men, live with those who are despised, love other men and serve them instead of making them serve you. Do not fight them when they push you around, but pray for those that hurt you. Do not look for pleasure, but turn away from things that satisfy your senses and your mind and look for God in hunger and thirst and darkness, through deserts of the spirit in which it seems to be madness to travel. Take upon yourself the burden of Christ's Cross, that is, Christ's humility and poverty and obedience and renunciation, and you will find peace for your souls.
>
> This is the most complete revolution that has ever been preached; in fact it is the only true revolution, because all the others demand the extermination of somebody else, but this one means the death of the man who, for all practical purposes, you have come to think of as your own self.[45]

The Church has survived over the many centuries when cultures and empires have come and gone. "The Church has ever proved indestructible. Her persecutors have failed to destroy her; in fact, it was during times of persecution that the Church grew more and more; while the persecutors themselves, and those whom the Church would destroy, are the very ones who came to nothing."[46]

While this endurance of the institution is not proof of God's existence, it does speak to the resiliency of the Church to adapt to an ever-changing world and the appeal of the spiritual principles that form its foundation.

✝

CHAPTER ELEVEN

THE BIBLE
(BIBLIOLOGY)

THE WORLD'S MOST UNIQUE BOOK

The Bible is the world's best-selling book. After millennia of study, it continues to reveal new insights. The Bible is an enlightening, inspiring, perplexing, unsettling compilation of individual books inspired by God and which reveal him to us.

There are many different translations of the Bible available to readers, but as the old adage goes, the best translation is the one you will actually read. That is, it is not as important whether a version honors the original wording or the original intent if one translation or another is incomprehensible to the reader.

Reading the Bible helps us to understand God better both individually and as a community of believers. Over the centuries, the Bible has served not only to set a standard for Church teaching and practices but also sometimes to admonish ecclesial excesses, behaviors, and practices inconsistent with sacred Scripture. That is because the Bible is the *norma normans non normata*, a Latin phrase meaning "the norm that norms" or the rule which rules.

Saint Jerome famously proclaimed that "Ignorance of Scripture is ignorance of Christ." But, we should never think we know the Bible so well that we have exhausted all it has to tell us. Even those who are intimately familiar with portions of Scripture need to come to each reading ready to learn something new. We can easily forget the Church existed for centuries without a completed Bible. There was, in the opinion of many ancients, a greater respect for oral tradition than for the written word. Remembering the enormous amount of labor, the expense, and the limited audience of literate people who could benefit from the written word, all helps to explain the high regard that was placed on the oral tradition. It was the early Christians who authored the New Testament. It was the Church that gave us the Bible and not the Bible that gave us the Church. Although the books of the New Testament were assembled as early as the fifth century, it was not until the Tridentine Council (1545-1563 AD) that the Church officially confirmed the canon of both the Old and New Testaments. The Bible, as we know it today, comes to us via a process that took nearly fifteen centuries and dozens of authors writing in multiple languages on three different continents. Nowhere in the Bible is there a list of all the books that should be included in the Bible, and it is the Church that exercised the authority to recognize what to keep in and what to leave out of the 73 books that form the official canon of the Catholic Bible.

In the early days of the Church, there were numerous writings that purported to offer authentic Christian teachings. From these hundreds of documents, the Church discerned, via the inspiration of the Holy Spirit, which texts should be included in the official canon of the New Testament. The earliest New Testament books were written by St. Paul and date to within 50 or 60 years of Jesus' death. The Gospels were written in the years that followed, with Mark composed as early as 65 - 71 AD.

This process of discernment was lengthy and complicated. The Council of Hippo (393) provided a listing of inspired books. Later, the Councils of Carthage, in the late-fourth and early-fifth centuries, confirmed this list. Yet, it was not until the Council of Trent (1545-1563) that the official canon was definitively closed. What this means is that God's revelation is complete—but, having been fully revealed does not equate, necessarily, with being fully understood.

Both the Old and New Testaments are comprised of ancient and nuanced writings authored over the course of centuries by authors who lived in cultures very different from our own.

While the Bible is certainly accessible to any literate person, the richness of this book cannot be overstated. Saint Thomas More said, ". . . the Scriptures have been crafted in such a way that they are plain and simple enough for every man to find in them what he needs to understand. Yet again, they are so lofty and difficult that no man is so cunning that he won't find there things far beyond his reach, things far too deep to fathom."

Although the Catholic Church teaches that "the task of interpreting the Word of God authentically has been entrusted solely to the Magisterium of the Church,"[1] at most there are a handful of Bible passages that have been authoritatively defined, at least partially.[2] More often, the Church will not define how a passage must be read but instead will declare as invalid certain novel interpretations.

I once visited a Unitarian Church, and one of the congregants said that there are so many different theories that he subscribes to the advice offered in Gershwin's famous opera *Porgy and Bess*. This opera includes the song "It Ain't Necessarily So," which recounts various stories from the Bible, followed by the skeptical chorus "De things dat yo' liable to read in de Bible, It ain't necessarily so."[3] This sort of skepticism is understandable given the plurality of interpretations we can access.

Saint Paul said that ". . . God is a God not of disorder but of peace" (1 Corinthians 14:33). So, why do so many apparently sincere Christians strongly disagree about some of the teachings of the Bible? Scripture promises that all who seek shall find, but so many of us keep finding different answers. As Shakespeare taught us in *The Merchant of Venice*, "The Devil can cite scripture for his purpose."[4] History has proven this to be all too true. The Bible has been used to justify every form of abuse, heresy, and vice. By taking verses out of context, a counterfeit argument can be made that will support almost any doctrine. So, believers ought to be able to honestly face the challenges presented by Scripture and avoid the temptation to dismiss or minimize difficult passages.

For example, in the Bible, Satan is described as a serpent (Revelation 12:9, Revelation 20:2), and elsewhere as a lion (1 Peter 5:8), and the morning star (Isaiah 14:12). Jesus, too, is described or associated with a snake (John 3:14-15), and a lion (Revelation 5:5), and the morning star (Revelation 22:16). Read out of context, it might appear that the devil and Jesus are one and the same, while the reality could not be further from this proposition. Jesus takes the evil symbols of Satan and transforms them by associating his holiness with them.

The Bible is not merely a code of statutes to be followed, though many throughout the centuries have read it this way and even tried to summarize the points they felt were most important into creeds or statements of faith. While these are important, they don't substitute for a living faith; the Bible is a guidebook for bringing about that faith. In other words, the Bible is necessary but not sufficient alone. There needs to be a body of believers too. This teaching represents a fundamental difference between Catholic and Protestant understandings of the Bible. One of the mottoes of the Reformation was "*Sola Scriptura.*" The Reformers wanted to strip away all the "unbiblical" trappings of Christian belief and worship and return to the Bible alone. There was a conception, which still permeates among some today, that the Church had a hostile relationship with respect to the Bible and the faithful. The image of a Bible being chained to a desk or lectern is the quintessential example.

Yes, the Bible was chained up, but because it was treasured, not because it was being locked away from curious believers—many of whom were illiterate. Remember that prior to the advent of the printing press, around 1440 AD, the laborious process of creating a new copy of the Bible was for the entire book to be painstakingly copied by hand.

The Church, however, was indomitably determined to share the Bible with the people. So, novel ways were created to expose as many people to as much of the Bible as often as was feasible. Even today, Catholics hear the Bible preached during the liturgy, and the liturgy itself incorporates many passages of Scripture, word for word. The Scripture readings for Mass (both daily and Sundays) are organized so that every three years a majority of the Bible is read aloud.

We also sing the Bible in hymns. Gregorian chant developed from the 600s AD through the 1400s AD, was a way of sharing the Bible through the singing of Scripture. We pray using the words of the Bible at each Mass and in private devotions, like the rosary. Go into nearly any Catholic church and look at the stained-glass windows. These luminous works of art originated as ways of visually sharing the faith, including Bible stories. Pope Gregory the Great, in a letter to the bishop of Marseilles, explained how such images are like words for the illiterate. "It is one thing to adore a picture, another to learn from narrative pictures what should be adored. For what scripture is to those who can read, a picture offers to the illiterate who look at it, for in it the ignorant see what should be imitated and those who do not understand writing read from it."[5] Icons provide another means for communicating biblical truths. Similarly, Catholics use other visual mediums to portray the Bible. Some of the world's most famous paintings and statues were commissioned by the Church to express famous stories from the Scriptures.

Another visual expression of the Bible came in the form of the pageant and passion plays of the Middle Ages. Not only did the people attend plays to learn about the Bible, but Catholics then and now participate in reenactments of events of Jesus' life to better understand the gospel. Pilgrims follow Jesus' way of the cross, and the faithful engage in sacred processions at certain times of the year.

When Christmas rolls around, we begin to see the familiar scenes of the crèche and the manger. This imagery comes directly from St. Francis of Assisi, who provided a visual expression of the Bible by initiating the nativity scene, which is a concept still used today. The scene is not meant to be historically accurate, however. For example, many manger scenes include three kings or wisemen. Tradition provides various names, the most popular being Melchior, Gaspar/Caspar, and Balthazar, as stated earlier. There is mention in the Bible of only three gifts being given to the baby Jesus, but no mention of only three gift-givers. So, St. Francis' nativity description helps to convey the story of Jesus' birth as presented in the Gospels, perhaps with some liberties taken to connect the dots provided by the words in the Bible.

In some instances, the confusion between what the Bible does and does not reveal extends all the way into fiction. For example, I was once asked where in the Bible the story of the little drummer boy could be found.[6] This extra-biblical story is meant to depict the humbling moment in history when the Savior was born, rather than any type of historical child musician present at the birth of Jesus.

To be clear, the Gospels are historical; they are nonfiction. In this way, the Bible differs from the fictional stories of the pagan religions of old. Mythological characters are one-dimensional and lack any true in-depth personality, whereas the Jesus presented in the New Testament is tangible and full of life.

> . . . the cumulative effect of reading his words is to be confronted by a wholly *distinctive* view and voice—distinctively Jewish, distinctively of its time, but distinctive. But it is more than the teachings of Jesus which make us blink our eyes and wish that we could adjust the focus a little more clearly on that figure who

is one moment transfigured in glory on a mountainside, and the next is squatting on the ground frying some fish.

It is the fish which lures us on. It is those little details—a man irrationally losing his temper with a tree. It is someone remembering that a little girl, when she recovers from a fever, will be extremely hungry. It is the man who, after his arrest, can turn to look at one of his best friends, and make that man weep with the knowledge that he has not been loyal to the end. These little novelistic details could all, of course, have been fabricated, though it is hard to see what purpose would have been served in inventing them.[7]

However, there are times when, to make a theological point, a Gospel writer, (John more than the others[8]) will express a truth in a way that is not to be taken as literal fact. To make any progress, we must embrace the idea that truth is what we seek, but the tools we are often most familiar with are not the only ones available to use. Abraham Maslow wisely pointed out, "If the only tool you have is a hammer, you tend to see every problem as a nail." So, we would do well to have more tools in our toolbox. We can borrow these tools from philosophy, history, linguistics, archeology, and many other disciplines.

To give an example of how the use of language can be confusing, the following two statements are both true. The first one is, "white is the combination of all color." The second is, "black is the combination of all color." Although these seem to contradict one another, the fact is they are both true—even if they do not seem to be. However, they can be true if they are put into the proper context. White is the combination of all color when we are talking about light. If you break down white light using a prism, you will see all the colors of the spectrum. However, if you are talking about color in terms of pigments, when you mix all of the colors together you will come out with black.

We see, from the example above, that context and specificity of language are critical to understanding the point being made. Language is not always precise but can be vague and ambiguous. When words are available that more tightly define a concept, it is an indication that this concept is very important. For instance, I've been told that certain native tribes in Alaska and northern Canada have dozens of words for the different kinds of snow. There are words for old snow, new snow, snow that is wet, snow that is powdery, snow that is wet that falls on top of old snow, snow that is powdery that falls on top of new snow—you get the point. In English, there are relatively few words for snow, because snow is not usually at the center of most English-speakers' lives. The point is, both individually and collectively, we take time and expend resources to describe what is important to us. With that in mind, we should give thought to the words used in sacred Scripture. We might ask, after reading a verse, why was this term used and not another? Reading the Bible exposes us to ideas and words that help draw us out of our everyday existence to ponder the word of God.

To truly appreciate the Bible's message, we should explore the phrase "word of God." The Bible is the word of God,[9] comprised of books written over a period of close to a thousand years. As the "word of God," the Church recognizes and proclaims the Bible to be *Theopneustos* (Greek: God-breathed), inspired, and infallible. However, each book of Bible has a dual authorship: human and divine (2 Timothy 2:16). (Actually, some books of the Bible have multiple authors. Most scholars agree that Isaiah, for example, was written over more than a century by more than one author, giving us Isaiah, Deutero-Isaiah, and Trito-Isaiah.) The human authors were a diverse group made up of kings, prophets, fishermen, and people from many backgrounds, who wrote in a variety of styles and genres (e.g. poetry, history, and liturgy). Though inspired by God in a wholly unique way, since the Bible is a compilation of books that have human authors, we must take seriously every writer's worldview, including the time and culture in which he or she wrote. Moreover, we must not insist on foisting our preconceived notions of narrative onto the text. For example, if we read the account of Jesus' trial before Pilate, we encounter a record of a historical event, but, perhaps, we are also encountering editorial commentary on a miscarriage of justice. Separating the reportage from the potential inserted reflections of the author can be a challenge. But, it is not a challenge that should trouble us.

More than just reading the Bible as a book written in a specific time and place, we ought to remember that it is a book that also transcends these limitations. On the one hand, it is essential that we resolve to read the Bible through the lens the authors intended. But, we must also recognize that the book transcends any one particular author. The Bible is comprised of a series of books written by ancient authors, many of whom followed literary styles and conventions that are foreign to most modern readers, who are used to reading narratives that follow the norms of Aristotelian logic and maintain an internal consistency. For example, in 1 Samuel 9:10-11, we read how Saul and his servant meet with some young women. We can infer from the text that Saul is an attractive man, and the girls in the story are eager to talk with him. The conversation that ensues is, in the original Hebrew, quite confusing. Some scholars point to this confusion as an example of a flaw in the biblical narrative. However, as the biblical scholar Avi Hurvitz points out:

> Now if we judge the quality of the style employed in the passage solely according to strict formal linguistic standards of grammar and syntax, we would undoubtedly conclude that this is deficient Hebrew. However, if we consider the peculiar circumstances of the episode, it becomes clear that the confused speech created here by the biblical writer is an attempt to reproduce the effect of the girls all talking at once in their excitement at meeting Saul. The confused style is thus a deliberate device intended to reflect the heroines' mood and feelings.[10]

All of these insights into Scripture merely scratch the surface. More importantly, they scratch the surface of only one side of a two-sided coin. There is also a long tradition of "*lectio divina*," or "sacred reading." Sacred reading is not about analysis, critique, inquiry, or any other academic pursuit. Instead, this sort of reading of sacred Scripture focuses on exactly what the name implies: the "sacred." In it, the reader seeks to appreciate, contemplate, and even encounter and absorb the text. This is, or at least can be, a more mystical and less scholastic approach to the Bible.

The Bible's riches have proven inexhaustible over the millennia, though it is not necessary to be a scholar to read and benefit from Scripture. As Pope St. Gregory the Great said, "Holy Scripture is a stream in which the elephant may swim and the lamb may wade."[11] Certainly, we should seek to constantly grow and learn and use new knowledge to expand our understanding of the Bible if we truly wish to appreciate its message.

For instance, it is quite useful to have a working knowledge of Hebrew cosmology to appreciate certain passages, especially in the Old Testament, but we ought not to exchange their pre-scientific ideas for contemporary ones. The challenge is for us to read what they were saying, not always to adopt what they believed—except in the case of faith and morals.

This means, in part, that the Bible is much more than a haphazard anthology of disconnected narratives. Instead, the individual books of the Bible address overarching themes; they present a grand metanarrative about creation, sin, and redemption. In the shortest of summaries, we can say that the Bible, taken as a whole, tells the story of a progressive history of God's original creation, his relationship with that creation, and, finally, his restoration and consummation of the created order. The Bible presents a big story where God created the world and desired to be in fellowship with his creation. Humans sinned and turned away from that friendship, with consequences for all of creation. Throughout the writings of the prophets, we find God repeatedly chastising Israel for not being faithful to him and his commandments. It is only a slight exaggeration to argue that Israel's entire history is a repeated cycle of the people turning away from God and then returning after a chastisement. (Reading the continual warnings of the prophets brings to mind the story of Cassandra, a prophetess in Greek mythology. Cassandra was blessed by the gods with the gift of true and accurate prophetic powers, but she was cursed so that no one who ever heard her prophecies would believe her.) God then set about restoring that broken relationship through covenants with individuals and with the nation of Israel. These having failed, he came personally, as Jesus, to do for us what we were unable to do for ourselves. This, in a nutshell, is the story the Christian Scriptures tell.

Too often, the Old Testament is caricatured as portraying a wrathful God, while the New Testament portrays a God of love. Both testaments present the same God. The Old Testament is filled with accounts of God's tenderness (read the books of Hosea and Psalms, for example), and in the New Testament Jesus spoke about hell more than any Old Testament prophet. The creation in Genesis and new creation written about by St. Paul are intertwined. The stories of the Old Testament are not disconnected tales only fit for Sunday school, but they are like pieces in an extraordinarily complex yet elegant puzzle, depicting God's continuous work in history. Another example is from John's Gospel, which begins with the phrase "In the beginning . . ." which parallels the opening lines of the first book of the Bible, Genesis 1:1, which also opens with the words, "In the beginning . . ." John does this, in part, to show that Jesus is the same God of creation, come to us to restore that creation. In Genesis, we read how God created the world in seven days. In John's Gospel, we start with day one, "In the beginning"; move to day two in John 1:29, "the next day . . ."; and, carefully, the text reveals a third, fourth, fifth, sixth, and seventh day to parallel the week recounted in Genesis.

The connection being made is not just between the Old and New Testaments but between the Hebrew way of seeing the world and pagan paradigms. As Thomas Cahill put it:

> The Jews started it all—and by 'it' I mean so many of the things we care about, the underlying values that make all of us, Jew and gentile, believer and atheist, tick. Without the Jews, we would see the world through different eyes, hear with different ears, even feel with different feelings. And not only would our sensorium, the screen through which we receive the world, be different: we would think with a different mind, interpret all our experience differently, draw different conclusions from the things that befall us. And we would set a different course for our lives.[12]

Judaism is extraordinarily unique in the ancient world for many reasons, including the concepts of monotheism[13] (there is only one God); creation ex nihilo (creation out of nothing, instead of creation out of preexisting matter); the observance of sacred time (the Sabbath)[14] as opposed to the pagan practice of merely observing sacred places (e.g. Stonehenge); and historicity, (e.g. Abraham and Moses were living breathing historical figures, unlike Hercules).

Just read the Hebrew Scriptures and you will get a sense of the uniquely Hebrew worldview. As the *Abingdon Bible Commentary* explains:

> First, it was practical. . . . There are in the Hebrew Scriptures no arguments that seek to prove the existence of God or the possibility of our knowing him. His being and self-revelation were taken for granted. The heavens might declare his glory (Psa. 191), but this was, because people already believed in his existence. There was in ancient Israel no theoretical atheism or agnosticism.
>
> In the second place, the Old Testament conceived of God as personal. . . . One reason for this theistic or personalistic cast of Hebrew thought was the fact that Jehovah from the very

beginning was regarded as primarily a God of history rather than of nature. . . . God everywhere in his relation to Israel is represented as a living, feeling, acting, Being. That He is also free is likewise everywhere assumed. Creation was his free act, and the course of human history is freely determined by Him. He is not bound by the laws of nature but through miracle can work out his own purposes. Nothing is more characteristic of Jehovah than what we call personality.

Another general characteristic of the Old Testament conception of God is found in its inherent tendency toward monotheism. This tendency appears from the very outset in the exclusiveness of Jehovah. 'Thou shalt have no other gods before me' was the foundation stone of the Mosaic religion and of the Israelitic religion as a whole. . . . it successfully resisted every attempt to introduce a female deity by the side of Jehovah and also every movement to break him up into a number of local Jehovahs. . . . The Hebrew heart insisted on absolute loyalty, and such loyalty could be directed only to one Being. Monotheism was thus implicit in Israel's religion from the very beginning.

A fourth characteristic of the Hebrew idea of God was its ethical quality. . . . There is nothing in the work of Moses more distinctive and more significant than the passionate and sustained devotion to Jehovah that he evoked among the Israelitic tribes. It was this that formed the basis of their national unity, it was this that differentiated them not only formally but qualitatively from other peoples, and it was this that made of Jehovah . . . the God of righteousness and the Creator of the world.[15]

He is a moral God and he desires us to be a moral people. The law of Moses gives us guidelines, and Jesus expands on this not by way of addition but intensification.

If God truly inspired the writers of the Old and New Testaments, then their messages would be authoritative not only for their initial audience, but for us and future generations as well. But, interpreting this authority can be difficult. Author A. J. Jacobs, who sincerely tried to live out all the rules of the Bible in a single year, found the task maddening and concluded that inevitably "everyone practices cafeteria religion . . . we pick and choose from the Bible."[16]

We find in its pages stories and prophecies that make it the most unique book in all the world. That authority does not merely come about through a list of "Thou Shall" or "Thou Shall Not" directives. But, instead, is the narrative through which the Holy Spirit speaks to us and instructs us, both individually and especially in the community of the Church. So then, if I pick up the Bible and read a passage and think, "OK, I've understood this," I'd want to check to see if others reading the same or similar passages came up with similar understandings. And not just my peers. G. K. Chesterton talks about the democracy of the dead, meaning, Christians who came before ought not to be automatically dismissed. "Tradition means giving votes to the most obscure of all classes, our ancestors. It is the democracy of the dead. Tradition refuses to submit to that arrogant oligarchy who merely happen to be walking around."[17] Additionally, Tradition can develop with an eye toward the future. In my graduate studies in Theology, I once wrote a paper speculating on how the Mass might be celebrated in the challenge of zero gravity in outer space.[18] (As an interesting aside, I was inspired during my research when I discovered that astronaut Buzz Aldrin brought Communion, provided by his Presbyterian pastor, with him into space.) Perhaps it will be a moot point if artificial gravity exists; the point is that the Church plants seeds today, which will bear fruit in the future. "A civilization flourishes when people plant trees under which they will never sit," is an old Greek proverb. The same can be said of the Church.

It is not enough to ask, "Is the Bible true?" but we must ask, "How is it true?" There are many tools that can be employed in one's search for biblical truth. The tools of linguistics, rhetoric, logic, anthropology, history, and even the natural sciences can all serve to flesh out any narrative, but too heavy a reliance on these tools could forsake the text in favor of an analysis devoid of its subject matter. Look at the Gospel of John and see the rich Christological symbolism throughout. John is seeking to reveal Jesus to the reader via a mystical Christology. Does he do so using the *ipsissima verba Jesu* ("very words of Jesus")? Some scholars believe John may be accrediting words to Jesus which were not actually spoken verbatim by him. If John does not always give us a word-for-word transcript of Jesus, he provides the *ipsissima vox Jesu* ("very voice of Jesus") in the form of an accurate synopsis of what Jesus really said.

However, it is also true that the Gospels were written during a time when oral storytelling was considerably more disciplined than we might find today. Few people in the ancient world were able to read and write, so careful preservation of oral traditions was quite necessary. Jesus was a great preacher who employed a panoply of rhetorical devices including comparisons of himself with common things such as bread (John 6:35) and a door (John 10:7).

We can begin to realize that the Bible was written for us, but it was not written to us. Instead, the Bible was written to audiences in the ancient world, and that fact must be kept in the forefront of our minds when reading Scripture. Each book has its own purpose, whether to inform, chastise, encourage, or resolve a dispute. There are numerous tools we can employ to help us in our understanding of the Bible; concordances provide a detailed index to Scripture, commentaries offer insights into specific passages, copies of the original language[19] of the text help provide a more precise interpretation, etc. (Some readers will want to consider pericopes, uncials, and other pertinent aspects of structure of the passages.) Yet, even when we have access to a very literal translation of the Bible, we are still faced with the challenge of deciphering the connotative and denotative ideas of the authors. Additionally, it can be a challenge to differentiate between historical narrative and stylized reasoning.

The rule of "First Mention" teaches that a particular word might be best understood if we look at the very first time that word is used in the Bible. This first usage may set a context for the later usage. Another technique is observing repetitions. A concept or story told once is not as rich as one retold from different perspectives. Finding out if a theme or narrative is repeated in the Bible is essential to grasping the breadth of the subject.

This sort of critical thinking about Scripture has been employed for centuries, but some major advances in biblical scholarship took place during and after World War II when soldiers (from Allied and Axis armies) used free time in between fighting to carefully read and expound upon the Bibles they carried with them into battles. Much of the biblical scholarship of this era centers on hermeneutics. Hermeneutics is the discipline of discovering how to correctly interpret a text. Closely related, yet distinct, is the work of exegesis. Exegesis is the discipline of actually doing that interpretation—finding the meaning of a text. Many biblical scholars believe much of the Old Testament was compiled around the time of the Babylonian exile, thereby influencing both the content and tone of certain books. Analyzing this background data is part of the process of exploring the meaning of Scripture. This can take the form of exegesis (from the Greek for "to draw out of") or eisegesis (from the Greek for "to read into"). Eisegesis sees authorial intent as irrelevant. I know of a seminary professor who half-jokingly tells his students that too often exegesis really becomes "extra-Jesus," meaning some people read a passage with bias and draw out of the text anything they want; in other words, bad exegesis becomes eisegesis. William Blake quipped, "We both read the Bible day and night, only you see black where I see white."

This is a valid point, but the fact is that reading the Bible within its historical context and taking the original language, the author's intent, and surrounding culture into account, is no simple task.

Throughout history, Christians asked if a verse should be taken literally, allegorically, as a moral instruction, or in an anagogical or mystical sense. Scholars today offer even more categories for consideration including historical criticism, psychological criticism, etc.

Sometimes, this sort of critical evaluation can be challenging. There may be passages that are saying something true about a real historical event, but the author is using poetry or some other device to provide an answer. We have to be careful, however, not to impose our own desires onto a text under the pretense of this principle. When an author states "X," and we wish him to have stated "Y," we have to avoid the temptation to distort the authorial intent. The difference between denotative definitions and connotative definitions is key.

The challenge is discovering when the Bible is being literal (as in references to Jesus' resurrection; 1 Corinthians 15:17) and when it is being metaphorical (as in 1 Chronicles 16:30, where we read that the earth is fixed and unmovable). Sometimes, it can be both. The story of Noah and the flood was for centuries believed to be an account of a literal global flood, while modern scholars predominantly argue that the narrative employs phenomenological language—meaning the flood story is about a local event that may have appeared global from the author's perspective. Regardless, the symbolism remains the same; the ark is symbolic of the Church and the flood waters the chaos of sin.

For another example of a different sort, read the story of Jesus' triumphal entry into Jerusalem toward the end of his ministry.

Matthew 21 records how he entered the city riding on a humble ass. We don't encounter Jesus riding on a mount at any other time. Yet this one time that he rides instead of walks, he does not travel in a regal chariot or saddled on a noble steed. He rides on an ass. Only the text actually implies he rode on the ass and a colt, the foal of an ass. Did Jesus ride two animals into the city? Was this some kind of circus trick with him riding two mounts simultaneously? Obviously, this detracts from the dignity of this important event in Jesus' life. What is really going on is that Jesus is fulfilling a prophecy of Zechariah 9:9: "Rejoice greatly, O daughter Zion! Shout aloud, O daughter Jerusalem! Lo, your king comes to you; triumphant and victorious is he, humble and riding on a donkey, on a colt, the foal of a donkey." This double reference to both a colt and a donkey is not uncommon in Hebrew writing. When reading the Old Testament, we often encounter pairings, parallelisms, and poetic licenses of this sort. This is one of numerous examples of how we ought to read the Bible precisely but not always literally. What we are looking for is the *sensus plenior*, or fuller sense. The point being made about Jesus riding on a donkey is to focus the reader's attention on his humility and the type of kingdom he is inaugurating.

Those who insist that every word of the Bible is to be taken literally usually fall into one of two extremes. Both types identify with an "us" versus "them" mentality. They set clear boundaries for membership in their communities and reject, sometimes even punish, members who violate those boundaries. Some retreat from the modern world and live in communities of like-minded followers. Others choose not to flee from the world but instead hope to dominate it, to bring in an age of universal obedience. This second group falsely claims that such a system of rule would restore us to an imagined golden age of Christian life—or advance us into an idealized future. The irony is that these myriad of fringe groups can never seem to agree on that same set of essential truths of the faith. It is, however, possible to take the Bible extremely seriously, without always taking it literally.

The Bible contains material that, upon first encounter, may seem superfluous, but thoughtful reflection often reveals a deeper purpose and meaning. Take the story of Peter having fished all day without catching anything. Jesus commands him to throw in the net once more. Miraculously, Peter hauls in an impressive 153 fish (John 21:11). Why? Saint Jerome thought (incorrectly) that it was the exact number of all the different species of fish. Scholars and, quite frankly, quacks, have offered an impressive number of other opinions about the reasons or numerological symbolism for this number. (See note 83 on page 331.) It does seem unlikely that the number is random. This is but one example of the richness of the biblical narrative. Sometimes, this richness is discovered by comparing one book in the Bible with another. There are numerous parallels between Genesis—the first book of the Bible—and Revelation—the final book. Genesis chapter 1 recounts how the earth was created; in Revelation, chapter 21 foretells how the earth will pass away. Genesis chapter 3 discusses how sin, suffering, and death come into our world; Revelation chapter 21 declares that sin, suffering, and death will cease.

These are more than interesting parallels—they represent fulfillment. Here is an example. In Genesis 9:13, God identifies a rainbow as a sign of his covenantal promise. In Ezekiel 1:26-28, and in Revelation 4:3 and 10:1, we see that same sign—the rainbow—surrounding the throne of God. The promise made in the beginning is both remembered and fulfilled at the end. Entire books have been written to explore such comparisons, but let's visit just one example in a bit more detail. There is an adage among some Christians that the Old Testament foreshadows the New Testament, while the New Testament fulfills the Old Testament. Motifs are repeated both within and across the two testaments. Consider the Gospel of Matthew. The depth of this one book would take years to plumb. There is the narrative itself, and the allusions comparing Jesus to Old Testament figures such as Moses[20] or Adam. More abstractly, there are scholars who find, in Matthew's Jesus, a reflection, perhaps, even an embodiment of the Jewish writings that nearly personify Sophia or "Wisdom."[21] The Old Testament is comprised of the Torah[22] (books of law), the books of the major and minor prophets, and some additional books. The order of these books differs in the Old Testament when compared to the Hebrew Bible. The Christian Old Testament parallels much of the Hebrew Bible, the Tanakh.[23] There are, however, certain differences between the two.

The Christian Old Testament ordering, based on the Masoretic text, is purposeful. In short, the metanarrative of the Old Testament tells the story of God and his chosen people, beginning with Abraham. We learn that God is a creator who loves, cares for, and enters into a covenant with his creation, and he has certain expectations of them. We also learn that when his chosen people fail to meet those expectations they are judged but then reconciled to God.

The author of the Gospel of Matthew knew well this pattern and sought to write his account of the life of Jesus in light of the Old Testament. The first book of the New Testament begins like the first book of the Old Testament, with the word "*geneseos*," (Greek: "generations"). Matthew is giving us a new Genesis. He is telling the reader that we are looking at God's new creation, in light of the stories of the Hebrew Scripture. Matthew picks up his narrative with a genealogy of Jesus, going all the way back to Abraham, the great Patriarch and Father of the Hebrews. What follows is an account of 42 generations. Why 42? Matthew is playing out another motif from Genesis. God created the world in six days, and his final and greatest act was the creation of Adam. So, by listing 42 generations, the Gospel author is saying "Let's see Jesus as the new Adam,"[24] as we have six sets of seven generations, culminating with Jesus, just as the creation story culminated with Adam.

The repeated cycle of the creator God entering into a covenant, played out over and over again in the Old Testament, is playing out once again, but this time with finality: the dawn of the kingdom of God, the entrance of God's new creation. In the story of Genesis, Adam is tested and fails, and the penalty is death. ("But of the tree of the knowledge of good and evil you shall not eat, for in the day that you eat of it you shall die" Genesis 2:17.) Matthew recounts how Jesus, crucified on a Friday, lay dead on a Saturday, the Hebrew Sabbath. But, on the seventh day, the new Sabbath, Jesus was resurrected.

With this, we encounter not just a new ending to the story of Adam in Genesis, but Matthew is telling a grander narrative and retelling the entire story of the Hebrew Scripture. Space does not allow for an exploration of the fascinating parallels found in Matthew between the lives of Moses and Jesus. Both men were born under an order for babies to be murdered, but they each escaped being killed. Jesus and Moses fasted for 40 days and 40 nights. They both proclaimed God's law from atop a mountain.

The connections continue as Matthew juxtaposes Joshua and Jesus, who shared the same name, and each led their people into the Promised Land. These and other parallels of the Hebrew Bible are found throughout Matthew. In short, then, Matthew is presenting Jesus as the embodiment of Israel, the one who faithfully fulfills God's covenant.

In Christian circles, there is a fallacy known as "proof texting." Proof texting is a technique where a person who is arguing for a particular point, and wishes to use the Bible as evidence, will point to one or perhaps a few verses to support the argument, as if the conclusion is inevitable and incontrovertible. While using isolated verses can be helpful in some circumstances, serious theological arguments rely on much more. Context within the totality of Scripture is often needed for a clear picture.

Much of the drama in the Bible is lost on us because most of us live lives of abundance, and we are unfamiliar with day-to-day life in ancient Judea. For example, the challenging story of Abraham's call to sacrifice Isaac is all the more dramatic given the circumstances surrounding Isaac's birth. Abraham and Sarah were thought to be incapable of having children together, and Isaac was conceived late in their lives. For a couple to be childless was a great burden in ancient times. Or, consider the story of the unforgiving servant (Matthew 18: 23-24): one talent is equal to 60 denarii, and one denarius was what an average man got paid for a day's labor. The servant was forgiven a huge debt of 600,000 denarii, but the servant himself refused to forgive a debt of a mere 100 denarii.

However, even when we do have a clearer understanding of Scripture, we encounter some difficult material. To ignore this is not only self-deception but it is to deprive ourselves of the opportunity to struggle to learn and reconcile our faith. In the Bible, we read about men and women living for hundreds of years, a talking snake and a talking mule, a fiery chariot that takes a man into the heavens, a cheater who is rewarded, a father who is commanded to murder his son, children who are devoured by bears for teasing a man about his baldness, and Jesus claiming to be the planet Venus. There are passages that appear at odds with Catholic teachings—passages that prohibit, for example, calling a man "Father," or using repetition when praying.

As stated before, the key is to take Scripture seriously, but not always literally. An overly literal reading of certain passages can vex a person who struggles to obey one command but consequently must ignore or violate a contrary teaching. Blatant manipulation of the text can make the Bible appear to support the most absurd positions.

For example, Jeremiah 18:11 reads, "Now, therefore, say to the people of Judah and the inhabitants of Jerusalem: Thus says the Lord: Look I am a potter shaping evil against you and devising a plan against you making a plan . . ." The misreading? That God is evil. In John 10:34, we read, "Is it not written in your law, 'I said you are gods'?" The misreading? That every human being is, in fact, a god. Proverbs 23:13-14 says, "Do not withhold discipline from your children: if you beat them with a rod, they will not die. If you beat them with the rod, you will save their lives from Sheol." This misreading? Child abuse is encouraged by God. According to Isaiah 11:12, "[God] will raise a signal for the nations, and will assemble the outcasts of Israel, and gather the dispersed of Judah from the four corners of the earth." The misreading? The earth is a flat square.

Sometimes, the misreading is of a different sort. In Genesis 3:15, there is a prophetic passage about the crushing of a serpent's head and the bruising of the heel of the person(s) doing the crushing. The original Hebrew pronoun can be legitimately translated as masculine or feminine, gender neutral, and even plural. For many years, certain key Catholic translations of the Bible chose to use the feminine "she," thereby investing rich Mariological significance in this passage. There are countless statues and images in devotional art depicting Mary standing, usually barefoot, atop a serpent's head. The "she" being referenced then was understood as typifying Mary; the serpent is the devil. Modern scholars, for good reasons, translate the pronoun as "he," thereby investing rich Christological significance to the passage. This newer translation is likely more loyal to the original text, yet some Catholics find the change disheartening, perhaps, not realizing that the use of "he" does not remove Mary from the equation.

We can see how another mistranslation affected art and theology. There is a famous statue of Moses with a set of horns on his head, which was carved by the great Michelangelo. Why would this Renaissance master add to Moses a symbol associated more with demons than with holy prophets? There is a story in the Pentateuch of Moses radiating light from his face after an encounter with God. When St. Jerome was translating the Bible into Latin he translated the Hebrew word "*keren*" as "horns" instead of as "radiated." "Keren" can mean horns, and some scholars believe Jerome did not mistranslate as much as he chose wrongly, for theological purposes. Jerome may have believed only Jesus is worthy of radiating light.

We could move beyond the misreading of individual passages to the misunderstanding of entire themes. Countless passages have been misapplied in order to argue heresies and blasphemies of every sort. The trick to making an absurd argument is not limited to mere quotation of a verse out of context; it also includes the stringing together of unrelated texts, ignoring the historical circumstances in which the passages were written, and taking no account of the author's style or the culture in which he wrote. In interpreting sacred Scripture, it is wise to keep in mind that the Bible is God's word, not merely human insights.

THE RICHNESS OF SCRIPTURE

■ The Bible is a library of books divided into the Old Testament[25] and the New Testament. The relationship between these two testaments is complex. In short, we can declare that oftentimes the Old Testament foreshadows the New Testament while the New Testament fulfills the Old Testament. All four Gospels, for example, refer back to the Old Testament.

■ The Catholic Bible is made up of a collection of 73 books. Although the early Church did not have a uniformly set canon, the same can be said of first- and even second-century Judaism. The Council of Rome (382) established which books made up the official Catholic canon. For Protestants, the Bible has fewer books—only 66. The reformer Martin Luther, in 1529, removed from the official canon the books of Baruch, portions of the book of Daniel, portions of the book of Esther, Judith, 1 and 2 Maccabees, Sirach, Tobit, and Wisdom, often referred to as Deuterocanonical books. He based his decision primarily on the fact that there were no Hebrew copies of these books. Fragments of three of these books, written in Hebrew, were found in Qumran, in the Dead Sea scrolls in 1947.

■ The Bible contains many different literary genres[26]: history, parable, poetry, liturgy, legal material, etc., and also employs various literary devices: alliteration, archetype, chiasmus, foreshadowing, hyperbole, inclusio (or bracketing), metaphor, paradox, personification, point of view, puns, and more. Despite this variety, there is a unity to the Bible such that Genesis through the book of Revelation form one big story, or metanarrative.[27]

Additionally, the Bible contains literary styles found nowhere else in the ancient world. The Gospels present us with an entirely unique literary genre by offering history viewed through the lens of faith. Although there are commonalities with ancient biographies, Greco-Roman aretalogies,[28] and historical accounts, there is nothing that compares to the richness and style of the prose of the Gospels.[29] Jesus' parables are wholly unique forms of storytelling, different from fables or other moral tales of the time. And, as previously mentioned, the inclusion of details such as Peter's tears is wholly distinctive in ancient writing.

■ The word "Bible" is from the Greek words "*ta biblia*" meaning "the books." The Bible brings together literature from many centuries; it includes material written by many different authors from different cultures. When we read a passage, the author, as well as the period, culture, and original language in which the author wrote must be taken into consideration. We cannot always identify an author by name, given the Jewish practice of pseudepigraphical writing. That is, an author would adopt the name of a famous figure in order to lend credibility to the text. This is neither an attempt at deception nor is it a form of ghostwriting, but pseudepigraphical works were not uncommon in biblical times.

■ Biblical authors were, in some instances, ignorant of knowledge we take for granted. The lands they lived in still exist but are very different now. Consider that Israel and parts of the Middle East are now largely deforested but once were homes to great forests.

■ Most of us read the Bible in translation.[30] We need to remember that the Bible was originally written in ancient languages (Hebrew, Aramaic, and Greek); only those original texts are inerrant. Translating ancient words and ideas into modern words and ideas can be difficult. The Greek of the New Testament is not elegant but rustic, even awkward. The Hebrew of the Old Testament is also challenging, given that early Hebrew used no vowels, hindering modern translation efforts. Defining a translated word also can be difficult, especially if the word appears only once ("*hapax legomenon*").[31] Also, Hebrew uses no punctuation, and so discerning where a verse (called a pericope) begins and ends can be difficult. Some versions translate the words literally; other versions focus on meanings. For example, Psalm 16 literally translates to read: "being instructed by kidneys," but most translators use the word "heart," not "kidneys," to preserve the intent of the author. Sometimes, it is not the original language but an old translation that poses the problem. The King James Version of Psalm 23 starts off with the famous, "The Lord is my Shepherd, I shall not want." The word "want" has a different definition today than it did in the time of the writing of the King James Bible. "I shall not want" meant "I shall not need anything." Equally important is the fact that the Hebrew mindset and the Greek mindset were very different. The Bible has no power in and of itself. It is not a magical book. The Bible has authority only because God, as the primary author, has authority, and the Bible is his word. It is not, however, merely an inert ancient document. The Bible identifies itself as alive: "Indeed, the word of God is living and active, sharper than any two-edged sword, piercing until it divides soul from spirit, joints from marrow; it is able to judge the thoughts and intentions of the heart" (Hebrews 4:12).

- The Bible is inerrant and so does not, in fact cannot, contradict itself; neither can it contradict sacred Tradition or reason, though it can surpass human reason.

- When the Bible is ambiguous, those passages are to be read in light of more comprehensible passages.

- The Bible contains nothing that is unnecessary or irrelevant. Comparing passages and reading the Bible with an attention to detail can reveal much. For example, it is not an accident that there were twelve tribes in Israel and twelve Apostles of Jesus, the new Israel.

- There are many legitimate techniques for reading the Bible. Textual criticism looks at the actual words of the Bible in their original language. Source criticism considers the sources of the text. Form criticism focuses on oral sources. Genre analysis looks to the style of writing, seeking identifiable similarities and common traits and forms. The historical-critical method examines the sources of the original biblical words and phrases and the cultural milieu surrounding the author to uncover the rich history and varied connotative and denotative meanings of the text. In addition, insights from psychology, archeology, anthropology, and a host of other disciplines can inform our reading of Scripture.

The Bible tells a story, and every high-quality story has both a good and bad version. I've had professors talk about the glory days of ancient Rome in terms of its architecture, literature, and art; yet we can just as validly discuss it in terms of the barbarity of its arena games and the cruelty of Rome's many emperors.

Each version of these stories is truthful but incomplete. Communications scholars refer to this as selective perception. This phenomenon played and continues to play itself out, tragically, in the division among Christians, though progress continues to be made. The Eastern Orthodox and the Catholic Churches split in 1054, when a Bull of Excommunication was placed upon the altar of the cathedral of Hagia Sophia. The Patriarch of Constantinople, a Byzantine Synod, responded in kind. These mutual excommunications were lifted over nine hundred years later when the Catholic–Eastern Orthodox Joint Declaration of 1965 was issued.

The next great split in Christendom occurred in 1517, when Martin Luther ignited the Reformation by nailing his 95 Theses to the door of the Wittenberg Castle Church. One year shy of the five-hundredth anniversary of this event, Pope Francis visited Sweden to join the Lutheran Church in inaugurating a yearlong celebration of Luther's action.

Mao Tse-Tung, the leader of the People's Republic of China (1949–1976), was once asked about his thoughts regarding the famous French Revolution of 1789. Mao's response was along the lines of: 'It is still too soon to tell.' Mao was a historian, and he knew that to truly appreciate the consequences of important events, much time needs to pass.

The Church, having been around for over two millennia, recognizes the need for patient assessment. "Thoughts are like living organisms. They need not only their special soil, but also their due time, so that they may strike root and develop. And the Church has abundance of time. She does not reckon in decades, but in centuries and millennia." Some of her roles will never change—preaching the gospel, celebrating the sacraments, serving the needy—but other roles might adapt through time. (Distinguishing what can change and what cannot change is a matter of some controversy.)

Unsurprisingly, this diversity can and sadly has led to dissent, mistrust, and deep misunderstandings. Interestingly, however, while it is true that Christianity has been around for over two thousand years and controversies still abound, in large part, the controversies of today are not those of years past. Those Creedal statements of faith previously mentioned helped to quell controversies of the early Church, controversies that no longer plague us today. So, with time, our contemporary dilemmas may also give way, though, perhaps, they will be replaced by new debates.

Moreover, because the canon of sacred Scripture was officially closed at the Council of Trent, and due to the fact that Jesus is the full and final revelation of the Father, the official position of the Church is that no new revelation, public or private, is forthcoming. So, even if a heretofore undiscovered ancient scroll were suddenly discovered, one that purported to be a missing Gospel or another epistle of Paul or a lost book of the Hebrew Scriptures, there is no chance that it would become part of the Catholic Bible.

Yet, we are still left with the nagging question: Why is there so much diversity of opinion over what the Bible "really" teaches when this book claims to be divinely inspired? There are many reasons. First, diversity does not always, or even often, mean disagreement. If one person understands Jesus' sacrifice on the cross in terms of payment of a debt, while another understands his death as analogous to a physician curing a disease, these are diverse opinions but not contradictions.

While it is true that the Bible speaks to us all in a personal way, it would be improper to confuse devotional reading with scholarly investigation. You don't have to be a scholar to be a Christian, but study and investigation are rewarded. Karl Barth (it is said) recommends, "Read the Bible in one hand, and the newspaper in the other." Actually, to really get something out of Scripture, it can be useful to do more than mere reading. Imagining sights and sounds can help us relate to the time and place we are reading about. We might think about what it would be like to be one of the characters in a passage or story. For example, in Matthew 17:5, the voice of God proclaims, "This is my Son, the Beloved . . ." What would it be like to hear God speak those words to you?

†

CHAPTER TWELVE

HUMANKIND, CREATION, AND LAST THINGS
(ANTHROPOLOGY, COSMOGONY, AND ESCHATOLOGY)

In those respects in which the soul is unlike God it is also unlike itself.[1] —Saint Bernard of Clairvaux

COSMOGONY - BEGINNING

Christianity has no theogony—story about God's origin—because God is eternal, uncreated, and without beginning. Christianity does, however, have much to say about cosmogony—the origin of the universe—but in a theological, not a scientific, sense.

Gerard Manley Hopkins was correct: "The World is charged with the grandeur of God."[2]

God's relationship to the world, however, is complicated. Many pagans, both ancient and modern, envision a world that was animated and, some even believed, sentient. Judeo-Christian tradition, however, insists that God is separate and distinct though simultaneously passionately and actively connected with his creation. This realization calls to mind the hymn "Lord of the Dance," where Jesus is identified as both the Lord of the Dance and the Dance itself.

Creation both discloses and conceals God. Saint Thomas Aquinas taught that, in some ways, the created order keeps God hidden from us (*Deus absconditus*). Looking to nature to understand the Creator can lead to all sorts of insights but also presents misinformation. When asked what nature reveals about God, the famous biologist J. B. S. Haldane purportedly responded, "The

Creator has an inordinate fondness for beetles."[3] Yet, in some ways, God is revealed through his creation (*Deus revelatus*). It is by this balance that God reveals himself without forcing us to have faith in him.

The creation account in Genesis is often compared with other Ancient Near East creation stories such as the Babylonian creation myth, the *Enuma Elish*. The story of Noah and the flood, also found in Genesis, is often compared with the story of Utnapishtim and the flood, recorded in the *Epic of Gilgamesh*.

However, a close reading of the text shows that the author(s) wrote the story in such a way so as to counter certain beliefs of the surrounding pagan cultures. For example, in the myths of the Mesopotamian region, both the sun and the moon were actual deities; in Genesis, they are only illuminating bodies created by God and are not gods themselves. So, Genesis does not initially use the words "sun" and "moon"—which may have been understood by some to be actual gods, but instead describes a greater light to rule the day and a lesser light to rule the night.

Correctives of this sort can be found throughout the first chapter of Genesis, which is presented as a type of Hebrew poetry. The material is written with a rhythm and meter that lends itself to being sung or chanted in seven verses. Just like a song with a repeated chorus, we see the phrase, "and God saw that it was good," repeated until the poem ends with the climax, "and it was very good."

This poetry, or mythopoeic style, has been widely interpreted throughout the centuries for rich theological content and symbolism. For example, the act of creation being divided into seven days is not random but may be indicative of God entering into a covenant with his creation. The Hebrew words for the noun "seven" and the verb "to swear" both stem from the same source. So, we see "God covenanting himself to the cosmos in the very act of creating it, deliberately in a sevenfold way."[4]

These types of narrative clues are embedded into the text, and millennia of both Jewish and Christian study of the Genesis story have revealed many interesting details. Mystic Simone Weil profoundly understood that: "On God's part creation is not an act of self-expansion but of restraint and renunciation. God and all his creatures are less than God alone."[5] This concept is similar to certain Kabbalistic writings describing God's "*Tzimtzum*," his self-contraction or withdrawal to make space for creation.

This theme of God making room for and creating that which is other than himself is recounted in the creation narrative of humans. Adam was made from the earth, from the dust of the ground. We are part of God's good creation but also stewards of that creation. We are the sons and daughters of the earth, ("For you are dust, And to dust you shall return" Genesis 3:19), but, through grace, we are invited to become children of God.

Genesis need not be read as being in conflict with current scientific theories about human origins. Some Christians, however, seek to find literal truth there, worrying that if we dismiss Genesis as a mere parable what's to stop us from doing the same regarding the stories Moses or even of Jesus? Scholar Raymond Brown provides a helpful answer.[6] He reminds us that we know the minutest details of the life of Queen Elizabeth II of England; we know less detail about her ancestor, King William the Conqueror; and we can barely separate myth from reality when it comes to the story of legendary King Arthur. Why? Because of the amount of and the quality of the information we have about each sovereign differs. Similarly, there are accounts in the Bible that offer great details and others that provide scant information.

The Church, when reading Genesis, the first eleven chapters in particular, recognizes that this material was not written in typical Hebrew prose with poetic elements. The narrative's purpose is not to provide a natural history of modern human origins, but rather, in highly stylized fashion, the text communicates certain truths about God and creation. Therefore, it is no conflict for a Catholic to accept current data that modern humans, *Homo sapiens*, may have existed for over two hundred thousand years (although civilization is only a relatively recent phenomenon, having begun about ten thousand years ago.[7])

Modern scientific and historiographic methods were simply not available to the author(s) of Genesis. The very name "Adam" may be a play on words with the Hebrew word for earth, which is "*adamah*." Prior to Genesis 4:25, the word "Adam" was not used as a proper name but simply an identifier coterminous with "the person." Actually, the first chapter of Genesis does not mention Adam and Eve by name, and so, perhaps, the story of their creation in the subsequent narrative is not, as many have claimed, a retelling of the first creation story but a separate account of a distinct event allowing us to hypothesize humans predating a historical Adam and Eve who were selected as representatives of the race. For some more fundamentalist Christians, tracing each and every human, biologically, back to a common ancestor is essential. Others are less concerned with this relationship, pointing out that we are not biologically related to Jesus, yet his actions have a universal effect upon humanity.[8]

The story of the creation of both Adam and Eve is very different than God's other acts of creation, which came about by God's fiat, him merely saying, "Let it be." God spoke into being the light, earth, and water, but human beings were not created by utterance. Instead, they were fashioned by God himself into his own image and likeness. Adam was formed from the dust of the ground, and Eve was then formed from Adam. The text identifies an intimate connection between humans and the earth but more so between humans and the God whose vivifying breath brings life.[9] God crafted humans in an intimate way. Since humans were made from the earth, the story indicates not just a special relationship between man and God but between man and the earth from which he was formed. (The Genesis narrative purposefully shows the sequence of God's creative act; first the heavens and then the earth, and then living creatures of the earth, with humans coming as the grand finale.)

Saint Gregory the Theologian pointed to the Genesis narrative as indicating that we are microcosms of the entire created order; that is, humans are so closely identified with creation that if we move toward or away from God, so too does the rest of creation. According to the description used most famously by the great theologian St. Maximus the Confessor, we are *methorios* (Greek for "a boundary"), the representatives—even in a limited sense, the priests of all creation; mediators between the physical and the spiritual realms.

If Adam and Eve served in priestly roles, then where was the temple in which they served?

> That Eden represents God's temple, the intersection of heaven and earth, is evident from tabernacle and temple descriptions elsewhere in the Bible (e.g. Ex 25-40; 1 Kings 6; Ezek 47; Rev 21-22). More specifically, Eden closely resembles the holy of holies. Both are populated with fruit trees (Gen 2:9; 1 Kings 6:29-35), with the Tree of Life occupying the center (Gen 2:9, 1 Kings 6:29-35, Rev 22:2). Rivers flow out of Eden as they flow out of the temple (Gen 2:10; Ezek 47:1, Rev 22:1), an especially relevant

concept since the Tigris and Euphrates flow into the Persian Gulf rather than out of a common source. Both Eden and the temples were adorned with precious metals (Gen 2:11-12; Ex 25:10-31; 1 Kings 6:20; Rev 21:18-21). Angels guard the entrance (Gen 3:24; Ex 25:17-22, Ezek 1:5-11; Rev 21:12). All these factors point to the conclusion that Eden was not simply paradise for Adam and Eve; it was the intersection of heaven on earth. Eden was God's sanctuary. It was the center of the cosmos.[10]

So, Eden was God's temple, and Adam and Eve, God's image-bearers, were his priests.

> As in all ancient temples (except the one in Jerusalem . . .), there was an 'image' or statue of the god in question, so the creator God places into the 'temple' of his heaven-and-earth creation his own 'image,' human beings made to reflect him, to bring his creativity to birth in his world, and to reflect the praises of the world back to the creator. That, of course, is the heart of the story, which is then spoiled by the rebellion of God's image bearing creatures.[11]

ANTHROPOLOGY

Ralph Waldo Emerson observed: "Jesus Christ belonged to the true race of prophets. He saw with open eye the mystery of the soul. Drawn by its severe harmony, ravished with its beauty, he lived in it, and had his being there. Alone in all history, he estimated the greatness of man. One man was true to what is in you and me."[12]

Jesus did not merely recognize what others before him missed, but he elevated human dignity in manner that pagans found scandalous. This radical egalitarianism is an essential part of the good news Jesus shared. He leveled the playing field, so to speak, explaining that the kingdom of God is open to all people; the poor and rich, the educated and ignorant, the healthy and sick all are loved by God.

The Hebrews, among all ancient peoples, recognized human dignity. Read through the pagan myths of the ancient world and you will find that mortals are mostly considered nuisances by the gods, useful, perhaps, for some menial services.[13] In the

Hebrew Bible though, we are God's decisive creation. We are neither nuisances nor servants as the pagan myths posit, but the
"image-bearers" of God. In Genesis, we read how God created the
heavens and the earth and that, contained therein, is his last
work of creation, the culmination of it all: humans. This sequence
communicates to the reader that God saved the best for last.

In a shocking affront to many pagan creation stories, God bestows equal dignity to both Adam and Eve, both men and women.
Adam and Eve were companions, not master and slave. Eve came
from Adam's rib, flesh of his flesh and bone of his bone. Genesis
2:22 reveals that God brought Eve to Adam; that is, the Father
escorted Eve to Adam as his bride. A loving father walking a bride
to her betrothed is an ancient custom that continues to be practiced even in our present time.

In contrast to this low view of mortals, Psalm 8 tells us we are
all crowned with glory and honor, while Psalm 139:14 declares
we are all "fearfully and wonderfully made." So, using Hebrew
hyperbole, the Old Testament declares our lofty status and God's
gift of being and self-determination. There is no single biblical
anthropology (not in terms of natural or social science); instead,
we find different insights into personhood.

The high regard for humankind is, elsewhere in the Bible, balanced with sobering assessments. Isaiah 64:6 declares that our
sinful behavior can be compared to filthy rags in the sight of God,
and the book of Job reminds us of our smallness in the universe
(38:26). Nonetheless, the general theme is that humans are made
by God and thereby endowed with an innate dignity. In Genesis
1:26, we read that humans are made in the image and likeness
of God. This means we can look to God to learn something about
ourselves, and, conversely, we can look to ourselves to learn some
things about God.

These Jewish understandings of what it means to be human
influenced and informed early Christians, but so did certain philosophical concepts borrowed from other cultures. Throughout
Christian history, anthropological questions were debated and
reformulated, including some explication of what it means to be
the image of a God who is a Trinity. Saint Irenaeus, for example,
sought to differentiate "image" and "likeness" as two separate categories. In the West, St. Augustine explored how our image and
likeness relate to the faculties of memory, intellect, and will. The
Cappadocian Fathers[14] emphasized our ability to make choices.

As the book of Sirach 15:14 reminds us, "It was he [God] who created humankind in the beginning, and he left them in the power of their own free choice."

We are tasked with co-creating with our God. He invites us to share in his work of shaping not only the events of our lives but our very identities. Participating with him in this great endeavor requires attentiveness to God's providential actions in our lives and commitment to his teachings—his law of love. The correlation between God's law and our will is not passive, but in our freedom we are invited to adopt God's life-affirming will, integrating it into our own beliefs and actions. It is a labor that involves sacrifice and sorrow but also elicits blessings and grace.

We are creatures made in the *imago Dei* ("image of God;" cf. e.g. Genesis 1:26–27; Wisdom 2:23). This is an important reference point that distinguishes the Christian from the secular understanding of the human person. This reverence, however, was balanced with the recognition that our dignity as "image-bearers" of the Creator was damaged through human rebellion. This damage has affected each one of us, and, to an extent, all of creation. Humanity became fragmented—lacking self-control, even self-understanding. Saint Paul wrote, "I do not understand my own actions. For I do not do what I want, but I do the very thing I hate" (Romans 7:15). I do what I hate in part because the "I" that engages in action is constantly shifting.

Great scholar of religion Huston Smith echoes similar sentiments by saying, "We are born in mystery, we live in mystery, and we die in mystery."[15] Yet these mysteries are not completely impenetrable. Imagine if your best friend were to stop over to say she suddenly had been called out of town on an emergency and would, then, be incommunicado. She hands you a box with air holes in it and asks you to take care of her pet while she's gone. Her taxi to the airport is waiting, so she gives the box to you and promptly leaves. Now that your friend has gone, you decide to open the box and see what is inside. You lift the lid, and to your amazement, you see that her pet is a creature you have never seen before. It is neither a cat nor a dog nor any kind of animal you recognize. So, not knowing anything about it, how would you take care of it?[16]

This scenario provides a good analogy for our own lives—except, the unknown creature is each one of us. What does it mean to be "human"? Christian anthropology borrows insights from sociology, psychology, biology, and other disciplines, recognizing that we see ourselves as alternating between expressions of our "public self" versus our "intimate self," our "biological self" versus our "spiritual self." The subject is sometimes tied to the idea that the human person is divided into a trichotomy: body, soul, and spirit (appealing, for example, to 1 Thessalonians 5:23 and Hebrews 4:12). If we do not know at least some of these fundamental characteristics, then how can we live well?

> For man, to 'be' means to 'be on the way'—he cannot be in any other form; man is intrinsically a pilgrim, 'not yet arrived,' regardless of whether he is aware of this or not, whether he accepts it or not. . . . Subconsciously, and apart from any specific act of the will, but also in the innermost core of all our conscious exercise of the will, we yearn for perfect happiness. In this lies man's fulfillment, man's good, the beckoning aim and destiny of his unfolding existence! The ultimate object of the human and the process itself of becoming, by which we approach yet never quite reach this goal . . . can never be adequately described in words, neither the destination nor the journey.[17]

The Greek philosopher Heraclitus claimed that a person can never step in the same river twice; since the water is constantly flowing, the river is necessarily changing. In a way, we, too, are always changing. The incidental things about us, such as age and weight, change. But, in another sense, the substantial things about us remain the same. Like rivers, we are simultaneously static and dynamic.

"In a higher world it is otherwise, but here below to live is to change, and to be perfect is to change often."[18] We must find ways to change what ought to be changed while remaining steadfast in those areas of our life that require constancy. Consider the famous Serenity Prayer: "God, grant me serenity to accept the things I cannot change, courage to change the things I can, and the wisdom to know the difference."[19]

In ancient Greece, in the city of Delphi, there once stood a temple dedicated to Apollo, the god of light, poetry, healing, and music. The words, "*gnōthi seauton*" ("Know yourself!") were carved on the entrance of the temple. The call to know yourself seems like a strange assertion, but there is wisdom in this invitation. Of course, the words were written centuries before we defined "knowledge" in a strictly rationalistic manner. There are different ways to know: intellectually, intuitively, etc. Plato's (and, more directly, Socrates') reflections led him to adopt the admonition that the unexamined life was not worth living.[20] That is a strong reproach: He does not say the unexamined life is trivial or vain—but that it is not worth living!

One way of avoiding the kind of deception mentioned above is through an examination of conscience. Socrates' self-examination led him to conclude that he knew nothing, except the fact of his own ignorance.[21] Socrates' insight into self-knowledge may have served as a faint foreshadowing of Descartes' statement: *Cogito, ergo sum* ("I think, therefore, I am"). Descartes' ideas about substance dualism—i.e., the mind and body are separate and distinct—is also found (though, perhaps, in "proto-form") in much of Greek philosophy. This is most famously identified with Cartesian Dualism. This perspective sees humans as if we were all ghosts in machines. The alternate view, Monism, simply posits that the mind and body form a single reality.

The paradox of Socratic ignorance was a profound and humble insight. Correctly understood, he was not saying he was ignorant in terms of a mere lack of knowledge. But, he was admitting that he did not have all the answers and was, thus, committed to discover truth, despite his preconceived ideas. It is very hard to learn anything new when you think you already have all the answers. In the worst cases, self-awareness is not just avoided but rebelled against because such self-revealing knowledge can be painful. Turning our attention to thoughts and emotions that are often ignored can unleash a host of negative results. So, we create elaborate excuses and find sometimes harmful distractions from becoming self-aware. As Brother Thomas Merton wrote:

> My false and private self is the one who wants to exist outside the reach of God's will and God's love—outside of reality and outside of life. And such a self cannot help but be an illusion.
>
> We are not very good at recognizing illusions, least of all the ones we cherish about ourselves—the ones . . . which feed the roots of sin. For most of the people in the world, there is no greater subjective reality than this false self of theirs, which cannot exist. A life devoted to the cult of this shadow is what is called a life of sin.[22]

Christians believe that everyone possesses an immortal soul.[23] There is an essential aspect of each person that is neither the product of biology nor anything in nature. The creation of our souls and the issue of "ensoulment" (i.e., when the soul unites with a body) is hotly debated.[24] Sometimes, the word, "spirit" (Greek: "*pneuma*"; Hebrew: "*ruach*"), is used synonymously with, "soul" (Greek: "*psychē*"; Hebrew: "*nepesh*"); but, sometimes the words "spirit" and "soul" denote different realities. The Bible does not offer a clear answer on the origin of our souls; and, throughout the centuries Christians have been in disagreement on the subject. Christianity rejects the speculation that the human soul somehow evolved from a more primitive form. This rejection is not a rejection of natural evolution, per se, but it is grounded in the recognition that souls are spiritual in substance and, therefore, are not subject to machinations of biological evolution. Also, we do not see any pantheistic arguments, namely, that all souls are just bits and pieces of God or that we are all just individual drops of the divine essence.[25]

A person's flesh-and-blood body is the material expression of the soul, while a person's soul is the spiritual manifestation of the body. What this means is that both our bodies and our souls are redeemed. Since we are the union of the physical and spiritual in one nature, our bodies express certain realities of our souls just as the states of our souls affect our physical bodies. (Pope St. John Paul II provided a rich theology described as a "Theology of the Body," which has been described as "a kind of theological time bomb set to go off, with dramatic consequences."[26])

As G. K. Chesterton reminds us, "A corpse is not a man; but also a ghost is not a man."[27] Both the "corpse" and the "ghost" are incomplete beings. That is part of the unique message of Christianity: The soul is not the prisoner of the flesh and the material world is not vile. (That is the heresy of the Gnostics.) The orthodox, Christian view is that we are a unity of flesh and spirit. Focusing solely on either aspect has its dangers. Therefore, the Church has always reverenced both the human soul and the body.

Related to this issue is the question of ensoulment. In general, there are three main theories:

- CREATIONISM[28]. God created each individual soul *ex nihilo* (Latin: "out of nothing"). There are many verses in Scripture that support this position, for example, Genesis 2:7 (cf. also Isaiah 42:5; Zechariah 12:1).[29]

- TRADUCIANISM. The human soul was co-created by or derived from an individual's parents. The word comes from the Latin word, "*tradux*" ("vine branch," "shoot"). It was espoused by Tertullian and (perhaps) St. Gregory of Nyssa, among others.

- PRE-EXISTENCE. God has created all human souls at once and keeps them in a heavenly storehouse of sorts. (This idea emanates from noncanonical Jewish mystical writings, which refer to a place, named the "Hall of *Guf*," as the name for this storehouse.) There is scant evidence in the Bible to support this view; it brings with it numerous theological dilemmas.[30]

These three theories represent the majority of Christian opinion on the topic, though other orthodox options have also been proposed. (Some heretical ideas, such as belief in reincarnation, are categorically rejected by the Church[31] and all orthodox Christianity.[32])

The origin of the soul is one debate within the Church. Another revolves around the topic of how the body and soul interrelate. There are three primary theories:

- "PURE SUBSTANCE" DUALISM. The person is not both body and soul, but a simple entity. One's identity is indistinguishable from one's soul.

- "COMPOUND SUBSTANCE" DUALISM. The person is made up of a body and a soul that are united.

- HYLOMORPHIC DUALISM. The person is made up of a body and soul. The soul forms the body.

Theories about the origin and form of the human soul are tangentially related to the topic of non-human souls. Do animals have souls? Do all dogs go to heaven? The Church has never proclaimed a definitive teaching on the issue. However, the Bible teaches that God created the animals, that he was pleased with them, and that he cares for them. (See Wisdom 11:24-26 and Matthew 10:29; Romans 8; Ephesians 1:10; Colossians 1:20; and Revelation 5:13.)

In Genesis we read, "And all flesh died that moved on the earth, birds, domestic animals, wild animals, all swarming creatures that swarm on the earth, and all human beings; everything on dry land in whose nostrils was the breath of life died" (7:21-22). The implication of the phrase "in whose nostrils was the breath of life" is that animals, like humans, share in the same God-given breath of life. The difference between humans and animals may be one of degree but not necessarily in kind.[33] In the penetrating opening of the Gospel of John we read that the Word (God the Son) became flesh (1:14). The verse does not read "the Word became human." Why? Some scholars speculate that the Gospel is cluing us in to the fact that Jesus' incarnation, his fleshy existence, was a partaking in the redemption of the entire created order. Saint Paul supports this idea in some of his writings. "We know that the whole creation has been groaning in labor pains until now" (Romans 8:22).

ESCHATOLOGY – END

Unsurprisingly, just as there is a large body of theological insights into the beginning of all creation, there is an equally rich corpus of Christian literature on the topic of the end of all things—apocalyptic literature.[34] (The word "eschatology" comes from "*eschatos*," a Greek word meaning "last.") The world as we know it will eventually end.[35] Speculating, and in some cases, distressing, about the end of the world is a longstanding pastime. Since the start of recorded history, humanity has contemplated last things, both individually and as the world as a whole. The great myths of ancient peoples are populated with stories about how the world will end. The Egyptians, captivated with the afterlife, have many stories about the end of the world, but early in their culture, they believed that the chaotic waters from which the world sprang would destroy all life. Ragnarök, the story of the end depicted in Norse mythology, describes an awesome final battle in which mortal life is consumed.

Fascinations with Christian apocalyptic scenarios date back to the earliest days of the Church and continue today. The Gospels recount Jesus discussing the end times, and more broadly, the New Testament ends with the book of Revelation—a book filled with mystical visions, prophetic warnings, and apocalyptic imagery.

This interest in the end of the world was present in Jesus' time and has resurged sporadically. For example, there was much angst throughout Christendom in the year 999, as many, subscribing to a superstitious numerology, thought the end was near. In the thousand years since then, innumerable end-of-time conjectures have flooded both the religious and secular realms. There are countless cultural references to the end of the world that saturate our everyday lives.

The Bible[36] provides numerous passages that address the apocalypse, especially in the last book of Scripture, the book of Revelation. The strange imagery and apocalyptic prophecies address the culmination of God's creation in terms of the great war of Armageddon (or Megiddo), global natural disasters, the Antichrist, the number six-six-six (666), the four horsemen, and more.

Scripture scholars from a variety of denominations read the prophecies of Revelation differently, but in general, their interpretations can be divided into four categories. Most would agree that the first three chapters of the book apply to historical events that occurred in the first century AD. The remainder of the book is approached in the following ways:

- PRETERISM. This position argues that the language of Revelation is deeply symbolic of events that already took place. Preterists believe the Apostolic Era, the first centuries after Jesus, was tumultuous for early Christians and that these experiences were recorded in a coded manner in Revelation.[37]

- HISTORICISM. Proponents of this approach understand Revelation as addressing the entire history that takes place between Jesus' first and second coming.

- FUTURISM. As the name indicates, the futurists believe Revelation is a book of prophecy about future events that will play out in a short time frame preceding Jesus' imminent return.

- ALLEGORICALLY. Followers of this position read Revelation as an allegory that does not refer to actual peoples and events but instead provides the reader with stories meant to communicate some truth about the Christian faith.

Not only is the entire corpus of apocalyptic writings analyzed according to different methods, but various passages in this literature have inspired divergent theological camps. For example,

Revelation 20 discusses a period of a thousand years when Jesus will reign on earth. This thousand-year reign has been interpreted according to premillennial, postmillennial, and amillennial theologies. (The word "millennial" refers here to a period of a thousand years as opposed to the newer generational term.) The premillennialists believe Jesus will physically return and rule the earth for a thousand years. Postmillennialists reject the idea of an actual thousand-year reign and believe God's kingdom will come about through a gradual betterment of our world. Lastly, the amillennialists also reject an actual thousand-year reign but argue that Jesus' second coming will inaugurate the new heavens and the new earth.[38]

Actually, all Christians believe in some version of Jesus' return and the coming of a new heaven and new earth. The questions of when and how Jesus will return have been endlessly speculated for centuries. What we can say is that the time will be at God's pleasure and not our desire. What's more, each of us individually must face our own end times in the form of our own deaths, and that date is much more certain.

One point we can say for sure is that just as Jesus' incarnation occurred in the fullness of time, so will his second coming. The apocalypse, like all of history, is Christocentric. "Christ doesn't come again, because it is the end of time; it is the end of time, because He comes again. Christ is not relative to time, Time is relative to Christ."[39] How will this second coming manifest? The Church refers to the event as the *parousia* (Greek for "presence" or "coming"). Jesus is already present among us. He is present sacramentally in the Eucharist; he is present in the Church, his Body; he is present wherever two or more are gathered in his name (Matthew 18-20).

All this rich symbolism regarding Jesus' departure from earth reemerges with speculations about his return; including the very Protestant idea of a rapture—that believers will brought up into the heavens while unbelievers will be left here on earth. Here are two of the few Bible passages that allude to this event.

- "Then we who are alive, who are left, will be caught up in the clouds together with them to meet the Lord in the air . . ." (1 Thessalonians 4:17).

- "Then two will be in the field; one will be taken and one will be left" (Matthew 24:40).

The notion that these and other verses refer to an event deemed "the rapture" is foreign to Christian thought prior to the 1830s, when an Anglican clergyman named John Nelson Darby conceived of the idea. Another Anglican, N. T. Wright, explains a more Catholic interpretation of these passages.

> When the emperor visited a colony or province, the citizens of the country would go to meet him at some distance from the city. It would be disrespectful to have him actually arrive at the gates as though his subjects couldn't be bothered to greet him properly. When they met him, they wouldn't then stay out in the open country: they would escort him royally into the city itself. When Paul speaks of 'meeting' the Lord 'in the air,' the point is precisely not—as in the popular rapture theology—that the saved believers would then stay up in the air somewhere, away from earth. The point is that, having gone out to meet their returning Lord, they will escort him royally into his domain, that is, back to the place they have come from.[40]

This eschatological experience will happen at a point in history, but no one knows the day or the hour (Matthew 24:36) when the end will come. What is undeniably certain, however, is that each one of us will face our own personal end at some point. Catholic tradition holds that there are four last things: death, judgment,[41] heaven, and hell.

Death holds great terror for many. Even to those of us who hope for eternal life, death is seen as the enemy. Nonetheless, death is unavoidable. From the Middle East comes an old folktale about a man who is in the marketplace with his servant. He turns and is startled to see Death standing a few feet away. The man abandons his servant, mounts his horse, and rides at top speed for hours until he reaches the far-off city of Babylon. Meanwhile, Death approaches the servant the man left behind and tells him how surprised she had been to see his master here in the marketplace this afternoon because she had an appointment with him later that evening in Babylon!

Death brings everything into perspective. Being filled with fear, resentment, and anxiety over dying makes it difficult to think about preparing for it. Legend has it that Plato, the consummate philosopher, was asked on his deathbed to sum up his philosophy. "Practice dying," he replied! Saint Ignatius of Loyola put it differently when he counseled "Just as taking a walk, journeying on foot, and running are bodily exercises, so we call 'spiritual exercises'; every way of preparing and disposing the soul to rid itself of all inordinate attachments . . ." [42]

An element of our fear of death comes from the realization that our actions have consequences both here and now and in the hereafter.[43] It is no coincidence that religions across the globe and throughout recorded history have envisioned judgment scenes for the dead. Consider how the ancient Egyptians envisioned the jackal-headed god, Anubis, weighing the hearts of the deceased. If the heart was lighter than a feather, the deceased would continue to exist in the afterlife. If, however, the heart was heavier than a feather, weighed down by misdeeds in life, then the person would be destroyed. A funerary goddess named Ammut, depicted as a mishmash of a crocodile, a lion, and hippopotamus—creatures feared by the Egyptians—would devour the heart, and the person would cease to exist.

When we die we are judged, or, in some traditions, we judge ourselves and are either rewarded or punished. The standard by which our deeds are measured is also similar. Without devolving into a naïve syncretism, it is reasonable to compare the ancient concepts of *maat* from Egypt, *logos* from Greece, and *Tao* from China.

Both Scripture and Tradition confirm that we all will be judged by God. Some people believe that when the deceased stand before God to be judged, they cannot speak. They are silent because God knows everything; there is nothing we can tell him by way of excuse or mitigation that he does not already know. As a lawyer who loves to argue my way out of trouble, this thought terrified me. Then I learned more about this theory, about the so-called "silence of the dead" before God. Yes, perhaps we don't get to speak—but Jesus does. He serves as our intercessor with his father. Jesus is our defense attorney! ". . . but if anyone sins, we have an Advocate with the Father, Jesus Christ the righteous" (1 John 2:1). The Holy Spirit, too, is our "Counselor." In the Gospel of John,[44] Jesus tells his disciples he will send "another Helper." Jesus is their helper, but the Holy Spirit is the other helper (*parakletos*) he sends.[45] (The Greek word "parakletos" translates to mean "attorney" or "legal advocate.")

The Christian imagery of final judgment is distinctly different in many respects, however. Too often, Christian symbolism can perpetuate certain misconceptions, such as portraying God the Father as an angry judge just waiting to condemn us all, requiring Jesus to intercede for us to try to get us a reprieve. That is not the biblical picture. The Father we are facing is not a judge who delights in condemning but one who delights in being merciful. He is the forgiving father who embraces his rebellious son as in the parable of the Prodigal Son.

An all-too-common misconception is that at the final judgment God sends good people to heaven and bad people to hell. While it is true that heaven is a meritocracy, the only way to get there is to earn it—and we cannot do that for ourselves. The problem then with the good-guys-go-to-heaven-while-the-bad-guys-go-to-hell paradigm is that there are no good guys. None of us can merit heaven. But, we don't have to because Jesus already did by living a totally sinless life. As R. C. Sproul poetically observed, "We need to see that not only did Jesus die for us, He lived for us."[46]

HELL: THE MISERIFIC VISION

The Bible uses terrifying language when describing hell, but the reality is worse than we think. The very idea that unrepentant reprobate souls are cast into an eternal, unquenchable fire is unfathomable. Yet, we do not have to look far for Christians who believe that the great majority of people go there after death. Jonathan Edwards, an eminent Protestant preacher of Colonial America, is famous for a hellfire and brimstone sermon: *Sinners in the Hands of an Angry God*. Although not Catholic, warnings similar to those in Edwards' sermon can easily be found in the works of Catholic preachers.

This metaphysical pessimism is often justified by biblical passages that reference how the gate to life is narrow, but the gate to destruction is wide.[47] To some extent, this is quite understandable, given the reality that Jesus not only taught about hell more than anyone else in the New Testament (mentioning hell over 70 times in the New Testament), but also he spoke about hell more than he discussed heaven. It is worth noting, however, that much of the time he was talking to the hypocritical, self-righteous religious leaders of his day.

Consider this excerpt of a description from the author James Joyce:

Hell is a strait and dark and foul-smelling prison, an abode of demons and lost souls, filled with fire and smoke. . . .

—They lie in exterior darkness. . . . at the command of God, the fire of hell, while retaining the intensity of its heat, burns eternally in darkness. . . .

—The horror . . . is increased by its awful stench. All the filth of the world, all the offal and scum of the world, we are told, shall run there as to a vast reeking sewer when the terrible conflagration of the last day has purged the world. The brimstone, too, which burns there in such prodigious quantity fills all hell with its intolerable stench; and the bodies of the damned themselves exhale such a pestilential odour. . . .

The torment of fire is the greatest torment. . . . Place your finger for a moment in the flame of a candle and you will feel the pain of fire. . . . Moreover, our earthly fire destroys at the same time as it burns, so that the more intense it is the shorter is its duration; but the fire of hell has this property, that it preserves that which it burns, and, though it rages with incredible intensity, it rages for ever [sic].

And this terrible fire will not afflict the bodies of the damned only from without, but each lost soul will be a hell unto itself, the boundless fire raging in its very vitals. O, how terrible is the lot of those wretched beings! The blood seethes and boils in the veins, the brains are boiling in the skull, the heart in the breast glowing and bursting, the bowels a red-hot mass of burning pulp, the tender eyes flaming like molten balls.

Every sense of the flesh is tortured and every faculty of the soul therewith: the eyes with impenetrable utter darkness, the nose with noisome odours, the ears with yells and howls and execrations, the taste with foul matter, leprous corruption, nameless suffocating filth, the touch with redhot [sic] goads and spikes, with cruel tongues of flame. And through the several torments of the senses the immortal soul is tortured eternally in its very essence amid the leagues upon leagues of glowing fires kindled in the abyss by the offended majesty of the Omnipotent God . . .[48]

Beyond all the torture imagery lies the true horror that hell is our eternal separation from God. It is that place or state of being where we eternally reject God's invitation to love. Hell is where God respects a person's demand that he simply leave us alone.

That loneliness is referred to by the Latin term *"poena damni"*—the pain that comes from being forever denied heaven. This misery is so unfathomable because we were created to share in the joy and happiness of God. Not only is this eternally denied to a soul in hell, but that soul knows that he or she is to blame for the current torment, that it will never end, and that God and the blessed in heaven are enjoying eternal bliss instead of anguish. This fact stirs great hatred in the damned, but it is a rage incapable of harming any in heaven.

In addition to this pain of loss, *poena sensus*, "pain of sense" in Latin, references the sensory torments of hell: the fire, the stench, the darkness, the horrible sights and sounds of the damned.

Perhaps this hell is allowed by God, but it is not imposed by him against the will of the sinner. A hellish soul in the heavenly realm would do nothing more than increase the punishment of the damned. For an unrepentant sinner, heaven would be a more miserable torment than hell. Cardinal John Newman expresses it this way:

> . . . for an unholy, reprobate soul, we, perhaps, could not fancy a greater (punishment) than to summon it to heaven. Heaven would be hell to an irreligious man. . . . How forlorn would he wander through the courts of heaven! He would find no one like himself; he would see in every direction the marks of God's holiness, and these would make him shudder. He would feel himself always in His presence. He could no longer turn his thoughts another way, as he does now, when conscience reproaches him. He would know that the Eternal Eye was ever upon him; and that Eye of holiness, which is joy and life to holy creatures, would seem to him an Eye of wrath and punishment. God cannot change His nature. Holy He must ever be. But, while He is holy, no unholy soul can be happy in heaven.[49]

The poet Milton understood this when he penned, "The mind is its own place, and in itself can make a Heaven of Hell, a Hell of Heaven."[50] He further made this point in *Paradise Lost* by noting that Lucifer and his allies were not cast out from heaven, but they threw themselves out: "headlong themselves they threw/ Down from the verge of Heav'n."[51] Although it may sound absurd, heaven and hell have been understood by some as actually being the exact same place![52] Think about an earthly analogy. Haven't you ever gone to a movie that you loved, but the person you were with absolutely hated it? Maybe you know someone who seems to be perpetually in a bad mood. If it's sunny out, she's too hot; if it's raining, she hates wet weather. Hell is, in many ways, self-chosen. Hell, in other words, is not merely some torture chamber located on the outskirts of the kingdom of God for those who won't play by the correct rules, but it is self-imposed isolation and rejection of God. "The fire of God, which is His essential being, His love, His creative power, is a fire unlike its earthly symbol in this, that it is only at a distance it burns—that the further from Him, it burns the worse."[53]

This theology, espoused by some Eastern Orthodox, posits that, objectively, each person who dies goes to the same place; each person comes face-to-face with God. For those people who love God, encountering his love and light is pure bliss. For those who hate him, the encounter must be avoided at all costs. And so, they become branches cut off from the vine; they shrivel and lie dying but never fully die. Originally made in the image and likeness of God, they have retained the image of eternal God but have chosen to discard his holy likeness, and so they retain their immortality and never completely cease to exist. Instead, they turn themselves inward and refuse to cast their eyes toward God. They rebel against the light and the truth and seek a place of refuge. But, God is everywhere, and the only place to hide is in the darkness of their own sin. This turning inward, this isolation, is the epitome of sin. A damned soul would then exist in a state of *incurvatus in se*, which is Latin for to "turn in on oneself."

Hell exists as a place or state of being where we are eternally separated from God. Hell, however, cannot exist in and of itself in the way heaven can and once did. Heaven can and did exist without hell, but hell cannot exist without heaven for the same reason that evil cannot exist without good. Evil does not exist on its own, as good does; evil is a perversion of the good. It is an absence, not a presence; a corruption or overindulgence of a thing, not a thing itself. Hell is not a kingdom of equal size and worth in opposition to heaven. It is nearly nothing, a mass of eternal introverts who turn in on themselves to avoid light and love. Still, one wonders how the blessed can endure the knowledge of the eternal sufferings of the damned, especially those whom they loved in life. Do they forget their beloved? Do they look on in resigned apathy? Clearly not.

Mass damnation may have been a popular theory among some saints but quite a few also hinted at universal salvation.[54] Consider Matthew 5:29-30, for example, where Jesus explains that it is better to gouge out your eye or cut off your hand in order to avoid hell. Elsewhere, Jesus warns that the road to hell is broad and crowded, while the road to heaven is narrow and few make it. "But 'few' here does not mean that less than half of mankind will be saved. For God speaks as our father, not our statistician. Even one child lost is too many, and the rest saved are too few. The good shepherd who left his ninety-nine sheep safe at home to rescue his one lost sheep found even 99 percent salvation too 'few.'"[55]

Catholic theology does not allow for a dogmatic belief in *apokatastasis*—the certain belief in the restoration of all creation, including the devils and all human souls—nor in universalism—the idea that all humans will be definitely be saved. However, Catholics may, actually must, hope. There are many more passages that reference hope than reference damnation. One could point to passages in Scripture that reinforce God's universal salvific will. So, too, could the writing of various early Christians, Church fathers, as well as saints and mystics throughout the ages who attested to God's will to save everyone. Couple this truth with the fact that in over two thousand years of Christian history, the Church has declared thousands of men and women to be saints, who are now reigning in heaven, but not one human, not Judas, not Hitler, no one, has ever been declared to be in hell. But, our concern must remain, not just for others though, because it is too easy to fool ourselves with the idea that hell is only possible for somebody else.

Perhaps then all those dire biblical warnings about hell are written in the tradition of some other Hebrew prophecies. God relented of his intent to destroy the Hebrew people when Moses intervened. He spared Nineveh because the inhabitants responded to Jonah's preaching. "What do you think?" Jesus asked: "If a shepherd has a hundred sheep, and one of them has gone astray, does he not leave the ninety-nine on the mountains and go in search of the one that went astray? And if he finds it, truly I tell you, he rejoices over it more than over the ninety-nine that never went astray. So it is not the will of your Father in heaven that one of these little ones should be lost'" (Matthew 18:12-14).

So then, why doesn't God simply forgive the souls in hell and eventually let them into heaven? Saint Thérèse of Lisieux purportedly asked God to let her enter into hell so that at least one soul there might love him. But, God replied that he would have to empty out all of hell before such a thing could happen because it is not possible for love to exist in that place. There are no damned who, looking back on their decisions, repent of having rejected God; they simply hate him all the more. The damned say no to God as loudly and forcefully now as then.

This horrible option should not be considered an equal alternative to heaven. As Hans Urs von Balthasar points out, our "no" to God, our refusal of him, cannot be compared with his "yes" to us. Interestingly, all of Jesus' discussions on hell took place prior to his resurrection. Perhaps this fact is important? The Paschal experience did not alter Jesus' teachings, but it certainly impacted his followers in ways that allowed them, and us, to more fully grasp the profound mystery of his salvific love.

PURGATORY – PURIFICATION

Although at the moment of death a person will be judged to either spend eternity in the beatific (life with God) or the miserific vision (life absent from God), some souls, destined for life with God, must first be cleansed. Purgatory is as a place or state of being whereby a person who dies in the state of grace but attached to the debt of sin is cleansed.

In hell, no sins are forgiven, as no one there seeks forgiveness. The damned obstinately deny that they need forgiveness. They may regret and lament but never repent. In heaven, no one is in need of forgiveness, as it has already and eternally been granted through Jesus. So, that leaves us with this third option known as purgatory.

The Bible does not directly make use of the word "purgatory," but then again neither does the Bible mention the word "Trinity." What we do find are numerous allusions to purgatory's existence. For example, in 2 Maccabees 12:39-46, we read about prayers being offered for the sins of the dead. We hear Jesus preach about sins that cannot be forgiven in the next world—meaning some sins can be so forgiven there (Matthew 12:32). Elsewhere, Jesus references a jail in which a sinner is imprisoned until full restitution is made (Matthew 5:25 -26). Then we read St. Paul talk about being saved through fire (1 Corinthians 3:11-15). And, in Revelation 21:27, we find echoes of numerous Old Testament passages declaring that nothing unclean can enter into God's presence in heaven.

We experience similar bittersweet joys in our own lives. Every year, when graduation rolls around, many of my students experience a mixture of sadness and joy. They long to move into the next phase of life but are sad about a special time in their lives coming to end. Purgatory is filled with souls who painfully long for a reunion with the Father but who nonetheless know that some necessary labor must first be completed. C. S. Lewis wrote,

> Our souls demand purgatory, don't they? Would it not break the heart if God said to us, 'It is true, my son, that your breath smells and your rags drip with mud and slime, but we are charitable here and no one will upbraid you with these things, nor draw away from you. Enter into the joy.' Should we not reply, 'With submission, sir, and if there is no objection, I'd rather be cleaned first.' 'It may hurt, you know'—'Even so, sir.'[56]

The reality of purgatory is alluded to in both the Old and New Testaments.

Although purgatory appears to be a distinctively Catholic doctrine, hints of similar teachings can be found in other religious traditions. Jews have a long history of praying the Mourner's Kaddish, recited for eleven months after a loved one's death. Some rabbis understand this prayer to be one of petition to God on behalf of the recently deceased.[57]

Purgatory is not a "second chance."

> The process of Purgatory is a negative one, a purification of the soul, a removal of those blemishes that remain in it, because of the imperfection of its earthly life; it is not a positive process, an elevation and perfecting of the soul. And, because death is the end of all creative moral initiative and meritorious activity, this removal of defects can be effected only by the way of passive punishment. It is not an active satisfaction for sin (*satisfactio*), but a satisfactory suffering (*satispassio*).[58]

The notion that we shall be judged on our actions should not conjure fears of Pelagianism (that is, that we can earn salvation). Purgatory, instead, is where one encounters the truth of personal sin and is transformed because of that encounter. We know from earthly experience that oftentimes the truth can be painful.

The notion of purgatory's pain reminds me of W. H. Auden's poem, "The Cave of Making":

> God may reduce you on Judgment Day
> To tears of shame, reciting by heart
> The poems you would have written,
> had Your life been good.

This truth can be difficult for us to bear. Purgatory is an unembellished encounter with our choices in life. It may be that we visited that sick relative—not just as an act of kindness, but as insurance that we would be remembered in the will. Such immoral decisions will, upon reflection from the perspective of eternity, seem quite irrational.

We are called to pray for these souls, to offer sacrifices for them, and to ask for their prayers for us. They can intercede for us, but their time for self-effective prayer has ended. There is no self-help in purgatory. But, through indulgences and other graces, we can lessen another person's time of cleansing—or our own. George MacDonald asks, "And why should the good of anyone depend on the prayer of another? I can only answer with the return question, 'Why should my love be powerless to help another?'"[59]

Purgatory is both rehabilitative and retributive. Although there is a rich tradition within the Church that describes purgatory as punishment, the traditional notion of a purging fire does not perfectly portray the reality of purgatory. This symbolism conjures images of hell, and the Church teaches that a soul's experience in purgatory is entirely different than what would be experienced in hell.[60] Especially in later medieval theology, we see purgatory as a place of joy. Dante's *Purgatorio* points to a less-punitive purgatory, a place where souls "train to leap unto joy celestial."[61] Surprisingly, in purgatory, souls suffer willingly, even joyfully. "I don't believe it would be possible to find any joy comparable to that of a soul in purgatory, except the joy of the blessed in paradise. For it is a joy that goes on increasing day by day as God more and more flows in upon the soul, which He does abundantly in proportion as every hindrance to His entrance is consumed away."[62]

Of course, going to purgatory at all need not be a foregone conclusion. Death itself may be a sufficient purging experience for some. Other curatives include availing ourselves of a rich prayer life, regular penance, offering up our sufferings and good works to God, frequent reception of the sacraments, utilizing indulgences,[63] avoidance of sin, and by fostering deep, abiding, unconditional trust in the mercy of God.

HEAVEN – THE BEATIFIC VISION/ THE NEW HEAVEN AND EARTH

The worst kinds of definitions are those that tell you what something does not mean instead of explaining what the word actually means. To define a cat as an animal that is not a dog isn't really helpful. In this case, however, I think it is best to begin describing what heaven is not.

Saint Paul taught in 1 Corinthians 2:9, that heaven is "What no eye has seen, nor ear heard, nor the human heart conceived, what God has prepared for those who love him."

Heaven is not a white cloud city with golden gates and cute cherubs buzzing about playing harps. (Incidentally, while Victorian cherubs may be cute, the original Middle Eastern version was quite fierce looking, often being depicted as a winged bull or lion with a human face.)

We can say that heaven is that place or state of being where we participate in the beatific vision, where we come to share in God's light, love, and joy. Saint Thomas Aquinas tells us that, "God's love for us is not greater in heaven than it is now."[64] He is not waiting for us to shed this loathsome physical shell. Jesus told St. Gertrude, "My heaven would not be complete without you."[65]

Some argue that if we all just stopped believing in a heaven after death, we would all start making life a heaven here on earth. However, I think the exact opposite is true. If we all lost our faith in heaven, most wouldn't try to make an earthly paradise. As St. Francis de Sales pointed out, "The world is only peopled in order to people heaven."[66]

Thinking about the reality of heaven begs a number of questions, such as: How is heaven going to be heavenly if we become bored with having everything so wonderful, or frustrated by a lack of change? Part of the answer, I think, relates to the fact that ancient peoples knew nothing of boredom. "The word 'boredom' does not exist in any ancient language. It first appears in the seventeenth century."[67] There is no time in heaven or hell, only eternity. There is no succession of days (sempiternity), only an eternal now. So, that verse in the famous hymn, "Amazing Grace"—

> When we've been here ten thousand years . . .
> bright shining as the sun.
> We've no less days to sing God's praise . . .
> then when we've first begun.[68]

—is not quite accurate. And just to be clear: Only God is eternal because he has no beginning; we will exist in a state of *aeviternity*—that is, we have a beginning but no end.

Tempus Fugit ("Time Flies"), the ancient Romans used to say. Perhaps that is relative. I worked for a man who had a theory about birthdays. He said that, as a kid, the year from one birthday to the next felt incredibly long; birthdays were so slow in coming. As an adult, he cannot believe how fast the years pass by. He thought it had to do with the percentage of life. In other words, when you are five years old, a year is 20 percent of your life, but when you are 50, a single year is only one percent. This is as interesting a psychological theory as any I've heard before. A theological speculation is that we process time in larger amounts in preparation for the timelessness of eternity. Furthermore, our earthly notion of time is not operative in heaven. Remember that eternity is not an endless succession of days (that is sempiternity), rather, it is an eternal now.

Here on earth, the rule seems to be that our natural desires are often greater than the things we most desire. There is no food as strong as hunger, no drink so sweet as thirst, says one philosopher. An even greater philosopher, Winnie-the-Pooh, said it better in this example from Milne's children's classic:

> 'Well,' said Pooh, 'what I like best,' and then he had to stop and think. Because although Eating Honey was a very good thing to do, there was a moment just before you began to eat it which was better than when you were, but he didn't know what it was called.[69]

But, in heaven, the exact opposite is true; the fulfillment will be infinitely greater than our desire. One sage says that, just as a winding river takes silt from one of its banks and deposits it on the other, the virtues we practice on earth are deposited as

treasures for us in heaven. This analogy about treasure notwithstanding, heaven really has no attraction for covetous souls.

In Scripture and the writings of the saints, heaven is described
as the realm of eternal silence, rest, and peace, yet there are also
references to music, banquets, and boisterous joy. So, heaven is
diverse.

C. S. Lewis wrote:

> If He had no use for all these differences, I do not see why He
> should have created more souls than one. . . . Your soul has a
> curious shape, because it is a hollow made to fit a particular
> swelling in the infinite contours of the divine substance, or a key
> to unlock one of the doors in the house with many mansions.
> For it is not humanity in the abstract that is to be saved, but
> you. . . . All that you are, sins apart, is destined, if you will let
> God have His good way, to utter satisfaction. . . . Your place in
> heaven will seem to be made for you and you alone, because you
> were made for it.[70]

Heaven is delight, and we experience a foretaste of heaven's
bliss through countless earthly expressions. Saint Bonaventure
surmised that "Heaven is not divided by the number of those who
reign, nor lessened by being shared, nor disturbed by its multitude, nor disordered by its inequality of ranks, nor changed by
motion, nor measured by time."[71]

Although all in heaven are completely fulfilled, we are not
necessarily equally fulfilled. An example often used is that of a
drinking glass and a shot glass. If both glasses are filled to the top
they don't hold the same amount, but they are both completely
filled. So it is with our experience of heaven; some will be filled
with much, others will be filled with less, but all will be completely filled and fulfilled, and even overflowing. Yet, this analogy
may be too pedestrian because it does not adequately account for
our infinite capacity for God. Saint Paul refers to our capacity to
increase in degrees of glory (2 Corinthians 3:18).

Of what will this utter satisfaction consist? Heaven is a community; more so, it is a family with God the Father as our father,
(our "Abba," or loving papa); God the Son, Jesus, as our brother;
and all of us united together in God the Holy Spirit.

Our primary joy will be God, but a secondary joy will be sharing in and rejoicing in the happiness of the angels and saints. The

bonds of love we form on earth are not dissolved in heaven but shared by the "great cloud of witnesses" spoken of in Hebrews 12:1. Names are important in the Bible, and we sometimes see names being changed. Genesis 32 recounts how the patriarch Jacob's name is changed to Israel. In John 1:42, we find Jesus changing the apostle Simon's name to Peter. The intimacy that God has with each of the redeemed is beautifully expressed in the book of Revelation, where God declares: "I will give a white stone, and on the white stone is written a new name that no one knows except the one who receives it" (Revelation 2:17).

C. S. Lewis asks,

> What can be more a man's own than this new name which even in eternity remains a secret between God and him? And what shall we take this secrecy to mean? Surely, that each of the redeemed shall forever know and praise some one aspect of the divine beauty better than any other creature can. Why else were individuals created, but that God, loving all infinitely, should love each differently? And this difference, so far from impairing, floods with meaning the love of all blessed creatures for one another, the communion of the saints. If all experienced God in the same way and returned Him an identical worship, the song of the church triumphant would have no symphony, it would be like an orchestra in which all the instruments played the same note.[72]

Sir Henry Taylor once said, "No siren did ever so charm the ear of the listener as the listening ear charmed the soul of the siren."[73] No matter how much joy the pianist's music might bring to an audience, it will never match the joy the admiring audience gives to the pianist simply by listening and delighting in the music. I once went to one of those giant stadium rock concerts at which the band got the audience to sing the chorus of one of their hit songs. The band would sing, the audience would echo back; the band would get louder, and the audience would get louder; the audience got a thrill, and the band got an even bigger thrill. So it went until the song ended. This is a pale example, but the choirs of heaven might function in much the same manner, drawing life and joy from God and returning glory to him by their songs of praise, becoming all the more joyful as they see how their song is pleasing to God. Heaven may be like that concert, only the song never ends!

Actually, the Bible teaches that heaven and the new earth will unite, and we shall dwell in this new creation as a resurrected people, body and soul. Jesus said, "In my Father's house are many mansions: if it were not so, I would have told you. I go to prepare a place for you. And if I go and prepare a place for you, I will come again, and receive you unto myself; that where I am, there ye may be also" (John 14:1-3 KJV). This is an interesting passage because we find two references to houses—the "house" of the Father and the "mansions" Jesus goes to prepare. The Greek word for the Father's house is "*oikia*," which expresses the intimacy of a family home, a household. In other words, John reveals to the reader that Jesus is God the Father's true son. The homes or mansions (sometimes translated as "rooms") Jesus goes to prepare are "*monaī*" in Greek, from the verb "*meno*," which can mean to stay only temporarily. Why would Jesus use this transitory language? Because heaven, as glorious as it is, is not our final home; the new creation is our home.

> We have belittled the cross, imagining it merely as a mechanism for getting us off the hook of our own petty naughtiness or as an example of some general benevolent truth. It is much more. It is the moment when the story of Israel reaches its climax; the moment when, at last, the watchmen on Jerusalem's walls see their God coming in his kingdom; the moment when the people of God are renewed so as to be, at last, the royal priesthood who will take over the world not with the love of power but with the power of love; the moment when the kingdom of God overcomes the kingdoms of the world. It is the moment when the great old door, locked and barred since our first disobedience, swings open suddenly to reveal not just the garden, opened once more to our delight, but the coming city, the garden city that God had always planned and is now inviting us to go through the door and build with him. The dark power that stood in the way of this kingdom vision has been defeated, overthrown, rendered null and void. Its legions will still make a lot of noise and cause a lot of grief, but the ultimate victory is now assured.[74]

The garden city Wright talks about is the merging of elements of Eden with Jerusalem. In Genesis, we often see cities as places of evil while the garden was a place of joy and bliss. In the book of Revelation, the imagery of the New Jerusalem with the Tree of Life and rivers flowing through the city unites the city and the garden in a utopian world free of pain and sorrow and death (Revelation 21-22).

The Gospels, too, speak to this hope. Both Jesus' parables and miracles testify to Jesus' power over nature and the entire created order. All of his miracles serve the purpose of either inaugurating or advancing the restoration of creation that is the kingdom of God, which will culminate in the new heaven and the new earth, described in surprising ways: "Then I saw a new heaven and a new earth, for the first heaven and the first earth had passed away, and there was no longer any sea" (Revelation 21:1). That there will be no sea in the new heavens and new earth is troubling for us ocean lovers. The point here is not that God does not like the oceans or sea creatures. The sea, for many in the ancient world, represented evil, chaos. The flood of Noah, the leviathan, all point to this symbolism. Jesus' calming of the sea was a declaration of his sovereign power over creation. Jesus reminds us of the world as it was meant to be, prior to the fall, and the way it will one day be again. So, I suspect the celestial equivalent to earthly oceans will be more magnificent—not less so.

While the first creation was *creatio ex nihilo*, the new creation is not brought out of nothing by God's fiat but instead is *creatio ex vetere*, a creation formed from God's original work. What we experience on earth points to a greater reality in the new heavens and the new earth. The symbols we interpret will be gone as we come face-to-face with the reality they symbolized, not gone by destruction but gone the way an acorn is gone after it bursts forth into a tree.

The new creation takes all that was good from the old creation and restores it—perhaps improves upon it. Moreover, we learn that reunion with God, that final surrender to our creator, will not feel foreign but will be like coming home. So, the end of all things recalls the beginning of all things. As previously addressed, the book of Genesis starts with the words "In the beginning . . ." and the Gospel of John starts with the words "In the beginning . . ." Clearly, John is identifying Jesus with the God who created the world—the One who brings about a new creation.

According to Genesis 2:1, "on the seventh day God *finished* the work that he had done" (italics mine). Jesus, from the cross, says, "'It is *finished*'" (italics mine; John 19:30). The point being made by John is that all creation was made through the Son of God, and so through him all creation will be restored and transformed (1:1–3). During Jesus' ministry, many of his miracles displayed this restorative work: the calming of the sea; the healing of the sick; walking among wild beasts, which were presumably tame in his presence. Like all miracles, these are not best understood as the wondrous but occasional interventions of a normally non-interfering God. In the words of Ralph Waldo Emerson: ". . . the word Miracle as pronounced by Christian churches, gives a false impression; it is a Monster. It is not one with the blowing clover and the falling rain."[75]

The miracle of the blowing clover and the falling rain, of the calm sea and the tame beast, are all glimpses of God's restorative kingdom. Some of Jesus' followers displayed these same healing powers over creation. Numerous stories are told of fierce animals becoming gentle in the presence of holy men and women (e.g. St. Francis and the wolf of Gubrio.) This kind of heavenly fellowship is promised to us after Christ's triumphant return, when all of the redeemed will be restored not just to a right relationship with God but to a healed relationship with all of creation.

> The wolf shall live with the lamb, the leopard shall lie down with the kid, and the calf and the lion and the fatling together, and a little child shall lead them. The cow and the bear shall graze, their young shall lie down together; and the lion shall eat straw like the ox. The nursing child shall play over the hole of the asp, and the weaned child shall put its hand on the adder's den. (Isaiah 11:6-8)

We do not need to wait for the restoration of the original bliss of Eden. The good news Jesus came to share is that, by his love, we can experience a foretaste of this joy and share it with others.

Saint Paul, in his First Letter to the Corinthians, wrote:

> Love is patient; love is kind; love is not envious or boastful or arrogant or rude. It does not insist on its own way; it is not irritable or resentful; it does not rejoice in wrongdoing, but rejoices in the truth. It bears all things, believes all things, hopes all things, endures all things. (1 Corinthians 13:4–7)

Reread this passage again, except, replace the word "love" with "Jesus" or "God": Jesus is patient; Jesus is kind; and, God does not rejoice in wrongdoing, etc. You'll see that the change matches perfectly. Go back once more and exchange the word "love" with your own name.[76] Did your name fit in with the Corinthians passage?

The entire point of the Church is to make us more like Christ. He desires to illuminate and transfigure our beliefs, our behaviors, our very selves for our benefit and that of the entire world. Karl Barth, one of the great theologians of the last century, wrote volumes of dense and complicated theology. When asked to summarize his vast work, without skipping a beat he simply said, "Jesus loves me . . ." Jesus is not attracted to humanity *en masse* but loves individuals. He is the light of the world, who came to illuminate and set the world afire with God's love. *Ite Incendite*[77] was the battle cry of St. Ignatius Loyola. It means, "Go set the world aflame!"

†

NOTES

PREFACE

1. C. S. Lewis, *Mere Christianity* (NY: Macmillan, 1952), 5–6.
2. Saint Anselm of Canterbury, *Proslogion* (Oxford: Clarendon Press, 1965), quoted in Daniel L. Migliore, *Faith Seeking Understanding: An Introduction to Christian Theology* (Eerdmans, William B. Publishing Company), 2.
3. Technically only a Catholic may truly act as a sponsor, or "godparent," for another's baptism (cf. *CIC* can. 874 §1 n. 3).
4. Oscar Wilde, *The Importance of Being Earnest*, in *Oscar Wilde: The Major Works*, ed., intro., & annot., Isobel Murray, Oxford World's Classics (Oxford: Oxford Univ. Press, 2000), 485.
5. This claim, often considered the inception of the "Correspondence Theory of Truth," can be traced back to his *Metaphysics* (cf. bk. IV—sometimes, called "Gamma"—pt. 4).
6. William Shakespeare, *Hamlet* (London: William Heinemann, 1904), 34.
7. Saint Thomas More, quoted in Ronda Chervin, *Quotable Saints* (CMJ Marian Publishers, 1992), 207.

INTRODUCTION

1. William James, *The Principles of Psychology* (Henry Holt and Company, 1890), 488.
2. Within the Church, one can find: philosophies (e.g., Platonic, Aristotelian, Phenomenological); theologies (e.g., Scholastic, Mystical); ritual churches (e.g., Latin, Melkite); religious orders (e.g., Benedictine, Carmelite, Dominican, Franciscan, Jesuit); spiritualities (e.g., Franciscan, Ignatian); and so forth.
3. Cardinal Henri de Lubac, *Paradoxes of Faith* (Ignatius Press, 1987), 157.
4. C. S. Lewis, *The Problem of Pain* (NY: Touchstone, 1996), 35.
5. Cardinal John Henry Newman, *The Church of England Quarterly Review: Vol. II* (R. Clay, Bread-Street-Hill, 1837), 174.
6. Saint John of the Cross, quoted in *The Wisdom of the Saints: An Anthology*, ed. Jill Haak Adels (Oxford University Press, 1987), 74.
7. Father Joseph Girzone, *Joshua and the Children* (Scribner Paperback Fiction; Simon & Schuster Inc., 1989), *dedication.*
8. The catechism is available online on the Vatican's website at: www.vatican.va/archive/ccc/index.htm.
9. The catechism does try to remedy this not just by providing an index, but also in the formatting of the text (for example, using small print in places where the text "indicates observations of an historical or apologetic nature, or supplementary doctrinal explanations"). Furthermore, following each thematic unit, there is an "In Brief" section, which "sums up the essentials of that unit's teaching in condensed formula" (cf. *CCC*, nos. 18–22 passim).
10. Karl Adam, *The Spirit of Catholicism*, rev. ed., trans. Justin McCann (Garden City, NY: Image Bks. for Doubleday & Co., 1954; reprint, 1958), 206–07.

11. Blaise Pascal, *Œuvres Complètes de Blaise Pascal*, ed. Louis Lafuma, L'Intégrale series (Paris: Éditions du Seuil, 1963), 619.

12. For example, the word "grace" can simply be defined as God's unmerited favor. However, "grace" also has nuanced meanings within academic circles: There is "actual grace" (i.e., God empowering an individual to act in a certain way); there is also "sanctifying grace" (i.e., the disposition of one's soul in relationship to God).

13. The relevant canon reads: "A person who is to receive the Most Holy Eucharist is to abstain for at least one hour before holy communion from any food and drink, except for only water and medicine" (*CIC*, can. 919 §1). For the sick and the elderly, as well as for those caring for them, this church law does not apply (see §3 of the same canon).

    The Code (in English) can be found on the Vatican's website at:
    http://www.vatican.va/archive/ENG1104/_INDEX.HTM.

14. The Precepts of the Church are:
    1. You shall attend Mass on Sundays and holy days of obligation and rest from servile labor.
    2. You shall confess your sins at least once a year.
    3. You shall receive the sacrament of the Eucharist at least during the Easter season.
    4. You shall observe the days of fasting and abstinence established by the Church.
    5. You shall help to provide for the needs of the Church.

15. J. R. R. Tolkien, *The Fellowship of the Ring* (Boston: Houghton Mifflin Co., 2004), 170.

16. The very fact that Peter's tearful sorrow was even included in the Gospel narrative is astounding. Modern readers are not surprised by this little detail, but, prior to this story, ancient narratives simply did not take seriously the sufferings of someone of Peter's social class. The German scholar Erich Auerbach wrote: "A scene like Peter's denial fits into no ancient genre. It is too serious for comedy, too contemporary and everyday for tragedy, politically too insignificant for history—and the form which was given it is one of such immediacy that its like does not exist in the literature of antiquity." E. Auerbach; *Mimesis: The Representation of Reality in Western Literature* (ET. 1935) (page 45) quoted in A. N. Wilson's *Jesus: A Life* at page 213.

17. Gregory the Great, Ephraim Syrus, and Aphrahat, *Nicene and Post-Nicene Fathers: Second Series, Volume XIII*, ed. Philip Schaff and Rev. Henry Wallace (Cosimo Classics, 2007), 42.

18. Marco Antonio de Dominis, *De Republica Ecclesiastica Libri X* (London, 1617), 676.

19. J. B. Phillips, *Your God Is Too Small: A Guide for Believers and Skeptics Alike* (NY: Simon & Schuster, 1952; Touchstone, 2004), 35.

20. John Calvin, *Institutes of the Christian Religion* (Devoted Publishing, 2016), 51.

21. "The Cost of Discipleship [*Nachfolge*]," Advent 1937, in Geffrey B. Kelly and F. Burton Nelson, eds., *A Testament to Freedom: The Essential Writings of Dietrich Bonhoeffer*, rev. ed. (San Francisco: HarperCollins; HarperSanFrancisco, 1995), 308.

CHAPTER ONE

1. *Humanist Manifestos I and II* (NY: Prometheus Books, 1973).

2. Pope John Paul II, *Fides Et Ratio: On the Relationship Between Faith and Reason: Encyclical Letter of John Paul II* (United States, Third Printing, 2005), 3.

3. The term "dogmatic slumber" is taken from Immanuel Kant, who coined the phrase in reference to the writings of David Hume.

4. Karl Adam, *The Spirit of Catholicism*, rev. ed., trans. Justin McCann (Garden City, NY: Image Bks. for Doubleday & Co., 1954; reprint, 1958), 10.

5. Western philosophy can be broadly divided into Pre-Socratic Philosophy, Classical Philosophy, Medieval Philosophy, Modern Philosophy, and Postmodern Philosophy. Each of these schools can be generalized as presenting four major ideas about how we experience and interact with reality.
   1. Materialism – The theory that only material reality exists.
   2. Idealism – The theory that only mental concepts are real and physical reality only exists through our perceptions; there is no real world out there. Idealism is anti-realism.
   3. Naïve Realism – The theory that mind-independent reality exists but that such reality is as it appears to us. Naïve realism is sometimes called Common Sense Realism.
   4. Critical Realism – The theory accepts objective reality but also fully acknowledges that the person experiencing this reality has a very subjective experience.

6. Friedrich Nietzsche, *The Portable Nietzsche* (Viking Penguin Inc., 1954), 52.

7. Cardinal John Henry Newman, *The Idea of a University* (Longmans, Green and Co., 1917), 466.

8. Saint Ambrose, quoted in *The American Ecclesiastical Review; A Monthly Publication for the Clergy, Vol. XXV*, ed. Herman Joseph Hueser (NY: American Ecclesiastical Review, 1901), 387.

9. Thomas Merton, *New Seeds of Contemplation* (New Directions Paperbook, 1972), 177.

10. Carl Sagan, *Broca's Brain, Reflections on the Romance of Science* (NY: Random House, 1979), 62.

11. C. S. Lewis, *God in the Dock* (William. B. Eerdsmans Publishing Company, 1970), 102.

12. Dr. Martin Luther King Jr., quoted in K. D. Gangrade and R. P. Misra, *Conflict Resolution Through Non-violence: Science and ethics* (Concept Publishing Company, 1990), 25.

13. Saint Augustine, quoted in Jonathan F. Bayes, *The Apostles' Creed: Truth With Passion* (Wipf & Stock, 2010), 6.

14. C. S. Lewis, *Mere Christianity* (1952; HarperCollins: 2001), 198.

15. C. S. Lewis, *George MacDonald An Anthology 365 Readings* (HarperSanFrancisco, 2001), 110.

16. Believers are not without uncertainties. Being a Christian is not just about unreservedly buying into a message but about unreservedly loving a person; Jesus. In the Gospels we read how "Jesus invited unbelieving, misbehaving, troublemaking men and women to follow him and to embrace something new, and they accepted his invitation."
   Andy Stanley, "Five Reasons People Leave the Church," https://www.foxnews.com/opinion/five-reasons-people-leave-the-church (accessed October 11, 2018).

17. Saint Thomas More, quoted in Paul Thigpen, *A Dictionary of Quotes from the Saints* (TAN Books, 2017), 83.

18. Saint Cyprian of Carthage, *The Writings of Cyprian, Bishop of Carthage,* ed. Alexander Roberts and James Donaldson (T&T Clark, 1770), 423.

19. George MacDonald, *Unspoken Sermons* (London: Longman, Green, and Co., 1885), 12.

20. Saint Francis of Assisi, quoted in *The Westminster Collection of Christian Quotations,* ed. Martin H. Manser (Westminster John Knox Press, 2001), 168.

21. David Bentley Hart, *A Splendid Wickedness and Other Essays* (William B. Eerdsmans Publishing Company, 2016), 211.

ॠॅ

22. Friedrich Nietzsche, quoted in Ernest L. Father Fortin, *Human Rights, Virtue and the Common Good* (Rowman & Littlefield Publishers, Inc., 1996), 122.
23. Just one example, the enormous role St. Patrick played, is recounted in Thomas Cahill, *How the Irish Saved Civilization: The Untold Story of Ireland's Heroic Role from the Fall of Rome to the Rise of Medieval Europe.* (This book could have appropriately been titled, *How Irish Catholics Saved Civilization.*)
24. Thomas E. Woods Jr., *How the Catholic Church Built Western Civilization* (Regnery Publishing, Inc., 2005), 47.
25. This practice dates back to ancient times when shepherds used to pour olive oil on the heads of their flock. This practice served a number of purposes including keeping the sheep's nostrils well lubricated to dissuade insects from laying eggs in the animal's nasal passages.
26. The sign is made differently in the various rites of the Church. For example, in the Latin Rite the practice has become somewhat casual, but the Melkite Rite is more formal and has a tradition of signing one's self using three fingers held together in remembrance of the Holy Trinity with the two remaining fingers (fourth finger and pinky) pressed into one's palm, in remembrance of Jesus' two natures.
27. Of course, Western jurisprudence owes a debt to many ancient pagan cultures; specifically, the Code of Hammurabi and Greco-Roman law.
28. For further reading: Thomas E. Woods Jr., *How the Church Saved Western Civilization.*
29. Christopher Kaczor, *The Seven Big Myths about the Catholic Church: Distinguishing Fact from Fiction about Catholicism* (Ignatius Press, San Francisco, 2012), 19–20.
    Kaczor is quoting, in part, from Thomas E. Woods Jr., *How the Church Saved Western Civilization.*
30. Galileo Galilei, quoted in Kenneth I. Pargament, *The Psychology of Religion and Coping: Theory, Research, Practice* (The Guilford Press, 1997), 179.
31. Gould uses the pejorative "Doubting Thomas," a moniker that has followed St. Thomas down the centuries. It may be the defense attorney in me coming out, but I think Thomas is maligned by the nickname. In John 11:16, we read how Thomas told the rest of the disciples that they should all follow Jesus to Jerusalem, even if it meant following Him into death. What greater statement of faith can one find?
32. Stephen Jay Gould, *Rock of Ages: Science and Religion in the Fullness of Time* (The Random House Publishing Group, 1999), 16.
33. Cardinal John Henry Newman, *The Idea of a University Defined and Illustrated: In Nine Discourses* (Longmans, Green, and Co., 1901), 465.
34. For further reading: J. L. Heilbron, *The Sun in the Church: Cathedrals as Solar Observatories Paperback.*
35. David Bentley Hart, *The Story of Christianity: A History of 2,000 Years of the Christian Faith* (Quercus Publishing, Inc., 2015), 288.
36. Susan Neiman, *Evil in Modern Thought: An Alternative History of Philosophy* (Princeton, NJ: Princeton University Press, 2002).
37. God is the best of all possible gods. As such, he is totally free, totally good, and totally powerful, and so there is nothing to constrain him from creating the best possible world. However, that does not mean we necessarily do live in the best of all possible worlds. Some philosophers argue that God, being omnipotent, can always create a better world than the one that currently exists.
38. Christians, too, need to take responsibility for a rise in atheism. A distorted version of Christianity throughout the ages has instilled a sense of despair among some—those who believe that an all-powerful God, whose sovereignty is not coterminous with his goodness, directly wills the good but also all of the malice

and evil and tragedy in the world. This grave misunderstanding has certainly contributed to many turning away from religion.

39. An equally important catalyst for the Reformation was the Renaissance, which swept through Europe from approximately the thirteenth to the seventeenth century. The Renaissance was a time when scholars, dissatisfied with secondary sources such as medieval theology, sought out original works. This same inclination led Protestant reformers to return to the original Hebrew and Greek texts of the Bible instead of the Church's official Latin Vulgate translation (which, admittedly, did not always offer the most precise translation).

CHAPTER TWO

1. C. S. Lewis, *Letter to Arthur Greeves* (September 12, 1933), 465, quoted in *The Quotable Lewis*, ed. Wayne Martindale and Jerry Root (Wheaton, IL: Tyndale House Publishers, Inc., 1989), 265.

2. Blaise Pascal, quoted in Paul Crittenden, *Reason Will and Emotion: Defending the Greek Tradition against Triune Consciousness* (Palgrave Macmillan, 2012), 99.

3. Helen Keller, *The Story of My Life* (NY: Grosset & Dunlap, 1904), 203.

4. C. S. Lewis, *The Weight of Glory: and Other Addresses* (NY: Macmillan Co., 1949), 12–13.

5. C. S. Lewis, *The Problem of Pain* (NY: HarperOne for HarperCollins Pub., 2001), 150–51.

6. Oscar Wilde, quoted in *Complete Works of Oscar Wilde*, ed. Robert Ross (Boston: Wyman-Fogg Co., 1921), 22.

7. Søren Kierkegaard, *The Sickness unto Death: A Christian Psychological Exposition for Upbuilding and Awakening*, ed., trans., intro., & annot. Howard V. Hong & Edna H. Hong (Princeton, NJ: Princeton Univ. Press, 1980), 27–28.

8. C. S. Lewis, *The Weight of Glory*, quoted in *The Weight of Glory: and Other Addresses* (NY: HarperOne for HarperCollins Pub., 2001), 26.

9. Gilbert K. Chesterton, *Orthodoxy* (NY: John Lane Co., 1909), 298–299.

10. Simone Weil, *Gravity and Grace*, trans. Emma Crawford and Mario von der Ruhr, with an Introduction & Postscript by Gustave Thibon, 1st complete English language ed. (NY: Routledge Classics, 2002; reprint, 2004), 70.

11. The story is recounted in Plutarch's *Lives* (see *Caesar*, I.3–II.4).

12. Saint Vincent de Paul, *Virtues and Spiritual Doctrine of St. Vincent de Paul* (Suspension Bridge, NY: Niagara Index Pub. House, 1877), 163.

13. M. Scott Peck, *The Road Less Travelled* (Simon & Schuster, 1978), 156.

14. M. Scott Peck, *The Road Less Travelled* (Simon & Schuster, 1978), 53.

15. Aesop, quoted in Roger L'Estrange, *Fables of Aesop and Other Eminent Mythologists with Morals and Reflections*, 6th ed. (London: R. Sare et al., 1714), 48.

16. Alfred, Lord Tennyson, quoted in *Wisdom for the Soul: Five Millennia of Prescriptions for Spiritual Healing,* ed. Larry Chang (Washington DC: Gnosophia Publishers, 2006), 545.

17. Cited in Ronda de Sola Chervin, ed., *Quotable Saints* (Oak Lawn, Ill.: CMJ Marian Publishers, 1992), 174.
The book's compiler was contacted, but she could not confirm the quote's association with Augustine [email communication; November 2, 2017].

18. C. S. Lewis, *Infatuation* (1964), 75, quoted in *The Quotable Lewis*, ed. Wayne Martindale and Jerry Root (Wheaton, IL: Tyndale House Publishers, Inc., 1989), 496.

19. The Christian philosopher Boethius expresses this truth with these words: "Good, then, is the sum and source of all desirable things. . . . Whereby it comes

to pass that goodness is rightly believed to be the sum and hinge and cause of all things desirable. . . . From all which it is transparently clear that the essence of absolute good and of happiness is one and the same." (*The Consolation of Philosophy of Boethius*, trans. H. R. James, New Universal Library Series [NY: E. P. Dutton & Co., 1900], 107.)

20. Frederick Buechner, quoted in Philip Yancey, *A Skeptic's Guide to Faith* (Zondervan, 2009), 58.

21. Bertrand Russell, "The Conquest of Happiness," https://www.youtube.com/watch?v=sL-mF_FwPnI (accessed August 31, 2018).

22. Saint Teresa of Avila, *The Complete Works of Saint Teresa of Jesus*, trans. Silverio de Santa Teresa, ed. E. Allison Peers (NY: Sheed & Ward, 1946), 192–93.

23. Other terms, such as "Blessed Sacrament," "Host," and "holy Communion," may be used interchangeably with the word "Eucharist."

24. "The Eucharist is not a question of the substance of bread becoming the substance of a human body (this kind of substantial change is familiar enough and takes place whenever we eat a slice of bread); it is a miraculous transformation at a deeper level, which Aquinas compares to creation, in which the *esse* (the existence) of this piece of bread and this cup of wine becomes the *esse* of Christ. This transformation of a substance into another particular existent, as distinct from a different kind of thing (as in ordinary substantial change) would have been completely unintelligible to Aristotle as, of course, was the notion of creation and, indeed, the whole notion of *esse* in Aquinas's sense." (*God Still Matters* (Continuums Icons) Paperback– March 1, 2005 by Herbert McCabe (Author), pp. 125-126.)

25. ". . . humanity by nature is an icon or image of deity: The divine image is in all humanity. Through sin, however, this image and likeness of God was marred and we fell.

     "Because of the incarnation of the Son of God, because the fullness of God has inhabited human flesh, being joined to Christ means that it is again possible to experience deification, the fulfillment of human destiny. That is, through the union with Christ, we become by grace what God is by nature—we 'become children of God' (John 1:12). His deity interpenetrates our humanity.

     "Historically, deification has often been illustrated by the 'sword and fire' example. A steel sword is thrust into a hot fire until the sword takes on a red glow. The energy of the fire interpenetrates the sword. The sword never becomes fire, but it picks up the properties of fire."
     (*The Orthodox Study Bible New Testament and Psalms Discovering Orthodox Christianity in the pages of the New Testament* [Thomas Nelson Publishers], 561.)

26. "The Order of Mass" in *The Roman Missal: Renewed by Decree of the Most Holy Second Ecumenical Council of the Vatican, Promulgated by Authority of Pope Paul VI and Revised at the Direction of Pope John Paul II*, 3rd ed. (n. p.: International Commission on English in the Liturgy, 2011), 529.

27. It was St. Peter who brought together Gentiles and Jews to share in the Lord's Supper. Previously, Jewish dietary law forbade such a commingling. However, Peter (Acts chapters 10 and 11) experienced a mystical vision that resolved this conflict.

28. Saint Thomas Aquinas' teaching that God's grace perfects human nature is tied closely to this theology (cf. *S. T.* I, q. 1, art. 8, ad. 2). As Anna N. Williams notes: "Indeed, the doctrine of deification pervades the *Summa*. If Western readers have failed to notice it, we may conjecture they have done so for two reasons. The first is that it is precisely pervasive and not localized: one finds no question 'Whether Human Persons Are Deified?' in the pages of the *Summa*. Second, Western readers may be unable to see the doctrine simply because they are unfamiliar with it. Because this model of sanctification has been absent from

Western theology for so long, Western readers do not recognize either the para-digmatic structure of the doctrine or the language that traditionally conveys it." ("Deification in the *Summa Theologiae*: A Structural Interpretation of the *Prima Pars*," *The Thomist* 61/2 [April 1, 1997]: 291–55, at 220.)

29. Karl Adam, *The Spirit of Catholicism*, rev. ed., trans. Justin McCann (Garden City, NY: Image Bks. for Doubleday & Co., 1954), 114.
30. Saint Irenaeus of Lyons, quoted in Paul Thigpen, *A Dictionary of Quotes from the Saints* (TAN Books, 2017), 139.
31. This healing that occurred when the woman touched the fringe of Jesus' garment may have been the fulfillment of a prophecy. "But unto you that fear my name shall the Sun of righteousness arise with healing in His WINGS; and ye shall grow up as calves of the stall" (Malachi 4:2). The term "wings" in Malachi and "fringe" in the Gospels may refer to the same part of a garment.
32. Francis de Sales, *Letter to a Superioress of the Visitation* (July 24, 1621), quoted in *Library of St. Francis de Sales*, trans. Henry Benedict (NY: Benziger Bros., 1909), 215.
33. Jean Paul Sartre, quoted in David W. Wilbur, *Power and Illusion: Religion and Human Need* (David W. Wilbur, 2010), 191.
34. George Orwell, *1984* (Houghton Mifflin Harcourt Publishing Company, 1949), 26.
35. The one source can be divided into two categories: public revelation and private revelation. By way of example, the category of public revelation would include the Bible. The second category would include messages given to a specific individual that were not necessarily meant to be shared with a wider audience.
36. The charism of infallibility is often confused with the concept of impeccability. The Church does not claim the pope is free from all sin or even free from all error, that he is impeccable. Instead, as originally defined in 1870 by the First Vatican Council, infallibility is a gift of assurance that, under specific circumstances, a pope can officially proclaim with certainty specific teachings on the matter of faith or morals.
37. Avery Dulles, "Infallibility: The Terminology," in *Teaching Authority and Infallibility in the Church,* ed. Paul C. Empie, T. Austin Murphy, and Joseph A. Burgess (Minneapolis: Augsburg Publishing House, 1978), 72.
38. "Nescience" is a separate category, and is a term used to explain a lack of some specific knowledge that is irrelevant to a person's life. Of course, we are all ignorant of some knowledge. Technically speaking, the word "nescience" is used for information a person does not possess, because it is not needed. For example, I am unable to read and understand Egyptian hieroglyphics not due to ignorance, but due to nescience.
39. Bernard Lonergan, *Method in Theology* (University of Toronto Press, 1991), 23.
40. John Henry Newman, "Letter to the Duke of Norfolk," December 27, 1874, in *Certain Difficulties Felt by Anglicans in Catholic Teaching*, 2 vols., new impression (NY: Longmans, Green, & Co., 1914), 250.
41. John Henry Newman, quoted in John. R. Connolly, *John Henry Newman: A View of Catholic Faith for the New Millennium* (Rowman & Littlefield Publishers, Inc., 2005), 112.
42. George Weigel, "Mourning and Remembrance," *Wall Street Journal*, April 4, 2005, A8.
43. Thomas D. Williams, *Knowing Right From Wrong: A Christian Guide to Conscience* (Faithwords, 2008), 85.
44. The Seven Capital Virtues are: 1. Humility 2. Generosity 3. Brotherly love 4. Meekness 5. Chastity 6. Temperance 7. Diligence.

   Additionally, the Church enumerates the Spiritual Works of Mercy: 1. Convert the sinner 2. Instruct the ignorant 3. Counsel the doubtful 4. Comfort the sorrowful 5. Bear wrongs patiently 6. Forgive injuries 7. Pray for the living and the dead;

And the Corporal Works of Mercy: 1. Feed the hungry 2. Give drink to the thirsty 3. Clothe the naked 4. Shelter the homeless 5. Visit the sick 6. Visit those in prison 7. Bury the dead.

45. The deadly sins have not always numbered seven, and throughout Church history the list of included sins has varied.

46. The "gifts" of the Holy Spirit are: wisdom; understanding; counsel; fortitude; knowledge; piety; and fear of the Lord.

47. The "fruits" of the Spirit are: charity; joy; peace; patience; kindness; goodness; generosity; gentleness; faithfulness; modesty; self-control; and chastity.

48. Saint Thomas Aquinas, quoted in M. I. Seka, *Life Lessons of Wisdom & Motivation* (Providential Press, 2014), 35.

49. George MacDonald, *Sir Gibbie*, quoted in *Great Thoughts From Masterminds, Volume 8* (A. W. Hall, 1887), 274.

50. Thomas D. Williams, *Knowing Right From Wrong: A Christian Guide to Conscience* (Faithwords, 2008), 6.

51. Saint Francis de Sales, quoted in *The Wisdom of the Saints: An Anthology*, ed. Jill Haak Adels (Oxford University Press, 1987), 161.

52. C. G. Jung, *Memories, Dreams, Reflections*, ed. Aniela Jaffé, trans. Richard and Clara Winston, rev. ed. (NY: Random House; Vintage Bks., 1989), 247.

53. Saint Francis de Sales, *An Introduction to the Devout Life*, new ed. (Dublin: M. H. Gill & Son, 1885), 12.

54. G. K. Chesterton, quoted in *The Collected Works of G. K. Chesterton*, ed. George J. Marlin, Richard P. Rabatin, & John L. Swan (San Francisco: Ignatius Press, 1987), 225.

55. John A. Hardon, *The Catholic Catechism* (Garden City, NY: Doubleday & Co., 1975), 293.

56. Saint Thomas Aquinas distinguished two faculties of the conscience: *synderesis* and *conscientia*. Synderesis is our ability to perceive and comprehend the Natural Law. Conscientia the ability to assess the morality of situations.

57. *Summa Theologiae*, I-II, q. 94, art. 2.

58. Jeremy Bentham, quoted in K. G. Binmore, *Game Theory and the Social Contract: Just Playing* (The MIT Press, 1998), 3.

59. Mahatma Gandhi may not have uttered these words, as reliable sourcing has proven elusive.

60. G. K. Chesterton is oft quoted as the source of this quip, but reliable sourcing has proven elusive.

61. Joseph Stein et al., *Fiddler on the Roof* (NY: Crown Publishers, 1964; reprint, 1970), 21.

62. I was first introduced to this quandary in Irwin Altman & Dalmas Arnold Taylor, *Social Penetration: The Development of Interpersonal Relationships* (n. p.: Irvington Publishers, 1973), 9.

63. Maxim 276, quoted in George H. Powell, intro. & annot., *The Moral Maxims and Reflections of the Duke de La Rochefoucauld*, 2nd ed. (London: Methuen & Co., 1912), 86.

64. Karl Adam, *The Spirit of Catholicism*, rev. ed., trans. Justin McCann (Garden City, NY: Image Bks. for Doubleday & Co., 1954; reprint, 1958), 67–68.

65. "Negative and Positive Morality," *Illustrated London News*, January 3, 1920, quoted in *The Collected Works of G. K. Chesterton*, ed. George J. Marlin, Richard P. Rabatin, & John L. Swan (San Francisco: Ignatius Press, 1987), 18.

66. Some theologians, William of Occam for example, held a different view. He argued that God's will, not his intellect, was the source of laws. Thus, God is capricious.

67. Oliver Wendell Holmes, quoted in Guido Herrmann Stempel, *Media and Politics in America: A Reference Handbook* (ABC-CLIO Inc., 2003), 137.

68. There is no definitive list of the 613 laws. The number, 613, is thought to be related to the word "*torah*." Each letter of the Hebrew alphabet has a numeric

value. When the letters of the word "torah" are added up, the sum is equal to 611. (*Tav* has a value of 400; *vav* has a value of 6; *resh* has a value of 200; *he* has a value of 5. These equal: 611.) The remaining two laws represent the two commandments that predate the Torah: "I am the Lord, your God," and "You shall have no other gods before Me."

69. Saint Francis de Sales, quoted in *A Year with the Saints* (P. J. Kenedy & Sons, 1891), 396.

70. Saint Thomas Aquinas, quoted in *St. Thomas Aquinas: Philosophical Texts* (Oxford University Press, 1951), 317.

CHAPTER THREE

1. Thomas Merton, *New Seeds of Contemplation* (NY: New Directions Pub. Co., 1961), 260-261.

2. Homer, *Odyssey* XI, ll. 593 ff. The Greek myth of Sisyphus recounts the story of a king who is condemned to perpetually roll a boulder up a hill—only to see it roll back down when he reaches the apex. After that, Sisyphus chases down after the boulder, starting the whole process over again.

3. Elton Trueblood, *The Life We Prize* (NY: Harper & Bros., 1951), 58.
   The *idea*, however, appears in various forms even before Trueblood. Its earliest example seems to have been with the Roman comic poet, Caecilius Statius (+ 168 BC; cited in Cicero's *On Old Age*, sec. VII).

4. J. R. R. Tolkien, *The Return of the King* (New Line Cinema, 2003).

5. John Wesley, *Sermons on Several Occasions*, 2 vols. (NY: Carlton & Phillips, 1855), 328.

6. Thomas Merton, *Conjectures of a Guilty Bystander* (NY: Random House, 1966), 81.

7. This motto's first appearance in a book can be traced to the Roman poet Horace's *First Book of Letters* but may predate this work as Latin maxim.

8. See St. Augustine, *The City of God.*

9. Simone Weil, *Gravity and Grace*, trans. Emma Crawford and Mario von der Ruhr, 1st complete English language ed. (NY: Routledge Classics, 2002; reprint, 2004), 99–100.

10. Herman Melville, *Billy Budd, Sailor, and Selected Tales*, ed., intro. & annot. Robert Milder (n. p.: Northwestern Univ. Press & Newberry Library, 1987; reprint, Oxford Univ. Press, 1998), 334.

11. Thich Nhat Hanh, *The Miracle of Mindfulness: An Introduction to the Practice of Meditation*, trans. Mobi Ho, with 11 drawings by Vo-Dinh Mai (Boston: Beacon Press, 1987), 3–4.

12. C. S. Lewis, *The Screwtape Letters, with "Screwtape Proposes a Toast"*, rev. ed. (NY: Macmillan Pub. Co.; Collier Bks., 1982), 116.

13. Søren Kierkegaard, *Works of Love*, 3 vols., trans. David F. Swenson & Lillian Marvin Swenson, with an Introduction by Douglas V. Steere (Princeton, N.J: Princeton Univ. Press, 1946; reprint, 1949), I:31.

14. Saint Francis de Sales, quoted in Shirley Carter Hughson, *Spiritual Guidance: A Study of the Godward Way* (Holy Cross Press, 1948), 108.

15. C. S. Lewis, *The Weight of Glory: and Other Addresses* (NY: Macmillan Co., 1949), 14–15.

16. Blaise Pascal, *Pensées*, no. 930-*513*, quoted in *Œuvres Complètes de Blaise Pascal*, ed. Louis Lafuma, L'Intégrale series (Paris: Éditions du Seuil, 1963), 623.

17. Saint Ignatius of Loyola, quoted in Gabriel Hevenesi, *Scintillae Ignatiani, sive Sancti Ignatii de Loyola, Societatis Jesu Fundatoris Apophtegmata Sacra* (Mexico: Regalis & Antiq. Divi Ildefonsi Collegii, 1756), 2.

The translation is taken from: J. P. M. Walsh, "Work as if Everything Depends on—Who?," *The Way*, Supplement 70 (Spring 1991): 125–36, at p. 130.

18. Saint Teresa of Avila, *The Life of St. Teresa of Jesus of the Order of Our Lady of Carmel, Written by Herself*, trans. David Lewis, ed., annot. & intro. Benedict Zimmerman, 5th ed. (NY: Benziger Bros., 1916), 58.

19. Saint Augustine, quoted in *We Believe in the Holy Spirit*, ed. Joel C. Elowsky (InterVarsity Press, 2009), 109.

20. Thomas Merton, *New Seeds of Contemplation* (NY: New Directions Pub. Co., 1961), 206.

21. Peter Kreeft, "Time," http://www.peterkreeft.com/topics/time.htm (accessed August 31, 2018).

22. Josef Pieper, *Leisure: The Basis of Culture*; *The Philosophical Act*, trans. Alexander Dru (San Francisco: Ignatius Press, 2009), in the epigraph to the former.
    The Hebrew verb, *rapah* ("to be still"), used by the Psalmist, does bear the interpretation of "idleness" or "leisure."

23. Josef Pieper, *Leisure: The Basis of Culture*; *The Philosophical Act*, trans. Alexander Dru (San Francisco: Ignatius Press, 2009), 35–36.

24. George MacDonald, *Wilfrid Cumbermede: An Autobiographical Story* (Philadelphia: David McKay Pub., 1911), 435.

25. The Right Honorable Lord Avebury [John Lubbock], *The Use of Life* (NY: Macmillan Co., 1894; reprint, 1900), 66.

26. Josef Pieper, *Leisure: The Basis of Culture*; *The Philosophical Act*, trans. Alexander Dru (San Francisco: Ignatius Press, 2009), 67.

27. In this case, the translation has been taken from the NABRE. It renders better than the NRSV does the Hebrew verb, *sachaq*, which means: "to laugh," "to play," "to make merry."

28. Hugo Rahner, *Man at Play* (Burns & Oates, 1965; NY: Herder & Herder, 1967), 96–105.

29. Nevertheless, cf. Elton Trueblood's book, *The Humor of Christ* (NY: Harper & Row, Pub., 1964).

30. Bede the Venerable, quoted in Paul Thigpen, *A Dictionary of Quotes from the Saints* (Charis Books, 2001), 160.

31. C. S. Lewis, *George MacDonald An Anthology 365 Readings,* (HarperSanFrancisco, 2001), 144- 145.

32. J. B. Phillips, *Your God is Too Small: A Guide for Believers and Skeptics Alike* (Simon & Schuster, 1952; reprint, 2004), 18.

33. Saint John Vianney, "The Blessed Curé of Ars in His Catechetical Instructions," https://www.ewtn.com/library/CATECHSM/CATARS.HTM (accessed August 31, 2018).

34. Saint Teresa of Avila, quoted in Michael E. Moynahan, *Once Upon a Mystery: What Happens Next?* (Paulist Press, 1998), 43.

35. Hail Mary, full of grace, the Lord is with thee. Blessed art thou amongst women and blessed is the fruit of thy womb, Jesus. Holy Mary, Mother of God, pray for us sinners, now, and at the hour of our death. Amen.
    (Latin: *Ave Maria, gratia plena, Dominus tecum. Benedicta tu in mulieribus, et benedictus fructus ventris tui, Iesus. Sancta Maria, Mater Dei, ora pro nobis peccatoribus, nunc et in hora mortis nostrae. Amen.*)

36. The sacrament of penance can be administered in private, communally, or, most rarely, general absolution can be granted to large numbers of people in emergency situations with the stipulation that individual private confessions must be made when possible.

37. The Bible provides numerous examples of how our bodies participate in prayer. The great patriarch, Abraham, abased himself before God by falling upon his face in prayer (Genesis 17:3). David sometimes sat to pray (2 Samuel 7:18), and

other times he danced (2 Samuel 6:14). Moses stretched out his hands (Exodus 9:29); others knelt (Psalms 95:6); and the tax collector beat his breast (Luke 18:13).

38. Robert M'Cheyne, quoted in *The Westminster Collection of Christian Quotations,* ed. Martin H. Manser (Westminster John Knox Press, 2001), 206.

39. Alfred, Lord Tennyson, *Poems of Tennyson,* ed. Henry Van Dyke and D. Laurance Chambers (Boston: Ginn & Company, Publishers, 1903), 96.

40. Saint John Vianney, quoted in *The Wisdom of the Saints: An Anthology,* ed. Jill Haak Adels (Oxford University Press, 1987), 40.

41. C. S. Lewis, *George MacDonald: An Anthology 365 Readings* (HarperSanFrancisco, 2001), 55.

42. The Transfiguration of Jesus is a theophany that reveals his hidden glory. Just as when Moses radiated after receiving the Ten Commandments on Mount Sinai, Jesus, too, was luminous on the Mount of the Transfiguration. However, Moses radiated God's glory; Jesus radiated with his own.

   Matthew tells us: "And He was transfigured before them. His face shone like the sun and his clothes became as white as the light" (Matthew 17:2). Then both Moses and Elijah appeared by his side. Moses represents the law and Elijah represents the prophets—the unspoken point being Jesus fulfills both the law and the prophets.

   Some Jewish folklore indicates that Adam and Eve, prior to the fall, were vested in a luminosity that darkened when they broke their relationship with God.

43. Saint Francis de Sales, quoted in Wade Menezes, *Four Last Things* (Irondale, Alabama: EWTN Publishing, 2017), 7.

44. There is a theological point being made in this story as well, namely that the God of the Israelites is very different from the nature deities of the pagan world. The God of Abraham, Isaac, and Jacob is above nature, outside nature. Unlike Ra or Zeus or Marduk, YHWH is not worshiped merely as god of the sun or the sky but as sovereign over all nature and all of history too.

45. Cardinal John Henry Newman, *Selection: Adapted to the Ecclesiastical Year From the Parochial and Plain Sermons* (Waterloo Place, London: Rivingtons, 1877), 240.

46. Although Christian history is wrought with examples of saints who have had mystical encounters with God, either through visions, apparitions, interior locutions, or some other communication, these phenomena are rare.

47 Alan W. Watts, *Behold The Spirit: A Study in the Necessity of Mystical Religion* (Random House Inc., 1947), 91.

48. Ed Spielman and Howard Friedlander, *Kung Fu,* "Pilot" (1972).

CHAPTER FOUR

1. Søren Kierkegaard, *The Sickness unto Death: A Christian Psychological Exposition for Upbuilding and Awakening,* ed., trans, intro. & annot. Howard V. Hong & Edna H. Hong (Princeton, NJ: Princeton Univ. Press, 1980), 67.

2. C. S. Lewis, *George MacDonald: An Anthology 365 Readings,* (HarperSanFrancisco, 2001), 125.

3. The word *"confiteor"* is a Latin word that translates to "I confess," which opens the prayer.

4. *International Commission on English in the Liturgy rendition,* 2011.

5. Cardinal John Henry Newman, quoted in *The Contemporary Review, Volume 49* (London: Isbister and Company, 1886), 347.

6. Saint John Vianney, *The Little Catechism of the Curé of Ars* (Saint Benedict Press, 1951), 101.

7. Total depravity doesn't mean we are as bad as we can possibly be, as in "utter depravity."

   The doctrine of Total Depravity goes hand in hand with other teachings that are often described using the acronym "TULIP." The letters stand for: 1. Total Depravity, 2. Unconditional election, 3. Limited atonement, 4. Irresistible Grace, and 5. Perseverance of the Saints.

8. This latter interpretation more closely aligns with the Eastern Orthodox Church teaching on "Ancestral Sin."

9. Genesis 46:26 and Exodus 1:5 refer to the descendants of Jacob as issuing forth from Jacob's loins in a manner that suggests they were more closely united with Jacob than merely having him as an ancestor. Hebrews 7:9-20 discusses how Levi was seminally present in Abraham. So, the concept is not foreign to the Bible.

10. Pope St. John Paul II, *Crossing the Threshold of Hope*, ed. Vittorio Messori (NY: Alfred A. Knopf, 1994; reprint, 2005), 228.

11. See, Gustavo Gutierrez, *A Theology of Liberation: History, Politics, and Salvation: 15th Anniversary Edition with New Introduction by Author* (Orbis Books, 15th ed., 1988).

12. Just like a mime imitates others, we, too, are imitators. What our neighbor has, we, too, wish to have. Girard argues that this covetous desire gives way to rivalry and then eventually to violence. This violence is, according to Girard, fueled by a "mimetic contagion," or agreement among the ignorant crowd.

    Girard's brilliant insight is that when a group or culture reaches the point of "mimetic crisis," then someone is picked out of the crowd to bear the full onslaught of the crowd's wrath. In other words, in order for society to survive the violence that would otherwise be spread among many, it is focused on one: a scapegoat who is eventually sacrificed. This ritual murder then brings a temporary peace, which is attributed to the appeasement of the gods resulting from the offering of the scapegoat victim. But, eventually the cycle begins again. The story of Jesus is the story of the final breaking of this cycle.

    "To break the power of mimetic unanimity, we must postulate a power superior to violent contagion. If we have learned one thing in this study, it is that none exists on the earth. It is precisely because violent contagion was all-powerful in human societies, prior to the day of the Resurrection, that archaic religion divinized it. They had good reason to mistake violent unanimity for divine power.

    "The Resurrection is not only a miracle, a prodigious transgression of natural laws. It is a spectacular sign of the entrance into the world of a power superior to violent contagion. By contrast to the latter it is a power not at all hallucinatory or deceptive. Far from deceiving the disciples, it enables them to recognize what they had not recognized before and to reproach themselves for their pathetic flight in the preceding days. They acknowledge their guilt in the violent contagion that murdered their master."

    Source: Rene Girard, *I See Satan Fall Like Lightning*, trans. James G. Williams (Orbis Books, 2001), 189.

13. Perhaps the demons were so loath to encounter Jesus due to the unbearable shame they must have experienced knowing that, as the Son of God, he knew each of them by name in their splendiferous, pre-fallen angelic form.

14. Saint Francis de Sales, quoted in *The Wisdom of the Saints: An Anthology*, ed. Jill Haak Adels (Oxford University Press, 1987), 46.

15. James Goldman, *The Lion in the Winter* (Samuel French, Inc., 1966), 63.

16. Thomas Merton, *New Seeds of Contemplation* (NY: New Directions Pub. Co., 2007), 176.

17. Saint Francis de Sales, quoted in *A Year with the Saints* (P. J. Kenedy & Sons, 1891), 24.

18. Dante Alighieri, quoted in Michael Haag, *Inferno Decoded* (Gallery Books, 2013), 21.
19. Cardinal John Henry Newman, *Parochial Sermons. Six Volumes, London Edition, In Two Volumes, Vol. 1.* (NY: D. Appleton and Co., 1843), 7.
20. *United States Catholic Catechism for Adults* (Washington DC: United States Conference of Catholic Bishops, 2006), 317.
21. Saint Francis de Sales, quoted in Mike Hickey, *Get Goodness: Virtue is the Power to do Good* (University Press of America Inc., 2011), 74.
22. John Hardon, *The Question and Answer Catholic Catechism* (Doubleday, 1981), 173.
23. C. S. Lewis, *The Screwtape Letters* (HarperOne, 1996), 88–89.
24. R. C. Sproul, *Essential Truths of the Christian Faith* (Illinois: Tyndale, 1998), 160.
25. George MacDonald, *Unspoken Sermons*, 3rd ser. (NY: Longmans, Green, & Co., 1889), 53, emphasis in original.
26. Guru Gobind Singh Ji, *The Creation of the Khalsa: The Saint Soldier* (Hemkunt Press, 1999), 101.
27. Thomas More, quoted in Gerard B. Wegemer, *Thomas More: A Portrait of Courage* (Princeton: Scepter Publishers, 1995; reprint, 2005), 218.
28. C. S. Lewis, *Reflections of the Psalms* (Geoffrey Bles, Lted., 1958), 25.
29. Catholics do not subscribe to the belief that Original Sin makes us utterly depraved—as sinful as possible—nor the Calvinist doctrine that Original Sin makes one totally depraved—radically sinful.
30. Karl Adam, *The Spirit of Catholicism*, https://www.ewtn.com/library/CATECHSM/CATARS.HTM (accessed August 31, 2018).
31. Previously, some theologians speculated that if an unbaptized baby should die then he or she would spend eternity in limbo. Limbo is a concept that has lost favor in recent years, not even appearing in the most recent official catechism. Instead, we simply entrust unbaptized babies to God's mercy, recognizing that while baptism is a normative element of the Christian life, God is not bound by his sacraments.
   According to the *Catechism of the Catholic Church*:
   "Holy Baptism is the basis of the whole Christian life, the gateway to life in the Spirit . . . and the door which gives access to the other sacraments. Through Baptism [human beings] are freed from sin and reborn as sons of God; [they] become members of Christ, are incorporated into the Church and made sharers in [the Church's] mission. . . .
   "This sacrament is called *Baptism*, after the central rite by which it is carried out: to baptize (Greek *baptizein*) means to 'plunge' or 'immerse'; the 'plunge' into the water symbolizes the [person's] burial into Christ's death, from which he rises up by resurrection with [Christ], as 'a new creature' [citing 2 Cor 5:17 and Gal 6:15] . . .
   "Baptism not only purifies from all sins, but also makes the neophyte 'a new creature,' an adopted son of God, who has become a 'partaker of the divine nature' [citing 2 Cor 5:17 and 2 Pet 1:4], member of Christ and co-heir with him, and a temple of the Holy Spirit" (nos. 1213–14, 1265; italics in original).
32. Thomas More, quoted in Paul Thigpen, *A Year With The Saints: Daily Meditations with the Holy Ones of God* (Charlotte, NC: Saint Benedict Press, 2013), Day 158.
33. This soteriology sounds suspiciously like Calvinism, but Molinism sounds suspiciously like Pelagianism. In fact, both Thomism and Molinism are distinct from these caricaturized comparisons.
34. Jesus taught his disciples to pray the Our Father, but there is no record of him praying this prayer with them. The way in which God is the father of Jesus is quite different from the way in which he is ours; he is a son by nature; we are sons and daughters by the grace of adoption.

35. Although there are numerous covenants in the Bible, many scholars point to six primary covenants between God and humans that are mentioned in Scripture. Three of these covenants, the Adamic (pre-fall is Edenic and post-fall is Adamic), the Noahic, and the New Covenant of Jesus Christ, are universally applicable. The remaining three covenants, the Abrahamic, the Mosaic, and the Davidic are all specific to Israel. Yet even these Israel-specific covenants where entered into so that Israel could be a light unto all nations and all peoples.

36. See, *Declaration "Dominus Iesus" on the Unicity and Salvific Universality of Jesus Christ and the Church.*

37. Pope Paul VI, *Declaration On The Relation Of The Church To Non-Christian Religions: Nostra Aetate* (October 28, 1965).

38. David Bentley Hart, *Christ and Nothing* (October 2003).

39. C. S. Lewis, *George MacDonald: An Anthology 365 Readings* (HarperSanFrancisco, 2001), 152.

40. See *Declaration "Dominus Iesus" On The Unicity And Salvific Universality of Jesus Christ And The Church.*

41. Karl Rahner, *Karl Rahner in Dialogue* (Crossroad, 1986), 35.

42. There was, for some time, a question of whether the ransom was being paid out to the devil, who had a claim on sinners' souls, or to God, since all sin is inevitably an offense against God. In his famous work on satisfaction atonement, *Cur Deus Homo?* (Latin: *Why was God a Man?*), St. Anselm of Canterbury pointed out the absurdity of arguing that the devil is due a ransom.

43. Because the writing style and word usage in the book of Revelation is so different from the other works of John the Apostle, some scholars believe he may not be the author.

44. R. C. Sproul, *Classic Teachings on the Nature of God* (Hendrickson Publishers, 1985; reprint, 1998), 24.

45. The phrase "*ex opere operato*" comes from Latin and means "from the work done." First used by Peter of Poitiers (c. 1130- 1215), the phrase quickly gained popularity within the Church and was employed by Aquinas and others. This language expresses the theological reality that a sacrament's efficacy is not dependent on the personal holiness of the one who administers the sacrament. This is because the source of the sacrament is Jesus, not the administrator of the sacrament. However, the recipient of the sacrament must be properly disposed in order to benefit from the sacrament's grace.

The sacraments of baptism, confirmation, and holy orders confer upon the recipient a permanent seal that cannot be erased or repeated.

46. Passages including John 10: 28-30 and John 16:22 are cited by some Protestants as bases for this belief a of "once saved, always saved" assurance. However, the Church counters with other passages such as Matthew 24:13 and numerous Pauline passages (e.g. Romans 11:22 and I Corinthians 10:11-12), which confirm the Church's stance that assurance is not offered; instead we are given hope.

CHAPTER FIVE

1. Henri de Lubac, *Paradoxes of Faith* (San Francisco: Ignatius Press, 1987), 171.

2. Manichaeism shares some commonalities with Zoroastrian dualism, however there are important differences as well. These differences were so acute that the founder of Manichaeism, Mani, was cruelly executed at the instigation of Zoroastrian priests who saw him as a heretic.

3. "I do not doubt that it would be easier for fate to take away your suffering than it would be for me. But you will see for yourself that much has been gained if we succeed in turning your hysterical misery into common unhappiness." *Studies*

on Hysteria (1895), (co-written with Josef Breuer) as translated by Nicola Luckhurst (2004).

4. Herman Melville, *Redburn: His First Voyage* (NY: Harpers and Brothers Publishers, 1850), 367.

5. Percy Bysshe Shelley, "To a Skylark," quoted in Frank P. Adams, *Grammatical Diagrams and Analyses* (Indianapolis, Indiana: Normal Publishing House, 1886), 101.

6. J. B. Phillips, *Your God Is Too Small: A Guide for Believers and Skeptics Alike* (NY: Simon & Schuster, 1952; Touchstone, 2004), 48.

7. Unknown Author; attributed to St. Francis of Assisi.

8. THE OUR FATHER: Our Father, Who art in heaven, hallowed be Thy Name. Thy kingdom come. Thy will be done, on earth as it is in heaven. Give us this day our daily bread. And forgive us our trespasses, as we forgive those who trespass against us. And lead us not into temptation, but deliver us from evil. Amen.

9. David Bentley Hart, "Tsunami and Theodicy", March 2005, https://www.firstthings.com/article/2005/03/tsunami-and-theodicy (accessed August 31, 2018).

10. Bach's "Jesu, Joy of Man's Desiring" explores this in music.

11. Although the actual words "ex nihilo" do not appear anywhere in the Bible, the idea is strongly implied throughout the Old Testament and the New Testament. The very name and titles of God used throughout Scripture reference him as the beginning and end of all things. More specifically, we read numerous allusions to creation ex nihilo throughout the Bible. (Proverbs 8:22–26 uses the literary device of personification of Wisdom, which predates the primordial chaos, the "depths" of Genesis 1:2. In the New Testament we read in 1 Corinthians 8:6, "God, who created all things.") So, the early Christian creeds refer to God the maker of "all things visible and invisible." The language of creation ex nihilo became the official teaching of the Church in 1215 at the Fourth Lateran Council.

12. Austin Farrer. This insight, when coupled with Farrer's profound thesis of double agency, provides an interesting thesis for understanding the relationship between God's providence and the potentiality of creation as well as human freedom.

13. C. S. Lewis, *The Four Loves* (NY: Harcourt Brace & Company, 1960), 121.

14. Douglas John Hall wrote in *God & Human Suffering: An Exercise in the Theology of the Cross*, that the creation stories of the Old Testament mention loneliness, limitations, anxiety, and temptation as four aspects potential in God's good creation.

15. In Genesis 3:21, we read how God clothed Adam and Eve in animal skins, indicating those animals had died. Admittedly, this takes place immediately after the fall and subsequent curse. There is a tradition that the animal garment was made from a shed snake's skin. The Jerusalem Targum (circa 11th century) specifically identifies snakeskin as the material used for the garments given to Adam and Eve by God.

16. See, Dietrich Bonhoeffer, *Creation and Fall: A Theological Exposition of Genesis 1-3* (Minneapolis: Fortress Press, 1997).

17. Jeffrey Burton Russell, *Lucifer: The Devil in the Middle Ages* (Cornell University Press, 1984), 173.

18. C. S. Lewis, *Words to Live By: A Guide for the Merely Christian* (HarperCollins, 2007), 63.

19. See, Sheldon Vanauken, *A Severe Mercy*.

20. Distinguishing between God's active will and his permissive will does not actually resolve the dilemma of an all-powerful and all-good God allowing evil; instead this distinction only regresses the problem until further comment is made about the distinction between the two expressions of God's will.

21. J. R. R. Tolkien coined a term to describe this kind of surprising resolution: "Eucatastrophe."

"I coined the word 'eucatastrophe': the sudden happy turn in a story which pierces you with a joy that brings tears (which I argued it is the highest function of fairy-stories to produce). And I was there led to the view that it produces its peculiar effect because it is a sudden glimpse of Truth, your whole nature chained in material cause and effect, the chain of death, feels a sudden relief as if a major limb out of joint had suddenly snapped back. It perceives—if the story has literary 'truth' on the second plane (. . .)—that this is indeed how things really do work in the Great World for which our nature is made. And I concluded by saying that the Resurrection was the greatest 'eucatastrophe' possible in the greatest Fairy Story—and produces that essential emotion: Christian joy which produces tears, because it is qualitatively so like sorrow, because it comes from those places where Joy and Sorrow are at one, reconciled, as selfishness and altruism are lost in Love."

"Letter 89" is a letter written by J. R. R. Tolkien and published in *The Letters of J. R. R. Tolkien.*

22. John Haught, "Darwin, God, and the Drama of Life", OnFaith, https://www. onfaith.co/onfaith/2009/11/30/darwin-god-and-the-drama-of-life/6813 (accessed August 31, 2018).

23. The phrase "Dark night of the soul" refers to a treatise written by St. John of the Cross, which addresses the topic of doubt and despondency in the life of a Christian. The individual feels alone, forsaken by God. Saint John's work is only one among a plethora of similar writings in Catholic spirituality. Mother Teresa wrote letters in which she expressed the torment of her own doubts; these letters are compiled in the book *Mother Teresa: Come Be My Light: The Private Writings of the Saint of Calcutta.*

Simone Weil brilliantly stated, "He who has not God in himself cannot feel His absence." Simone Weil, *Gravity and Grace* (Routledge & Kegan Paul, 1952), 27.

24. For those who wish to simply state that sin was caused by Adam's disobedience, this begs the question of the serpent's presence in the garden. If the serpent is Satan, his fall is equally opaque to us.

25. Paul Claudel, quoted in Mary C. Earle, *Days of Grace* (Morehouse Publishing, 2009), 21.

26. Herman Melville, *Moby Dick* (Norton, 1892), 504.

27. G. K. Chesterton, *The Book of Job* (North Charleston, SC: Createspace, 1907), 8.

28. Robert Frost, quoted in Jesse Zuba, *Robert Frost* (Philadelphia: Chelsea House Publishers, 2003), 173.

29. G. K. Chesterton, *The Book of Job* (North Charleston, SC: Createspace, 1907), 6.

30. Austin Farrer, *Said or Sung* (London: World, 1960), 27-28.

31. Simone Weil, quoted in Eric O. Springsted, *Simon Weil and The Suffering of Love* (Wipf & Stock Publishers, 1986), 42.

32. "To the question then: 'How did Christ save us?' the answer is: 'by making us part of Himself.' And when we ask: 'How are we to save ourselves?' the answer is: 'by making ourselves part of Christ.' Obviously such expressions need careful understanding. They could be understood in a heretical or in a pantheistic sense by taking them too literally; but they can also be interpreted in a metaphorical, or even sentimental sense that is utterly inadequate." M. Eugene Boylan, *This Tremendous Lover* (Ave Maria Press, 2009), 28.

33. Pope John Paul II, "Apostolic Letter, Salvifici Doloris Of the Supreme Pontiff John Paul II to The Bishops, To the Priests, To the Religious Families and To the Faithful of The Catholic Church on The Christian Meaning of Human Suffering," http://w2.vatican.va/content/john-paul-ii/en/apost_letters/1984/documents/hf_jp-ii_apl_11021984_salvifici-doloris.html (accessed August 31, 2018).

34. Saint Augustine, *The Confessions of St. Augustine,* trans. F. J. Sheed (NY: Sheed & Ward, 1943), 66-68.
35. Thomas Howard, *Christ the Tiger* (Hodder & Stoughton, 1967), 15.
36. Some have argued that Jesus' use of spit in some of his miracles points to similarities with other purported magicians and alleged healers of the pagan world. It is true that ancient authors believed in the curative powers of "saliva jejuna" (the saliva of a person who is fasting), especially regarding eye conditions.

    There is a Talmudic tradition, with which Jesus' audience would likely have been familiar, which held that the spit of the firstborn had healing powers. This, too, adds a layer of symbolism to Jesus' use of spit. Moreover, in one of his miracles (John 9:6) in which he used his own spit, Jesus mixes his saliva with some dirt. In this action we think back to Genesis and God's creation of Adam out of the dust of the ground. The very dust, which was now cursed, is being restored.
37. Isaac Watts, "Joy to the World," 1719.

CHAPTER SIX

1. Although God is neither male nor female, I use the traditional masculine pronouns in reference to him. While the Bible infrequently uses feminine images for God, (cf. e.g. Psalms 131:2) never, though, does it apply the feminine to God in its Hebrew verbal structures or pronouns. God may act like a mother (cf. Isaiah 66:13), but is always referenced in the masculine.
2. Charles de Secondat Montesquieu, *Persian and Chinese Letters: Being the Lettres Persanes* (M. Walter Dunne, Publisher, 1901), 122.
3. Voltaire, *Le Sottisier, suivi des Remarques sur le Discours sur L'Inégalité des Conditions et sur le Contrat Social,* new ed. (Paris: Garnier Frères, 1883), 151.
4. Fourth Lateran Council, can. II, quoted in H. J. Schroeder, *Disciplinary Decrees of the General Councils: Text, Translation, and Commentary* (St. Louis, MO: B. Herder Bk. Co., 1937), 241.
5. The *CCC* states: "God transcends all creatures. We must therefore continually purify our language of everything in it that is limited, image-bound or imperfect, if we are not to confuse our image of God . . . with our human representations. Our human words always fall short of the mystery of God" (para. 42).
6. Saint John Chrysostom, quoted in *The Faith of the Early Fathers, Volume 2,* trans. W. A. Jurgens (The Liturgical Press, 1979), 92.
7. "Thomism" is an entire school of thought that developed around the teaching of Aquinas, which can, in some cases, be differentiated from what Thomas Aquinas himself taught and believed.
8. There are some who begin with a philosophical presumption that we finite creatures living in the natural world have no access to anything outside the phenomenal world (the world of our senses). This thinking is in line with Immanuel Kant's arguments in the *Critique of Pure Reason,* where he differentiates between the noumenal and phenomenal realms. Bernard Lonergan corrected this erroneous thinking.
9. William Shakespeare, *Othello* (Simon & Schuster Paperbacks, 1993), 147.
10. David Hart points out that many contemporary atheists write objections to arguments for the existence of God without understanding those arguments, "Not knowing the scholastic distinction between primary and secondary causality, for instance, [Dawkins] imagined that Thomas's talk of a 'first cause' referred to the initial temporal causal agency in a continuous temporal series of discrete causes. He thought that Thomas's logic requires the universe to have had a temporal beginning, which Thomas explicitly and repeatedly made clear is not the case. He anachronistically mistook Thomas's argument from universal

natural teleology for an argument from apparent 'Intelligent Design' in nature. He thought Thomas's proof from universal 'motion' concerned only physical movement in space, 'local motion,' rather than the ontological movement from potency to act. He mistook Thomas's argument from degrees of transcendental perfection for an argument from degrees of quantitative magnitude, which by definition have no perfect sum. (Admittedly, those last two are a bit difficult for modern persons, but he might have asked all the same.)"

David Bentley Hart, *The Experience of God: Being, Consciousness, Bliss*. (New Haven: Yale University Press, 2013), 21–22.

11. Saint Augustine, *Sermones ad Populum*, LII.6.16 (in *PL*, vol. 38, col. 360). Cf. also *Sermo* CXVII.3.5.

The translation is my own from the Latin.

12. The statement is attributed to the British politician Arthur James Balfour (cf. Robert Hugh Benson, *Christ in the Church: A Volume of Religious Essays* [St. Louis, MO: B. Herder, 1911], 165).

13. In the ancient Mideast, a ceremony was conducted to formalize a contract. The ceremony involved the killing of an animal, the dividing of its carcass, and the parties to the contract walking between the two halves of the dead animal. In the case of God's covenant with Abraham, only God walked between the two halves because the contract, in this case the covenant, was a gracious gift. There were terms that Abraham had to follow, but Abraham offered nothing as payment. He had nothing to offer the infinite God.

14. Saint Augustine, Jacobus de Voragine, *The Golden Legend, or Lives of the Saints*, trans. William Caxton, 7 vols., Temple Classics, ed. F. S. Ellis (London: J. M. Dent & Co., 1900), 5:66.

15. *ST* I, q. 4, art. 2 (cf. also q. 3, art. 4): "*Deus est ipsum esse per se subsistens*." Aquinas' works in Latin can be found at: www.corpusthomisticum.org/iopera.html.

16. Pierre Teilhard de Chardin, *The Divine Milieu: An Essay on the Interior Life* (NY: Harper and Row, 1968), 112.

17. N. T. Wright, *Pauline Perspectives: Essays on Paul, 1978–2013* (Minneapolis, MN: Fortress Press, 2013), 472.

18. *Best-loved Negro Spirituals: Complete Lyrics to 178 Songs of Faith*, ed., Nicole Beaulieu Herder and Ronald Herder (Mineola, NY: Dover Publications, 2001), 54–55.

19. Catherine of Siena, *The Dialogue of the Seraphic Virgin, Catherine of Siena: Dictated by Her, While in a State of Ecstasy, to Her Secretaries, and Completed in the Year of Our Lord 1370; Together with an Account of Her Death by An Eye-Witness*, trans. & intro. Algar Thorold, new & abridged ed. (London: Kegan Paul, Trench, Trübner & Co., 1907), 275.

20. Fr. John A. Hardon, quoted in *Modern Catholic Dictionary*, ed., John A. Hardon (Bardstown, KY: Eternal Life, 1999; reprint, 2004), s. v. "Simplicity of God."

21. The fact that the Second Person of the Trinity took on a human nature in the person of Jesus adds another dimension to this discussion. Jesus certainly experienced emotions, and in that sense, emotion is not foreign to God.

22. Peter Kreeft, "Love," http://www.peterkreeft.com/topics/love.htm (accessed August 31, 2018).

23. *The New Dictionary of Theology*, ed. Joseph A. Komonchak, Mary Collins, & Dermot A. Lane (Collegeville, MN: "A Michael Glazier Book" for Liturgical Press, 1990), s. v. "Apophatic Theology."

The Greek term means, "turning away from speech." It has been a hallowed aspect of Eastern Christian theology since (at least) the time of Pseudo-Dionysius the Areopagite (sixth century AD). The converse process of being able to assert something positively of God—He is righteous; He is loving; etc.—is called: "Kataphatic Theology" (cf. *The Westminster Handbook to Patristic Theology*, ed. John Anthony McGuckin, Westminster Handbooks to Christian Theology [Louisville, KY: Westminster John Knox Press, 2004], s. v. "Apophaticism").

24. Cf. the footnote above.

25. According to Gary A. Rendsburg, professor of Jewish Studies at Rutgers University:

"An important point to be noticed is the presence of demythologizing, that is, the conscious avoidance of words that can be associated with pagan deities.

A. This is seen especially on day 4, where the words *sun* (*shemesh*) and *moon* (*yareah*) are consciously avoided.

B. Even the singular form *sea* (*yam*), which was also the word for the sea god of the ancient Canaanites, is studiously avoided in favor of the plural *seas* (*yamim*).

C. The author does not want the reader to think for a moment that God is responsible for the existence of pagan deities." (*The Book of Genesis: Part I* [n. p.: Teaching Co., 2006], 5; available from *Internet Archive* at: archive. org/details/BookOfGenesis.)

26. The word is derived from the Latin phrase, "*a se*," meaning "from itself."

27. C. S. Lewis, *The Problem of Pain* (NY: HarperOne for HarperCollins Pub., 2001), 157.

28. The ancient Christian theologian Tertullian (+ ca. 240 AD) is credited with having been the first to use the word in his work, *Adversus Praxean* (ch. II; cf. *The New Dictionary of Theology*, ed. Joseph A. Komonchak, Mary Collins, & Dermot A. Lane [Collegeville, MN.: "A Michael Glazier Book" for Liturgical Press, 1990], s. v. "Trinity").

29. Cf. also e.g. Exodus 15:11; Deuteronomy 10:17; Psalms 86:8 and 96:5; Isaiah 46:9.

30. Cf. also Genesis 3:22 and 11:7 as well as (intriguingly) Isaiah 6:8.

31. The traditional understanding of "person" comes from Boethius: "an individual substance of a rational nature." Cf. *The New Dictionary of Theology*, ed. Joseph A. Komonchak, Mary Collins, & Dermot A. Lane (Collegeville, MN: "A Michael Glazier Book" for Liturgical Press, 1990), s. v. "Nature" and "Person, Divine."

32. The knowledge that God is Trinity is revealed truth, not the result of reason. If we forget this, we could begin to adopt all sorts of errors. For example, since God the Holy Spirit proceeds from the Father and the Son, why does not yet another divine person proceed from the Son and the Holy Spirit, resulting in a quadrinity (four persons)? The answer is that we are discussing divine mysteries not mathematical formula.

33. Cf. *The New Dictionary of Theology*, ed. Joseph A. Komonchak, Mary Collins & Dermot A. Lane (Collegeville, MN: "A Michael Glazier Book" for Liturgical Press, 1990), s. v. "Homoousios."

34. This notion is tied to heresies such as *patripassionism* and *theopaschitism*. God is impassible; that means he cannot suffer, but that does not mean God is apathetic. Since God is infinite and eternal, there is nothing outside of him that can influence him. Still, God the Son suffered in the person of Jesus, and if we take the Bible seriously, while still avoiding heretical theodicies, we must affirm that in some way God the Father and God the Holy Spirit suffered too. What human father would not suffer at the sight of his only son in great pain? How much more, then, does God react to the suffering of Jesus, his only Son?

"The scriptures . . . are not concerned with an abstract ideal of perfection but with the living God who 'knew' in a personal and intimate way (Ex 2:23-25) the sufferings of the people and who sought to free them from oppression. This is a God of compassionate love who walks with the people, covenants with them, endures their rejection, and brings them to the promised land. The God of Israel is not distant and apathetic, uncaring and unaffected by the fortunes of the beloved community. This God is deeply involved and deeply affected by the history of Israel and indeed by the history of all peoples." Michael L. Cook, *Responses to 101 Questions About Jesus* (Paulist Press, 1993), 80.

35. Cf. *The Westminster Handbook to Patristic Theology*, ed. John Anthony McGuckin, Westminster Handbooks to Christian Theology (Louisville, KY: Westminster John Knox Press, 2004), s. v. "Monarchianism."

36. *Modern Catholic Dictionary*, [ed.,] John A. Hardon (Bardstown, KY: Eternal Life, 1999; reprint, 2004), s. v. "Monarchianism."

37. See *The Concise Oxford Dictionary of the Christian Church*, ed. E. A. Livingstone, rev. 2nd ed., Oxford Paperback Reference ([Oxford]: Oxford Univ. Press, 2006), s. v. "Tritheism" and "John Philoponus."
   Surprisingly, as late as 1857, the Church has had to condemn such views: see *Modern Catholic Dictionary*, [ed.,] John A. Hardon (Bardstown, KY: Eternal Life, 1999; reprint, 2004), s. v. "Tritheism."

38. Sermon preached by Dr. Maurice Boyd on file with the author.

39. *The Westminster Handbook to Patristic Theology*, ed. John Anthony McGuckin, Westminster Handbooks to Christian Theology (Louisville, KY: Westminster John Knox Press, 2004), 26.

40. For example, the scholastic theologians had a tendency to create categories (i.e. Dividing Grace into Actual Grace, Efficacious Grace, Habitual Grace, and Sanctifying Grace and contrasting these types of graces with nature) that may not always serve as helpful distinctions.

41. Pope St. Gregory I, quoted in *Morals on the Book of Job*, 3 vols., A Library of Fathers of the Holy Catholic Church (London & Oxford: John Henry Parker, 1845), II:496.

42. Dame Julian of Norwich, *Revelations of Divine Love* (NY: Divine Love, 2007), 48.

43. Dame Julian of Norwich, *Love's Trinity: A Companion to Julian of Norwich*, trans., John-Julian (Collegeville, MN: Liturgical Press), 170.

CHAPTER SEVEN

1. One of my favorite absurdities is the claim that Jesus was not an actual historical person but the creation of a first-century fertility cult, whose members ingested mind-altering, hallucinatory mushrooms. Cf. John M. Allegro, *The Sacred Mushroom and the Cross: A Study of the Nature and Origins of Christianity Within the Fertility Cults of the Near East* (London: Hodder & Stoughton, 1970).

2. Albert Camus, *The Fall*, trans. Justin O'Brien (NY: Vintage Bks. for Random House, 1956), 111 ff.

3. Few serious scholars deny Jesus' very existence, but some note that there is not much written, non-Christian evidence of Jesus. However, we find a few lines mentioning him in the writings of Flavius Josephus, Pliny the Younger, and in Tacitus. Regardless, there are numerous ancient Christian texts that attest to Jesus' historicity.

4. In *The Human Christ: The Search for the Historical Jesus* (NY: Free Press, 1998), 5. The comment by Rev. Fr. George Tyrrell can be found in his book: *Christianity at the Cross-roads* [sic], 4th printing (NY: Longmans, Green & Co., 1913), 44.

5. Romano Guardini, *The Humanity of Christ: Contributions to a Psychology of Jesus*, trans. Ronald Walls (NY: Pantheon Bks. for Random House, 1964), xxi–xxii.

6. Edward Schweizer, *Jesus*, trans. David E. Green (Richmond, VA: John Knox Press, 1971), 13.

7. The closest parallel of this phenomenon stems from the way Roman emperors adopted 'Caesar' as a cognomen. In other words, the name "Caesar" was originally the surname of Julius Caesar, essentially Rome's first emperor. Julius was

so closely identified with his office as ruler of Rome that his surname became a title that subsequent emperors adopted. The title was so identified with rulers that variants of the word came to be used in other countries, (e.g., "Kaiser" in German, "Tsar" in Russian).

8. Similarly, there are those who see God's creative work as a one-time event, and others, Doctor of the Church Hildegard of Bingen and St. Maximus for example, who understand God's creative work as continuous.

9. *Ep.* CI (*NPNF²* 7:440). Gregory was writing to the priest Cledonius, in opposition to the views of Apollinaris of Laodicea (ca. 315–92 AD). Apollinaris, or Apollinarius, claimed that, when becoming man, the Son inhabited, and hence, effectively replaced the soul of the human Christ. That view was condemned: cf. *CCC* para. 471.

10. In Greek thought, the Platonic and/or Gnostic God would not take on the nature of a mortal man, let alone die on a cross; such an act would be sheer folly. To the Jewish mind, the Messiah was to come in victory, not in humiliation and the apparent defeat of crucifixion. More importantly, anyone hung on a tree, as Jesus was, would be considered cursed by God (Deuteronomy 21:23).

11. Monothelitism was the heresy that taught that Jesus had only one will, namely, the divine. This is a version of Monophysitism, the heresy that taught that Jesus has only one nature, which is the divine one. In modern times, this view remains prevalent amongst the so-called "Oriental Orthodox" churches.

    Nestorianism is the heresy that teaches that there is a distinction to be made between the divine person of the Son *per se*, who is God, and the divine person of the Son incarnate as Jesus, who is God-made-man. Thus, followers of this heresy preferred to call the Blessed Virgin Mary, the "Mother of *Christ*," rather than the "Mother of *God*." It still exists today in the Assyrian Church of the East.

12. So, after his crucifixion, it was Jesus' body that lay in the tomb, while his soul descended into the dead, yet he remained one person.

13. David Bentley Hart, *Atheist Delusions* (David Bentley Hart, 2009), 64.

14. This custom may not have been well observed throughout Jewish history.

15. "The Spirit of the Lord GOD is upon me, because the LORD has anointed me to bring good tidings to the afflicted; he has sent me to bind up the brokenhearted, to proclaim liberty to the captives, and the opening of the prison to those who are bound; 2 to proclaim the year of the LORD's favor, and the day of vengeance of our God; . . ." (Isaiah 61:1-2).

16. But, Jesus did not just fulfill prophecies; he also fulfilled the law. More astoundingly, it can be said that he fulfilled Israel's role. Generally speaking, Jesus' life parallels many of the figures of ancient Israel. He is the second Adam; he is the creator of a new covenant, reminiscent of Abraham. Like Moses, who delivered the Jews from slavery, Jesus delivered us from the slavery of sin. The parallels continue. The Gospel of John declares: "The Word became flesh and made his dwelling among us" (1:14). The language of dwelling among us, really, pitched his tent, alludes to the Shekinah or visible glory of God referenced throughout the Old Testament.

17. The Gospels of Matthew, Mark, and Luke share much in common. A comparison of these books, along with historical analysis, reveals that Mark was likely the first Gospel, which both Matthew and Luke used as a primary source for their texts. In addition, Matthew and Luke provide information not found in Mark's Gospel. This insight has led scholars to posit the existence of a source, *Quelle*, which means "source" in German, for this information. The Q document, as it has become known in academic circles, is a hypothetical collection of written material about Jesus including stories and sayings.

    In addition to the hypothetical Q document, there are various other sources that purport to report authentic sayings of and stories about Jesus. The *Agrapha* (Greek: "non-written") offer material not found elsewhere in the New

Testament but are nonetheless quoted by certain early Christian sources. These sayings are not easily authenticated, however.

Likewise, there are early Christian texts that claim to provide unique information about Jesus. Although the Church has deemed these sources to be noncanonical, there may be some authentic information, mixed in with fictional material, contained therein.

18. The English word "gospel," comes from the Greek word "*euangelion*," which means: "good news (or, message)." It was translated literally into Anglo-Saxon as, "*gōdspel*," which became our modern, "gospel" (see *Merriam-Webster Dictionary*, s. v. "gospel; available at: www.merriam-webster.com/dictionary/gospel).

19. Saint Augustine, Bishop of Hippo, *The Works of Saint Augustine: Sermons,* ed., John E. Rotelle, trans., Edmund Hill (NY: New City Press, 1991), 343.

20. George Sylvester Viereck, "What Life Means to Einstein: An Interview by George Sylvester Viereck," *Saturday Evening Post*, October 26, 1929, 117.

21. Albert Einstein, quoted in Kaustuv Roy, *Rethinking Curriculum in Times of Shifting Educational Context* (Palgrave Macmillan, 2018), 154.

22. Christmas is always celebrated on December 25, but Easter's date changes from year to year. Saint Augustine speculated, in the fourth century, that the fixed date for Christmas is tied to the solar and lunar cycles. There is great significance in that December 25 marks the day when the sun ascends to a point where light begins overtaking the darkness of night. Additionally, December 25 is the same day as the pagan Saturnalia festival. In the year 274 AD, the Roman Emperor Aurelian inaugurated the feast of Sol Invictus on December 25, celebrating the Roman sun god. Sometimes, Christians purposely tried to supplant pagan holidays with Christian ones as a tool of evangelization. However, it is possible that Christmas was established first and Emperor Aurelain established the *Natalis Solis Invicti* (birth of the unconquered sun) to help counter the mass conversions to Christianity by offering a pagan alternative to the popular Christian holy day.

23. Mythologist Joseph Campbell wrote about the pagan rite of baptism:
    "And the rite of baptism . . . was an ancient rite coming down from the old Sumerian temple city Eridu, of the water god Ea, 'God of the house of Water,' whose symbol is . . . Capricorn (a composite beast with the foreparts of a goat and body of a fish), which is the sign into which the sun enters at the winter solstice for rebirth. In the Hellenistic period, Ea was called Oannes, which is in Greek Ioannes, Latin Johannes, Hebrew Yohanan, English John. Several scholars have suggested, therefore, that there was never either John or Jesus, but only a water-god and a sun-god."
    Joseph Campbell, *The Masks of Gods: Occidental Mythology* (pp. 349-350).
    While these connections are intriguing, they are not surprising. Early Christians often noted such similarities. What is missing in Campbell's critique are the extraordinary differences between the historical John the Baptist and the mythical Oannes. Followers of Oannes may have been ritually washed in the name of or to please Oannes, but John did not baptize in his own name. What's more, the similarities between these two rituals are exaggerated by Campbell's use of the word "baptism." This is a distinctly Judeo-Christian concept, heavy with theological meaning.

24. This fallacy occurs when a complex idea is simplified so much that the original idea becomes lost or distorted.

25. In Deuteronomy 32:11, we find the same Hebrew verb for hovering to denote an eagle watching over its young; again, a revelation of the intimacy God has with his creation.

26. After David's reign, his son, Solomon, took the throne, but the twelve tribes of Israel, which had constituted one nation, split into the northern kingdom, called Israel (made up of ten tribes), and the southern kingdom of Judah (made up

of the two remaining tribes). In 720 BC, the northern kingdom was conquered, and the ten tribes were lost, or more likely assimilated into the neighboring cultures. Later, Judah, which dominated a small region of the southeastern Levant, also fell in 587 BC. By the time of Jesus' birth, the kings of Judah, albeit not forgotten, were certainly a distant memory. So, Jesus' royal ancestry did not provide him with any clear advantages, such as wealth or power. We have no record of Jesus making any claim to reestablish the Davidic monarchy. As far as we know, he simply did not publicize his descent from that great king. Nevertheless, it would become theologically important.

27. Luke's Gospel connects Jesus to King David in several ways, noting they were both born in Bethlehem—which Luke identifies as the City of David—they were both shepherds, and they were both kings.

28. The wise men, or Magi, are neither named nor numbered, but since three gifts are mentioned—gold, frankincense, and myrrh—there has been a tradition of naming three Magi. Gaspar (or Casper), Balthazar, and Melchior are three of the most popular names attributed to these mysterious men from the East. Some scholars believe they were Zoroastrian astrologers, which, if true, speaks to Jesus' invitation to all peoples from the onset of his life.

29. Origen provided this useful symbology of the three gifts.

30. Jesus was born in Bethlehem, which means "city of bread." He is the bread of life, come from heaven.

31. Today's date is measured in relation to Jesus' birth. Events that happened before the incarnation are labeled BC (Before Christ), or more recently BCE (Before the Common Era). Events that happened after Jesus' death are labeled as AD (*Anno Domini*; Latin: "Year of the Lord"), or ACE (After the Common Era).
    A Jesuit by the name of Dionysius Petavius introduced the acronym "BC" and popularized the use of "AD," which originated centuries earlier.

32. James Allan Francis, *"The Real Jesus" and Other Sermons* (n. p.: Judson Press, 1926).

33. Herod the Great was the man responsible for the murder of the innocents; that is, he was the ruler visited by the wise men, and he is the one who ordered the slaughter of the firstborn sons right around the time Jesus was born. After the passing of Herod the Great, his heir, Herod Antipater (a.k.a. Antipas) took the throne. His realm was to the south and the west, while his half-brother, Philip, had jurisdiction of the adjoining lands—until Rome claimed immediate rule there too.

34. There are noncanonical books, such as those discovered in 1945 at Nag Hammadi, which recount dubious stories about Jesus' childhood.

35. Romano Guardini, https://www.ewtn.com/library/CHRIST/HUMAN.TXT (accessed August 31, 2018).

36. Jesus was familiar with Jewish history from the stories of Genesis through his own time. Importantly, he knew about God's covenants and the history of how the Hebrews lived contentedly in Goshen under Egyptian rule but were eventually enslaved when an unsympathetic pharaoh took the throne. It was Moses who led the Jews from slavery into the Promised Land. In their new home, the Israelites developed a government of rule by judges, then, after about three centuries, a series judges gave way to kings—the greatest of which were David and Solomon. After King Solomon died, the kingdom split (796 BC) into two realms with Israel in the north and Judea in the south. Further divisions occurred when the land was conquered by different enemies. These conquests (especially the Babylonian Exile, 586 BC) proved pivotal in the life of the Jewish people, and much of the Hebrew Bible was either composed or compiled during the Babylonian Exile or in light of that event.

37. The Pharisees included the House of Shammai (known for its rigidity) and the House of Hillel (known for its lenience). In the debates recorded in the Gospels,

we find Jesus siding with the House of Hillel most often, though not always—for example, his position on the issue of divorce.

38. Adam prefigures Jesus. Here are some connections.

   ■ Origin: Adam was not born through the procreative act of a man and woman; nor was Jesus the product of a conjugal act—though he was the biological child of Mary.

   ■ Ribs: Genesis (2:21-23) recounts the story of how God caused Adam to fall into a deep sleep, after which he opened Adam's side in order to remove a rib, from which he created Eve. In the Gospel of John (19:33), we read how Jesus' side was pierced after he was already dead (sleeping, so to speak). From this postmortem wound flowed water and blood, which symbolized the inauguration of his church. Eve was to Adam what the church is to Jesus. Jesus' side was opened on the cross to create the church. Adam's side was opened, from which his rib was taken to form Eve.

   ■ Title: In Genesis 1:14, Adam is described as "the man," and in John 19:5, when Pontius Pilate presents Jesus to the crowd he says, "*Ecce Homo*," which is Latin for "Behold the Man."

   ■ Courage: A juxtaposition: When Adam was confronted in the Garden of Eden by God he hid himself (Genesis 3:8). When Jesus was confronted in the garden of Gethsemane by soldiers he announced himself (John 18:5).

   ■ Jesus, the second Adam, was to substitute obedience for the original Adam's failure; he was to replace Adam's self-centered choice to follow his own desires with a God-centeredness; to completely submit to the will of the Father.

39. An overlooked irony pointed out by some scholars is that Adam and Eve did not know the serpent was Satan. Conversely, while Satan knew Jesus was a holy man, he may not have known or else may have refused to believe Jesus was the incarnation of God.

40. John Henry Newman ponders the question why Jesus wept at the grave of Lazarus. ". . . the question naturally arises in the mind—*why* did our Lord weep at the grave of Lazarus? He knew He had power to raise him, why should He act the part of those who sorrow for the dead? In attempting any answer to this inquiry, we should ever remember that the thoughts of our Saviour's mind are far beyond our comprehension. Hardly do we enter into the feelings and meaning of men like ourselves, who are gifted with any special talent; even human philosophers or poets are obscure from the depth of their conceptions. What then must be the marvellous abyss of love and understanding in Him who, though partaker of our nature, is the Son of God?"

   John Henry Newman, *Tears of Christ at the Grave of Lazarus*

41. Romano Guardini, *The Humanity of Christ: Contributions to a Psychology of Jesus*, trans. Ronald Walls (NY: Pantheon Bks. for Random House, 1964), 145.

42. C. H. Dodd, *The Parables of the Kingdom* (London: Nisbet and Company, 1935), 16.

43. Jesus' reluctance to be publicly identified as Israel's Messiah has been the subject of scholarly inquiry. An interesting but outdated body of scholarship arose in 1901, referencing the Messianic Secret. A scholar named William Wrede proffered the hypothesis of the Messianic Secret, which is a reference to a theme found mostly Mark's Gospel, where Jesus repeatedly admonitions his disciples not to reveal him as Messiah.

44. Romano Guardini, *The Humanity of Christ: Contributions to a Psychology of Jesus*, trans. Ronald Walls (NY: Pantheon Bks. for Random House, 1964), 47–48.

45. Romano Guardini, *The Humanity of Christ: Contributions to a Psychology of Jesus*, trans. Ronald Walls (NY: Pantheon Bks. for Random House, 1964), 6.

46. Not all the disciples were uneducated. Luke was a physician, and his mentor, St. Paul, was educated under the famous first-century rabbi Gamaliel (cf. Acts

22:3). Nevertheless, Paul was not one of the Twelve Apostles, nor was he the author of any of the Gospels.

47. Romano Guardini, *The Humanity of Christ: Contributions to a Psychology of Jesus*, trans. Ronald Walls (N. Y.: Pantheon Bks. for Random House, 1964), 12.

48. P. Carnegie Simpson, *The Fact of Christ* (James Clarke edition, 1952) 23-24.

49. J. B. Phillips, *Your God Is Too Small: A Guide for Believers and Skeptics Alike* (NY: Simon & Schuster, 1952; Touchstone, 2004), 80.

50. J. B. Phillips, *Your God Is Too Small: A Guide for Believers and Skeptics Alike* (NY: Simon & Schuster, 1952; Touchstone, 2004), 54.

51. Jesus rose from the dead to live forevermore, but Lazarus was not resurrected in the same permanent manner. Lazarus eventually died again. Lazarus' rising does point to Jesus' own resurrection, however. For example, Lazarus' body was in the tomb for over three days, and his body began to stink from decomposition (cf. John 11:39). This detail suggests that Jesus' rising on the third day, before his body started corrupting, is indicative of his innate dignity.

52. The prayer is called the "Shema," because the first word of the prayer is "hear," or "listen," which is rendered as "*Shema*" in Hebrew. "Hear O Israel, the Lord is our God, the Lord is One" is translated from the Hebrew, "*Shema Yisrael Adonai eloheinu Adonai ehad.*" See Deuteronomy 6:4.

53. The Our Father is reminiscent of God's original creation, and references to God as our father, to his holy character, to his kingdom, to his providential love in giving us food to eat, to his forgiveness, and to his help in overcoming temptations, all echo back to the very good creation written about in the Genesis narrative.

54 John Hardon, *The Catholic Catechism: A Contemporary Catechism of the Teachings of the Catholic Church* (Doubleday, 1981), 431.

55. The entire idea of slaughtering tens of thousands of animals to appease God seems foreign to modern readers. After leaving Egypt, some of the Jews formed for themselves an idol in the form of a golden calf. It may not be a coincidence that after this event the Jews began to sacrifice actual calves and other animals. Perhaps this was a reminder of the folly of worshiping animals, or animal-human hybrids such as the zoomorphic deities of the Egyptian pantheon. Hosea 6:6 and Psalm 51:16 indicate that God does not delight in such sacrifices, however.

56. In John's Gospel, there is an account of the cleansing of the temple that takes place not toward the end of Jesus' ministry but at the beginning. John may have been writing thematically instead of chronologically, or possibly there could have been two cleansings.

57. In Jesus' time, the temple was not the original building built by Solomon. That temple was destroyed by the Babylonians. A second temple was built in the time of King Cyrus, but that building, too, was demolished by King Herod. Herod then renovated the second temple, which was the structure contemporary with Jesus.

58. Palms were a common symbol in the land where Jesus lived. The Greeks, Romans, and Hebrews identified palm fronds with ideals of victory or peace.

59. There is a debate among theologians about whether Jesus' presence is that of his pre-resurrection or his post-resurrection body. One may ask how Jesus could offer his glorified body before the resurrection. "In the Eucharist, the faithful are nourished with the Body of the Risen Christ. In each Eucharistic celebration throughout the world, the Risen Lord, conqueror of sin and death, goes beyond the limits of time and space and is really present under the elements of bread and wine. Therefore, it is the Body of the Glorified Lord" [*Instrumentum Laboris*, 11th General Synod of Bishops].

60. After the resurrection of Jesus, the remaining Apostles were ordained. (See John 20:21-23.)

61. Passover is celebrated on only one day, and the feast of Unleavened Bread is celebrated for seven days.

62. Scott Hahn, "The Fourth Cup: The Sacrament of the Eucharist," Trinity Communications, http://zuserver2.star.ucl.ac.uk/~vgg/rc/aplgtc/hahn/m4/4cp.html (accessed August 31, 2018).
63. A. N. Wilson, *Jesus: A Life* (W. W. Norton & Company, 2004), 51.
64. Temptations were still manifest, as temptation is not only from the devil but our own inner struggles.
65. The Evangelist who authored this story may be telling us both a fact—that Peter, James, and John slept while Jesus was agonizingly praying—while also providing the reader with a symbol. The Apostles, Jesus' inner circle, his three closest friends, could not even overcome mere sleep as Jesus was preparing to overcome Death itself! The connection between death and sleep is obvious, but it held particular currency in the mythologies of the Middle East. In the *Epic of Gilgamesh*, for instance, we find the hero, Gilgamesh, seeking immortality. He meets Utnapishtim, who survived the great flood, and Gilgamesh is offered his prize of immortality if he can stay awake for seven days. The point is that if he can overcome the small death, sleep, he would be worthy to overcome true death.

    One may ask how the story of Jesus' agony came to be recorded if the only witnesses were sleeping during the ordeal. A few explanations come to mind. First, Jesus himself must have shared the information with his followers. Alternately, the disciples may have slept intermittently. Lastly, some scholars speculate that the Gospel accounts of the agony in the Garden are literary creations. If this is the case, then the accounts are among the finest that have ever been written in all of history.
66. Luke may be referencing hematidrosis, a medical condition where a person sweats blood.
67. Examples of some of the other "I am" statements of Jesus include:
    1. "I am the bread of life; he who comes to Me shall not hunger" (John 6:35).
    2. "I am the good shepherd; the good shepherd lays down His life for His sheep" (John 10:11).
    3. "I am the resurrection and the life; he who believes in Me shall live even if he dies" (John 11:25).
    4. "I am the way, and the truth, and the life; no one comes to the Father, but through Me" (John 14:6).
    5. "I am the true vine, and My Father is the vinedresser" (John 15:1).
68. There are numerous comparisons to be made between the life of Moses and the life of Jesus; here are a few. They were both born at time when other children were ordered to be killed (Exodus 1:16/Matthew 2:16); they left their home countries (Exodus 2:11-15/Matthew 2:15); both returned to Israel from Egypt (Exodus 13:3/Matthew 2:15); Moses fasted and prayed in solitude for 40 days and then wandered the desert for 40 years, and Jesus spent 40 days in the solitude of the wilderness fasting and praying (Deuteronomy 8:2/ Matthew 4:1).
69. The Gospels are unclear as to whether Jesus was completely naked or if he wore a loincloth. In Matthew 27:28 and Luke 10:30 we read that Jesus was stripped and soldiers gambled for his garments. However, in Jesus' time, wearing a loincloth was synonymous with being naked.
70. Simone Weil, *Gravity and Grace* (Lincoln: The Bison Books Edition. 1997), 140.
71. N. T. Wright, *Simply Jesus* (HarperOne, 2011), 186.
72. The supreme irony of the story is that by his death he destroyed Death's power.
73. The fact that innocent Jesus was executed, and guilty Barabbas was set free, is indicative of the substitution offered to us all: Jesus taking on the penalty each one of us deserves.
74. The New Testament is the only ancient text that records the practice of Rome's token gesture of releasing a criminal in honor of the Passover holiday.
75. There is an additional irony. In Aramaic, Jesus' name would have been Joshua Bar-Joseph: Joshua, son of Joseph—his foster father. It was a common practice

of the time to be known in this way. "*Abbas*" is a variant of the Aramaic word "*Abba*" (father); Barabbas thus is "*Bar-Abba*," son of the father. Some early Christian documents indicate that Barabbas shared the same first name with Jesus, so the crowd called for the release of "Jesus Bar-Abbas" (*Joshua* being rendered as *Jesus* in these Greek writings). At the request of the crowd, Jesus Barabbas (Jesus, son of the father) was released. Jesus, the source of all life, was rejected, while the crowd accepted a murder, a destroyer of life. Jesus, the true son of God the Father was killed, while the imitator was set free.

76. We see here the fulfillment of prophecy. One prophecy is from the book of Isaiah, which portrays the coming Messiah as a lamb "led to the slaughter" (Isaiah 53). In addition, the book of Genesis recounts God testing Abraham's faith by asking Abraham to sacrifice his son, Isaac. In the story of the Binding of Isaac (the Aqedah), when Abraham and his son went to offer a sacrifice to God, Isaac asked where the lamb was for the sacrifice. "Abraham answered 'God himself will provide the lamb for the burnt offering, my son.' And the two of them went on together" (Genesis 22:8). This passage is prophetic in that it reveals that God would provide a sacrificial lamb not only then for Abraham but for the entire world in the person of his son as the Lamb of God.

77. Tradition identifies one of these women by name: Veronica. According to the account, the woman approaches Jesus with a handkerchief or cloth. When she wipes his face of blood and sweat, the image of his face is purportedly imprinted on the cloth. The Bible does not give the name of any of the women mentioned, but the name "Veronica" may be a moniker originating from the Latin word "*vera*," which means true, and "*icon*," which means image.

78. Hans Urs von Balthasar, *You Crown the Year with Your Goodness: Radio Sermons*, trans. Graham Harrison (San Francisco: Ignatius Press, 1989), 85.

79. Saint Faustina Kowalska, quoted in Paulette Honeygosky, *Top Ten Questions that Jesus Asked: As Recorded in the Gospel of John* (AuthorHouse, 2010), 165.

80. Pope St. John Paul II, in a general audience of November 30, 1988.

81. Sergeï Nikolaevich Bulgakov, *The Holy Grail and the Eucharist*, ed., trans., Boris Jakim (Lindisfarne Books, 1997), 33.

82. Hans Urs von Balthasar, *You Crown the Year with Your Goodness: Radio Sermons*, trans. Graham Harrison (San Francisco: Ignatius Press, 1989), 78-79.

83. The Gospel of John, 21:3-12, recounts the story of the post-resurrection Jesus ordering his disciples to cast their nets into the water. Though they had been fishing throughout the night without catching anything, they obeyed. Soon, they hauled in a catch of 153 fish.

    Theories abound about the meaning of the number 153, but there may be a connection to the symbol of the fish. One of the first symbols of Christianity was a simple drawing of fish, made by the intersection of two half circles. We find this image in early Christian tombs, and some scholars link the fish pictogram to Jesus' miraculous multiplication of the fishes and loaves of bread (John 6:1-14). The Greek word for fish is "*Ichthys*," the letters of which form the acronym "*Iesous Christos Theou Yios Soter*," which is Greek for "Jesus Christ the Son of God, Savior."

    The "*Vesica Piscis*" (Latin: "bladder of a fish") is a symbol made when two circles of the same size partially overlap. A measurement of the intersection of these two half circles produces a ratio, known as the measure of the fish, of 153:265.

84. Saint Catherine of Siena, quoted in *Love Came Down*, ed. Christopher L. Webber (Morehouse Publishing, 2002), 71.

85. Saint Augustine, quoted in Melissa Perez, *Living Loved* (Melissa Perez, 2017), 19.

86. Adrienne von Speyr, *The Boundless God* (San Francisco: Ignatius Press, 2004), 24.

87. Jesus' resurrection is wholly unique in the Bible. Although we occasionally read about other miracles when someone is raised from the dead—Lazarus being the most famous—they are different. Lazarus eventually died again.

There is a curious passage found in Matthew 27:52, which describes how old tombs were opened and many saints were raised from their graves. This account could be Matthew using the literary convention of midrash, somewhat like Jesus used parables, to make a theological point.

It is also possible the account is historical and that the vivifying power of Christ's resurrection affected these righteous dead. If so, then those resurrected dead would not die again and presumably they ascended to heaven as Jesus did.

88. John 2:18-22, Matthew 12:39-40, Matthew 16:21, John 10:17-18, Matthew 27:62-64.

89. Joseph Ratzinger/Pope Benedict XVI, *Jesus of Nazareth, Holy Week: From the Entrance Into Jerusalem to the Resurrection* (Catholic Truth Society, 2011), 228.

90. Joseph Ratzinger/Pope Benedict XVI, *Jesus of Nazareth, Holy Week: From the Entrance Into Jerusalem to the Resurrection* (Catholic Truth Society, 2011), 228.

91. Charles Spurgeon, *Sermons Delivered in Exeter Hall* (London: Alabaster & Passmore and James Paul, 1855), 137.

92. The New Testament does not give a reason why "Saul" became "Paul," but he may have been born with two names given he was both a Roman citizen and a pious Jew of the tribe of Benjamin.

93. The text tells us that Jesus' disciples did not recognize him, which is odd since they knew him so well. The point being made is not that they mistook his physical form, but they still failed to recognize Jesus as the Messiah. Jesus actually admonishes them as being "foolish" and "slow to believe" (v. 25).

94. Early Christians struggled with the concept of resurrection. Athenagoras of Athens, an Ante-Nicene Church father, wrote one of the earliest defenses of the resurrection of the flesh. He was among the first Christians to address questions about the resurrection of bodies that are torn apart in war or consumed by other animals. Aquinas points out that we trim our hair and nails, but we are still the same material being, thus we need not have every molecule of our flesh restored to ensure our bodies are resurrected.

95. Additionally, in the ancient culture of Jesus' time, the highest place of honor was the seat at the right hand of a king or lord. The symbolism also directs us to the legal system of ancient Israel, where the verdict of the Sanhedrin was recorded by one of two individuals. If the judgment of the court was guilty then the scribe sitting to the left of the court recorded the verdict. However, if the judgment of the court was not guilty then the scribe seated at the right hand recorded the verdict.

96. Joseph Ratzinger/Pope Benedict XVI, *Jesus of Nazareth, Holy Week: From the Entrance Into Jerusalem to the Resurrection* (Catholic Truth Society, 2011), 275–290.

CHAPTER EIGHT

1. Edith Wharton, "Vesalius in Zante," https://public.wsu.edu/~campbelld/wharton/whartpoe2.htm#Vesalius%20in%20Zante.%20(1564), (accessed August 31, 2018).

2. Mary is depicted as having been set apart from all other women by Allah. ". . . O Mary! Indeed God has chosen you, and purified you, and has chosen you above all other women of the worlds. O Mary!" (Quran 3:42-43).

3. Pius XII, "Ineffabilis Deus: Defining the Dogma of the Immaculate Conception," http://www.papalencyclicals.net/pius09/p9ineff.htm (accessed August 31, 2018).

4. Many people confuse the immaculate conception of Mary with the miraculous conception of Jesus. Adding to the confusion, perhaps, is the fact that the Gospel reading for the feast of the immaculate conception recounts the story of the Annunciation: the communication between the archangel Gabriel and Mary, regarding God's choice of Mary to be the mother of Jesus.

5. A good way to think about this is to compare the title "Immaculate Conception" with Jesus, who said, "I am the Resurrection and the Life." How can Jesus be "the Resurrection?" How can a person be an event? Think about the way we commonly speak. A really fun person is said to be "the life of the party." Someone experiencing turmoil might be called a "train wreck."

6. William Wordsworth quoted in *Ave Maria* (Notre Dame, Indiana, 1883), 523.

7. Adrienne Von Speyr, *Handmaid of the Lord*, trans. Alexander Dru (Harvill Press, 1956), 49.

8. Other similarities to pagan myths can be traced to the millennia of tradition of worship of the *Magna Mater*, the great mother goddess, going back to prehistoric times. However, none of the purported similarities were lost on the early Church fathers who were well aware of them. Therefore, orthodox teachings about Mary are precise and nuanced. She is the Theotokos, the Mother of God, but she is not the goddess mother.

9. See, Raymond Brown, *The Virginal Conception and Bodily Resurrection of Jesus* (Paulist Press, 1973).

10. Adrienne Von Speyr, *Handmaid of the Lord*, trans. Alexander Dru (Harvill Press, 1956), 15–16.

11. There is a short vignette that takes place while Jesus is dying on the cross. He looks down at his apostle John and his mother, who are standing nearby. "When Jesus saw his mother there, and the disciple whom he loved standing nearby, he said to her, 'Woman, here is your son,'" (John 19:26).

   Joseph likely died earlier, and it was Jesus who cared for his mother, in accordance with Jewish custom. Had Jesus actually had any brothers he would not likely have passed care for his beloved mother to John but to one of them.

12. The Ark of the Covenant may also legitimately be compared to Jesus himself. In ancient Semitic culture, wood represented humanity while gold represented divinity. It is then no coincidence that the Ark is wood covered in gold, symbolizing Jesus' human nature and divine nature. This sort of Old Testament symbolism playing out anew in the New Testament is replete throughout Scripture. Take, for example, Moses' encounter with God via the burning bush. Reading the passage carefully, we see the bush was aflame but was not being consumed by the fire. Here, too, we find a connection with Jesus, as the wood of the bush can represent humanity and fire is symbolic of divinity. Jesus was both human and divine, but his divinity did not consume his humanity.

13. See the book of Revelation, which discusses the Ark of the Covenant in chapter 11, then references a woman typifying Mary in chapter 12.

14. Her statement in Luke 1:38 exemplifies this.

15. Saint Ephrem wrote: "'Mary is made for us a heaven bearing the divinity, which Christ, without leaving His Father's glory, shut up within the narrow limits of her womb. . . . She is the temple of the Son of God . . . that mystical *new heaven*, wherein dwelt the King of kings as in His mansion'. She is the new Eden, in which the tree of life is planted, the ladder of Jacob, whereby God has descended to us."

16. Was the Blessed Virgin free from stain because she did not offend God, or because she was impeccable and incapable of sin? The latter is common teaching in Catholic Tradition, while distinguishing it from the impeccability enjoyed by Christ. His may be called absolute and derived from the union of his human nature with the divinity. He could not sin because he was God, and God is infinitely holy. Mary could not sin by reason of an inherent quality, which some

place midway between the state of souls in the beatific vision and that of our first parents before the fall.

Concretely this quality may be identified with perseverance in grace as regards grave sin, and confirmation in grace for lesser sins. In either case, however, her incapacity for sin differed radically from that of Christ. Where his was based on the fact that he is a divine person, hers was an added prerogative. It was absolutely necessary that he could not sin, since God is sinless. It was a free gift of God's mercy that Mary could not sin, but only because she was protected by divine favor."

(John A. Hardon, *The Catholic Catechism* [Garden City, NY: Doubleday & Co., 1975], 159–160)

17. Adrienne von Speyr, *The World of Prayer* (San Francisco: Ignatius Press, 1985), 115–116.
18. Mary's spiritual formation came about through outward instructions and interior insights. Catholic theologians sometimes refer to "infused grace" and "infused contemplation" as two privileges enjoyed by Mary. These terms refer to God working in Mary's life in a way that is not usually perceived by the five senses.
19. Adrienne Von Speyr, *Handmaid of the Lord*, trans. Alexander Dru (Harvill Press, 1956), 7.
20. Adrienne Von Speyr, *Handmaid of the Lord*, trans. Alexander Dru (Harvill Press, 1956), 116–117.
21. The beginning of the prayer that begins "Hail Mary" is a combination of Bible verses, repeating the words Gabriel, the archangel, spoke to Mary (Luke 1:18) as well as the words spoken to Mary by Elizabeth her cousin (Luke 1:42).
22. *Memorare* (Remember)
    "Remember, O most loving Virgin Mary, that never was it known that anyone who fled to your protection, implored your help, or sought your intercession was left unaided. Inspired with this confidence, we turn to you, O Virgin of virgins, our Mother. To you we come, before you we stand, sinful and sorrowful. O Mother of the Word Incarnate, do not despise our petitions, but in your mercy hear and answer us. Amen." —Saint Bernard
    Salve Regina (Hail Holy Queen)
    "Hail, holy Queen, mother of mercy; hail, our life, our sweetness and our hope. To thee do we cry, poor banished children of Eve; to thee do we send up our sighs, mourning and weeping in this valley of tears. Turn then, most gracious advocate, thine eyes of mercy towards us; and after this our exile, show unto us the blessed fruit of thy womb, Jesus. O clement, O loving, O sweet Virgin Mary. Amen." www.vatican.va/special/rosary/documents/misteri_luminosi_en.html (Accessed October 16, 2018).

CHAPTER NINE

1. C. S. Lewis, *The Complete C. S. Lewis Signature Classics* (HarperOne, 2002), 174.
2. A biography of a saint is called a hagiography. The term "hagiography" can sometimes be used dismissively as in "that story is mere hagiography," meaning that story is a pious folktale and not a historical reality. Although many hagiographies are laced with embellishments, the lives of the saints are also filled with true but nonetheless phenomenal events. There are countless other examples of saints who performed miracles, experienced miracles, and had visions, interior locutions, or other mystical experiences.
3. Saint Teresa of Avila, quoted in Helene Ciaravino, *How to Pray: Tapping Into the Power of Divine Communication* (SquareOne Publishers, 2001), 203.
4. Saint Augustine of Hippo, *The Confessions of St. Augustine*, trans. F. J. Sheed (NY: Sheed & Ward, 1943), 236.

5. Oscar Wilde, *The Plays of Oscar Wilde, Volume 1* (John W. Luce & Company, 1905), 59.

6. Thomas Merton, *New Seeds of Contemplation* (New Directions Paperbook, 1972), 24.

7. Just because a person is declared to be a servant of God or venerable or blessed does not guarantee that individual will eventually be declared a saint. Thomas á Kempis, author of the perennially popular devotional book *Imitation of Christ* had a great reputation for holiness. His cause for sainthood was opened twice but to date has been unsuccessful. There is an unsubstantiated rumor that after his body was disinterred it was discovered that there were scratch marks on the inside of the coffin, purportedly indicating he was buried alive and may have been despondent with this situation. Some scholars have dismissed this claim as scandalous calumny.

8. Just because a person is declared a saint that does not mean everything that person has said or written is approved by the Church. While a saint has to hold to the orthodox tenets of the faith, it would be an easy task to find contradictory opinions held by any number of saints.

9. On rare occasions a saint will be disinterred only to discover the body has not suffered corruption. These are called incorruptibles.

10. There are various holy men and women whose identities are lost to history but whom tradition has identified by various names. For example, the name of the good thief crucified with Jesus is St. Dismas in Catholic tradition. But in certain noncanonical writings and other Christian traditions he is called Titus, or Demas or Rakh.

11. Saint Francis de Sales, *Library of St. Francis de Sales: Letters to Persons in Religion,* trans. Henry Benedict Mackey (London: Burns and Oates, 1888), 217.

12. Henri de Lubac, *Paradoxes of Faith* (San Francisco: Ignatius Press, 1987), 81.

13. Saint Francis de Sales, quoted in *A Year with the Saints* (P. J. Kenedy & Sons, 1891), 25.

14. It is worth repeating that Mary, queen of angels and saints, surpasses every other saint, regardless of how devout or wonderfully virtuous the person may have been.

15. Karl Adam, *The Spirit of Catholicism,* https://www.ewtn.com/library/CATECHSM/CATARS.HTM (accessed August 31, 2018).

16. Humans do not become angels. They are of two distinct orders in creation. But, confusion can arise since some angels are referred to as "saints" and certain humans as "saints."

17. This is not a biblical distinction and may have some connection to Aristotelian cosmology, which presumed nine spheres in the heavens. Dante, too, wrote about nine spheres in heaven. Interestingly, Dante also divided his version of hell into nine circles, perhaps, in an effort to have the infernal imitate the celestial.

18. There is a hypothesis among some theologians that humans were created in order to replenish the missing population of heaven, which was diminished when the reprobate angels fell.

19. "To Him shall bow / All knees in Heav'n" (V. 607-608).

20. See Quran 2:34, 7:11-13, 17:61-62, etc.

21. In his weighty treatise, "On the Fall of the Devil," St. Anselm of Canterbury explores the how any being created by an all-good God could sin. Anselm's conclusion is in harmony with St. Augustine and St. Paul, that God is not the author of evil but is the creator of free beings who may choose evil.

22. Nigel Wright, *The Satan Syndrome* (Grand Rapids: Zondervan, 1990), 163.

23. Father Delaporte of the Society of Mercy, *The Devil: Does He Exist and What Does He Do?* (TAN Books, 1982), 24-25.

24. This is not meant to imply the ancient Greeks were naïve. Both mythological thinking (*mythos*) and logical reasoning (*logos*) were intertwined in ancient Greek thought, like the snakes of a caduceus symbol.

25. Many scholastic theologians speculated that humans were created to replace the lost angels, but this theory is not currently popular.
26. There are some theologians who posit that some angels neither fell from heaven nor remained there but are in prison elsewhere awaiting judgment—meaning some could return to heaven. This is based on a passage in Peter, and it is a speculative notion.
27. Saint Francis de Sales, *Letters to Persons in Religion,* trans. Henry Benedict Mackay (Eugene, Oregon: Wipf & Stock, 2017), 58.

CHAPTER TEN

1. A Church was built on the legendary site of this encounter in Rome, the Church of *Domine Quo Vadis.*
2. Roy H. Schoeman, *Salvation is of the Jews* (San Francisco: Ignatius Press, 2003), 9.
3. In general, the holy Mass can be divided into four parts:
   1. The Introductory Rite: Procession, Greeting, Penitential Rite, and Gloria (except during Advent and Lent).
   2. The Liturgy of the Word: First Reading from the Old Testament (except during Easter, when the reading comes from the book of Acts), the Responsorial Psalm (read or sung), Second Reading from a New Testament Letter or from the book of Revelation (usually taking up where last week's reading left off), the Gospel Reading, a Homily, the Creed, the Prayer of the Faithful. (The Old Testament and Gospel passages are read not at random but equate in some way with each other.)
   3. Liturgy of the Eucharist: Presentation of the Bread & Wine and Altar Preparation, Consecration, the Lord's Prayer, Recitation of the Lamb of God, Communion.
   4. The Concluding Rites: Final Prayer, Departing Blessing.
   5. Each of these parts is interlaced with music.
4. Saint Cyprian of Carthage, quoted in Paul Thigpen, *A Dictionary of Quotes from the Saints* (Charis Books, 2001), 36.
5. Although both the Church and the Eucharist can rightly be identified as the body of Christ, they are distinct. The Church is the mystical body of Christ while the Eucharist is Christ's sacramental presence: Body, Blood, Soul, and Divinity.
6. See Avery Dulles' models of the Church.
7. Pope John XXIII, *Mater Et Magistra Encyclical Of Pope John XXIII* (St. Paul Publications, 1962).
8. Pope Paul VI, "Lumen Gentium," http://www.vatican.va/archive/hist_councils/ii_vatican_council/documents/vat-ii_const_19641121_lumen-gentium_en.html (accessed August 31, 2018).
9. Henri de Lubac, *Paradoxes of Faith* (San Francisco: Ignatius Press, 1987), 234.
10. Jesus admonishes his followers to "Call no man on earth your Father . . ." (Matthew 23:9). However, the Church has understood his meaning to be figurative, not literal, as evidenced by the repeated use of the word "father" by St. Paul and other authors of the New Testament.
11. William L. Countryman, *Living on the Border of the Holy, Renewing the Priesthood of All* (Harrisburg, PA: Morehouse Publishing, 1999), 58.
12. There were many different pagan religions from which to choose, but few were exclusivist. A devotee could legitimately belong to multiple cults simultaneously. In some cases, these cults even blended. For example, the messenger of the gods, the Greek Hermes, and the ibis-headed Egyptian god of writing, Thoth, became almost synonymous in parts of the Hellenized world.

13. Saint Paul in particular was well traveled. He set out on missionary journeys across Europe and Asia Minor, establishing congregations across the region circa 48 AD.
14. Some other religious traditions also do not rely solely on miracles. Mohammed spread the word of Islam across the planet through a book, the Quran. The Buddhist Koans are invitations to think deep thoughts.
15. Some scholars believe Paul actually only wrote as few as eight of the books attributed to him.
16. Paul's writings are, at times, luminously brilliant, and at other times, opaque and confounding. Saint Paul was indisputably one of history's greatest minds, as evidenced by his seamless blending of Hebrew theology, Greek philosophy, and concepts of his own origin. One of the reasons Paul's writings are notoriously difficult to interpret is that while some of his letters make up part of the New Testament, we do not have access to the other party's correspondence; we're missing out on half of the exchange.
17. The designation "prophet" in the Hebrew Scriptures identifies a man or woman who was enlightened by God and who both spoke and acted on God's behalf. Sometimes that speech included predictions of future events, but at other times prophets served as interpreters of dreams and signs and more often as heralds who warned, admonished, and encouraged others to be faithful to Yahweh the God of Israel.
18. Elaine Pagels, *The Gnostic Gospels*, (NY: Vintage, 1989), xxii-xxiii.
19. The word *"Didache"* means "Teaching" in Greek and is the common reference used for a text titled: *The Teaching of the Twelve Apostles.*
20. Garry Wills, *What Jesus Meant* (Penguin Books, 2007), 49–50.
21. Tertullian, quoted in Joyce E. Salisbury, *The Blood of Martyrs: Unintended Consequences of Ancient Violence* (Taylor & Francis Books, Inc., 2004), 1.
22. Rodney Stark, *The Rise of Christianity: A Sociologist Reconsiders History* (Princeton, NJ: Princeton University Press, 1996), 161.
23. Some early debates centered on Gnostic teachings. Marcionism is the heresy that rejected the Old Testament and Jesus' incarnation. Docetism is the heresy that Jesus was not a human person with a body of flesh and bones. Arianism is the heresy that Jesus was not truly divine, consubstantial with the Father, but was instead created by God the Father. Manichaeism is the heresy that posited a dualistic power struggle between opposing powers; good and evil.
24. John A. Hardon, *Modern Catholic Dictionary*, ed. John A. Hardon (Bardstown, KY: Eternal Life, 1999; reprint, 2004), s. v. "Heresy."
25. The current translation reads:
     I believe in one God,
     the Father almighty,
     maker of heaven and earth,
     of all things visible and invisible.
     I believe in one Lord Jesus Christ,
     the Only Begotten Son of God,
     born of the Father before all ages.
     God from God, Light from Light,
     true God from true God,
     begotten, not made,
     consubstantial with the Father;
     through him all things were made.
     For us men and for our salvation
     he came down from heaven,
     [At the words that follow up to and including 'and became man,' all bow.]
     and by the Holy Spirit
     was incarnate of the Virgin Mary, and became man.

For our sake he was crucified under Pontius Pilate,
he suffered death and was buried,
and rose again on the third day
in accordance with the Scriptures.
He ascended into heaven
and is seated at the right hand of the Father.
He will come again in glory
to judge the living and the dead
and his kingdom will have no end.
I believe in the Holy Spirit,
the Lord, the giver of life,
who proceeds from the Father and the Son,
who with the Father and the Son
is adored and glorified,
who has spoken through the prophets.
I believe in one, holy,
catholic and apostolic Church.
I confess one baptism
for the forgiveness of sins
and I look forward to the resurrection of the dead
and the life of the world to come. Amen.
New Roman Missal at Mass Beginning, Nov. 27, 2011.

26. The Council of Jerusalem, described in the book of Acts, can be termed a pre-ecumenical council in that it was not attended by representatives of the entire Church the way ecumenical councils since the time of Nicaea have been. Nonetheless, this meeting was authoritative due to the participation of some of Christ's Apostles, and it was exemplary in that it provided authority for later ecumenical councils.

27. The "gifts" of the Holy Spirit are: wisdom; understanding; counsel; fortitude; knowledge; piety; and, fear of the Lord. The "fruits" of the Spirit are: charity; joy; peace; patience; kindness; goodness; generosity; gentleness; faithfulness; modesty; self-control; and, chastity.

28. Catholics are not merely members of their local parish but are members of the universal Church.

29. *Decree on The Catholic Churches of The Eastern Rite Orientalium Ecclesiarum Solemnly Promulgated By His Holiness Pope Paul VI On November 21, 1964.*

30. Floyd Filson, *A Commentary on the Gospel According to St. Matthew* (New York, NY: Harper & Row, 1960), 243.

31. Jesus' teachings on both the law and tradition are admittedly complex. There are times when he approves or disapproves.

32. *The Catechism of the Catholic Church* (1994), quoted in Robert L. Reymond, *A New Systematic Theology of the Christian Faith* (Nashville, TN: Thomas Nelson, Inc., 1998), 26.

33. The word "*Filioque*" comes from Latin for "and the Son." It refers to a line in the Nicene Creed that explains how the Holy Spirit proceeds from the Father and the Son. The Eastern Orthodox use the original Nicene formula, which omits this line. So, basically, the argument has to do with the question of whether the Holy Spirit proceeds from the Father alone or from the Father and Son. In 1995, the Pontifical Council for Promoting Christian Unity issued a clarification that reads, in part, "The Father alone is the principle without principle (*arch anarcos*) of the two other persons of the Trinity, the sole source (*peghe*) of the Son and of the Holy Spirit. The Holy Spirit therefore takes his origin from the Father alone (*ek monou tou Patros*) in a principal, proper and immediate manner." This clarification has satisfied many who still struggled with the Filioque controversy.

34. Since the earliest days of Christianity, some of the faithful have sought to more closely follow Jesus in a consecrated life. This life choice is made when an individual freely elects to be bound by certain temporary or perpetual vows. These vows are separate and distinct from the sacrament of holy orders. There is a distinction between solemn vows and simple vows. (Both types of vows are made publicly.)

    Consecrated life is divided into two distinct types of organizations: religious institutes and secular institutes. The four types of religious orders are Monastic Orders, Mendicant Orders, Canons Regulars, and Clerks Regulars. Canon law also allows for individuals to live the consecrated life identifying men as hermits and women as consecrated virgins.

35. The "Liturgy of the Hours" (commonly referred to as the "the divine office") are eight distinct prayers offered throughout the day. This practice, which dates back to the early sixth century, begins in the morning with *"Mattins,"* followed by *"Lauds,"* then *"Prime,"* *"Tierce,"* *"Sexte,"* and *"Nones,"* ending with the prayers of *"Vespers"* and *"Compline."* These terms, odd to a modern audience, reflect either the time a prayer is offered or the reason behind the prayer.

36. R. W. Southern, quoted in Jean Porter, *Natural and Divine Law: Reclaiming the Tradition for Christian Ethics* (William B. Eersmans Publishing Company, 1999), 42.

37. E. Michael Jones, *The Jewish Revolutionary Spirit and Its Impact on World History* (South Bend: Fidelity Press, 2008), 156.

38. Some Catholics were not enthusiastic about the secular art produced by the Renaissance. For example, Girolamo Savonarola, a Dominican friar, became famous for his Bonfire of the Vanities. However, he was later excommunicated from the Church.

39. Peter Kreeft, *Fundamentals of the Faith* (San Francisco: Ignatius Press, 1988), 277–281.

40. The word "Protestant" can be traced back to the root word "protest," as in to protest against the Church of Rome, or it can be linked to the words "pro," meaning "in favor of," and "testament" or "testimony."

41. Saint Thomas Aquinas taught that laws should not force citizens to practice every sort of virtue and avoid every kind of vice. "The purpose of human law is to bring people to virtue, not suddenly, but step by step. Therefore, it does not all at once burden the crowd of imperfect men with the responsibilities assumed by men of the highest character, nor require them to keep away from all evils, lest, not sturdy enough to bear the strain, they break out into greater wrongs." (*Summa Theologica*, I, II, Q. 96 Article 2, 3" New Advent Thomas Aquinas, February 2010, http://www. newadvent. org/summa/2096. htm#article6.)

42. Henri De Lubac, *Paradoxes of Faith* (Ignatius Press, 1987), 157.

43. Admittedly, Pope Innocent III annulled the Magna Carta with his bull *Etsi Kavissimus*. However, the Magna Carta was subsequently edited several times and finally reissued in 1225, garnering the acceptance of the Catholic Church.

44. Bishop Fulton Sheen, "The Decline of Controversy," April 2, 2007, http://catholicism.org/sheen-decline-controversy.html (accessed August 31, 2018).

45. Thomas Merton, *New Seeds of Contemplation* (NY: New Directions Pub. Co., 1961), 142–144.

46. Saint Thomas Aquinas, *The Aquinas Catechism: A Simple Explanation of the Catholic Faith by the Church's Greatest Theologian* (Manchester, NH: Sophia Institute Press, 200), 81.

CHAPTER ELEVEN

1. *The Catechism of the Catholic Church,* 100.

2. For example, the Council of Trent, in response to certain Protestant challenges, officially defined the meanings of certain Bible verses. Yet, even these definitions were not meant to be exhaustive.

3. George Gershwin, "It Ain't Necessarily So," 1935.

4. William Shakespeare, *The Merchant of Venice* (Wordsworth Edition Limited, 2000), 44.

5. Pope St. Gregory the Great, *S. Gregorii Magni Registrum Epistularum*, CCSL 140-40A (1982), 874.

6. The story originated in 1941 as a song composed by Katherine Kennicott Davis.

7. A. N. Wilson, *Jesus: A Life* (W. W. Norton & Company, 2004), 68–69.

8. An example of Johannine symbology is the absence of any narrative concerning Jesus' Last Supper. John recounts the foot-washing scene but not the Passover meal itself. Why? The Gospel author is making a Christological point equating Jesus with the Passover lamb; so, he is himself the Passover meal, the Lamb of God.

9. The Bible is called the Word of God, but it is the *created* word of God. The second person of the Trinity, referred to as the "*Logos*" or the "Word," is the uncreated God himself.

10. Avi Hurvitz, *Ruth 2:7. —. A Midrashic Gloss* (ZAW 95, 1983), 122.

11. Pope St. Gregory the Great, *Edge-tools of Speech,* ed. Maturin Murray Ballou (Houghton, Mifflin, and Company, 1899), 42.

12. Thomas Cahill, *The Gift of the Jews: How a Tribe of Desert Nomads Changed the Way Everyone Thinks and Feels* (Anchor Books, 1998), 3.

13. Some scholars speculate that Abraham and the early Israelites were henotheists: persons who believe in one particular god, usually their own tribal god, without necessarily denying the existence of other gods. It was not uncommon in the ancient world for people to believe in native deities who ruled a particular geographic area. This hypothesis posits that originally the Hebrews were not, technically speaking, monotheistic, but instead they practiced monolatrism. Monolatrism is the exclusive worship of one god while being open to the possibility that other deities also exist. Given that Abraham's father was a maker and seller of idols this speculation makes sense, at least with respect to the early stages of Abraham's faith journey.

14. Paganism was diverse and multifaceted, and certainly there were regular pagan feasts and holidays, but nothing like the weekly Sabbath of Judaism.

15. *The Abingdon Bible Commentary*, ed. Frederick Carl Eiselen Edwin Lewis and David G. Downey (Abingdon Press. New York/Nashville: The Abingdon Press, Inc., 1929), 158-159.

16. A. J. Jacobs, *The Year of Living Biblically* (Simon & Schuster Paperbacks, 2008), 328.

17. G. K. Chesterton, *Orthodoxy* (NY: John Lane Company, 1909), 85.

18. See, Aldrin, Buzz Jr., McConnell, Malcolm, *Men from Earth: An Apollo Astronaut's Exciting Account of America's Space Program* (NY: Bantam Books, 1989).

19. Translating the Bible from the original text(s) to current vernacular is not the only challenge; grammar and punctuation are also important topics for scholars. After all, the original manuscripts did not have chapter and verse divisions. The innovation of organizing the books of the Bible into various chapters and verses originated with Archbishop of Canterbury Stephen Langton (1150–1228).

20. Jesus is presented in Matthew's Gospel as the new Moses. Moses presided over the miraculous ten plagues of Egypt; Jesus performed, according to Matthew, ten consecutive miracles. Moses crossed the Red Sea through a miracle; Jesus calmed the stormy sea via a miracle. Some further points of similarity include:

    1. The Pharaoh of Egypt ordered the death of all male Hebrew babies; however, Moses escaped this fate (Exodus 1:22; 2:1-2).

Herod ordered the death of all male Hebrew babies; however, Jesus escaped this fate (Matthew 2:16-18).

2. After fleeing to Egypt for safety, Moses returned to his people (Exodus 2:15; 4:18).

After fleeing to Egypt for safety, Jesus returned to his people (Matthew 2:13-23).

3. Moses delivered God's law after receiving it atop a mountain (Exodus 24:1-3). Jesus delivered God's new law preaching from a mountain (Matthew 5:1-3).

4. Moses is the central figure of the Old Covenant's blood sacrifice (Exodus 24:8).

Jesus offers himself as the new and perfect blood sacrifice (Matthew 26:28).

5. Moses fasted 40 days and 40 nights (Exodus 34:28).

Jesus fasted 40 days and 40 nights (Matthew 4:2).

21. Cf. Matthew 11: 25-30.

22. The Torah is comprised of the five books of Moses. Some scholars find in Matthew's Gospel five distinct discourses given by Jesus. This would be another example of Mosaic typology.

23. The word "Tanakh" is actually an acronym comprised of three letters T+N+K. The acronym derives from the three primary categories of Jewish Scripture, which are *Torah* (Law), *Nevaiim* (Prophets), and *Kethuvim* (Writings).

24. The details are even more profound. Adam was made in the image of God; Matthew presents Jesus as the image of the Father. Adam was created by God breathing life into him and Matthew references Jesus being born by the breath of God (Matthew 1:20). In Genesis, God rested on the seventh day, the Sabbath; Matthew's Gospel portrays Jesus as inaugurating the new Sabbath.

25. The first five books of the Bible are known as the "Pentateuch," or the "Torah," in the Jewish faith. The remainder of the Jewish canon, which closely parallels the Christian Old Testament, is called the Tanakh, by Jews. Tradition held that Moses was the author of the Pentateuch, but scholars, since the time of Baruch Spinoza in the seventeenth century, have posited the Documentary Hypothesis: that the Torah has four different authors. (The author(s) are referred to as "J," who refers to God as Yahweh; "E," who refers to God as Elohim; "D," which refers to the which the author of Deuteronomy; and "P" references the priestly authors.)

26. Even within a single book we find differing literary techniques. The book of Psalms, for example, is a collection of 150 lyrical poems meant to be sung. Scholars divide them into post-exilic psalms, penitential psalms, desolation psalms, and monarchic psalms. The poetry of the Psalms uses personification, anthropomorphism, and other literary devices. The lyrical structure most commonly found in the Psalms is called parallelism, meaning comparisons are made that either point to similar (synonymous parallelism) or to dissimilar (antithetic parallelism) ideas. Sometimes an idea is started in one verse and finished in a later verse (synthetic parallelism).

27. It is no coincidence that Genesis tells the story of creation while the Book of Revelation tells the story of the last days and new creation.

28. Though no precise definition has ever been found, an "aretalogy" seems to have been the name given in the ancient Mediterranean world for any collection of miracle stories. Cf. Morton Smith, "Prolegomena to a Discussion of Aretalogies, Divine Men, the Gospels and Jesus," *Journal of Biblical Literature* 90/2 (June 1971), 174–99.

29. The transcendence of the Gospels in particular and of the New Testament and entire Bible in general has inspired some of the greatest minds throughout history. Authors who have been inspired by the Bible and have sought to integrate—sometimes imitate—the Bible include: Blake, Chaucer, Dickens, Dostoevsky, Dante, Hemingway, Joyce, Marlowe, Milton, Shakespeare, Spencer, Tolstoy, and numerous others. This inspiration was not just "content-based."

For example, Hemingway's famous staccato sentence structure was influenced by the paratactic style of the King James Version of the Bible. Parataxis is a form of writing where two or more short sentences, each having a syntactic value, are joined together by a coordinating conjunction (usually the coordinator "and," in biblical style). This type of writing is used throughout the Bible to great effect. For example, when telling of Judas' forthcoming betrayal of Jesus, the Gospel of John uses these words: "[Judas] then having received the sop went immediately out: and it was night" (13:30 KJV). That short bit at the end, "and it was night," is a double entendre, heavy with meaning. Hemingway masterfully used the same style of writing.

30. The Bible has been translated into over two thousand languages.
31. "*Hapax Legomenon*" is a technical term describing a situation when a word appears only once in a given body of literature.

CHAPTER TWELVE

1. Saint Bernard of Clairvaux, quoted in Aldous Huxley, *The Perennial Philosophy* (London: Chatto & Windus; reprint, 1947), 18.
2. The Church rejects both pantheism (creation is a manifestation of God) and panentheism (creation is contained within God).
3. Scholars debate whether Haldane actually said this, but it is true that the most numerous animals on earth are insects and the most numerous insects are beetles.
4. Scott Hahn, *A Father Who Keeps His Promises* (Servant Books, 1998), 51.
5. Simone Weil, trans. Emma Crawford, *Waiting for God* (Perennial Classics, 2001), 89.
6. Raymond E. Brown, *Responses to 101 Questions on the Bible* (Paulist Press, 1990), 37.
7. See, Nicholas Wade, *Before the Dawn.*
8. The papal encyclical *Humani Generis,* issued by Pope Pius XII, declares that Catholics may accept evolution; however, there is language that states that it is unclear how Original Sin can be understood without reference to a historical Adam and Eve. *Humani Generis* is skeptical but not fully condemning of polygenism (the hypothesis that all humans trace back to multiple ancestral couples).
9. God breathed life into the dust of the ground to form Adam; Eve, however, was formed from Adam. In the noncanonical Hebrew folklore and myth there is a character, Lilith, whom was purportedly formed from the ground as was Adam. Their story is of discord. The intimacy of the two, Adam and Eve, is preserved from the first in the Genesis account.
10. Kyle Greenwood, *Scripture and Cosmology: Reading the Bible Between the Ancient World and Modern Science* (InterVarsity Press, 2015), 111–112.
11. N. T. Wright, *How God Became King* (HarperCollins Publishers, 2012), 87.
12. Ralph Waldo Emerson, *The Works of Ralph Waldo Emerson*, vol. III, *Society and Solicitude; Letters and Social Aims; Addresses*, The York Library (London: George Bell & Sons, 1904), 397.
13. Some contemporary secular views see each person as mere accidents of nature, the remnants of stardust that by sheer happenstance gained sentience in this ultimately meaningless universe.
14. Amazingly, the great saints Basil and Gregory of Nyssa had a holy mother, St. Macrina the Older, and a devout sister, St. Macrina the Younger, who produced erudite writings in theology. They were also close friends with St. Gregory of Nazianzus.

15. Huston Smith, quoted in *The Way Things Are: Conversations with Huston Smith on the Spiritual Life,* ed. Phil Cousineau (Los Angeles, CA: Univ. of California Press, 2003), 30.

16. I am indebted to Dr. Anthony Santamaria of the College of St. Elizabeth (Madison, NJ) for coming up with this example.

17. Josef Pieper, *Only the Lover Sings* (San Francisco: Ignatius Press, 1990), 43-44.

18. Cardinal John Henry Newman, quoted in *Wisdom for the Soul: Five Millennia of Prescriptions for Spiritual Healing,* ed. Larry Chang (Washington DC: Gnosophia Publishers, 2006), 112.

19. The Serenity Prayer is attributed to Reinhold Niebuhr.

20. Cf. Plato, *Apology,* 38a.

21. Cf. Plato, *Apology,* 21d.

22. Thomas Merton, *New Seeds of Contemplation* (NY: New Directions Pub. Co., 1961), 34.

23. Plato taught that there are three elements of the human soul. Aristotle proposed five. Scholastic theologians also identified five (vegetative, sensitive, appetitive, locomotive, and intellectual). Aquinas pointed out that these are not synonymous with the soul itself but are empowered by the energy of the soul; they are not self-energized.

24. The language of "creation of the soul" is a bit misleading, as it betrays a Platonic dualism. True, a soul is united to a corporeal body now and will one day be eternally united to a resurrected body. As the soul animates the body, it is possible to analogize how God animates the soul.

25. Something quite different are the claims of great Christian mystics, who so identified with God that they could claim (for example, in the words of "Meister" Eckhart von Hochheim): "*The eye with which I see God is the same with which God sees me. My eye and God's eye is one eye, and one sight, and one knowledge, and one love*" (Serm. IV, in Claud Field, trans., *Meister Eckhart's Sermons,* Heart & Life Booklets, no. 22 [London: H. R. Allenson, n. d.], 32; italics in original).

26. According to papal biographer George Weigel in his book: *Witness to Hope: The Biography of Pope John Paul II (1920–2005),* updated with new preface (NY: HarperCollins; Harper Perennial, 2001), 343.

27. Saint Thomas Aquinas, quoted in *The Collected Works of G. K. Chesterton,* ed. George J. Marlin, Richard P. Rabatin, & John L. Swan, vol. II, *St. Francis of Assisi; The Everlasting Man; St. Thomas Aquinas,* ed. Lawrence J. Clipper (San Francisco: Ignatius Press, 1987), 433.

28. The term "Creationism" used here does not refer to "creationists"—those who reject evolutionary theories.

29. Cf. *ST,* I-II, q. 82 ff.

30. Then, there is a fourth proposal: "Differentiated Unity." It rejects anthropological dualism. In other words, some theologians decry as false the teaching that humans are comprised of both a body and a soul; the soul is autonomously immortal, while the body is corruptible and, thus, of less importance to both God and (presumably) to our very selves.

31. See *CCC,* para. 1013.

32. Clive Staples (or, "C. S.") Lewis compares living life to taking an exam. He knows that multiple chances (like with reincarnation) don't necessarily mean a student has a better chance of passing: "A simpler form of the same objection [i.e., to the finality of death and judgment] consists in saying that death ought not to be final, that there ought to be a second chance. I believe that if a million chances were likely to do good, they would be given. But a master often knows, when boys and parents do not, that it is really useless to send a boy in for a certain examination again. Finality must come some time, and it does not require a very

robust faith to believe that omniscience knows when" (*The Problem of Pain* [NY: HarperOne for HarperCollins Pub., 2001], 126).

33. The Church will flesh out this topic when biologists spawn viable animal-human hybrids, or chimeras.

34. The most famous biblical example of this genre is the New Testament book of Revelation and the much shorter Marcan apocalypse found chapter 13 of the Gospel of Mark. However, there are examples found in the Old Testament in the apocalyptic literature of Isaiah (24-27), in Joel (2), Daniel (7-12), and Ezekiel (37), etc.

35. Just as the Genesis account of creation is not a scientific treatise, neither is Christian eschatology. Modern cosmology has much to say about how the earth and even the universe may come to an end. There are currently three theories: 1. The universe will continue to expand indefinitely. 2. The universe will simply stagnate and grow cold. 3. Gravity will eventually dominate other cosmic forces, causing everything to retract back into a single point; a quantum singularity. This contraction, or Big Crunch, may not even be the end of the story. If the conditions are right, that new singularity may explode all over again in a new Big Bang.

36. Some of the apocalyptic themes that resonate throughout the New Testament can be traced to texts from the deuterocanonical period, referred to as the intertestamental period by some scholars. This is the time after the canon of the Hebrew Scriptures was closed but before the time of the events of the New Testament.

37. Given that some books of the Old Testament may have been written later than their sequential order and then inserted back into the Old Testament, another way to interpret prophecy, especially the book of Daniel, is by viewing a foretelling passage as *vaticinium ex eventu* ("prophecy in hindsight," after the event occurred).

38. Millennialism differs from Millenarianism. The first term, "Millennialism," which references a forthcoming era of peace, can fully comport with Catholic doctrine. "Millenarianism," however, is a heresy that teaches that Jesus will return to earth and reign as king of the world for one thousand years, after which time there would be a falling away of the faithful. Then, after a period, Satan is purportedly set loose upon the earth to wreak havoc, after which, Jesus establishes his permanent victory.

39. Peter Kreeft, *The Catholic Register,* November 18, 1990.

40. N. T. Wright, *Surprised by Hope* (HarperOne, 2009), 132-133.

41. The judgment referenced here is the particular fixed judgment each person will face. There is also a general judgment that does not alter anyone's particular judgment but does reveal and proclaim God's ultimate judgment of all.

42. Saint Ignatius of Loyola, quoted in *An Ignatian Spirituality Reader,* ed. George W. Traub (Chicago: Loyola Press, 2008), 122.

43. Our acts of virtue are pleasing to God and beneficial to ourselves. While in the state of grace, the good works we do open us to new graces now and future blessings in the life to come. If we sin mortally, all of those past acts are, in a sense, nullified. If the person in mortal sin participates in the sacrament of reconciliation and makes a good confession, then by rights his or her account of merit should start from scratch. However, it is reasonable to assume that the God of mercy does not allow the commission of mortal sin to forever obliterate our past good deeds but instead restores to the repentant sinner the treasury of merit previously earned.

44. See John 14:16, John 14:26, John 15:26, and John 16:7.

45. The language Jesus uses is that he and the Father will send "another" *Paraklete.* Jesus is the first Paraclete, the Holy Spirit another, who continues the work of Jesus after his ascension.

46. R. C. Sproul, *The Truth of the Cross* (Orlando, FL: Reformation Trust Publishing, 2007), 95.

47. "Enter through the narrow gate. For wide is the gate and broad is the road that leads to destruction, and many enter through it. But small is the gate and narrow the road that leads to life, and only a few find it" (Matthew 7:13-14).

48. James Joyce, *A Portrait of the Artist as a Young Man* (NY: B. W. Huebsch Inc., 1922), 139.

49. Cardinal John Henry Newman, *Selection: Adapted to the Ecclesiastical Year From the Parochial and Plain Sermons* (Waterloo Place, London: Rivingtons, 1877), 281.

50. John Milton, *Milton's Paradise Lost: Books I and II* (Boston: Ginn, Heath, and Co., 1883), 30.

51. John Milton, *Milton's Paradise Lost: Books I and II* (Boston: Ginn, Heath, and Co., 1883), 13.

52. Some Christians, many Church fathers included, reject the view that the suffering of hell is self-imposed and insist the locus of the torment is God's righteous judgment.

53. C. S. Lewis, *George MacDonald An Anthology 365 Readings,* (HarperSanFrancisco, 2001), 74.

54. Saint Gregory of Nyssa, St. Isaac of Nineveh, Origen, Edith Stein, Maximus the Confessor, and others hint at the idea.

55. Peter Kreeft, "Hell," http://www.peterkreeft.com/topics/hell.htm (accessed August 31, 2018).

56. C. S. Lewis, *Letters To Malcolm: Chiefly on Prayer* (California: Harcourt, 1973), 108–109.

57. Others disagree and note that Kaddish, the "Mourner's Prayer," never even mentions the name of the deceased nor the topic of death.

58. Karl Adam, *The Spirit of Catholicism,* http://www.ewtn.com/library/theology/spircath.htm (accessed August 31, 2018).

59. C. S. Lewis, *George MacDonald An Anthology 365 Readings,* (HarperSanFrancisco, 2001), 53.

60. Some theologians speculate that hellfire and the flames of purgatory are one in the same. The catechism, however, states that "The Church gives the name Purgatory to this final purification of the elect, which is entirely different from the punishment of the damned." *CCC* 1031.

61. Dante Alighieri, *The Comedy of Dante Alighieri, the Florentine: Purgatory,* trans. Dorothy L. Sayers (Penguin Books, 1955), 73.

62. Saint Catherine of Genoa, quoted in William Griffin, *Endtime: The Doomsday Catalog* (Collier Books, 1979), 38.

63. "An indulgence is a remission before God of the temporal punishment due to sins whose guilt has already been forgiven, which the faithful Christian who is duly disposed gains under certain prescribed conditions through the action of the Church which, as the minister of redemption, dispenses and applies with authority the treasury of the satisfactions of Christ and the saints. An indulgence is partial or plenary according as it removes either part or all of the temporal punishment due to sin. The faithful can gain indulgences for themselves or apply them to the dead."
   CCC 1471, "What is an indulgence?" http://www.vatican.va/archive/ENG 0015/_P4G.HTM (Accessed October 18, 2018).

64. Saint Thomas Aquinas, quoted in Gerard P. Weber and Janie Gustafson, *Jesus Send Your Spirit* (Benziger, 1989), 46.

65. Saint Gertrude the Great, quoted in Ronda Chervin, *Quotable Saints* (CMJ Marian Publishers, 1992), 47.

66. Saint Francis de Sales, quoted in Paul Thigpen, *A Dictionary of Quotes from the Saints* (Charis Books, 2001), 113.

67. Peter Kreeft, *Christianity for Modern Pagans*, (London: Penguin Classics, 1966), 187.
68. John Newton, "Amazing Grace," 1779.
69. A. A. Milne, *The Complete Tales of Winnie-the-Pooh* (Penguin Books, 1994), 336.
70. C. S. Lewis, *The Complete C. S. Lewis Signature Classics* (HarperOne, 2002), 640.
71. Saint Bonaventure, quoted in Paul Thigpen, *A Dictionary of Quotes from the Saints* (Charis Books, 2001), 112.
72. C. S. Lewis, *The Problem of Pain* (HarperOne, 1996), 154.
73. Sir Henry Taylor, quoted in Mardy Grothe, *Never Let a Fool Kiss You Or a Kiss Fool You* (Penguin Books, 2002), 83.
74. Tom Wright, *How God Became King* (HarperOne, 2012), 237.
75. Ralph Waldo Emerson, *The Collected Works of Ralph Waldo Emerson: Nature, addresses, and lectures,* ed. Alfred R. Ferguson (The Belknap Press of Harvard University Press, 1971), 81.
76. This technique follows closely on the technique of *lectio divina*, that is, reading Scripture as if you were actually present—there to see Jesus' miracles, there to hear the Sermon on the Mount, there at the cross.
77. Saint Ignatius Loyola, quoted in Evonne Levy, *Propaganda and the Jesuit Baroque* (University of California Press, 2004), 151.

About the Author

DR. DANIEL AGATINO is an award-winning author, attorney, and professor. He is a popular speaker who has lectured throughout the United States and abroad and has appeared on numerous television programs such as CNN's *Headline News*, and on Court TV and TruTV as an expert commentator. When not in the studio, the courtroom, or the classroom, Daniel enjoys time with his wife and their twin sons.

www.ingramcontent.com/pod-product-compliance
Lightning Source LLC
Chambersburg PA
CBHW031603110426
42742CB00037B/818